World Peace Foundation

40 MT. VERNON STREET, BOSTON, MASSACHUSETTS

Founded in 1910 by Edwin Ginn

THE Foundation operates upon the policy that the actual facts concerning international relations and official international cooperation constitute the best possible arguments for lasting peace and improved international understanding. Its activities are, therefore, focused upon the task of making these facts available in clear and undistorted form.

Board of Trustees

GEORGE H. BLAKESLEE, *President*

WILLIS J. ABBOT	STEPHEN P. DUGGAN
GEORGE W. ANDERSON	HARRY A. GARFIELD
FRANK AYDELOTTE	ALANSON B. HOUGHTON
ISAIAH BOWMAN	MANLEY O. HUDSON
LEONARD W. CRONKHITE, JR.	A. LAWRENCE LOWELL

GEORGE A. PLIMPTON

General Staff

RAYMOND THOMAS RICH
Director

DENYS P. MYERS
Research

FARRELL SYMONS
Publications

MARIE J. CARROLL
Reference

HAZEL C. BENJAMIN
Librarian

MARY J. MACDONALD
Treasurer

RECENT WORLD PEACE FOUNDATION PUBLICATIONS

THE REPARATION SETTLEMENT, 1930
By DENYS P. MYERS

LATIN AMERICAN RELATIONS WITH THE LEAGUE OF NATIONS
By WARREN H. KELCHNER

HANDBOOK OF THE LEAGUE OF NATIONS SINCE 1920
By DENYS P. MYERS

INTERNATIONAL CONTROL OF AVIATION
By KENNETH W. COLEGROVE

THE SOVIET PLANNED ECONOMIC ORDER
By WILLIAM HENRY CHAMBERLIN

THE WORLD COURT, 1921–1931
By MANLEY O. HUDSON

HAITI UNDER AMERICAN CONTROL, 1915–1930
By ARTHUR C. MILLSPAUGH

WORLD DISARMAMENT

ITS PROBLEMS AND PROSPECTS

By
DENYS P. MYERS

WORLD PEACE FOUNDATION
BOSTON · MASSACHUSETTS
1932

Copyright, April, 1932
By WORLD PEACE FOUNDATION
BOSTON, MASSACHUSETTS

PRINTED IN THE UNITED STATES OF AMERICA

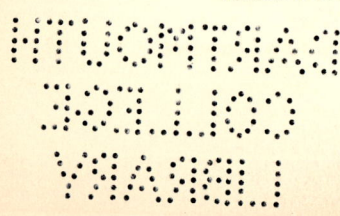

CONTENTS

PART ONE
ELEMENTS OF THE PROBLEM

CHAPTER		PAGE
I.	THE HEART OF INTERNATIONAL "POLITICS"	1
	"Moral Disarmament" First	3
	The Extent of Preparation	5
	Clearing the International Decks	8
	Conference Will Change the Problem	10
	Most Countries Not Heavily Armed	17
	Control of Conference Agreement	19
	Unanimity Rule of Constructive Value	21
	Why Great States are More Active	22
II.	MILITARY AND NATIONAL FACTORS	24
	Products of Military Use	24
	Organization of "War Potential"	26
	Technological Obsolescence	29
	Increasing Cost Cramps Style	32
	Peace and War—Conversion Lag	34
	Civilian Control Superseding Military	36
	Technical Naval Policy of the United States	40
	The Soviet Union and the Draft Convention	42
III.	PRESENT ARMAMENT CONTROLS	46
	A. Admitted Members of the League	46
	B. Demilitarization and Nonfortification	49
	C. Revision of Peace Treaties	55
	D. Private Manufacture of Arms	61
IV.	ARBITRATION AND NATIONAL SECURITY	69
	I. The Record as to Safety	70
	I. Use of Council	73
	II. Consultation of States	74
	The Convention on Financial Assistance	74
	Application to Actual War	76
	Application to Threat of War	77
	Unoffending State Commands Credit	78
	Operation of Guaranties Automatic	80
	Further Prevention of War	83
	Threat of War—Conservatory Measures	85

CONTENTS

CHAPTER		PAGE
II.	The Record as to Pacific Settlement	88
	I. Multilateral	89
	II. Bilateral Conventions	90
	War Possible Only by Treaty Violation	92
	Pacific Settlement and War Possibilities	94

PART TWO
THE MEETING OF THE WORLD'S MINDS

V.	THE GROWTH OF THE DRAFT CONVENTION	103
	(1) A Practical Task	104
	(2) Mechanism	105
	(3) Coordination of Policy	105
	(4) Change of View	106
	(5) Increase of International Order	106
	(6) Technical Homologation	106
	(7) "Security" an International Problem	106
	Steps of Progress	108
	Military Approach, 1920	108
	Civilian Inquiry, 1921	109
	Guaranty Approach, 1922	109
	"Aggression a Crime," 1923	110
	Pacific Settlement	111
	"Arbitration, Security, Disarmament"	112
	All-in Guaranty, 1924	113
	Regional Guaranty, 1925	114
	Security by Arbitration, 1927	115
	Renunciation of War, 1928	117
	Resistance Lessens, 1929–1930	118
	Data for the Conference	121
	Amount of Data to be Furnished	124
	Uniform but Limited Reports	125
	The Armament Truce	127
VI.	EFFECTIVES FOR ALL FORCES	130
	Purpose—Reduction, so Far as Possible	132
	"Average Daily Effectives"	133
	Formations Organized on Military Basis	134
	Significance of the Tables	139
	Problems of Conscription	142

CONTENTS

CHAPTER		PAGE
VII.	THE CONTROL OF MATERIAL	145
	A. Land Material	145
	Attitude of United States	147
	The Course of the Debate	150
	B. Naval Material	160
	C. Air Material	171
VIII.	CONTROL OF EXPENDITURE	176
	Models for Several Purposes	178
	To Prevent Shifting of Expense	182
	Effect of Currency Fluctuation	185
	Does Not Gauge Armed Strength	187
	Reanalysis of Budgets	188
	Account of the United States	190
IX.	CONTROLS BY PUBLICITY	197
	More Annual Details on Effectives	199
	Reports on Subsidiary Formations	201
	Expenditure by Material Categories Unsolved	204
	Budgetary Experts Analyze Problem	208
	Other Publicity—Civil Aviation	211
X.	CHEMICALS AND WARFARE	213
	The Commission's Discussions	215
XI.	THE PERMANENT DISARMAMENT COMMISSION	219
XII.	INSURANCE OF GOOD FAITH AND FULFILLMENT	227
	Case A. Notion of Circumstantial Menace	228
	Involves the Aggression Problem	230
	American Formula Adopted	232
	Full Responsibility for Derogation	235
	Case B. Violation the Concern of All	238
XIII.	THE PAST IN THE FUTURE: A NECESSITY AND PROBLEM	244
	The War-Guilt Issue	253
XIV.	DEVIATION AND NEW CONFERENCES	257

CONTENTS

APPENDICES

APPENDIX		PAGE
I.	DRAFT CONVENTION FOR THE REDUCTION AND LIMITATION OF ARMAMENTS, DRAWN BY THE PREPARATORY COMMISSION FOR THE DISARMAMENT CONFERENCE, DATED DECEMBER 9, 1930	265
	Draft Annex to Arts. 10, 24, 29 and 38 of the Draft Convention	306
	A. General Provisions	306
	B. Instructions on the Different Subheads	309
	Model Statement	317
II.	ARBITRATION AND SECURITY TEXTS	324
	1. General Act for the Pacific Settlement of International Disputes, Geneva, September 26, 1928	324
	Reservations	334
	2. Convention on Financial Assistance, Geneva, October 2, 1930	337
	3. General Convention to Improve the Means of Preventing War, Geneva, September 26, 1931	351
	Reservations on Signing	355
III.	STATISTICAL NOTES	356
	World Armament Strength	356
	National Expenditures on Armament	359
	Land Effectives	361
	Naval Tonnage	362
	Air Strength	363

PART ONE

ELEMENTS OF THE PROBLEM

WORLD DISARMAMENT
ITS PROBLEMS AND PROSPECTS

CHAPTER I

THE HEART OF INTERNATIONAL "POLITICS"

The first General Disarmament Conference has convened at Geneva, February 2, 1932. "For the first time in the history of the world, the problem of national armaments will have changed its character. It has hitherto been, and still is, an essentially domestic concern — a matter coming exclusively under the sovereign rights of each state. Henceforth it will become an international question, governed by laws which the states will have freely accepted."[1] Whatever the result of the conference respecting the measure of agreement, that essential principle has been automatically and inevitably established for all participating states by the mere assembling of the conference.

With the sole exception of engagements already in force respecting armament — which may be affected and perhaps modified by the agreements of the conference — the 64 participating governments will meet on the basis of the fullest equality. The invitation to the conference is issued to every autonomous government in the world which maintains any kind of military establishment.

Attendance at the conference includes the membership of the League of Nations, and an individual invitation was sent by its Secretary-General to some nine other states. The first General Disarmament Conference, when it convened on Tuesday, February 2, 1932, was the largest official gathering and the most important deliberation among governments in history. The participants are almost

[1] *Documents of the Preparatory Commission*, Series VIII, p. 197. The document is C.195.M.74.1929.IX.3.

exactly[1] the states which have renounced war as an instrument of national policy, condemned recourse to it and agreed to seek the solution of all disputes by only pacific means. Specifically the governments invited to participate are:

AFGHANISTAN	ESTONIA	NETHERLANDS
ALBANIA	ETHIOPIA	NEW ZEALAND
ARGENTINE REPUBLIC	FINLAND	NICARAGUA
	FRANCE	NORWAY
AUSTRALIA	GERMANY	PANAMA
AUSTRIA	GREAT BRITAIN AND NORTHERN IRELAND[2]	PARAGUAY
BELGIUM		PERSIA
BOLIVIA	GREECE	PERU
BRAZIL	GUATEMALA	POLAND
BULGARIA	HAITI	PORTUGAL
CANADA	HEJAZ AND NEJD[3]	RUMANIA
CHILE	HONDURAS	SALVADOR
CHINA	HUNGARY	SIAM
COLOMBIA	INDIA	SOUTH AFRICA
COSTA RICA	IRISH FREE STATE	SOVIET UNION
CUBA	ITALY	SPAIN
CZECHOSLOVAKIA	JAPAN	SWEDEN
DENMARK	LATVIA	SWITZERLAND
DOMINICAN REPUBLIC	LIBERIA	TURKEY
	LITHUANIA	UNITED STATES
ECUADOR	LUXEMBURG	URUGUAY
EGYPT	MEXICO	VENEZUELA
		YUGOSLAVIA

The United States Government accepted the invitation it received without equivocation or any qualification, and added:[4]

The American Government is happy to accept this invitation and welcomes the opportunity for cooperating with the other nations in a common effort to reduce the menace and to lighten the burden of armaments under which the world is suffering.

[1] Danzig and Iceland, having no armament, are not eligible attendants; Argentina and Brazil have not agreed to adhere to the treaty for renunciation of war.

[2] And all parts of the British Empire not separate Members of the League of Nations.

[3] Invited in accordance with resolution of the Assembly, September 28, 1931.

[4] Department of State, *Press Releases*, July 11, 1931, p. 50.

The importance of the conference can scarcely be exaggerated, since it cuts to the heart of the fundamental problem of all international relations. Ostensibly dealing with the physical structure and arrangements for defense adopted by the various states, the conference in reality will enjoin a searching examination of the national conceptions upon which the need for defense is based. Armament exists in part because of competitive conditions, but its essential base is the attitudes of peoples, organized in states, toward one another. The subject has not in 10 years of preparation for the conference, and can not in the conference itself, be handled without profoundly affecting those attitudes, which are customarily defined as national policies.[1] Without doubt, the discussions in the conference will bring to the surface elements of national policies previously unperceived by the general public. However, there is nothing in human nature or political science to indicate that open confession is not good for the soul, and the net effect of the conference, regardless of its actual decisions, will of a certainty serve to clarify the political relations between states.

" Moral Disarmament " First

The preparatory work for the conference has since 1922 proceeded on the conviction " that moral disarmament is an essential preliminary condition of material disarmament, and that this moral disarmament can only be achieved in an atmosphere of mutual confidence and security."[2] Some further contribution to that end the conference of 1932

[1] In the Third Plenary Session of the London Naval Conference, January 30, 1930, Dino Grandi, the first Italian delegate, expressed this idea with admirable directness:

"It has been stated and acknowledged in all the countries here represented, if I am not mistaken, that our problem is essentially a political one. This assertion is self-evident. The limitation of armaments means the acceptance by governments of restrictions to a fundamental right inherent in national sovereignty. The voluntary renunciation of freedom of action in the matter of armaments is essentially a political act. We should not fear to state that we are here not so much to solve a technical, but first and foremost, a political question." (*Documents of the London Naval Conference, 1930*, p. 149.)

[2] League of Nations, *Resolutions and Recommendations adopted by the Assembly during its Third Session*, p. 27. (*Official Journal*, Spec. Sup. No. 9.)

can not avoid achieving. The international regulation of means of national defense, which is the generic purpose of the conference, will bring into play in each country some conflict of points of view. National policies in the broadest sense emanate from the general attitudes of mind of the nationals of the respective states.

The renunciation of war — and in logic of its instrument, armament — as an instrument of national policy has been accepted as a world principle, but it can not be said that nations as a whole are yet thinking of the political, defensive and material aspects of armament in the terms of that premise. In so far as the publics of the states participating in the conference lack that conviction and the sense of cooperation and solidarity that it implies, the conference will exemplify the truth of Salvador de Madariaga's characterization:[1]

In effect every delegation goes to the conference determined to secure an increase in the *relative* armaments of its own nation, even though the conference may lead to an all-round reduction of *absolute* armaments. What matters for the expert is: (a) the national standing power in relation to that of the nation's potential adversary; (b) the national potential power (power for expanding armaments) in relation to that of the nation's adversary. It is clear that a cleverly conducted negotiation in conference may increase these two relative quantities even though the absolute values concerned be reduced.

This explains the atmosphere of profound mistrust which prevails in disarmament conferences. Every delegate scrutinizes the most innocent-looking proposals with the utmost anxiety, lest his own relative position be sacrificed by his acceptance thereof.

Dependent exclusively upon the knowledge, temperament and disposition of the peoples, whose views the delegates represent, is the extent to which the conference will be either a battle for national advantage and points of view or a cooperative effort to push forward " the possible measures which may, with mutual concession, help us toward the goal we all desire to reach."[2]

[1] *Disarmament*, p. 61–62.
[2] Hugh S. Gibson in the closing meeting of the Preparatory Commission, December 9, 1930, (*Documents of the Preparatory Commission*, Series X, p. 409 (C.4.M.4.1931.IX.1)).

When the Preparatory Commission for the Disarmament Conference closed its work, Viscount Cecil of Great Britain was hailed in the farewell speeches as the prophet of the effort which in various forms had continued without interruption for 10 years. In his remarks Viscount Cecil referred to the creation of those conditions which would be most favorable to success of the conference. "The last word," he said, "is with the peoples of the world. We have given them in this document a great opportunity. They have the opportunity to carry forward the disarmament of the world. What will they do with it? The world can be disarmed if the peoples wish. The question we have to solve in the next few months — and it will be part of the duty of every one of us to assist in that solution — is 'do the peoples wish for disarmament?' Only they can give an answer to that question."[1]

THE EXTENT OF PREPARATION

The document which was thus commended to the attention of the public by one of the foremost leaders of international thought was the Draft Convention for Limitation and Reduction of Armaments, drawn up by the direct representatives of 27 states[2] on December 9, 1930, in the course of six sessions[3] extending over four and one-half years.

During the progress of their meetings, those government delegates had exhibited very really, even though imperfectly, the attitude described above. In that commission, the significance of the conference as affecting a shift of the armament problem from the national to the international plane was enunciated; the many underlying political in-

[1] *Documents of the Preparatory Commission*, Series X, p. 408.

[2] Belgium, British Empire, Bulgaria, Canada, China, Cuba, Czechoslovakia, Finland, France, Germany, Greece, Italy, Irish Free State, Japan, Netherlands, Norway, Peru, Persia, Poland, Rumania, Spain, Sweden, Turkey, United States of America, Union of Soviet Socialist Republics, Venezuela, Yugoslavia.

The following countries were not represented at the second half of the sixth session of the Preparatory Commission for the Disarmament Conference: Argentina, Chile, Colombia, Guatemala, Uruguay.

[3] Really seven, since the sixth was in two parts and spread over two years.

hibitions were brought to light, and not a few of them were eliminated, while others were subjected to a change of form or nature or even became the basis of mutual concessions. The limited group of nations that possess substantially all[1] the armament that exists in the world — the so-called " great powers " — had considerable, and on the whole satisfactory, experience in modifying their self-assumed military requirements and in recasting their conceptions of national advantage in the presence of new principles of international relations. They developed to a notable extent the mechanism for the pacific settlement of international disputes as an essential foundation to enable them to make progress in the technical fields of disarmament.[2] They explored and acquired a fuller knowledge of facilities available to prevent hostilities or to stop hostilities already begun.[3] They saw security further enhanced by the completion of a convention on financial assistance to states victims of war.[4] During their deliberations, they were able to benefit from the new outlook afforded by the entrance into force of the treaty for the renunciation of war. And in other ways their individual and collective policies were given trends more assuredly peaceful, thus creating *imponderabilia* which conduce to more far-reaching agreement concerning limitation and reduction of the *ponderabilia* of the armament problem.

Nevertheless, so tremendously complicated is the armament problem that the Draft Convention for Limitation and Reduction of Armaments is still very far from being a

[1] See p. 17 *ff*.

[2] Through the coordinate Committee on Arbitration and Security, resulting in this connection in a much wider acceptance of the compulsory jurisdiction of the Permanent Court of International Justice and in the preparation of the General Act for pacific settlement of international disputes as a standard model form of engagement. See League of Nations Assembly resolution of September 26, 1928 (*Resolutions and Recommendations adopted by the Assembly during its Ninth Ordinary Session*, p. 16–57; *Official Journal*, Spec. Sup. No. 63).

[3] The work of the Committee on Arbitration and Security particularly with reference to Arts. 10, 11 and 16 of the Covenant of the League of Nations. (*Documents of the Preparatory Commission*, Series V, VI, VII, IX).

[4] League of Nations *Official Journal*, XI, p. 1648; discussed at p. 74, with the text in Appendix II. See also discussion of the general convention to improve the means of preventing war at p. 83, and text in Appendix II.

complete document. It is, as a matter of fact, only a framework, containing no figures, but yet covering in varying degrees of detail principles of some sort for the limitation or reduction of all forms of armament. Specifically, it is divided into six parts, which deal with personnel, material (land, naval and air), budgetary expenditure, exchange of information, chemical arms, and the miscellaneous provisions, which importantly provide for a permanent Disarmament Commission, establish procedure regarding complaints and include a provision for temporary derogation from the agreed terms.

Even this incomplete Draft Convention does not represent full unanimity of the 27 states which participated in its making. In general, however, its guiding principles represent a framework from which it is to be presumed that the peoples of the world will require their governments to erect in the Disarmament Conference the foundations of a real edifice. The Disarmament Conference is proceeding with its work from the primary basis of the Draft Convention as it stands, reviewing its text in the light of the specific studies of its significance and implications which have been made by each of the governments concerned in the interval.

Meantime, a thorough and systematic general preparation has gone forward. Most governments, as requested, forwarded to Geneva particulars as to the position of their armaments "and all data, technical or otherwise, which might help to inform the conference and to justify such concrete proposals as the governments may lay before it." As such data bear upon the figures for limitation and reduction which are to be inserted in the Draft Convention, they were circulated in advance to all governments invited to the conference, in accordance with the custom of the Secretariat of the League of Nations.

Further, since the preparation of the Draft Convention it has been completed in several respects by special committee reports.[1] The Preparatory Commission, in Art. 27

[1] The conclusions have been incorporated in the text of the Draft Convention as printed in the appendix.

of its Draft Convention, provided for the measurement of the horse power of aëroplanes and dirigible engines, but was unable to fix the rules for such measurement. This task was intrusted to a committee of experts called in by the Organization for Communications and Transit. The rules themselves were communicated to the governments as a preliminary basis for calculating figures respecting their air armaments. The Preparatory Commission was unable to attain agreement upon formulas for limiting directly the material of land armaments and was further unable to agree upon a model statement for the reporting of armament expenditures in general. This question, along with several other cognate problems, was left by the commission to the Committee of Experts on Budgetary Questions, which rendered a report on February 28, 1931,[1] which was immediately transmitted to governments for their study. The Draft Convention brings the development of military aviation to a standstill before the evolution of the "capital ship" of the air, but civil aviation "will continue its unrestrained march." Therefore, all possible information respecting civil aircraft development — technical and legal — is being turned in by governments for the use of the conference.[2] All the documents described above became the basis of exhaustive study by the governments of the word with a view to determining their technical attitude at the conference.

Clearing the International Decks

It is upon the foreign offices, rather than the military, naval and air experts, that the responsibility for reaching decisions of policy lies. It will be the foreign offices rather than the technical services which will be praised or blamed for the outcome of the conference. Delegates to the Preparatory Commission have in principle from the outset been diplomatic civilians. Since the abortive Coolidge conference for limitation of naval armament in 1927, military officers have not been heads of the delegations of

[1] C.182.M.69.1931.IX.3; *Official Journal*, XII, p. 676.
[2] See p. 211.

states to such gatherings, but have attended as advisers only.

Though the Disarmament Conference is expected to bring about a fundamental review and recasting of national policies with relation to their connection with methods of force, there could be no accurate specific knowledge of what the position of governments would be until the conference actually convened. However, there was no doubt of the existence of a general effort in many capitals to set their houses in order with respect to foreign relations before the great assize. Without going into detail, it may be said that every important nation was bending its efforts to that end. Said Secretary of State Stimson in a radio address May 9, 1931:

> A great stimulus has been given to the prospects for success of the conference on general disarmament which is set for February of next year. The nations of Europe are to-day busily engaged in endeavoring to clear up and get out of the way the various controversies and political problems which may jeopardize the success of that movement. Attention has everywhere been focused upon the necessity, as well as the possibilities for good, of the cause of arms limitation.

The clearance or attempted clearance of those problems went on apace during 1931, possibly encouraged by the modest frame of mind in which the depression put the great nations. The Hoover moratorium on intergovernmental debts, the support of German and British finance, the Franco-German and Franco-Italian *rapprochements*, the corrective admission of Mexico to the League of Nations, the increase of nonaggression pacts in eastern Europe, the decision for an armament building truce, the development of bases for European union, the various incidents of the movement toward European economic and tariff cooperation, the abandonment of the projected Austro-German customs union, the visits of United States cabinet ministers to Europe and of European ministers to Washington, the exchange of visits between French and German ministers and between German and Italian ministers, the establishment and functioning of the Franco-German Economic Commission, the renewed attention to the entire problem of intergovernmental debts — all these and other responsible expressions of policy indicated the extent to which those governments most able to interfere with the success of the conference have sought to straighten their own records in advance.

In a larger sense it is a mistake to assume that any degree of success in the conference can of itself settle, either completely or once for all, the armament problem. Hugh S. Gibson, who headed the American delegation to the Preparatory Commission, expressed a salient truth when he recently said:[1]

> I do not expect to see a final solution of the problem of armaments in my lifetime, for it is a problem of human relations, and those problems have to be attended to as long as the human beings involved are alive. The only human problems that can be definitely disposed of are those concerned with the dead. But as there is no finite answer to the problem, there is an infinite possibility of progress. We have in this country the fundamental stimulus to that progress.

Before entering upon a discussion of the details of the problem it may be well to weigh the probabilities of the general success of the conference. It is, of course, of vast importance that a conference is held at all, since it is the first of the kind in history, the largest conference ever held so far as participating states are concerned, and is certain to set a precedent for further meetings in the same series.

Conference Will Change the Problem

Whatever the outcome, the elements of the problem must emerge greatly changed from the conference; and that will be true whether the result is apparent success or apparent failure, for in problems of human relations there is always an advantage on the side of society in the mere comparison of attitudes with a view to agreement. If much agreement results, the indication is that the states involved were not as far apart in reality as they may have

[1] Address at Yale Commencement, *New York Times*, June 18, 1931, p. 22.

seemed before the opportunity to test each other's attitudes had been afforded. If the amount of agreement is slight, the indication is that the differences were of tougher fiber or more fundamental than they seemed to be before the opportunity to consult had occurred. Either type of result is a definite form of progress from which additional agreement is bound to develop, unless the conference itself should prove to be the last. So long as one conference or meeting is likely to lead to another, progress toward the desired end is not only possible, but measurably inevitable.

What this conference may accomplish is, of course, beyond detailed prediction, but if it results in any agreement whatsoever, it is clear — both from the temper of the world and from the tentative agreement recorded in the Draft Convention — that it can not do less than record a limitation of armament. That in itself will be a notable accomplishment, even though it is obvious that, for the great majority of the world, it would not satisfy the expressed demand. But since limitation at some level must result, from any convention containing figures, its significance may be stated for the sake of giving perspective.

In modern civilization it is still customary to justify the maintenance of armament by assumed liability to attack, a point of view which is further emphasized by the strategical dictum that the offense is the best defense. But attack in an actually unprovoked sense does not occur in modern times. The outbreak of war without a *casus belli* of sufficient substance to be convincing to the populace of the attacking state and capable of being argued with other nations, is inconceivable in these times, even if all the conciliatory functions of international organization are left out of account. On the other hand, the use of instruments of war as a makeweight in diplomacy has, until recent years, been a standard practice of the larger states, whose claims were predicated upon the eventual strength which they could throw into the scales in their favor. The existence of armament in international relations until the most recent times has, therefore, offered the opportunity for a state to make its wishes prevail either by employing force or by threatening to employ it.

The truth is that war can serve no useful or essential purpose in modern civilization. No government is on record otherwise, but public men are not averse to seeking the easy advantages of arousing suspicion in their own countries against the intentions of their neighbors, and publics are not averse to enjoying the emotional picture presented. All life consists of conflicts of interest, and modern civilization has not diminished their number. Its questions create conflicts of interest in which war, or even force, is incapable of itself producing a satisfactory solution. The most it can do is to determine — with a maximum of death, destruction and social disturbance — which contestant is in a position to dictate a solution. But in the nature of modern problems, the real solution depends not on who makes it but on its intrinsic qualities; and these can only be determined by referring to the substance and nature of the problem.

Before the Great War, the major value of armament was not its actual use, but the ability of its possessor to threaten a diplomatic antagonist with it. In other words, the chief value of armament was its use for purposes of international bullying. In taking the measure of the armament situation to-day, it is impossible to reach a realistic conclusion without full consideration of the effect that the improved possibilities of pacific settlement have upon the recent freedom of states to display their armed forces so as to turn the scale in securing their own ends.

Though the option of using or displaying armament has thus been considerably restricted in principle, it does not follow that the foregoing analysis of the present position is the prevailing basis of thought upon the matter. The adjustments of foreign offices to the new conditions which have come into existence in recent years is more thorough than that of the peoples. This is naturally so, since it is the foreign offices which have to understand most completely the various engagements taken by their states and which are further under the necessity of digesting the totality of them into practical lines of policy. It takes a long time for millions of people in a nation to assimilate the meaning of a new and changing set-up. The public is seldom able to see the picture as a whole or to take account of all the factors. It is, furthermore, disposed to discount the value of ameliorating agreements and to exaggerate the seriousness of expressed fears and unexpressed suspicions. It resulted that, on the eve of the General Disarmament Conference the element of fear, usually referred to euphemistically as a "lack of security," is as much in evidence as in the old days when a nation could fire off a gun at another without violating the canons of good international society. When a difference arises between states, their necessary first questions are what form of conciliatory machinery will be applied to it, and on whose initiative.

But the opposite is still true of most publics and of the great majority of the individuals of whom they are composed. In consequence, though the conditions justifying fear of one nation by another have greatly changed for the better, the people whom the governments serve indulge themselves in fear of supposititious enemies almost to the same extent that they did in the prewar period.[1]

In such a condition of mind, it is almost negligible whether it is the use or the threat of armament that is involved. The emotion is really called forth by the mere existence of armament, which everybody instinctively knows is not maintained for its appearance on gala occasions of dress parade. In reality, it is this element of fear which maintains the armaments. Everybody knows that no nation, however heavily armed, would limit its strength to its peace-time forces in the case of an actual war; but the peace-time forces are obviously adequate for any threats which a state might be suspected of wishing to make. No state can ever be adequately mobilized in

[1] It may be suggested that there is a certain psychological satisfaction obtained by indulgence in vicarious fear that encourages the continuance of the state of mind described.

peace time for war;[1] for the purpose of threats, they are always fully mobilized.

It is this elemental emotion of fear in the sense indicated which will be the skeleton at the conference, if it has any skeleton in its closet. The conference will surely disintegrate that skeleton in some degree. If it does nothing more than bring a limitation of armament, there will be such an effect. For the two essential characteristics of armament — particularly in these days of technological developments — are instability of value and a consequent tendency to increase. Fear extended throughout a people creates effectively the pressure which causes a government to respond to that historical tendency of increasing its armament. Limitation at any level creates a ceiling, above which the emotion of fear can not rise at all or above which it can rise only against constructive and corrective counter influences. Emotion in international relations is the most difficult of all elements to evaluate and control. Limitation of armament at any level affords an opportunity to control it, because it transforms a subjective feeling into the terms of an objective obligation.

A limitation will have this effect by eliminating in large part new competitive factors between states deeming themselves to be rivals. On this point, Admiral William V. Pratt, Chief of Naval Operations, may be quoted in remarks referring particularly to the London naval treaty:[2]

Perhaps one of the greatest factors in causing trouble is the item "fear." Before the Washington treaty, there was constant talk of trouble between the United States and Japan. The putting into effect of that treaty has been one of the most potent factors in

[1] In the early chapters of his book, *My Experiences in the World War*, General John J. Pershing expresses himself in no uncertain terms on what he deems the inexcusable negligence of the United States to "prepare" for eventualities. In the later chapters he is even more emphatic as to the lack of supplies furnished by a nation bending the every effort of the largest industrialized country in the world. It should be amply clear to others that any possible preparation in peace time can only satisfy the needs of the first weeks or months of an actual war and that therefore the anticipation is of slight military benefit, even though it would make a compound contribution to fear in international relations.

[2] Letter to Fred A. Britten, Chairman of the Committee on Naval Affairs, House of Representatives, December 20, 1930, reported in the press.

eliminating friction between ourselves and Japan that has been possible to devise. Instead of an atmosphere of mistrust, there has been substituted an atmosphere of confidence. The present treaty merely carries on to a completion the work inaugurated by the Washington treaty, and it may be said, with assurance, that in the course of a few years the mistrust, lack of confidence and suspicion which has in the past been such a potent source of trouble, will in future be partially allayed through the medium of treaties for limitation of competitive armaments.

What was true of the condition existing in the Pacific, to a minor degree existed in the Atlantic.

In another direction limitation, and nothing more, can not fail to have a salutary effect. It will reduce at once the pressure for expansion. One of the fundamental reasons for the existence of the state is given in all except the most recent constitutions as "national defense." War ministries around the world have had a disproportionate influence, as compared with foreign offices, upon defining what "national defense" required. Most of their arguments, whether legitimate or not, have been calculated to appeal strongly and persuasively to the latent fear of the people, and in most countries they have acquired an aptitude for securing appropriations from parliaments that approaches genius.

Limitation of armament levels creates a ceiling, stops competition, removes the tendency of expenditures to rise, shifts emphasis from increase to improvement of existing personnel and material — from quantity to quality — and in other ways eliminates technical pressures by the armed institutions of a government. The experience of the states affected by the Washington and London naval treaties is conclusive that the limitation of armament enjoins upon governments a caution[1] in not exceeding the limitations which amounts to a stabilization of strengths

[1] The practical effect of this consideration is illustrated by capital ship experience under the Washington and London treaties. United States construction permitted in 1930 and 1931 was 116,740 tons, of which 16,500 was utilized and 100,240 not; of 125,406 tons Great Britain had utilized 68,250, with 57,156 not used; Japan was postponing some of its 37,484 permissible building; France and Italy had not utilized any of their 30,000 tons. (*United States Daily*, September 14, 1931.)

arguably below the fixed limits. Construction propaganda is based on the demand to "build up to the treaty level." Additionally, limitation diverts attention from mere numbers and quantities to values and, as part of a consecutive process of limitation, inevitably results in an eliminative competition for quality on a reduced scale in the various departments of the armed forces. So much can surely be expected from the effect of the General Disarmament Conference.

The people of the world apparently want reduction as well as limitation of armament to result from the conference. They are particularly in favor of states other than their own reducing, for no people is completely convinced that other states really need, or will make entirely proper use of, the armament they possess. This understandable fact is sufficient to justify the statement that the conference will be subjected to a widespread demand for general reduction.[1] There are indications of popular interest of sufficient scope throughout the world to warrant the suggestion that this demand will create an atmosphere in which the conference will work.[2] All states concerned concentrated upon clearing their political decks before the conference so as to arrive at Geneva with as few outstanding differences as possible. It can, therefore, be concluded that the conference will make an extended and

[1] For petitions to the Preparatory Commission, see *Documents of the Preparatory Commission*, Series VIII, p. 215–221.

[2] Throughout the world during 1931 a remarkable number of organizations adopted resolutions in favor of disarmament and circulated many forms of petitions for signature. A special meeting of the conference on February 6, 1932, received petitions and resolutions and heard spokesmen for the various interested organizations. Petitions signed by over 8,000,000 women in 15 international organizations, having branches in 56 countries and representing a total membership of 45,000,000 women, were one offering from public opinion. The International Cooperative Alliance representing 70,000,000 persons in cooperative families and the international students' organizations, speaking for a combined membership of 10,000,000 persons, made their pleas. Persons speaking for 50,000,000 Methodist communicants as a whole and for 25,000,000 women through the International Union of Catholic Women's Organizations were but two among many from the religious groups. Professional, educational and labor groups handed in petitions by the thousands and spoke for organizations representing many other millions of members. Impressive national petitions were received from many countries, a particular feature being a telegram from Japan signed by 173,000 names.

laborious effort to effect a reduction of armament as well as a limitation.

Most Countries Not Heavily Armed

The possibilities of reduction will, of course, depend in large measure upon the solution of details and the application of the principles at present existing in the Draft Convention. But there are certain general considerations which are bound to work in favor of reduction. In the Appendix (p. 356) is a table compiled from the seventh *Armaments Year-Book* which gives chiefly the figures for 1930 and 1931 of official army strength, other military formations and of naval tonnage. The table is intended to show only the numerical relations of the forces of 62 out of the 63 states which will participate in the conference.[1]

From this table it may be seen that the armament problem affects states very unequally. The table shows a total world army strength of 5,782,000. The army of China, which no one can hold to be an international factor, accounts for 1,800,000, or nearly one-third of the total. Omitting it, the world's armed strength is 3,982,000 maintained by 61 states. Of the 61, the armies of 13 — Czechoslovakia, France, Great Britain, India, Italy, Japan, Poland, Rumania, the Soviet Union, Spain, Turkey, the United States and Yugoslavia—account for 3,047,000 of the total, while the other 48 states — with armies below 100,000 in strength — maintain only 934,000 men. Only 12 other states[2] have armies above 25,000 men, and they account for 559,000 more of the total. The 37 remaining states have 376,000 men under arms. It appears that 13 states out of 62 possess 53% of the world's armies, that 14 (including China) have 85% of them and that the 26 with armies above 25,000 men maintain 95% of the world's land forces.[3] With respect to land armament, therefore, it is clear that in the conference a group of 35 states will certainly use all of its influence to effect reduction all along the

[1] Statistics for Afghanistan are not available.
[2] Argentina, Belgium, Brazil, Bulgaria, Finland, Germany, Hungary, Mexico, Persia, Portugal, Siam and Switzerland.
[3] If China is omitted, the respective percentages are 77 and 91%.

line, while at least 48 states will support most moves in that direction. Since the majority of those 48 states feel the need of some military force, their national policy can only be directed toward improving their own security by seeking the reduction of the armament of others.

The discrepant world distribution of navies is even greater than that of armies. The accompanying table shows a total naval tonnage of 5,423,000, of which 4,249,000 (or 78%) is held by only five states — France, Great Britain, Italy, Japan and the United States. By tonnage, Germany and the Soviet Union are the only states with approximately half the tonnage of the lowest of that group. Further, 20 states which will be represented in the conference are navally nonexistent.[1] Only four others — Argentina, Germany, the Soviet Union and Spain — had over 100,000 tonnage each in 1930, the nine above that figure accounting for 4,797,000 out of 5,423,000 tons, or 88% of the total. The foregoing and eight others with fleets above 25,000 tons — Australia, Brazil, Chile, China, the Netherlands, Norway, Poland and Turkey — maintain all but 234,000 tons of the world's fleets. Thus 17 navies possess 96% of the tonnage, leaving 46 states whose only interest in the matter is to see the high-liners of the 17 with less.

Many civilians feel that the future of military effectiveness depends more upon air forces than upon the older land and naval forces. It has frequently been hinted that attention directed at controlling land and naval forces was "given to closing out moribund services and that militarism" would rise into the air with all its old brilliance. Whatever the future of military aviation may be, it is certain that there is at present world-wide agreement to keep civil and military air strength as separate as possible and that scien-

[1] The following have no navies: Afghanistan, Austria, Belgium (" the Belgian navy has been suppressed as a measure of economy," *Armaments Year-Book, 1929–1930*, p. 57), Bolivia, Costa Rica, Czechoslovakia, Dominican Republic, Guatemala, Haiti, Honduras, Hungary, Irish Free State, Liberia, Lithuania, Luxemburg, Nicaragua, Panama, Paraguay, Salvador and Switzerland.

In addition, Albania, Bulgaria, Canada, Colombia, Ecuador, Latvia, Persia and South Africa showed less than 2,000 tons each.

tific development tends distinctly to reduce the interchangeability of material. Of the 63 states to participate in the General Disarmament Conference, 16 of the smaller ones report no air forces at all, while Austria, Bulgaria, Germany and Hungary are prohibited by the peace treaties from having air forces.[1] France, Great Britain and Italy seem to be the only countries which maintain separate air forces. The 40 others assimilate air forces to their armies, and with rare exceptions, of which the United States is doubtless one, the indications are that their policy respecting air strength will follow that concerning land strength. The chances are that in this field also a great bloc of states will insist on reduction.

From this evidence of the attitude of the states participating in the conference respecting military, naval and air questions, it can be seen that a considerable pressure will exist among the official delegations in favor of reduction. Popular demands to that end will, therefore, have spokesmen.

Control of Conference Agreement

The interplay of forces in the conference itself merits a word, especially since there is a popular tendency to foreshorten the view and romanticize the action of a diplomatic gathering. A conference occurs for no other reason than that the conferring states are not in agreement, but wish to arrive at common decisions. Short of actual threats, which may be disregarded, the process of agreement among states is a complicated one of weighing points of view, of finding points of agreement and of recording them in agreeable formulas. Just in proportion to the difficulty of the subject matter is this process likely to be arduous. It will be extremely so at Geneva, but it will be a great mistake to misinterpret the general aspect of the conference, which will be a succession of antagonistic views, as anything other than a strenuous argument with the primary purpose of reducing divergency of opinion to har-

[1] Art. 144 of the treaty of St. Germain-en-Laye, Art. 89 of the treaty of Neuilly, Art. 198 of the treaty of Versailles and Art. 128 of the treaty of Trianon.

monious conclusions. The public, aided and abetted by the press, tends to disregard everything except conclusions, and plenty of them, and to exaggerate or get peevish at the necessary process of reaching agreement by airing national opinions. On the other hand, full public discussion of national opinions serves to determine what the policy of the state is to be, and foreign comment is an excellent corrective to extreme views or stubborn egoism.

The other misjudgment that customarily occurs is what has been referred to as romanticizing a conference. The most usual picture of a conference is a duel between some of the great states, the so-called great powers. What actually takes place should be kept clearly in mind. A conference is convened for the sole purpose of attaining agreement, and it is the most democratic form of gathering above the New England town meeting. Every state, great or small, has exactly the same rights, and no decision can be finally taken without the consent of all, express or implied.

The rule of unanimity is not necessarily the negative thing which it is usually assumed to be. It does afford any state of whatever size a free and unfettered opportunity to prevent itself being bound by an objectionable decision. It also prevents other states from taking a decision agreeable to them, and this is the side of it which is usually emphasized. However, the action of one state in preventing others from taking a decision desired by them throws upon the blocking state a heavy responsibility, which it is not likely to assume without grave reasons. In practice, in all the action of the League of Nations Assembly and Council there have been but two instances of the actual casting of a veto to prevent unanimity.[1] No state will cast such a vote except for fundamental reasons, and there is nothing to show that such reasons will not be respected, even though they are not accepted.

[1] The adverse vote of Persia respecting an interpretative resolution with regard to Art. 10 of the Covenant in the Assembly, September 25, 1923 (*Records of the Fourth Assembly, Plenary Meetings*, p. 87, *Official Journal*, Spec. Sup. No. 13). Japan prevented a draft resolution from being made executory on October 24, 1931. (*Official Journal*, XII, p. 2358).

Unanimity Rule of Constructive Value

The unanimous vote in reality puts a premium upon finding a basis of agreement, and in multilateral matters this is frequently of advantage. Numerous cases could be cited where the further effort at agreement brought about by the necessity of satisfying all points of view has resulted in a superior decision, while any decision under it is certain to be thoroughly representative.[1]

The responsibility entailed in preventing decision by employing the veto of a unanimous vote results in abstentions. An abstaining state exercises its option of not voting at all. Its reason may be mere lack of interest in the issue, but more often the reason is that, while it does not prefer the suggested solution of the point at issue, it does not set sufficient store upon its own point of view to take the responsibility of preventing agreement.

As has been mentioned, the General Disarmament Conference comprises 64 states, the great majority of which on almost every issue will either be disinterested or desirous of attaining the greatest possible measure of disarmament, which will be effected by others and inure to their own advantage. Any one of those states will cast a vote of exactly the same weight —since all votes are unitary — as the state with the greatest stake at issue in the vote. The disinterested states will be sure to associate themselves by affirmative votes with final decisions of which they really approve. As to others, they will abstain and thus fail to accord their moral support to decisions which they do not prefer, but which seem to them to be practical solutions of points at issue.

At the moment of a final vote, that may seem like a purely negative influence, but its true meaning lies farther

[1] Criticism on this aspect of the matter is usually based on the allegation that a "compromise" decision is unsatisfactory. But in that case the critic must justify his claim to know exactly what should have been decided. In practical international affairs the occasions are comparatively rare when it can be categorically asserted that precisely one decision was necessarily the correct one and that all other forms of reaching agreement or reaching toward agreement should be rejected. Empiricism must remain until rules of law or procedure have been developed in practice to provide definite measuring rods for international action.

back. In an international conference, the unanimous vote is employed only in the final stage of determining a text. Any states represented are entirely unrestricted in introducing proposals and all intermediate decisions in the committees, where the intimate negotiations take place, are subject to majority vote. The multiplicity of proposals reflects the dominant ideas among the delegates, and the debate reveals the general temper of the conference. Principles and proposals, as made or amended, are voted up and down and, aside from the value of the decisions, yield evidence of the general attitude of the membership of the conference, so that there emerges from the detail of committee labors an atmospheric tenor to which all delegates are sensitive and to which they try to conform either within their instructions or by seeking new instructions. It can not be doubted that in the General Disarmament Conference the influence of three-fourths of the states represented will be for constructive accomplishments in disarmament. They will have as their allies outside of the conference a huge, vocal and probably insistent mass of public opinion throughout the world.

Why Great States are More Active

The principle on which an international conference of states operates is the representation of interests. The states interested are represented. Degree of interest does not affect representation, but it positively affects activity. It is this circumstance which too frequently causes it to be said that certain states have controlled a particular conference. The truth in such a statement is applicable to no state or group of states, and the conference mechanism renders any influence beyond that of earnest conviction and the sheer value of ideas relatively harmless. Log-rolling as a means of making an idea prevail may be effective under a majority system of voting, but it can scarcely overcome the unanimous vote unless the subject can win on its intrinsic merit.

Nevertheless, the so-called great powers will in the General Disarmament Conference occupy the center of the stage for the simple reason that their interests are larger, more numerous and better defined than those of other states. A great number of propositions, and even the acceptance of principles, will depend upon the attitude of the great states, not because they are in a position to dictate, but because their governments happen to be the largest or even exclusive custodians of the interests involved in the decisions. It may not appear in the proceedings as currently reported, but it will be true at every stage of the conference that the smaller states will jealously prevent any decision from being taken which would jeopardize their own primary, and frequently only, interest in the proceedings, namely, that the conference take the longest possible step toward a thoroughgoing reduction of armament.

The small state plays frequently an important part through the personality of its delegates. The instances are many in which an individual representing a small state, by his innate ability, special training, aptitude for negotiation or other characteristics, has become an outstanding person in committee or conference work. To mention names might be invidious, but any extended study of the armament problem at Geneva will clearly divulge the fact that much of the progress so far attained has been due to the perspicacity and ability of persons representing states which only a few years ago would have been voiceless and ineffective in international affairs. Ability from the minor states can be counted on to be a constructive influence at the Geneva conference of 1932.

CHAPTER II

MILITARY AND NATIONAL FACTORS

The purpose of these pages being to present the armament problem in the form in which governments are giving it attention in the period before and during the General Disarmament Conference, various phases of the subject which are usually discussed have not been dealt with because they have not received official attention. There are, however, several conditions which so patently affect the problem as a whole that they may be said to be present though not mentioned, perhaps more present for not being mentioned. Notice of them is, therefore, warranted.

There is, first, the well-known fact that national military strength and policy are dependent upon material resources; there are now indications of what materials are contributive to military force. Secondly, there is the assimilation of industrial facilities to military requirements — the addition of the material factor to the long-standing "war potential" of personnel. Thirdly, there is a noticeable and salutary reduction of the influence of the professional military man on governmental policy. Fourthly, is the defining of the position of the Soviet Union with respect to equal participation in the conference.

Products of Military Use

A phase of the national defense problem which affects the attitude of states toward the subject is the production of and trade in raw materials of certain types. This phase of the question has not been officially discussed, though it is frequently present in the minds of all those who have debated physical phases of the problem in the various gatherings. By Art. 8 of the Covenant Members of the League "undertake to exchange full and frank information as to the scale of their armaments, their military, naval and air programs and the condition of such of their industries as are adaptable to warlike purposes."

The interchange that takes place in accordance with this provision is principally evidenced in the *Armaments Year-Book* which has been issued annually since 1924. The third part of the annual volume is published with reference to the condition of industries adaptable to war purposes. The governments have not defined the material to be included,[1] and the Secretariat comments that, "in view of the tendency of modern warfare to absorb all the industrial activity of the country, it would be difficult to define the limits to be given to this part of the Year-Book. Raw materials, manufactured products, existing manufacturing capacity, the quantity of technically specialized labor and the number of persons capable of undertaking work of a technical or organized character are all questions which have become of primary importance to-day from the point of view of preparation for war." Without authority to complete the relevant information, the Secretariat annually publishes statistics drawn from official sources relative to the production of and the import and export trade in the "principal products and raw materials of importance for national defense." The materials reported as to both production and trade are:

I. Fuel: coal, lignite, petroleum.
II. Ores and metals:
   (a) Ores: iron ore, copper ore, lead ore, zinc ore, tin ore.
   (b) Metals: pig iron and ferro-alloys, steel (ingots and castings), copper, lead, zinc, tin aluminium, nickel.
III. Chemical products: natural phosphates, sulphate of ammonia, nitrate of soda and nitrate of lime, cyanamide of calcium, sulphur, salt.
IV. Agricultural products: wheat, rye, barley, oats, maize, rice, potatoes.
V. Live-stock: cattle, sheep, horses, pigs, goats, asses and mules; meats.
VI. Various products: cotton, flax, wool, rubber.

The statistics are given by countries so that it is possible to work out what might be called the nonmilitary ability of

[1] Except for some reports in the early issues of the *Armaments Year-Book*.

the various states with respect to resources and normal command of markets.

Organization of "War Potential"

In dealing with the armament problem as a whole and particularly with the land phase of it, the new features of strategy should be kept in mind. Their significance is not widely recognized outside of technical circles, but within those circles they account for much of the feeling of competition which is known to exist.

An account of the action of the United States will illustrate the principal features of a change which has developed as a result of the Great War. In March, 1915, the United States Secretary of War instructed the War College Division, General Staff Corps, to make a complete and exhaustive study of military policy. In accordance with those instructions, a series of brochures was issued in September to November, 1915. To the principal one, entitled "Statement of a Proper Military Policy for the United States," were appended 30 special studies, many of which dealt with the mobilization and utilization of resources, industries, educational facilities, etc.[1] In consequence of these studies, a Council of National Defense was established by act of Congress of August 29, 1916,[2] "for the coordination of industries and resources for the national security and welfare." The duty of the Council was to supervise and direct investigations and make recommendations to the President on the following subjects:

The location of railroads with reference to the frontier of the United States so as to render possible expeditious concentration of troops and supplies to points of defense;

the coordination of military, industrial and commercial purposes in the location of extensive highways and branch lines of railroad;

the utilization of waterways;

the mobilization of military and naval resources for defense;

the increase of domestic production of articles and materials essen-

[1] For these brochures see War Department, Office of the Chief of Staff, Documents Nos. 506–535.
[2] *Code of Laws of the United States*, Title 50, Chap. 1, Sec. 3, p. 1689.

MILITARY AND NATIONAL FACTORS

tial to the support of armies and of the people during the interruption of foreign commerce;

the development of seagoing transportation;

data as to amounts, location, method and means of production, and availability of military supplies;

the giving of information to producers and manufacturers as to the class of supplies needed by the military and other services of the Government, the requirements relating thereto, and the creation of relations which will render possible in time of need the immediate concentration and utilization of the resources of the nation.

Following the close of the Great War, the War Department in 1922 began preparation of peace-time procedure for realizing military benefits from the recent experience. This action was consonant with the duties of the Council of National Defense and was under the National Defense Act as amended June 4, 1920, by which the Assistant Secretary of War was "charged with supervision of the procurement of all military supplies and other business of the War Department pertaining thereto, and the assurance of adequate provision for the mobilization of matériel and industrial organizations essential to war-time needs."[1]

It first concentrated on industrial mobilization.[2] The magnitude of this plan can be appreciated from the fact that the United States military shopping list in the Great War ran to 700,000 different items. That figure, to be sure, included many component parts and relatively nonessential items. The present "vitally essential list" includes 4,000 articles.

The country was organized into 14 procurement districts, to each of which the American Railway Association assigned an official so as to secure the advantages of unified transportation control. The assignment to industrial plants of war tasks, including a tentative schedule of production up to half of its normal capacity, and the preparation of factory war plans, were undertaken under the name of "survey and

[1] *Code of Laws of the United States*, Title 10, Sec. 1193, p. 214, as amended March 4, 1929; citation from *The National Defense Act* (Washington, 1929), p. 22; cf., War Policies Commission, *Hearings before the Commission*... p. 403.

[2] The *Plan for Industrial Mobilization* is printed as it existed in May, 1931, in War Policies Commission, *Hearings*, p. 395–470. The chief of staff made an extended statement on its purpose at p. 354–378.

allocation of facilities." By 1931, 15,000 large facilities had been surveyed. Allocation of facilities, intended to do away with competitive bidding, had reached 20,245 in 1927.[1]

For articles not familiar to manufacturers complete drawings and specifications are prepared from experiments at government arsenals and laboratories. Educational orders are contemplated to selected facilities, which would use these "descriptions of manufacture" and also maintain in the plant a complete set of dies, jigs and fixtures for producing the article in question.[2]

The collection, collation and evaluation of information pertinent to requisite commodities had been intrusted to 17 commodity committees. By 1931, 4,000 essential items had been listed. Standard contract forms for all purposes are kept constantly revised up to date, being based on a 6% rental of plant involved. A survey of the power resources gave the War Department adequate information on that subject.[3] By 1929, the staff of the Assistant Secretary of War in charge of "planning for procurement and industrial mobilization" had become highly efficient, and the complex industrial war plan was undergoing rapid change in detail as a result of the constant shift in industrial customs, practices, organization and character and the intermittently changing war plan.[4]

In 1928, it had become evident that certain raw materials were deficient in domestic production, and studies were inaugurated to determine which were the "strategic materials" whose importation would be necessary to insure proper supply.[5] Specific study of the list showed that some of these were strategic because they were found in certain parts of the world only, while others were subject to changes caused by new metallurgical developments, new manufacturing methods or by the adoption of new weapons and

[1] In the fiscal year 1930, 1,092 were canceled and 765 added. There were then 14,623 listed facilities assigned to branches, of which 13,019 had been surveyed.

[2] War Policies Commission, *Hearings*, p. 364–365.

[3] *Annual Report of the Secretary of War, 1925*, p. 26–28, and *1927*, p. 29–38.

[4] *Ibid., 1929*, p. 66.

[5] *Ibid., 1928*, p. 17.

MILITARY AND NATIONAL FACTORS

munitions. Each strategic material is the subject of a special procurement plan. The natural object is to decrease the list, which in 1931 contained the following:[1]

antimony	manganese	quinine
camphor	manila fiber	rubber
chromium	mica	shellac
cocoanut shells	nickel	silk
coffee	nitrates	sugar
hides	nux vomica	tin
iodine	opium	tungsten
jute	platinum	wool
	quicksilver	

CRITICAL RAW MATERIALS

copper	airplane spruce	tanning materials
kapok	white phosphorus	lead

All these preparations cost about $400,000 a year and provide complete plans and specifications, requiring only the appropriation of money to permit immediate production. As General Douglas MacArthur, the chief of staff, said:[2] "Modern war demands the prompt utilization of all the national resources. Measures for transforming potential strength into actual strength must work in emergency with the utmost speed and effectiveness."

TECHNOLOGICAL OBSOLESCENCE

By a resolution of Congress,[3] a War Policies Commission consisting of the Secretaries of War, Navy, Agriculture, Commerce, Labor and the Attorney-General and four members each of the Senate and House of Representatives was appointed, and by a further House resolution,[4] the commission was instructed to present to the 72d Congress (1931) a report[5] upon the state of national preparation. The hearings before this War Policies Commission dealt with

---

[1] War Policies Commission, *Hearings*, p. 469. This list is dated November 1, 1928, in a copy forwarded by the director, Planning Branch. A list in unofficial print contains cork, graphite, hemp, flaxseed, potassium, sodium nitrate and vanadium and omits cocoanut shells and nitrates. (*Report of Subcommittee of American Section, International Chamber of Commerce, on Thirty Years of Europe-United States Trade*, p. 11).

[2] War Policies Commission, *Hearings*, p. 376.

[3] Pub. Res. 98, 71st Cong. 2d sess.

[4] H. J. Res. 251.

[5] See House Doc. 264, 72d Cong., 1st sess.

many phases of the problem, especially those connected with industry.

On March 11, 1931, Newton D. Baker, the Secretary of War during the Great War, referred to one of the most salient considerations now affecting armament and its preparation. He said:[1]

> Modern war is essentially and inevitably a process of improvization, particularly if it lasts any length of time. I think two modern nations can undertake to engage in a war that will last three or four months and live on their antecedent preparations for that length of time; but everything about modern war changes very rapidly — its size, its economic demands, its effects on the civilian population, the kinds of arms that are used and the quantity of armament of various kinds. Everything changes as the war goes on. The World War is a typical example of it. The kind of new weapons which were used in the World War, at the end of the war, and their dominance over the old arms, is one of the striking characteristics of that war. The development of the submarine, the development of the airplane, the proportion of artillery used to infantry, the whole introduction of chemical warfare, changed the character of the war from the time it started to the time of its conclusion so profoundly that it was really a different war, for which antecedent preparation had not been made.
>
> As a war progresses under modern conditions the inventive faculty of the various nations is stimulated, its industrial capacity is developed, and these new agencies and new theories of combat necessarily change the whole character of it. I think this is also true about the economic situation. At the outset the economic demands of a war, no matter how imaginatively they are tried to be foreseen, are varied and changed to correspond with the other changes that go on in the making of the war itself. Having had that experience, my own very strong feeling is that there is only a limited amount of preparatory economic legislation or planning that can be done, and that it would be a mistake to have inelastic provisions of that sort attempted, just as it would be a mistake to have inelastic provisions made for arms.

The considerations set forth by the former Secretary of War have made a great impression upon the civilian mind, which has encountered them in many forms. In a period of scientific research and industrial development, when

[1] War Policies Commission, *Hearings*, p. 122.

technological obsolescence is a striking feature of mechanized civilization, it is obvious to all that warlike implements must be subject to the same conditions as other forms of mechanism.

This is the phase of the armament question which perhaps is most nearly affected by budgetary limitation. If a new machine is developed in a manufacturing industry, it is possible for a board of directors, by the use of surplus or by bond or stock issues, to replace present machines with improved ones, and the advantages of the new machinery rapidly justify the decision on a balance sheet. Rearming troops, however, can not be done on any such basis, but only by national appropriations, and it is usually inadvisable, as well as expensive, to attempt piecemeal rearming. Naval material, which is already limited in numbers, must be used in formations, and the extent to which new designs can be introduced from bottom to bottom is, therefore, limited.

In the days when armament competition was free and unlimited, and when war scares for the sake of military appropriations were an acceptable form of demagoguery, the adjustment of material to technological advances was a problem. It is a historical fact that the Russian tsar convened the Hague Peace Conference of 1899 in the hope that an armament agreement would obviate the necessity of undertaking the financial burden of rearming Russian artillery to meet the changes already made by Germany and France and about to be effected by Austria-Hungary.[1]

In more recent periods when army and navy departments were still unrestricted, they found the greatest difficulty in securing appropriations for keeping up with technological advances to their own satisfaction; in fact, it is probably true that they have not in a generation been satisfied with the quality of the armament obtainable. A permanent feature of technological improvements is that they increase costs. This is the principal reason why "national defense"

[1] *The Staggering Burden of Armament*, p. 331–332 (World Peace Foundation, IV, No. 4), citing E. J. Dillon, *The Eclipse of Russia*, p. 269–274; Sergius Witte, *Memoirs*, p. 96.

budgets tend so persistently to rise. Obviously, the mere limitation of budgets—not to speak of reduction—will definitely alter the problem of military men in this respect.

Increasing Cost Cramps Style

One of the interesting features of official consideration of armament limitation is the extent to which technical style is being cramped by the necessity of doing something. German armament, which is notoriously the *bête noire* of French political life, was limited respecting effectives and material by the treaty of Versailles, which made no stipulations respecting budgetary limitation. Germany was not to build any warship above 10,000 tons, but was free to spend as much as was needed to carry out plans on that size. As a natural consequence, the battle cruiser *Deutschland* was designed within that tonnage limit, with such marked technological improvements that it is admittedly equal to ships of much larger tonnage. Obviously, the budgetary limitation which is insisted upon as an antidote for such a situation will also cripple all other countries in making radical technological improvements in material.

All general staffs pay much attention to the development of new arms, but the armament actually in use is always approaching, and sometimes reaches, the obsolescent stage. The result has been to concentrate attention upon the development of experimental models. Arrangements for procurement and industrial mobilization are directed to this end. Even without any restrictions, the keeping of material abreast of technological standards in peace time lags, and it is destined to lag still more with the imposition of international restrictions, whether budgetary or otherwise.

From a military point of view, this is probably not as bad as it might seem, since the military people are the only ones in the world who approach the record of the proverbial plumber for going to the job with the wrong tools. As Secretary Baker correctly stated, "modern war is essentially and inevitably a process of improvization." As soon as the pressure which in peace time causes military experts to worry over the lack of "preparedness" is released by an actual state of war, all the improved plans that had to be kept in pigeon holes can be put to manufacture. A speedy effect is the introduction of new weapons.

"You must remember," says Gen. George V. H. Moseley, deputy chief of staff, "that in war we always go into the first battle with the ordnance equipment saved from the previous war. In this respect, we are always one war behind . . . We do not attempt in time of peace to produce these new guns in quantity. It would mean a great outlay of funds for equipment which might become obsolete."[1]

The competition respecting material being entirely free in actual war, the new weapons inspire improvements or new types, and any modern war is bound, like the Great War, to end in a dependence upon implements which were not thought of at its beginning. Campaign emergencies accelerate the process, the commandeering of Paris taxicabs to save the battle of the Marne being the historical prelude to the present development of mechanization of transport. Tactics and strategy alike create unforeseen demands. The open formations of the Boers in the South African War spelled the doom of the classic British square. Trench warfare in 1915–18 altered the functions of infantry, and machine guns changed the value of the rifle. The British grand fleet was parked in the North Sea, except for occasional furloughs to have the barnacles scraped off. The safety of the battleships required the assignment of a protecting cordon. Notwithstanding that the dreadnought was supposed by Admiral Fisher to be a great improvement in the prewar days, the huge mechanisms were used once at the battle of Jutland, when an inferior German fleet inflicted a superior damage upon the British, and successfully retired. The submarine and the transport with its attendant cruiser, original or converted, were the chief naval craft of the war.

So it will always and inevitably be. It is beyond the power of the human mind, in an inventive and technological world, to equip an army, navy or air force in advance with material that will prove to be of maximum use in actual

[1] War Policies Commission, *Hearings*, p. 389.

warfare. This important question of the genuine usefulness of implements, except as evolutionary exhibits, has not yet entered into the debates.

PEACE AND WAR — CONVERSION LAG

The relation of armament to the initial outbreak of a war has never been examined objectively. Instead, it is used as the canvas for painting the most lurid pictures of disaster, with the conclusion that the imaginary view of national misfortune indicates a lack of security necessary to be remedied. Major Victor Lefebure, in his excellent *Scientific Disarmament*, emphasizes effectively for the first time what he calls the "conversion lag," that is, the essential time required for getting a given thing into use after the decision to design, make or employ it. We are, he said, "faced, not with a spontaneous phenomenon, quite uncontrollable, but with a long, steady growth involving a number of specific steps, each of which permitted effective measures of control, and the integration of which gave real hope of disarmament in the true sense."[1] Major Lefebure's entire book lays the greatest stress upon this factor and goes a long distance toward exploding "the idea of the sudden emerging of the new agencies to threaten a peaceful world, somewhat on the lines of an epidemic of measles."

It takes time even to get a war declared, leaving out of account the important mechanism of pacific settlement, which can not fail to be applied in these days before there is a possibility of such a declaration. With the exception of Japan, no state of any importance in the armament problem is in a constitutional position to start a war without parliamentary authority, and no parliament responsible to a public would dare approve such a step unless the people's temper were generally known. There is a definite conversion lag between the state of peace and the state of war in a legal sense, and that, added to the conversion lag respecting effectives and material, together create a transitional period. It is possible that this element of the problem will get into the discussions at the conference.

[1] *Op. cit.*, p. 16.

MILITARY AND NATIONAL FACTORS

Another way in which the peace scale of equipment adds to the sense of insecurity is with respect to the outcome of the first battle. Peace-time equipment is comparatively evaluated only in terms of the first battle; for, as soon as actual war exists, the entire energies of a nation are devoted to supply, and all elements of warfare advance to a new level.[1] The real uses of peace-time equipment on land are for winning the first conflicts and for providing a skeleton organization to which fresh effectives and material can be added, which latter is the more important of the two.

When general staffs find themselves really hampered in continuing the maintenance of effectives, material and expenditures on the present or increasing scales, they are likely to make much of this false assumption in the elements of security. They are likely to discover that their business is not the winning of initial battles, but of campaigns and to plan their equipment to take the game rather than the initial trick. If that should become military policy, the emphasis of preparation would naturally shift from the material in hand at any given peace time to the means of providing effectives and material under conditions in which expenditure had none except national limits and the full resources of the state could be mobilized for their purposes. The effect would be to concentrate peace-time attention upon the training of officer cadres, so far as effectives were concerned, and of perfecting designs for the speediest possible manufacture of material, once the word was given. Planning for procurement and industrial mobilization is admirably adapted to achieve such ends. When that is the direction of the development of general military policy, the nation with the largest national resources and the highest industrial development would automatically and inevitably be the prime military state in the world.

[1] "The United States is a nation of 120,000,000 people. Its aggregate wealth is reckoned at $400,000,000,000. The industrial planning agencies are engaged in the task of developing methods whereby the combined efforts of this huge organization may be coordinated, and where necessary diverted from their normal pursuits of peace, toward the single purpose of winning a war." ("Plan for Industrial Mobilization," War Policies Commission, *Hearings*, p. 403.")

Civilian Control Superseding Military

One of the unnoticed changes in the armament problem has been the assumption of control over it by national conductors of foreign affairs instead of military men. The extent to which national defense was left to interested officers until recent years accounted in considerable part for the national state of mind respecting the subject. In the United States, it has been a fixed policy to choose only civilians as heads of the military departments, thus carrying on a long tradition of Anglo-Saxon suspicion of military influence in government. But until after the Washington conference, it could scarcely be said that anywhere was determination of the objectives of national defense really made where it ought to be, in foreign offices. The latter, in fact, either maintained methods of thought essentially strategic in a military sense or they substantially evacuated their proper position and left it to military experts to appraise the dangers to which a nation was subjected, as well as to perform their proper function of providing means to neutralize those dangers.

The great schoolmaster of war, Von Clausewitz, properly defined war as an extension of policy, realized by force instead of negotiation. The vigor and tenacity of strategists, and also national dispositions, brought it about that in the nineteenth century it was the general staff which determined policy rather than the foreign office, upon which the function rightly devolved.

The change that has occurred may be illustrated by an incident or two. It is well known that the annexation of Alsace-Lorraine in 1871 was due to Von Moltke. At Versailles in that year, when Bismarck "was in conflict with foreign, feminine and military influences,"[1] he had doubts about the retention of the Metz area. "If they gave a milliard more," he said one day, "we might perhaps let them have Metz. We would then take 800,000,000 francs and build ourselves a fortress a few miles further back. . . . We should thus make a clear profit of 200,000,000. I do

[1] *New Chapters of Bismarck's Autobiography*, p. 57.

not like so many Frenchmen being in our house against their will. . . . The military men, however, will not let Metz slip, and perhaps they are right."[1] After the resumption of diplomatic relations, he referred to this doubt and indicated the pressure upon him even more clearly in a conversation with the French chargé d'affaires at Berlin on August 14. "I am under no illusion," he then said. "It is absurd for us to have taken Metz, which is French. I did not wish to keep it for Germany. The General Staff asked me if I could guarantee that France would not take its revenge. I replied that I was fully convinced to the contrary. . . . In that situation, they said to me, Metz is a glacis behind which France can put 100,000 men. We had to keep it. I should say the same thing of Alsace and Lorraine. We made a mistake in taking it from you if peace was to be durable, for these provinces are an embarrassment for us."[2]

At Versailles, 50 years later, Marshal Foch, the generalissimo of the victors, was brushed aside by the French premier Clemenceau in a personal controversy that never relaxed during their lives and was given considerable notoriety after their deaths. Foch insisted on making the Rhine the western frontier of Germany.[3] Whatever else can be said about the treaty of Versailles, its strategical determinations were made by the civilian governments and not their military advisers. The peace treaties as a group indicate the extent to which after the Great War the military consideration was a part of the policy of governments, representative of their respective peoples. The negotiations demonstrated the subordination of the military adviser, who was not permitted to dictate terms of settlement, even though his point of view materially affected the terms.

There remained both the influence of the military on the conduct of foreign relations and a more or less fixed habit of officers acting as spokesmen for governments concerning

[1] Charles Lowe, *Prince Bismarck*, Vol. I, p. 631.
[2] France, *Ministere des Affaires Etrangeres. Commission de Publication des Documents Relatifs aux Origines de la Guerre de 1914. Documents Diplomatiques Francais (1871–1914)*. 1re Série (1871–1900). Tome premier, p. 62.
[3] André Tardieu, *The Truth about the Treaty*, p. 145.

the needs of defense. The fault was largely that of the foreign office, since its silence upon matters of fearsome interest to the public created a vacuum which the professional soldier, whether loquacious or not, was under a professional temptation to fill. By long habitude, it had become fairly customary for generals and admirals to tell their publics when and where some other country was going to start the next war. Chronologically, these open confidences usually took place when budget figures were being fixed.

At the Washington conference on limitation of naval armament, officers were brought to their proper function. The proposals made to that conference were worked out by the conductors of foreign relations from data furnished by the experts. The significance of the facts and their working into a program was effected without the aid of naval experts and in connection with the functional appraisal of policy situations by experts in foreign relations. It took general staffs years to recover from the shock that they were no longer setting up the target as well as being expected to hit it.

The extent to which officers continued to discuss questions of policy was not yet satisfactory. It apparently irked even President Coolidge, for he rather went out of his way to define an officer's duty in his address before the graduating class of the United States Naval Academy on June 3, 1925. On that occasion he said:

> It seems to me perfectly proper for any one upon any suitable occasion to advocate the maintenance of a navy in keeping with the greatness and dignity of our country. But as one who is responsible not only for our national defense, but likewise our friendly relations with other peoples and our title to the good opinion of the world, I feel that the occasion will very seldom arise, and I know it does not now exist, when those connected with our navy are justified, either directly or by inference, in asserting that other specified powers are arming against us, and by arousing national suspicion and hatred attempting to cause us to arm against them.

In following the reduction of professional military men to their normal stature, it is appropriate to recall that until after the abortive naval conference called by the United States in Geneva in 1927, it was customary to include high ranking officers in delegations as negotiators. The concentration of attention which they gave in that conference to matters of purely strategical advantage created a reaction which has since resulted in dominantly civilian delegations and the relegation of military men either to subordinate positions in delegations[1] or to rank as advisers only.

Another instance of the change in trend may be cited from another international situation. During the negotiations resulting in the Locarno treaties, the relaxation of inter-allied supervision over German military, naval and air forces became a necessary condition. The Conference of Ambassadors asked the Inter-Allied Military Control Commission, of which Marshal Foch was the head, for a statement of status. Marshal Foch handed in a memorandum in which he dealt with political considerations,[2] as well as strategical. The Conference of Ambassadors handed it back with the explanation that Marshal Foch's commission had exceeded its instructions and that, when a proper memorandum was presented, it would receive consideration. The note containing the demands remaining to be fulfilled and constituting conditions prior to the evacuation of the northern Rhineland zone was duly handed to the German ambassador on June 4, 1925, and the arrangement which resulted was effected by exchange of notes in the following October and November.[3]

Military influence in international affairs is illustrated in a different way by Japan. When the Shogunate was abolished and the Empire established, it was decided that the German imperial constitution was a satisfactory model for that of Japan. One result of this were provisions that "the emperor has the supreme command of the army and navy" and "determines the organization and peace stand-

[1] Two excellent exceptions continued through the commission's sessions, General de Marinis of Italy and General Karprzycki of Poland.

[2] He still wanted to put France on the Rhine despite the wholly German character of the territory.

[3] For the correspondence on the conditions handed to Germany, see Great Britain, Parl. Papers No. 12 (1925) Cmd. 2527.

ing of the army and navy."[1] In consequence, the ministers of war and navy have not been civilians, but generals and admirals who are outside of the cabinet.[2] At the London Naval Conference the head of the Japanese delegation was a civilian, as were the other heads of delegations. When the resulting treaty reached Tokyo for acceptance, the naval authorities, notwithstanding the presence of the minister of the navy at London, were in several instances opposed to its provisions. An internal political struggle ensued, but the cabinet eventually had its way, and the treaty was ratified, though a number of naval officers committed hara-kiri in unavailing protest.

TECHNICAL NAVAL POLICY OF THE UNITED STATES

An indication of the changing attitude respecting armament may be had from the record of the United States. Matters of foreign policy are, of course, within the jurisdiction of the Department of State, and properly enough, it was that Department alone which produced the program of limitation which was presented to the Washington conference in 1921 and became the basis of the naval treaty of 1922. The Secretary of the Navy in his Annual Report dated November 15, 1922, in referring to that treaty says:[3]

For the first time in the history of our country the navy and Congress have a definite naval policy and building and maintenance standard to work to, a standard which is proportionate to our position as a world power. The maintenance of this standard in all respects is necessary to our defense and to our prestige.

The prior "lack of definitely enunciated policies" was corrected in the light of that treaty by a statement prepared in the General Board and approved by the Secretary. The fundamental and general naval policies were expressed in two paragraphs:

[1] The text is quoted from W. W. McLaren, *Japanese Government Documents*, p. 137 (Transactions of the Asiatic Society of Japan, Vol. XLII. Part I, May, 1914), where many other pertinent documents may be found.
[2] Further to the constitutional position of the minister of war see Naokichi Kitazawa, *The Government of Japan*, p. 40–41; Tatsukichi Minobe, *Essentials of the Japanese Constitutional Law*, p. 219, 552–557.
[3] P. 1.

The navy of the United States should be maintained in sufficient strength to support its policies and its commerce, and to guard its continental and overseas possessions.

To create, maintain, and operate a navy second to none and in conformity with the ratios for capital ships established by the treaty for limitation of naval armaments.

Following the abortive conference called at Geneva in 1927 on the invitation of the United States, the Secretary began carrying in his report a statement of the objects which the operation of the naval forces had in view during the year. As published first in the 1928 report,[1] this consisted of four items, the first of which was "maintenance of battle efficiency." In the report for 1929 and subsequently, the employment of force has been defined by the Secretary as follows:

The operations of our naval forces during the past year had the following objects in view:

(a) Exercise and train the units of the fleet to the highest state of efficiency and provide a nucleus for expansion in case of national emergency.

(b) Protect American interests in disturbed areas.

(c) Cultivate friendly relations with foreign peoples.

Just after Armistice Day in 1928, the Navy Department announced the fundamental naval policy of the United States which is dated October 6. On August 5, 1931, a revision was announced.[2] In the latter revision appear the following principles:

The navy should be maintained in sufficient strength to support the national policies and commerce, and to guard the continental and overseas possessions of the United States.

General navy policy: To create, maintain and operate a navy second to none and in conformity with treaty provisions.

To organize the navy as far as possible so that expansion only will be necessary in the event of war.

To make strength of the navy for battle of primary importance.

To make strength of the navy for exercising ocean-wide control

[1] P. 3.
[2] *United States Daily*, November 13, 1928, and August 5, 1931.

of the sea for protection of American interests and overseas and coastwise commerce next in importance.

To determine emergency material needs. To plan for their procurement and to coordinate these plans with those of the War Department.

THE SOVIET UNION AND THE DRAFT CONVENTION

The first-reading text of the Draft Convention contained an article on reservations which might be made by Estonia, Finland, Latvia, Poland and Rumania, suspending with respect to them certain articles "until the accession of Russia to the present convention under the same conditions as the above-named powers."[1] This proposal, which is reminiscent of Art. 29 of the convention on traffic in arms of June 17, 1925, was made by the delegations of Finland, Poland and Rumania in April, 1927,[2] before the Soviet Union accepted the invitation to take part in the Preparatory Commission.

That proposal was submitted to the subcommittee, of which M. Politis was chairman, along with other final articles in November, 1930. The delegations concerned then still attached importance to the text and stated that they were unable to abandon it. The subcommittee did not recommend it for inclusion in the Draft Convention for the reason that it raised an essentially political question and also brought forward the extremely complex problem of reservations to a disarmament convention.[3] The Soviet delegate, M. Lunacharsky, regarded the omission of the article as a matter of course, since his country was now represented on the commission, but was "amazed to find that the article in question has not entirely disappeared." He wished the position to be made entirely clear.[4]

On December 9, the Preparatory Commission was revising the draft of the report which constitutes its authentic gloss on the text of the Draft Convention.

M. Lunacharsky, prefacing his remarks with the obser-

[1] *Documents of the Preparatory Commission*, Series X, p. 460.
[2] *Ibid.*, Series IV, p. 312–317.
[3] *Ibid.*, Series X, p. 282.
[4] *Ibid.*, p. 285.

vation that the Soviet delegation was not taking part in the drafting of the report, which it was leaving to the whole responsibility of the commission, objected that this treatment of the matter placed his government in an exceptional position, to which it could not agree. He trusted that the delegations concerned would have the tact to withdraw their reservation; if not, and his appeal to the commission was not acceded to, he would be obliged to protest on purely political grounds. His primary objection was the singling out of his country as the specific subject of a reservation, and he suggested that the report note that the text in question had been expunged from the Draft Convention because all reason for its maintenance had disappeared.

After a discussion of formulas for the report, the Soviet proposal was defeated 12 to 2, and a majority text adopted by 18 to 1. This recorded that an article, EC, had been adopted on first reading. The text adopted reads:[1]

> The commission decided that the study of this question should be left for the conference. This decision was dictated by two reasons. The first was that the text raised an essentially political question, and the second that it brings up a very complex problem: the effect of the reservations which the contracting powers will be allowed to formulate at the time of signature.

In his speech at the final meeting of the Preparatory Commission on the same day, the Soviet delegates vehemently protested against the commission's refusal to pronounce any final judgment on the article.[2]

The commission thus left an issue pending for the conference, which as an issue had assumed a somewhat different status in February, 1932, than was the case in December, 1930. On December 2–13, 1922, following the Genoa conference in which the Soviet Union participated, there was held at Moscow a conference on the limitation of armament in which Estonia, Finland, Latvia, Lithuania and Poland participated after various preliminary meetings of the non-

---

[1] *Report*, par. 280.
[2] *Documents of the Preparatory Commission*, Series X, p. 402.

Russian diplomats.[1] The six governments drew up a convention of nonaggression and arbitration and adopted it for signing,[2] but were unable to reach conclusions respecting the reduction of armaments, on which disagreement the conference broke up.

During the Genoa conference in April, 1922, Russia had signed the treaty of Rapallo with Germany.[3] In April, 1926, it was superseded by a political treaty, to which was attached an interesting pacific settlement clause providing for an annual mutual examination of outstanding differences and for their settlement by inquiry or arbitration. The following August a treaty of friendship and nonaggression was made by the Soviet Union with Afghanistan and in September one with Lithuania, a fourth following with Persia in October, 1927. The five-year term of the German, Afghan and Lithuanian treaties was attained in 1931, and they were all renewed, or new treaties were signed to replace them, during that summer. Following those prolongations, negotiations for a nonaggression pact were undertaken by Poland on August 23, in resumption of a proposal first made in August, 1926, on which discussion was continued until 1927. The Soviet attitude was that negotiations should proceed separately with Poland. At the same time a proposal for a treaty of nonaggression and conciliation between France and the Soviet Union[4] was made in connection with a general settlement of their outstanding questions, which was actively taken up again in October. At the same time also, the Soviet Union separately proposed the same sort of treaty with its other neighbors, Estonia, Finland and Latvia. Moscow has declined to deal with Rumania, with

---

[1] *Conférence de Moscou pour la Limitation des Armements* (Moscow, 1923).
Military experts of Estonia, Finland, Latvia and Poland met at Reval, August 1–4, and those Governments participated in a conference at Reval, September 8 preceding, while their military experts and experts from Rumania consulted at the end of September at Warsaw (*Bulletin de L'Institut Intermediaire International*, Vol. VIII, p. 185–188). The conference itself had been preceded by a meeting of delegates of Estonia, Latvia, Poland and Russia at Riga, March 29–30, 1922. (*Conférence de Moscou pour la Limitation des Armements*, p. 239).

[2] *Ibid.*,

[3] *Treaty Series*, XIX, p. 248.

[4] Moscow has proposed such a negotiation three times in recent years (*Le Temps*, August 29, 1931).

which the Bessarabia affair is outstanding, except singly.[1] Negotiations were begun with Rumania at Riga in January, 1932, and treaties were signed with Finland on January 21 and with Poland on January 25.

The form of engagement in these treaties is illustrated by that with the border state Lithuania:[2]

Art. 2. The Lithuanian Republic and the Union of Socialist Soviet Republics undertake to respect in all circumstances each others sovereignty and territorial integrity and inviolability.

Art. 3. Each of the two contracting parties undertakes to refrain from any act of aggression whatsoever against the other party.

Should one of the contracting parties, despite its peaceful attitude, be attacked by one or several third powers, the other contracting party undertakes not to support the said third power or powers against the contracting party attacked.

By another article, the parties undertake to settle all disputes arising between them by conciliation and inquiry, but remit to a subsequent treaty the establishment and procedure of the commission.

A recent form of the Soviet pact of nonaggression is built to the idea of developing and completing the Briand-Kellogg pact, which is applied between neighbors as follows:[3]

Art. 1. The two contracting parties, recalling that they have renounced war as an instrument of national policy in their mutual relations,

Reciprocally undertake to refrain from any aggression or attack against one another, both individually or jointly with other powers.

As an act contrary to the engagements of the present article shall be considered any act of aggression impairing the integrity and inviolability of the territory or the political independence of the other party, even if this act has been committed without declaration of war and by avoiding all its characteristics.

Art. 5. The two parties desiring to settle and solve all disputes and conflicts, of whatever nature and of whatever origin they may

[1] The Rumanian delegate to the Assembly of the League of Nations on September 8, 1931, announced that his Government was ready to negotiate nonaggression pacts with any country whatever.

[2] League of Nations *Treaty Series*, LX, p. 153.

[3] Translation from the French text initialed at Moscow January 25, 1932, on behalf of Poland and the Soviet Union.

be, which might arise between them, exclusively by pacific means, undertake to submit all contentious questions which it has not been possible to settle in the necessary periods by diplomatic means, to a procedure of conciliation, in conformity with the provisions of a convention concerning the application of the procedure of conciliation, which convention forms an integral part of the present treaty and is to be signed separately, then ratified, with the shortest possible delay, at the same time as the pact of nonaggression.

The Soviet Union was thus embarked prior to the conference upon a policy of establishing relations of nonaggression and pacific settlement with all border states. Upon the status of the negotiations during the conference depended in large measure the attitude of the states of eastern Europe toward each other.

CHAPTER III
PRESENT ARMAMENT CONTROLS
A. Admitted Members of the League

All states admitted as Members of the League of Nations — in distinction from the original members — are subject to prescriptions by the League respecting armaments. The admitted Member "shall give effective guaranties of its sincere intention to observe its international obligations, and shall accept such regulations as may be prescribed by the League in regard to its military, naval and air forces and armaments." This condition applies at the present time to Albania,[1] Austria,[2] Bulgaria,[3] the Dominican Republic,[4] Estonia,[5] Ethiopia,[6] Finland,[7] Germany,[8] Hungary,[9] the Irish Free State,[10] Latvia,[11] Lithuania,[12] Luxemburg [13] and Mexico.[14]

---

[1] *Proces-Verbal of the 11th session of the Council*, p. 134 (20/29/17).
[2] *Ibid.*, p. 133.
[3] *Ibid.*, p. 133.
[4] *Records of the Fifth Assembly, Plenary Meetings*, p. 470 (*Official Journal,* Spec. Sup. No. 23).
[5] *Proces-Verbal of the 10th session of the Council*, p. 109 (20/29/16).
[6] *Records of the Fourth Assembly, Meetings of the Committees, Minutes of the Sixth Committee*, p. 33 (*Official Journal*, Spec. Sup. No. 19).
[7] *Proces-Verbal of the 10th session of the Council*, p. 109 (20/29/16).
[8] *Records of the Special Session of the Assembly (March 1926)*, p. 46 (*Official Journal*, Spec. Sup. No. 42).
[9] *Records of the Third Assembly, Plenary Meetings*, II, p. 122.
[10] *Records of the Fourth Assembly, Meetings of the Committees, Minutes of the Sixth Committee*, p. 28 (*Official Journal*, Spec. Sup. No. 19).
[11] *Proces-Verbal of the 10th session of the Council*, p. 111 (20/29/16); *Proces-Verbal of the 11th session of the Council*, p. 134 (20/29/17).
[12] *Proces-Verbal of the 11th session of the Council*, p. 134 (20/29/17).
[13] *Proces-Verbal of the 10th session of the Council*, p. 113 (20/29/16).
[14] The resolution of September 12, 1931, admitting Mexico to the League mentions the invitation extended, and continues:
"Having by this exceptional invitation — which must not be regarded as establishing a precedent — formally indicated that it accepts as having been fulfilled from the outset in the case of Mexico the conditions governing the entry of states into the League as set forth in Art. 1 of the Covenant."

The duty of prescribing the regulations to be accepted by admitted states devolves upon the Council in the first instance and a report from a committee of the Assembly is always before that body when it acts upon an application for admission. The actual examination of the evidence with respect to armaments is made by the Permanent Advisory Commission for Military, Naval and Air Questions, and this has for some years been its most important function. Its duties in this connection have very largely been formal in character, since the states admitted have had small armaments and have had modest ambitions for their maintenance, but the duty is not only intrinsically important, but its fulfillment creates a continuing obligation.

The case of Finland is in point. The commission in a report of October 22, 1920, passed upon Finland's armament. The report[1] states that the army then consisted of 32,000 men, but the government wished to reduce it to 16,000; the commission recommended "the maintenance of these forces," and the last report of the country showed budgetary effectives of 31,575. Finland wished to maintain the six torpedo boats and four auxiliaries then in possession, reserving the right to replace them by modern vessels of about 1,000 tons each. The commission unanimously recommended their maintenance, and the present fleet consists of exactly those vessels. In addition, Finland asked for four submarines, and the subcommission, considering that the submarine is an economic method of defense for small countries, proposed the authorization of four submarines of less than 400 tons by a vote of 6 to 2. One submarine of the four was launched in 1930, and the three others permitted are now constructed.[2] As to air forces, Finland possessed 69 aëroplanes and wished to increase that number "in the future." The commission recommended the maintenance of the present force and reserved "the right of approving the later demands of Finland when it has received fuller information."

[1] *Proces-Verbal of the 10th session of the Council*, p. 109 (20/29/16).
[2] *Armaments Year-Book 1931*, p. 403; *Particulars Concerning the Position of the Armaments . . . Finnish Government*, C.655.M.267.1931.IX.25.

Here is an instance of setting a tentative limit and of retaining a right to pass upon an additional question of armament. Finland was admitted to the League by vote of the Assembly on December 16, 1920, in accordance with a report which records that the Finnish Government had given "a solemn assurance of its intention to observe international obligations in all sincerity" and that "no objection to Finland's naval and military program" had been raised.[1] Finland, in reporting the status of its armament for the *Armaments Year-Book*, recognizes the condition placed upon its air force by recalling in a note attached to the text that the maintenance of its 69 aëroplanes had been approved and that the League of Nations had reserved approval of any further demands. The country's air force consists of a staff, two aviation squadrons, three independent flights, a flying school and a school of noncommissioned officers, reported as 1910 average daily effectives.

With respect to the states defeated in the Great War, the procedure in carrying out the condition of admission to the League was the same and may be illustrated by the case of Germany. A subcommittee of the special session of the Assembly in March, 1926, was asked the customary question: "What had been the acts and declarations of the German Government regarding (*a*) its international engagements, and (*b*) the stipulations of the League with regard to armaments?" The Council, acting under Art. 9 of the Covenant, had from the Permanent Advisory Commission on Military, Naval and Air Questions a reply to question (*b*) that "the question of the status of the military, naval and air forces of Germany is regulated by the treaty of Versailles of June 28, 1919, and does not require to be considered by this commission." The Assembly's subcommittee's intention to seek additional information was anticipated by the Conference of Ambassadors which transmitted a declaration that "as far as it is concerned, and to the best of its knowledge, Germany is now giving effective guaranties of her sincere intention to discharge her obligations under the treaty of peace." As regarded land arma-

[1] *Records of the First Assembly, Plenary Meetings*, p. 609.

ments, the declaration of March 4, 1926,[1] stated that the condition on which the execution of the military clauses was to be completed were in an agreement "now in course of realization." The naval clauses had been executed and the final reports forwarded to the League, whose Secretary-General added a letter that no request had been received for exercise of the right of investigation by the Council. As to the air clauses, only certain arrangements for insuring general observance in the future remained to be completed.

It will be perceived that the Members of the League of Nations in such cases have regarded limitations of armament by treaty as a condition in fulfillment of the terms of admission to the League. The German application was not acted upon at the special session of the Assembly in March, 1926, but in the seventh ordinary session in September of that year. At that time, the vote to admit was taken without a reexamination of the conditions of the application.

The admission of Ethiopia[2] was voted following a declaration in which the country recognized as binding the system established with regard to the importation of arms and ammunition in conformity with the principles set forth by the protocol on that subject.[3]

B. Demilitarization and Nonfortification

While the Temporary Mixed Commission was exploring the armament problem, it gave some attention to the existence and usefulness of demilitarized zones. The prohibition of fortifying a particular area has occurred many times in history. Originally, it was imposed upon a defeated state as a strategical incident of victory. Since the Anglo-American agreement concerning naval forces on the Great Lakes of 1817, it has been increasingly accepted as a means of avoiding conflict.

The Anglo-American agreement has had an immense in-

[1] *Records of the Special Session of the Assembly* (*March 1926*), p. 47.
[2] *Records of the Fourth Assembly, Plenary Meetings*, p. 125 (*Official Journal*, Spec. Sup. No. 13).
[3] The protocol of St. Germain-en-Laye of 1919 has since been succeeded by the convention of June 17, 1925, to which Ethiopia is an ordinary contracting party.

fluence upon thought concerning the subject, and rightly so, for its effect upon both policy and national attitudes has far transcended the actual engagement. In a strictly technical sense, it is very questionable whether the agreement itself is legally in force, but it has always beyond question been morally in force, and its influence has extended far beyond its specific terms. The agreement in text limits war vessels on the Great Lakes according to the technique of 1817, which has long been obsolete. But the intent of its meaning has been followed not only on the Great Lakes, but on all other boundary waters between Canada and the United States. The agreement relates only to naval forces, but by a moral expansion, believed to be unconscious on the part of the contracting parties, the principle was extended to the longest boundary line in the world between two countries. And when the United States and Canada again became territorially tangent along the Alaska border, the principle was extended without question. It is not an insignificant circumstance in the consideration of security that an agreement over 100 years old to remove naval competition on certain boundary waters has been extended in practice to demilitarize frontiers totaling nearly 5,000 miles of land and water.

Neutralization is of a character similar to demilitarization. It consists of a treaty obligation on the part of contracting states not to use specified territory for warlike purposes. It may or may not involve the absence of military structures in the territory in question. It has the effect of legally removing the neutralized territory from the possibility of attack. It differs from neutrality in that the latter status is assumed at will, while neutralization is established in advance and creates a duty on the part of the neutralized area to maintain status. Neutralization has not been popular since the Great War, owing to the violation of Belgium's and Luxemburg's neutralization by Germany during that conflict, with the result that Belgium abrogated the status, and Luxemburg has allowed its claim to fall into desuetude. Nevertheless, there remain in the world some neutralized areas, and the principle, therefore, continues to exist in international relations.

The Council of the League of Nations in its handling of one of the first disputes before it brought about the demilitarization and neutralization of the Aaland Islands by the convention of October 20, 1921.[1] The Temporary Mixed Commission saw values in the principle involved, and the Geneva protocol of 1924 specifically contemplated the existence and increase of demilitarized zones. The treaty of mutual guaranty of the Locarno series demilitarizes the Rhine frontier. It can thus be seen that the principle of establishing areas in which hostilities are not to take place is one of the methods which can be used to enhance the feeling of security. The principle is established only for those states accepting it as a restriction upon their military freedom.

In comprehending the armament problem as a whole, the following list of demilitarized and neutralized areas may be studied :[2]

SWITZERLAND. *Neutralization.* Declaration of March 20, 1815, annexed to the treaty of Vienna of June 9, 1815.

CANADA AND GREAT BRITAIN-UNITED STATES. *Demilitarization.* Agreement of April 28–29, 1817.

STRAITS OF MAGELLAN. *Neutralization and demilitarization.* Treaty between the Argentine Republic and Chile of July 28, 1881.

SUEZ CANAL. *Neutralization and demilitarization.* International convention of Constantinople, October 29, 1888.

BURMA AND TIBET. *Demilitarization.* Convention between Great Britain and China, London, March 1, 1894.

THE PAMIRS. *Demilitarization.* Agreement between Great Britain and Russia, London, March 11, 1895.

SIAM. *Abnegation.* Declaration between Great Britain and France, London, January 15, 1896, engages neither of them to advance armed forces into the frontier river basins of the Kingdom of Siam.

---

[1] League of Nations *Treaty Series*, IX, p. 212.

[2] The texts of the documents establishing the status indicated are compiled in Annex I of the *Armaments Year-Book*.

ITANG. *Demilitarization.* This territory leased by Ethiopia to the Sudan is not to be used for any military purpose. Treaty between Great Britain and Ethiopia, May 15, 1902.

HELIGOLAND. *Demilitarization.* Treaty of Versailles, June 28, 1919, Art. 115.

GERMANY, maritime littoral. *Nonfortification.* No new structures to be erected within 50 kilometers of the coast, treaty of Versailles, June 28, 1919, Art. 196.

SAGHALIEN. *Nonfortification.* Treaty of peace between Japan and Russia, Portsmouth, September 5, 1905. Navigation of the Straits of La Perouse and Tartary is also free of military impediments.

NORWAY-SWEDEN. *Neutralization and demilitarization.* Neutral zone on either side of the common frontier established and demilitarized by convention of Stockholm, October 26, 1905.

MOROCCAN COAST. *Demilitarization.* Convention between France and Spain (Great Britain party in interest), Madrid, November 27, 1912.

NEW HEBRIDES ISLANDS. *Nonfortification.* Protocol between France and Great Britain, London, August 6, 1914.

GERMANY, left bank of Rhine. *Demilitarization.* Treaty of Versailles, June 28, 1919. Arts. 42-44, confirmed and guaranteed by the treaty of mutual guaranty, Locarno, October 16, 1925.

SAAR BASIN. *Demilitarization.* Treaty of Versailles, June 28, 1919. Saar Annex, par. 30.

IRAQ. *Nonfortification and demilitarization.* Under terms of mandate (Great Britain mandatory) and Art. 22 of the Covenant.

PALESTINE AND TRANS-JORDAN. *Nonfortification and demilitarization.* Under terms of mandate (Great Britain mandatory) and Art. 22 of the Covenant.

SYRIA AND THE LEBANON. *Nonfortification and demilitarization.* Under terms of mandate (France mandatory) and Art. 22 of the Covenant.

CAMEROONS. *Nonfortification and demilitarization.* Under terms of mandate (Great Britain mandatory) and Art. 22 of the Covenant.

CAMEROONS. *Nonfortification and demilitarization.* Under terms of mandate (France mandatory) and Art. 22 of the Covenant.

TOGOLAND. *Nonfortification and demilitarization.* Under terms of mandate (Great Britain mandatory) and Art. 22 of the Covenant.

TOGOLAND. *Nonfortification and demilitarization.* Under terms of mandate (France mandatory) and Art. 22 of the Covenant.

TANGANYIKA TERRITORY. *Nonfortification and demilitarization.* Under terms of mandate (Great Britain mandatory) and Art. 22 of the Covenant.

RUANDA-URUNDI. *Nonfortification and demilitarization.* Under terms of mandate (Belgium mandatory) and Art. 22 of the Covenant.

SOUTHWEST AFRICA AND ZIPFEL. *Nonfortification and demilitarization.* Under terms of mandate (Union of South Africa mandatory) and Art. 22 of the Covenant.

WESTERN SAMOA. *Nonfortification and demilitarization.* Under terms of mandate (New Zealand mandatory) and Art. 22 of the Covenant.

NAURU. *Nonfortification and demilitarization.* Under terms of mandate (British Commonwealth of Nations mandatory) and Art. 22 of the Covenant.

NEW GUINEA. *Nonfortification and demilitarization.* Under terms of mandate (Australia mandatory) and Art. 22 of the Covenant.

ISLANDS UNDER JAPANESE MANDATE. *Nonfortification and demilitarization.* Under terms of mandate and Art. 22 of the Covenant.

DANUBE. *Nonfortification.* Prohibition to Czechoslovakia respecting the right bank south of Bratislava. Treaty of Saint-Germain-en-Laye, September 10, 1919, Art. 56.

ESTONIA-RUSSIA. *Demilitarization and neutralization.* Specific frontier regions affected by the treaty of Tartu, February 2, 1920. Demilitarization of Lakes Peipus and Pskov.

SPITZBERGEN. *Demilitarization.* International treaty, Paris, February 9, 1920, Art. 9.

GULF OF FINLAND. FINNISH ISLANDS. *Neutralization.* Treaty of peace between Finland and Russian Soviet Republic, Dorpat, October 14, 1920, Art. 13.

LAKE LADOGA. *Demilitarization.* Treaty of peace between Finland and Russian Soviet Republic, Dorpat, October 14, 1920, Art. 16.

AALAND ISLANDS. *Nonfortification and neutralization.* International convention, October 20, 1921.

DANZIG. *Demilitarization.* Constitution of May 11, 1922, under guaranty of the League of Nations.

FINLAND-RUSSIAN SOVIET REPUBLIC. FINNISH-SOVIET FRONTIER. *Limited demilitarization.* Convention between Finland and Soviet Union, Helsingfors, June 1, 1922.

ANZAC (ARI BURNU). *Demilitarization.* Treaty of peace with Turkey, Lausanne, July 24, 1923, Art. 129.

GREEK ISLANDS IN ÆGEAN SEA. *Demilitarization.* Treaty of peace with Turkey, Lausanne, July 24, 1923 (Islands of Mytilene, Chios, Samos and Nikaria).

BULGARIA-TURKEY. *Demilitarization.* Convention, Lausanne, July 24, 1923, demilitarizes the European frontier to a depth of 30 kilometers on both sides.

GREECE-TURKEY. *Demilitarization.* Convention, Lausanne, July 24, 1923, demilitarizes the European frontier to a depth of 30 kilometers on both sides.

THE STRAITS. *Neutralization and demilitarization.* Convention establishing the régime of the Straits, Lausanne, July 24, 1923. Affects the Strait of the Dardanelles, the Sea of Marmora and the Bosporus. Both shores of the Bosporus and of the Dardanelles are demilitarized to varying, but effective, depths. Islands in the Sea of Marmora and the Islands of Imbros, Tenedos, Lemnos, Samothrace and Rabbit Island in the Ægean Sea outside the Dardanelles are also demilitarized (Art. 4).

TANGIER. *Neutralization and demilitarization.* Convention, Paris, December 18, 1923, Art. 3.

NEJD-TRANS-JORDAN. *Nonfortification of Kaf district.* Agreement, Bahra Camp, November 2, 1925.

DOMINICAN REPUBLIC-HAITI. *Nonfortification.* Treaty

of peace, friendship and arbitration, Feburary 20, 1929, Arts. 1-2, *Treaty Series*, CV, p. 215.

CHILE-PERU. *Nonfortification*. Morro de Arica. Protocol, Lima, June 3, 1929.

C. Revision of Peace Treaties[1]

In connection with this aspect, an undefined thesis of the necessity for revising the treaty of Versailles has popular currency and is the basis for some internal agitation in Germany. In viewing the matter objectively, it should be distinctly understood that the treaty of Versailles has been considerably revised, and will continue to be so, by the normal methods of adjustment if not by a formal conference. All treaties which deal with the details of international relations undergo frequent revision or change of status, and there are literally dozens of subsequent treaties dealing with the subject matter of Versailles which have as effectively superseded its text as the New Plan has superseded Part VIII, dealing with reparation.

Failure to recognize this cardinal fact has measurably created an unreal situation and brought forward a thesis of the necessity of maintaining the status quo of the "peace treaty," which corresponds to no practical or actual reality. In international affairs, there is no such thing as a status quo. Time changes if nothing else does. All the status quo means in reality is that its advocate is fully satisfied with conditions of to-day and does not wish to-morrow to change them. If the human race can not somehow manage to do better to-morrow than it does to-day, it is in a sorrowful state. The true test either for the maintenance of what is—or its discontinuance — is empiric usefulness, modified by the soundest principles which the parties in interest are able to apply.

The military, naval and air clauses of the treaty of Versailles have been extensively modified in practice, and on account of the discussion which persists respecting them, it

[1] The extent to which revision of the treaties of peace has taken place can be studied in very full detail by consulting the section "Exécution des traités de paix" in *Bulletin de l'Institut intermédiaire international* (La Haye, 1920–).

PRESENT ARMAMENT CONTROLS

may be well to mention the principal details of modification. Part V of the treaty consists of Arts. 159-213, divided into five sections.

Section IV establishes and defines the duties of the Interallied Military, Naval and Air Commissions of Control, which were abolished respectively on the following dates: military, January 31, 1927;[1] naval, September 30, 1924;[2] air, *circa* March 8, 1921.[3]

Section V has expired by limitation with the exception of Art. 213, which establishes the exercise of right of investigation by the Council of the League "so long as the present treaty remains in force" and in reality so long as the Council decides to exercise it.

Section III contains the air clauses, Arts. 199-202 of which were executed within time limits. Art. 198 prohibits air contingents in German armed forces, and was impractical without definite decisions distinguishing and recognizing the right of Germany to conduct civil aerial navigation. This was done by an agreement signed at Paris, May 22, 1926, which is effective.[4]

Section I of the part is the military clauses. They are full of time limits, all the original dates of which have, of course, expired and the extensions of which belong to history. The figures in the section have been extensively revised by agreements between Germany and the Conference of Ambassadors, and it is the revised figures only which are now effective. The revision of the military terms began with the protocol of January 10, 1920,[5] continued with the Spa protocol of July 9, 1920,[6] was advanced by numerous ex-

[1] See communiqué of the Conference of Ambassadors, Myers, *Seventh Yearbook of the League of Nations*, p. 260.

[2] *Official Journal*, VI, p. 304.

[3] *Ibid.*, V, p. 1011. An aëronautical committee of guaranty, however, functioned until August 9, 1926.

[4] League of Nations *Treaty Series*, LVIII, p. 331-374.

[5] *Protocols and Correspondence between the Supreme Council and the Conference of Ambassadors and the German Government and the German Peace Delegation between January 10, 1920, and July 17, 1920, respecting the Execution of the Treaty of Versailles of June 28, 1919* (Miscellaneous No. 15 (1921) Cmd. 1325).

[6] *Ibid.*, p. 171.

changes of notes up to June 4, 1925,[1] and the correspondence of October-November of that year,[2] closing with the records attached to the reports of July 22, 1927,[3] and March 16, 1931.[4] It will be noted from the character of the documents described that all changes have been the result of agreements between the Conference of Ambassadors, acting for the collective party of the first part on one side, and Germany on the other. The following changes of number are effective:

Art. 160. Effective strength of officers remains at 4,000, with 300 medical and 200 veterinary officers added.

Art. 161. Civilian administrative personnel increased from 901 to 1,636.

Art. 165. The maximum stocks have been changed as follows:

	Table No. III	Authorized
Rifles and carbines	102,000	156,080
Revolvers	none	52,000
Heavy machine guns	792	861
Light machine guns	1,134	1,475
Bayonets	none	106,080
Sabers	none	30,000
Lances	none	18,000
Ammunition, for rifles, carbines and machine guns	56,208,000	103,768,000
Hand grenades	none	2,000,000
Pistol cartridges	none	5,000,000
Blank cartridges	none	25,000,000
Medium trench mortars	63	63
Light trench mortars	189	189
Ammunition for trench mortars	176,400	201,000
Field artillery:		
7.7 cm. guns	204	204
10.5 howitzers	84	84
ammunition for, 7.7 cm. guns	201,000	239,000
ammunition for, 10.5 cm. howitzers	67,200	82,200

Art. 162 attempted to restrict the number of gendarmes and local or municipal police to the ratio of the population maintained in 1913 and provided that they might not be assembled for military training. The Conference of Ambassadors on June 20, 1920, agreed to an increase in police

[1] *Note presented to the German Government* (British Parl. Paper, Germany No. 2 (1925) Cmd. 2429).
[2] Miscellaneous No. 12 (1925) Cmd. 2527.
[3] *Official Journal*, VIII, p. 1058.
[4] *Ibid.*, XII, p. 783.

effectives from 80,000 to 150,000 men, and the police since 1926 have consisted of 105,000[1] under the jurisdiction of the states and 35,000 under the communes.

Art. 168. Establishments for the manufacture of arms, munitions and war material were not "closed down" by decision of February 10, 1921, of the Conference of Ambassadors; only those exclusively devoted to those purposes were suppressed. On December 26, 1921, the Conference of Ambassadors permitted transformation of the latter factories; following a long correspondence, on January 10, 1930, it postponed establishing definitive rules in that connection until the year 1932.

Art. 169 provides that all German "war material" must be surrendered for destruction or to be rendered useless, including special plant intended for its manufacture. The Conference of Ambassadors on May 28, 1920, permitted the retention of 25,000 machines used for making war material, but capable of other uses. On June 1, 1923, it ruled that automobiles, railroad material and nonmilitary clothing were not war material to be surrendered. On June 27, 1923, the conference permitted the retention by Germany of material for scrapping, instead of crediting such receipts to themselves.

There has been an acrimonious argument as to whether the "centers of instruction" established in each of the seven divisions of the German army are military schools permitted by Art. 176, or military academies of the sort prohibited by that article. Retirement of officers before attaining the age of 45, fixed by Art. 175, undoubtedly occurs, and French experts make the most of the evidence. There is constant bickering over the extent to which former officers and students are inducted into and promoted in the Reichswehr, the character of which is equally a matter of controversy. The argument on it is whether it is a reserve in the prohibited sense. The army itself has more superior officers per regiment than the French, on which fact the Parisian

[1] French military men are insistent that the state police are a military formation violative of the treaty, despite their authorization by the Conference of Ambassadors.

experts dwell at length, though the quota of officers is not definitely exceeded. Such details have been all too carefully played up, with the net result that French suspicions have been kept at an exaggerated level and German sensibility has been aroused. German private organizations offering military training have undergone a number of postwar transformations. In 1918, there were the Einwohnerwehren (armed units) and Sicherheitspolizei (safety police), followed by other Selbstschützorganisationen (self-protection organizations) and the notorious Orgesch. By 1922 these were mostly disbanded, partly because of allied insistence. Other organizations, such as the Hochschulring deutscher Art, Stahlhelm and Jungdeutscher Orden became popular and offered German youth particularly an opportunity to wear uniforms. Whatever is the truth as to the military value of these organizations, the victors have it in their power to raise any questions they see fit. Until they formulate objections through complaint of the Conference of Ambassadors to the Council of the League, it may safely be assumed that German good faith is at least equal to that of the others.

Section II includes the naval clauses. Art. 181 restricts the naval forces in commission to six battleships, six light cruisers and 24 destroyers and torpedo boats in commission. In addition, Germany maintains, with the knowledge and consent of the Conference of Ambassadors, one battleship, two light cruisers and five destroyers and torpedo boats uncommissioned and in reserve. The ships in reserve are to be commissioned only in replacement of vessels in commission. Submarines were and remain abolished.

Art. 183 establishes a fleet personnel of 15,000 which continues as a limit. The total strength of officers and warrant officers is there stipulated as 1,500. The Conference of Ambassadors recognized that the figure was wrong and the present officers and warrant officers number some 5,000.[1]

[1] French military journalists take the typical attitude that the German action is not in good faith. Having the facts, they claim concealment is going on and even blame the Germans for the concessions made by the Conference of Ambassadors. See particularly Lt.-Col. Reboul "Le Potentiel militaire de l'Allemagne," *Le Temps*, August 14, 18, 19, 23, 30 and October 3, 1931.

A phase of the flaunting of armament, established by Art. 429 of the treaty of Versailles, was the occupation of the west bank of the Rhine and of the bridgehead zones (20,927 square miles) by Belgian, British, French, Italian and United States troops at German expense, but at rates of expenditure exclusively determined by the occupying authorities. In three years the United States ran up a bill of $292,000,000. France quartered 60,000 troops in the zones, though at moderate cost to Germany. The zones have been evacuated after and before the due dates, as follows:

Zone	Evacuation due	Effected
Cologne	January 10, 1925	February 28, 1926
Coblenz	January 10, 1930	December 14, 1929
Mainz-Kehl	January 10, 1935	June 30, 1930

Austria has no need for a navy and both its navy and air forces were abolished by the treaty of St. Germain-en-Laye. The country has had other things than armament on its mind since the Great War and maintains an army of only 21,000 men, though it is entitled under the treaty to 30,000.

Bulgaria under the treaty of Neuilly has no navy, but only patrol boats on the Danube, and no air force. The land troops may attain 33,000 men, but do not. Bulgaria, however, shares the German insistence upon regaining unilateral control over its armament under multilateral agreement.

Hungary under the treaty of Trianon has only patrol boats on the Danube, but no navy. Air forces are prohibited. The treaty army of 35,000 effectives is maintained under the command of 26 generals and 75 colonels. Nearly half of the effectives — 15,300 — rank as noncommissioned officers.

Bulgaria, Germany and Hungary have been represented in the Preparatory Commission, so that they have had opportunity to participate under normal circumstances in laying the groundwork of the Draft Convention. The influence of their attitude in the conference will of a certainty be directed, constructively, at bringing the restrictions of the peace treaties into the universal convention; or, otherwise, to divest themselves of those servitudes.

Principles of the peace treaties which might be useful in fulfilling the pledge of the victors in the respective Parts V of the treaties are:

Fixation of the proportion of officers and men;

Limitation of administrative services;

Establishment of international agreement respecting methods of recruitment;

Abolition of reserves of all types;

Fixation of maximum amounts of material to be stocked in relation to effectives retained;

Abolition of freedom of international trade in arms, munitions and war material;

Limitation of military school enrollment to recruiting requirements;

Detailed international rules as to what constitutes measures of mobilization, and international cognizance of measures taken;

General application of demilitarization to border areas;

Regulation and control of military and naval aviation.

The other principles on which Part V of the peace treaties were built are believed to be implicitly or explicitly incorporated in the Draft Convention.

D. Private Manufacture of Arms

Another of the important features of armament control which will play a part in the whole picture at the General Disarmament Conference is the supervision of the private manufacture and publicity of the manufacture of arms and ammunition and of implements of war. The fifth paragraph of Art. 8 of the Covenant of the League reads:

> The Members of the League agree that the manufacture by private enterprise of munitions and implements of war is open to grave objections. The Council shall advise how the evil effects attendant upon such manufacture can be prevented, due regard

being had to the necessities of those Members of the League which are not able to manufacture the munitions and implements of war necessary for their safety.

Results under this provision are exactly in the same state as the general results. There is an incompleted Draft Convention which it is hoped that the conference will be able to finish.

Prewar experience created a widespread suspicion that the private manufacture of arms caused a competition in salesmanship which encouraged and maintained a militaristic rivalry and which had even been a direct incentive to actual war. On the scientific side, the private manufacture of arms undoubtedly contributed to the beginnings of the period of technological acceleration which is a current industrial feature. The commercial marketing of the product, however, raised the suspicions which are reflected in the Covenant. The Temporary Mixed Commission for the Reduction of Armaments in 1923, after a survey of the problem, recommended that private manufacture should be controlled, but not prohibited.

The Brussels act of July 2, 1890, regulated the traffic in arms and ammunition in colonial Africa, and its expansion and modernization in the convention of September 10, 1919, was not effectively ratified. In consequence, a conference on control of trade in arms was held at Geneva in 1925, resulting in a considerable expansion of the categories of controlled and prohibited arms.[1]

Following that action, the Council of the League transmitted a series of questions on private manufacture to states and prepared a preliminary Draft Convention.[2] Due to criticism of this text, a Commission on the Private Manufacture of Arms and Ammunition and Implements of War was set up in 1927. In that year, in August and November, 1928, and again in March, 1929, the commission struggled with the problem and finally in August, 1929, drew up a Draft Convention concerning which there was still a distinct difference respecting methods of securing publicity for state

[1] *Treaty Series*, XCIV, p. 65.
[2] *Official Journal*, VI, p. 554, 220; VII, p. 170.

manufactures. The 10th session of the Assembly in 1929 invited the Council to convene the commission once more, after having itself struggled fruitlessly to solve the outstanding phase of the problem. Inasmuch, however, as the problem of publicity raised the question of whether reports were to be made respecting quantity or value or both, a number of states expressed the opinion that they could not make up their minds before knowing the conclusions of the Preparatory Commission for the Disarmament Conference on the question of publicity of war material. That commission found the question of publicity insoluble even on the expenditure side in its own body and remitted that phase of its work to the Committee of Budgetary Experts, which did not report until after the commission produced the Draft Convention for the Disarmament Conference. In consequence of this interlocked series of complications, it was found that a positive solution of the method of publicity respecting privately manufactured arms could not be solved prior to the General Disarmament Conference. Moreover, the budgetary experts found themselves unable to recommend a detailed method of publicity by categories of material owing to the divergent accounting elements involved in the question. In consequence, the whole problem of agreement on private manufacture was, by a Council resolution of May 20, 1931, deferred until after the settlement of the question of publicity in the General Disarmament Conference.

The question of a control of private manufacture has thus become closely interrelated with the General Disarmament Conference and has by the natural processes of examination become welded to the additional question of publicity concerning manufacture. In this connection, it is pertinent to recall that since 1924 there has been issued a *Statistical Year-Book of the Trade in Arms and Ammunition* which in its successive editions has developed into a most elaborate conspectus of both the imports and exports of those materials by quantity and by value. Its information is, however, confined to private commerce and includes neither sales of military and naval materials to states nor any information respecting either quantities or values actually manufactured.

The Draft Convention with regard to the Supervision of the Private Manufacture and Publicity of the Manufacture of Arms and Ammunition and of Implements of War establishes five categories of weapons.[1] Category I includes arms, ammunition and implements of war exclusively designed and intended for land, sea or aërial warfare, comprised under 12 headings as follows:

1. Rifles, muskets, carbines.

2. (a) Machine guns, automatic rifles and machine pistols of all calibers;
   (b) Mountings for machine guns;
   (c) Interrupter gears.

3. Projectiles and ammunition for the arms enumerated in Nos. 1 and 2 above.

4. Gun-sighting apparatus, including aërial gun sights and bomb sights, and fire-control apparatus.

5. (a) Cannon, long or short, and howitzers, of a caliber less than 5.9 inches (15 cm.);
   (b) Cannon, long or short, and howitzers, of a caliber of 9.5 inches (15 cm.) or above;
   (c) Mortars of all kinds;
   (d) Gun carriages, mountings, recuperators, accessories for mountings.

6. Projectiles and ammunition for the arms enumerated in No. 5 above.

7. Apparatus for the discharge of bombs, torpedoes, depth charges and other kinds of projectiles.

8. (a) Grenades;
   (b) Bombs;
   (c) Land mines, submarine mines, fixed or floating, depth charges;
   (d) Torpedoes.

9. Appliances for use with the above arms and apparatus.

10. Bayonets.

11. Tanks and armored cars.

12. Arms and ammunition not specified in the above enumeration.

[1] *Official Journal*, X, p. 1601

Category II comprises arms and ammunition capable of use both for military and other purposes.

Category III comprises vessels of war and their armament.

Category IV comprises aircraft and aircraft engines.[1]

Category V includes explosives and arms and ammunition not comprised in Categories I and II and of general civilian use. These articles are subject only to such publicity as national legislation prescribes.

The categories are the same as those included in the convention of 1925 on the supervision of trade in arms. Private manufacture is defined as the manufacture of these articles in establishments of which the state is not the sole proprietor and which are to a large extent engaged in the manufacture of Categories I-IV on behalf of others than the state in which the factory is situated. Private manufacture as so defined of the articles included in Categories I-IV shall be licensed by the government.[2] The contractants undertake to forward to the Secretary-General of the League quarterly a list of licenses.

So far the Draft Convention represents general agreement. The draft of Art. 5 as it stands contains an undertaking to forward to the Secretary-General or to publish annually a return showing the total production under private manufacturing licenses in value, number and weight[3] of the articles in Categories I, II and IV. The parties undertake to report the text of all statutes, orders or regulations with regard to these categories and to continue making them public.

The controversial point on the subject is a provision that the publicity indicated for each contracting party to give respecting these three categories "shall also apply to the

[1] The United States suggested that this material should be limited to that manufactured under military specifications to include material manufactured for purely military purposes and that manufactured for commercial purposes on specifications designed to make it capable of military use.

[2] The Government of the United States has stated that it "is powerless to prescribe or enforce a prohibition or system of licenses upon private manufacture."

[3] The Japanese Government holds that the publicity should be in terms of value only.

production of the material manufactured for it in establishments of which the state is the sole proprietor, or in any other establishment on behalf of the state." This provision would serve to produce information, open to the world, respecting the amount of land war material actually in existence and destined for military use, whether in stock or reserve. The basis of traditional military secrecy would in large part disappear.

The Czechoslovak, French, Italian, Polish and Rumanian delegations stated that they could not accept the proposal. The reason given, which was also a Belgian argument, was that the question of state manufacture of state armament could only be determined in connection with the decisions taken under the resolution of the Preparatory Commission of May 4, 1929. That resolution recorded a decision that the limitation and reduction of land material "must be sought by means of publicity of expenditure" at a subsequent examination. It was a transactional resolution, as is clearly shown by the fact that it was proposed by the United States delegation which is itself not reconciled to budgetary limitation.[1]

So far as the Draft Convention on publicity is concerned, reporting of state manufactures stands at that point, and the Preparatory Commission in its Draft Convention did not advance the question beyond it in Art. 10 comprising Chapter A of Part II. Nevertheless, the precise question was affected by the debate in the final meeting of the Preparatory Commission in 1930, and it is practically certain to arise when the wide open problem of land armament is reached in the General Disarmament Conference. If agreement can then be had, it is quite possible that the Draft Convention on Private Manufacture and Publicity might be completed during the conference as a part of the general settlement.

Art. 6 of the 1929 draft deals with publicity respecting

[1] *Documents of the Preparatory Commission*, Series VIII, p. 179. The vote was 22 to 2 as follows: *For*, Belgium, Canada, Chile, Colombia, Cuba, Czechoslovakia, Finland, France, Great Britain and Northern Ireland, Greece, Italy, Japan, the Netherlands, Persia, Poland, Rumania, Spain, Sweden, Turkey, the United States, Venezuela, Yugoslavia. *Against* China, the Soviet Union. *Abstained*, Germany.

Category III, vessels of war and their equipment. Since this material is already limited and the same character of secrecy has not inhered in it, no difficulty was found in providing for publicity respecting all manufacture. In fact, the article of the Draft Convention under reference gives the details to be reported under conditions already controlled by Art. 21 of the Draft Convention, so far as state manufacture is concerned. That article repeats Art. 18 of the Washington treaty and prevents the disposal of a war vessel to the navy of any foreign state. Of course, publicity of naval construction by private manufacture raised no question of principle, secrecy never having been practical in that regard.

CHAPTER IV

ARBITRATION AND NATIONAL SAFETY

It is impossible to get a proper view of the armament problem without proper appreciation of the fact that since 1924 the theory on which a solution for it has been sought has been based upon the formula, "arbitration, security (safety),[1] disarmament." The arbitration and security elements are seldom understood as a whole; first, because the structure of pacific settlement which has developed is disjointed and, secondly, because it has not, possibly on that account, exercised its eventual effect upon the emotion of security.

The formula is arbitration, security (safety), disarmament; that is, the development of pacific settlement gives a basis for confidence in the national security (safety), and that confidence makes possible steps toward disarmament. The formula was first enunciated by France, but the entire

[1] The two words are used together, because the dispute over policy in this case, as in so many others, is measurably due to the choice of words and is therefore to that extent a difference over expression rather than intention.

The underlying idea, namely, that armament must bear a relation to national needs, was inevitable in establishing an international principle. The English text of Art. 8 of the League Covenant refers to the requirement of reducing armament "to the lowest point consistent with national safety," a criterion appearing in the House (Art. 23), Wilson's first (Art. IV), second (Art. IV), third (Art. IV), fourth (Art. IV), Percy (Art. V), Cecil-Miller (Art. IV) drafts and the draft from which the commission worked (Art. 8) (Hunter Miller, *The Drafting of the Covenant*, II, 10, 13, 72, 99, 146, 122, 134, 233). In those proposals — all officially presented except those of France and Italy — the phrase was "domestic safety," which was changed to "national safety" on a Japanese suggestion, (*Ibid.*, p. 264). In the French texts the noun everywhere appeared correctly as "sécurité," (*Ibid.*, p. 399, 431), and it so appears in the official French text of the Covenant in force.

When M. Herriot gave expression to the formula, "arbitration, security, disarmament," in 1924, he, of course, spoke in French in the Assembly, where "security," instead of "safety" got into currency in the English texts. Security in English is a more abstract conception than safety, involving a freedom from apprehension as well as mere immunity from harm. Safety, which is the condition of the Covenant, is a determinable factor; security is to a degree a psychological point of view, which is possessed by the governments laying the greatest stress on that element of the trinity.

membership of the League of Nations had been feeling for it, and its expression in 1924 seemed to be a classic statement of an obvious thing. However, in the interval since that time the order of progress has been somewhat debated, and Italy has become a definite advocate of a change of order, putting it disarmament, arbitration, security;[1] that is, the cutting of armament opens the way to broader pacific settlement, and national safety results from the doubly improved situation. The change of order might give rise to an interesting discussion as to the proper method of procedure, but either order leaves security as the result of the other two steps, and as a matter of international action both arbitration and disarmament are being pursued simultaneously.

I. THE RECORD AS TO SAFETY

The "security" element is emphasized solely by states which are nervous as to their position in the world or are devoted to the status quo. Exactly what would satisfy the insecure states has never been stated in actual terms; all that is known is that they believe their neighbors or near neighbors possess too much armament for their comfort or are pursuing an antipathetic policy. From the nature of that state of mind, it would be very difficult to get a statement — and still more difficult to obtain realization — of the exact degree of reform in the neighbor which would satisfy the complainant. "Security" has been many times identified in the Preparatory Commission as a subjective national feeling, and that is what it is. It is not so much an emotion called forth by tangible facts as a state of mind due to national attitudes. More or less imponderable, it has to be taken account of while it exists, but no one can predict when a national change of attitude or a combination of international circumstances will materially alter the emotion.

As "security" presents itself in the armament problem, it seems to call for satisfaction by one of two possibilities: either the insecure state would be satisfied with the in-

[1] *Documents Relating to the Organisation of a System of European Federal Union*, p. 25 (A. 46. 1930. VII. 4.)

dubitable assurance of permanent superiority over its *bête noire* — whatever that superiority might mean — or it would be satisfied with a positive assurance of wholesale international support in case it got into a run of trouble. The first alternative is obviously impractical and impossible.

The second alternative is worthy of attention because its mere expression necessitates a loyalty to the fundamental consideration on which the whole disarmament problem rests, the recognition of international solidarity. It is, moreover, capable of logical legal enunciation. International solidarity has resulted in the laying down of certain principles, which are accepted by most states and not denied by the others, as sound bases of international relations. So accepted, they have become standards of international society, and it behooves the members of that society to punish infractions of those rules and not to leave their defense solely to the individual state which happens to be the victim. Here is the same principle, argued in international affairs, that is accepted in municipal affairs, where a felony is not an offense against the individual who suffers by it, but an offense against the community, which prosecutes the offender through the organized mechanism of order. Appeal to the thesis obligates its advocate internationally to assume that it will not be an offender and thus encompasses that state very completely in the theory of international solidarity.

This theory of collective action against the military offender logically calls for sanctions, that is, a method of inducing the observance of the common law in case it is flouted. That is the essential idea back of Art. 16 of the Covenant of the League, which goes only to the extent of making refusal to resort to pacific settlement, prior to resort to war and to an incomplete acceptance of the results of such a reference, a sanctionable offense. It is an incomplete sanction, also, because it leaves the decision of each state to itself individually and, therefore, does not in terms insure a united front against an apparent offense. Art. 16 of the Covenant is in full force, though it has never been actually called into operation.[1] For the present purpose it may be referred to as a simple sanction, that is, a sanction which would operate automatically within specified limits under defined conditions. Since 1920, little progress has been made in developing that type of sanction.

States regarding themselves insecure at first vociferously demanded the development of the simple sanction to cover all cases. That demand was resisted in long and tedious debates in many forms on the primary ground that states ready and willing to come to the aid of virtue could not find any device capable of demonstrating instantaneously and positively that virtue would exist whence the call for help came.

In the many efforts to solve the problem, lines of positive advance have appeared. No government in the world questions that outright war would be an offense against international society and should command its own influences toward stopping it. But to determine which side to support in stopping a conflict is quite another matter. The continuous conference machinery of the League of Nations and the extensive development of pacific settlement, especially the conciliation method, have made it possible to go farther back than the actual outbreak of war in a solution of the problem.

The test of good will and good faith may now be said to be the extent to which a state places a dispute, which its own diplomacy has failed to settle, completely in the hands and under the jurisdiction of some type of pacific settlement machinery, before taking any overt acts or resorting to mobilization. In other words, the problem of war — the eventuality for which armament is ostensibly maintained — is now being positively attacked on its inner line, and it is the threat of war which a growing machinery of international agreement is being constructed for handling.[2]

In terms of sanctions, this development gives what may

[1] The convention establishing the International Agricultural Mortgage Credit Company, for instance, provides in Art. 6 for suspension of payments in accordance with it but not for such suspension on account of war.

[2] The term "aggression" has dropped out of the discussions. It has been generally accepted that, while aggression is apparently impossible to define

be called a complex sanction. The cooperating governments of the world recognize in their formal conventions that a threat of war is a constructive offense against the society of which they are members. They insist, and individually agree, that such a contingency be taken out of the hands of the interested parties into a forum of disinterested individuals or state representatives, who are able to bring to bear upon the question at issue the sense of solidarity and the concepts of justice. A decision resulting from such procedure would be one that in all likelihood would command the highest and fullest support. Taken at the moment of crisis and in the presence of all the facts, it would have that quality of moral appeal which it has been suspected that the operation of the simple sanction would not possess.

In accordance with this reasoning, two lines of action are of record, one under the League of Nations, using the Council as the deliberative body; and the other emphasizing the duty of states to consult, without being definite as to the forum they shall use. The following documents express these two lines of policy:

I. Use of Council:

A. Convention on Financial Assistance, October 2, 1930.

B. General Convention to Improve the Means of Preventing War, September 26, 1931.

C. Proposal to Amend the Covenant to bring it into Harmony, with the Pact of Paris, which is to be decided upon during the General Disarmament Conference.[1]

D. Arts. 50, 52 and 59 of the Draft Convention for Limitation and Reduction of Armaments (not exclusively dependent upon the Council).

---

satisfactorily, it is not difficult to distinguish the victim as the state which places its case unreservedly in the hands of organized pacific settlement. Identification of the victim is further aided by the development of means to deal with a situation threatening war, to the end that circumstances from which a violation of international obligations might emerge would develop under the observation of disinterested parties. They would thus be able to determine which disputant was acting with good will.

[1] *Resolutions and Recommendations adopted by the Assembly . . . 1931,* p. 9. (*Official Journal,* Spec., Sup. 92).

II. Consultation of states:
   A. Treaty relating to Insular Possessions and Insular Dominions in the Region of the Pacific Ocean, Washington, December 13, 1921.
   B. Treaty for Limitation of Naval Armament, Washington, February, 6, 1922 (Art. XXI).
   C. Treaty for Renunciation of War, August 27, 1928 (by admitted implication).
   D. London Naval Treaty, April 22, 1930.

On this phase of the subject it is clear that there is no essential disagreement among governments that their international solidarity requires concerted action. The disagreement lies in the method by which decisions are to be taken. As the question is approached under different conditions and from different angles the national obsessions which have repeatedly prevented agreement tend to disappear. It may be said that at the present moment the principle of international solidarity, in the face of violence or threatened violence, is accepted as a requirement in international relations. It can be seen from the above list that various phases of the problem have been given individual solutions, and it is more than probable that this process will continue until there is a network of engagements relating to the main situations in which concerted action, and the possible application of sanctions, might be called for.

THE CONVENTION ON FINANCIAL ASSISTANCE

On October 2, 1930, there was opened for signature at Geneva the Convention on Financial Assistance, which has a very real bearing upon the underlying conditions of "security" on which disarmament depends. The Preparatory Commission for the Disarmament Conference began work on the basis of a series of questions intended to summarize the elements of the puzzle as they were identified in 1926. As soon as the commission met, a number of additional questions were raised. The Finnish delegate was concerned with one phase of mutual aid, and on its suggestion the commission proposed that the Council "should undertake the examination of special arrangements whereby a reduction of armaments agreed to by states unfavorably placed, owing to geographical or other exceptional circumstances, might be compensated in order to meet their requirements for security."

This proposal was referred on September 4, 1926,[1] to the Committee of the Council, its directive machinery for the Preparatory Commission. The Financial Committee, thereupon came forward with a scheme for a report which was passed to the eighth session of the Assembly (1927). That body requested continued study of the matter and expressed a conviction "of the need for a system of financial aid for contributing to the organization of security, which is an indispensable preliminary to general disarmament." It was then referred by the Council to a joint committee of the Financial Committee and of the Committee on Arbitration and Security; that study of the problem resulted in September, 1929, in a draft convention being presented to the 10th session of the Assembly for consideration.

The hope that the scheme would be adopted at that time was not realized, owing to an old trouble. Some of the governments differed in their conception of the cases in which financial assistance should or should not be granted; others desired assistance to be confined to states actually attacked and not to those directly menaced by aggression. The debate[2] went over thorny ground traversed many times before, with the result that the text was again referred to the Joint Committee of the Financial Committee and the Committee on Arbitration and Security. A modified text was brought before the 11th session of the Assembly, and after an additional debate, a text generally agreeable to the various schools of thought was adopted. The importance attached to the convention was accentuated in the session of October 2, 1930, when the meeting of the Assembly was suspended for the signature of the convention by over two

[1] *Official Journal*, VII, p. 1238.

[2] See generally the Report of the Third Committee, *Records of the Tenth Ordinary Session of the Assembly, Plenary Meetings*, p. 503 (*Official Journal*, Spec. Sup. No. 75) and the debate on Art. 1 in *ibid.*, *Minutes of the Third Committee*, p. 19–43 (*Official Journal*, Spec. Sup. No. 78.)

dozen states. Always before, conventions perfected and opened for signature by resolution of the Assembly had been subscribed to outside of the meeting itself, in the president's room.

At the ceremony of signature, the Convention on Financial Assistance was hailed as a great international instrument, "one of the corner stones of the edifice which the League is slowly, but systematically erecting for the safeguarding of peace and the security of nations." It was described as giving peaceful and innocent states a real guaranty of security and providing a salutary warning to countries which might be tempted to violate their international engagements and disturb the peace.

Application to Actual War

In its contribution toward solving the armament problem, the convention[1] is notable for successfully defining the cases in which financial assistance is to be granted and for giving reality, to this extent, to the principle of solidarity in the face of a threat to peace. The essential purpose of the convention is to extend financial assistance automatically to any state entitled to receive it. The determination of that condition is not automatic, but depends upon the decision of the Council.

The scheme is based upon the full operation of the peaceful machinery of the Covenant intrusted to the Council.[2] The primary *casus foederis* is a resort to war by a state in violation of its international obligations, "despite the efforts which the Council of the League of Nations has found it possible to make for the maintenance or the reestablishment of peaceful relations." The contracting party against which such a resort to war takes place "shall at its request receive the financial assistance provided for in the present convention, unless the Council decides otherwise." The beneficiary party undertakes so far as it is concerned "to submit the dispute to judicial or arbitral settlement or to any other pacific procedure which the Council may deem

[1] *Official Journal*, XI, p. 1648.
[2] Arts. 11, 12, 13, 15 and 17.

suitable." The essential *casus foederis*, therefore, depends upon overt violative acts of the one party and the unrestricted submission of its case to the consideration of disinterested organs by the other party. It is clear that such conditions enjoin only one line of action, namely, support of the injured party by all states committed to peace. The world can scarcely be other than unanimous about that.

The question whether those conditions exist is left to the appraisal of the Council at the moment when decision is required and with all the special circumstances of the specific case before it. Here then, is a formula which meets the demands of the two prevalent views concerning solidarity of action. Those states desiring a system fixed in advance have it, and those states which object to pledging their future course of action in specific terms are met, since the system operates only by reason of a decision taking all conditions of an actual case into consideration.[1] The Member states of the League in their study of war long ago gave up the imaginary idea that a war is like a bolt of lightning from a clear sky. There are antecedent conditions from which it develops, and the Covenant itself recognizes this in prescribing that the time when a dispute should have attention is when it is "likely to lead to a rupture" rather than after it has done so.

Application to Threat of War

Art. 2 of the convention on financial assistance applies it at this preventive stage. The Council may have a dispute likely to lead to a rupture under consideration by reference from either party when it acts under the provisions of Art. 15 of the Covenant. It may consider a difference brought before it as involving a threat of war under Art. 11, par. 1, on the initiative of any Member of the League; or by reason of the mediatory action of a Member under Art. 11, par. 2. It may also be seized of disputes between states under general or special conventions. In any or all of these cases, the

[1] The formula seems to go far toward meeting the Anglo-Saxon objection to laying down rules in advance on the assumption that they tend to encourage a state of bad will to make its action conform to the definition, while actually antagonistic to its meaning.

procedure followed is essentially the conciliatory system of Art. 15 of the Covenant. In that article are the famous "fissures in the Covenant." If the Council fails to effect the settlement, by the terms of the article, it issues a report and, if the report is unanimous by par. 6, "the Members of the League agree that they will not go to war with any party to the dispute which complies with the recommendations of the report." If the Council fails to produce a report, unanimous except for the disputants, by par. 7 "the Members of the League reserve to themselves the right to take such action as they shall consider necessary for the maintenance of right and justice."

Art. 2 of the Convention on Financial Assistance is directed at such cases. It contemplates the case where the Council shall "have taken steps to safeguard peace, including resort to mediation or any other means of pacific settlement," that is, if its efforts extend beyond the formal provisions of the Covenant. In such a case, if one of the parties refuses or neglects to conform to the steps laid down by the Council, that body may at the request of the other party, which must be a party to the convention, grant it financial assistance if the Council "considers that peace can not be safeguarded otherwise." The beneficiary in this case undertakes to submit the dispute to judicial or arbitral settlement or to any other pacific procedure which the Council may deem suitable and also "to conform to any provisional measures that may be recommended by the Council with a view to safeguarding peace." Hence again the beneficiary is indubitably a party who meets every requirement prescribed for effecting the peaceful settlement of the difference, and here again also the appraisal of the conditions justifying assistance are considered with all the circumstances of the specific case at their acute moment.

Unoffending State Commands Credit

The convention is built to meet the need for immediate funds of an unoffending state which finds that an attack or threat of an attack makes it difficult if not impossible for it to raise funds. Such a state, by the decision of the Council under the specific circumstances, finds itself able to approach the financial markets of the world with an application for a loan on which the service (interest and amortization) are guaranteed not only by its own financial ability, but by the guaranties available to it through the action of the Council. Such a loan is not to be contracted for a period exceeding 30 years.[1] The contracting parties to the convention undertake to hold themselves liable for annual guaranties amounting to 100,000,000 gold francs, distributed among them on the ratio of their contributions to the League's expenses. The convention will enter into force simultaneously with the convention of the General Disarmament Conference so that it is to be regarded as an essential part of any agreement reached at Geneva in 1932. A further condition is that the ratifiers shall together cover a sum of 50,000,000 gold francs for annual service.[2]

An unoffending state, having been found by the Council entitled to benefit from the convention, would be authorized to issue a loan for an amount fixed by the Council and with the guaranties specified for the particular transaction. Full details of the contract are to be submitted for approval, and the guaranties are to be managed by five trustees of Swiss nationality appointed by the Council. It will be perceived that all this procedure is automatic.

The parties to the convention furnish ordinary guaranties and special guaranties, the obligation emanating directly from the convention. The ordinary guarantors are Members of the League, providing a total of 100,000,000 gold francs in 968[3] units of about 101,420 francs each in proportion to their contribution to League expenses. Great Britain, for instance, would assume 105 units; France and Germany 79 each; Italy and Japan 60 each and so on down to the states contributing one unit only. The obligation, however, would cost the guaranteeing state nothing until the beneficiary state should default, and the total is only a

[1] Interest at 5% and annual amortization at 1½% liquidate in substantially that period. The figure is mentioned only as an indication.

[2] Present signatories will cover more than this sum on ratification.

[3] Since the convention was signed, Mexico's admission to the League has resulted in the normal units being raised to 1,000.

contingent liability which would not be reached until loans requiring the full amount of the guaranty fund were not only issued, but also in default. Thus, financial credit can be mobilized on behalf of the maintenance of peace and against its violation.

Operation of Guaranties Automatic

In addition to the ordinary guarantors, special guaranties are to be provided by those permanent members of the Council who so decide and by other members who agree to become special guarantors on the unanimous invitation of the other special guarantors. The special guarantors, like the ordinary guarantors, are obligated in respect to any loans contracted under the convention "without any further action or consent" on their part. The special guaranty is created for the purpose of strengthening the security on which a loan is issued and covers the service of its full amount in addition to the similar cover afforded by the ordinary guaranty. In the case of a loan being contracted, no guaranty would operate until the borrowing state should default. Such default would occur under the convention if the borrowing state failed to provide loan service 30 days before its due date. The trustees would then call upon the ordinary guarantors for payment under the ordinary guaranty bond, previously executed by each guaranteeing party with respect to the loan in question. Should all ordinary guarantors respond, any moneys received under the cognate special guaranty bonds would be returned to the remitters. In case a special guarantor's payment should be required, it would be returned as soon as the ordinary guarantors met their obligations. All payments by guarantors draw interest at a rate 1% higher than the rate payable on the guaranteed loan.

Such is the broad outline of the system now determined for mobilizing the financial resources of the peaceful world against any government whatever which actually exhibits a warlike disposition. The operation of the convention runs against non-Members of the League as well as Members, It was made specifically as a convention of Member states of the League and has not been opened to signature or ratification by non-Members of the League. Its proper functioning obviously depends upon the acceptance of the obligations of the Covenant and that condition precedent does not exist for non-Members. However, Art. 23 provides that the Council, with the consent of the special guarantors, "may accept an offer by a state which is not a Member of the League to participate in guaranteeing the annual service of a particular loan which the Council decides to authorize." Thus, a non-Member state like the United States could exercise the influence of its financial power in favor of peace in a particular case if it should be so minded.

The British Government in a memorandum on the convention dated July 10, 1931, informed the Parliament that, after ratification of the convention, it intended to accept the obligations of a special guarantor. Undoubtedly with the United States in mind, Mr. Henderson said "His Majesty's Government would also use their endeavors to secure that other financially strong powers are invited to become special guarantors." He further forecast favorable action by the French Government, serious study by Italy and the expectation that Japan would ratify. Respecting his own country, he said that the London Government was "convinced that its ratification will have the support of all responsible sections of public opinion in this country."[1]

The convention was open for signature until December 31, 1931, after which it is open to accession by Members of the League of Nations. It will enter into force and be maintained in force as regards the authorization of new loans conditionally in respect of each contracting party upon entrance into force and maintenance in force by that party "of a plan for the reduction of armaments" in execution of Art. 8 of the Covenant. No party which "is not acting in conformity with its obligations under such plan" shall benefit from the financial assistance provided by the convention.

[1] *Memorandum respecting the International Convention on Financial Assistance*, p. 7, 8 (Miscellaneous No. 13 (1931) Cmd. 3906).

As stated, the convention met with unanimous approval of the 11th session of the Assembly. It has been very generally signed, by states which feel themselves both secure and insecure, by states which have insisted on guaranties and those which have objected to guaranties. The following are signatories as of February 1, 1932: Albania, Australia, Austria, Belgium, Bolivia, Bulgaria, Cuba, Czechoslovakia, Denmark (ratified), Estonia, Ethiopia, Finland (ratified), France, Germany, Great Britain and Northern Ireland and all parts of the British Empire not separate Members of the League of Nations, Greece, the Irish Free State, Italy, Latvia, Lithuania, the Netherlands, Norway, Persia, Peru, Poland, Portugal, Rumania, Spain, Sweden and Yugoslavia.

The contribution which the convention makes to the program for disarmament has been expressed on behalf of the British Government as follows:[1]

In the first place there will be provided a measure of "pooled security," enabling the smaller and less wealthy states to rely on speedy and effective aid. In the second, the authority of the Council would, in the event of the convention coming into force, be very greatly increased. Even a powerful "aggressor" might be impressed by the fact that his opponent could immediately borrow on the markets on favorable terms owing to the guaranties given by the other parties to the convention. Though it might be unlikely that the convention would ever be applied, the mere existence of machinery enabling the victim of aggression to raise substantial sums on such terms would undoubtedly exercise a salutary and deterrent effect. In the third place — and this is perhaps the most important aspect — it is by pointing to the increased chances of security as a result of disarmament that those who are working for peace are most likely to induce all nations to disarm.

Lastly, it would result that the "aggressor" would find its own credit ruined internationally by the mere alignment of the conventionally mobilized credits on behalf of its opposite.

[1] *Memorandum respecting the International Convention on Financial Assistance*, p. 7 (Miscellaneous No. 13 (1931) Cmd. 3906).

Further Prevention of War

The 12th session of the League of Nations Assembly opened for signature on September 26, 1931, the General Convention to Improve the Means of Preventing War. This convention was an outgrowth of the study by the Committee on Arbitration and Security of Art. 11 of the Covenant and was formulated on the original suggestion of Germany made in 1928. To the Assembly of that year the committee reported a model treaty relating to conservatory measures for the prevention of war, and the ninth session of the Assembly recommended it for consideration by states desiring to conclude such a treaty.[1] In 1929, the British delegation requested the Assembly to consider the question with a view to establishing a draft general convention on the broad lines of that treaty. The Committee on Arbitration and Security failed to solve that larger problem, and the Third Committee in the 11th session of the Assembly in 1930 was confronted with two texts representing alternative opinions. Reconciliation of the points of view was not effected then, and the question was reconsidered by a special committee, which on May 15, 1931, reported a draft which the Assembly revised, adopted and opened for signature.[2]

It will be recalled that Art. 11, par. 1, of the Covenant makes any war or threat of war a matter of concern to the whole League and places upon the Council a duty to safeguard the peace. Any Member of the League may call this provision into action, but there is no special provision outside of the general procedure for Council business to determine the exact position. In case of the existence of the condition, uncertainty might be a serious handicap to maintaining peace. When action occurred under Art. 11, par. 1, in the Greco-Bulgaro incident in 1925, the circumstances enabled the Council at the outset to secure the consent of the parties to the withdrawal of their troops across

[1] *Resolutions and Recommendations adopted by the Assembly . . . 1928*, p. 58 (*Official Journal*, Spec. Sup. No. 63).
[2] *Resolutions and Recommendations of the Assembly . . . 1931*, p. 24 (*Official Journal*, Spec. Sup. No. 92).

the border line. The Council at that time took the precaution of including the disputants in the adoption of the resolution to that effect. It is by no means certain that the desirable halting of every threat of war could be handled in such a way. The specific examination of conservatory measures is, therefore, one of the important elements in building up an assurance against surprise, lack of which in so large a measure accounts for suspicions of insecurity.

The debate in the 1930 Assembly made it clear that a draft general convention should be confined to the threat of war rather than to war itself. Outright war, the formal embarking of nations on the prosecution of their own will by force of arms, is assumed in all responsible international thought at the present time to be a condition which can take place only after the interposition of various preventive and interventional measures. The more efficient and definite such measures are, the less likelihood there obviously is that the condition of formal war will occur. The general convention consequently relates only to the problem of preventing war by establishing precise measures for handling situations which threaten war.

The object of the general convention is to facilitate the task of the Council in insuring peace and conciliation by undertakings assumed voluntarily in advance by the contracting parties. The intention is to add to the efficacy of the means of preventing war, of which the Council disposes under the Covenant, without in any degree restricting its powers. The convention is thus directed specifically at the problem of keeping a threatening situation from degenerating into actual conflict. On a multilateral scale it deals separately with that problem for the first time in history. Confining itself to conditions threatening war, the convention provides for conservatory measures of a military, as well as of a nonmilitary character, thus satisfying those states which are nervous unless they are assured that peaceful intentions can command some weapons.

Conservatory measures of a nonmilitary nature may be called for by the Council in the case of any dispute before it (Art. 1). Such measures relate to the substance of the dispute and not simply to its incidental features. They are to be recommended with the object of "preventing the aggravation of the dispute" and are to continue for a fixed time. The contracting parties undertake to accept and apply such measures.

Compliance with measures of a military character is more complicated. Three articles of the Covenant relate to war: Art. 11 declares any war to be a matter of concern to the whole League; Art. 16 would run if a Member state of the League should violate provisions to submit a dispute to pacific settlement before "resort to war," such resort is to be deemed as the commission of "an act of war against all other Members of the League;" Art. 17, par. 3, deals with the possibility of a non-Member state resorting to war against a Member of the League; in which case Art. 16 shall apply. It is to be noted that under Art. 16 the state resorting to war is at war, while the state against which the act has been committed is not necessarily at war since, though performing identical acts, its purpose is the upholding of international covenants. The Special Committee comments that "the powers and duties of the Members of the League and of the Council are defined in these articles, which will be applied should occasion arise." It, therefore, decided to deal only with the case of a threat of war.

THREAT OF WAR — CONSERVATORY MEASURES

In Art. 2 the convention recognizes the fact that the movement of troops does not of necessity create a state of war. If the Council is of the opinion that the circumstances do not create a state of war when the forces of one contracting state enter the territory or territorial waters of another, or a demilitarized zone or fly over them, it may prescribe measures to insure their evacuation. The parties obligate themselves to comply without delay with the measures prescribed to correct such an overt act. The border incident ceases to be a definite *casus belli*.

Whether troops are in contact as a result of an overt act or simply in a threatening posture, making contact possible, the Council by Art. 3 may fix lines which must not be passed by land, naval or air forces, and the states contract to comply with such recommendations.

The deadlines for land, naval or air forces are to be fixed by the Council by agreement with the parties, if possible; but if such agreement is not reached, the Council shall fix the lines "with the consent of the party whose forces are affected." Their retirement is not to be back of the exterior lines of existing defense organizations at frontiers and is not to involve the abandonment of any "work, position or line of communication essential to the security or the supplies of the party concerned." Fortified works are, therefore, not to be evacuated by decision of the Council, but the Council alone determines the period during which the lines fixed shall be maintained. The contracting parties agree to take all necessary precautions to avoid incidents.

The convention, either by the method of withdrawal or by fixing military lines, empowers the Council in effect to step between disputants and to keep them out of each other's reach. Though the provisions do not mention aggression, they substantially wipe out its possibility by obviating the physical contact from which alone it can occur. Before the conservatory measures of a military character are decided upon, either party to the dispute may request the appointment of commissioners by the Council to verify the execution of the measures to be taken. This obviates the customary objection in such circumstances that the other party would not execute the measures in good faith. The contracting parties undertake to afford the commissioners every facility for the performance of their duties, and a disputant, by making a reasoned request, may secure a regulation by the Council that the execution of the measures to be verified shall coincide with the arrival of the commissioners at the affected spot; in effect that execution shall be supervised by the Council's commissioners. Commissioners are not to inspect naval or air bases, and inspection of military works or establishments is to be confined to verification of withdrawal of forces. Rules for the working and composition of the commission are to be prepared by

ARBITRATIONS AND NATIONAL SAFETY

the competent organs of the League and to enter into force with the convention.

Violation of conservatory measures of either nonmilitary or military character is dealt with in Art. 5. If such violation continues in spite of the Council's injunctions, it shall consider "what means of all kinds are necessary." Should war break out as a consequence, the violation "shall be regarded by the high contracting parties as *prima facie* evidence that the party guilty thereof has resorted to war within the meaning of Art. 16 of the Covenant." All decisions and recommendations of the Council under the convention are to be taken by it without the concurrence of the parties to the dispute.

In matters involving a threat of war, the character of publicity given the circumstances is an element of considerable importance. It was not deemed desirable that various states should be encouraged to give out their views of the action, while it was regarded as desirable that the balanced and responsible statements of the Council should receive the widest publicity. Art. 6 of the convention is an undertaking by the high contracting parties to provide through the means at their disposal such publicity "as the Council may recommend for its proceedings, decisions and recommendations" under the convention.

The convention is not to be interpreted as restricting the powers of the Council under the Covenant, nor as affecting the right of free passage through the Suez Canal.

It was open for signature until February 2, 1932, by both Members and non-Members of the League and will enter into force 90 days after 10 ratifications or accessions are deposited.

The Special Committee, on the initiative of the delegate of Poland, adopted a recommendation for consideration by the Assembly as follows:

The Special Committee,

Being aware of the danger which, in the event of an international crisis, may arise from irresponsible press campaigns and publicity given in the press to inaccurate or tendentious information;

Recognizing that aggressive propaganda against a foreign power may in certain circumstances constitute a veritable threat to the peace of the world;

Requests the Assembly to consider this problem and examine the possibilities of finding a solution.

The Council on May 21, 1931, decided to transmit this resolution to the Assembly, at the same time calling attention to a Swedish proposal that states should "endeavor, so far as their national laws permit, to suppress all verbal or written propaganda designed to prevent a peaceful settlement of the crisis." The Polish representative in the Council emphasized that "aggressive campaigns of hate, contempt for foreign countries, the publication of false and tendentiously interpreted news, without any possibility of rectification, appeals to the lowest and most selfish instincts" and are "a real danger to good understanding among the peoples." The Assembly on September 24 adopted the following resolution :[1]

The Assembly,

Considering that the organization of peace demands an international spirit freed from all prejudices and misconceptions,

Convinced of the necessity of insuring that press information shall be as impartial and complete as possible,

Requests the Council to consider the possibility of studying, with the help of the press, the difficult problem of the spread of false information which may threaten to disturb the peace or the good understanding between nations.

II. The Record as to Pacific Settlement

Arbitration in the trilogy, arbitration, security, disarmament, is, of course, used in the broad sense, which includes all methods of pacific settlement. In international policy to-day, the trilogy emphasizes that disputes between nations can be settled by two means only, if their solution is beyond the diplomatic ability of the parties themselves: pacific means or warlike means. The prewar development of pacific settlement was characterized by limited agreements providing for the third-party handling of some, but seldom all types of, disputes. Postwar development has empha-

[1] *Resolutions and Recommendations adopted by the Assembly*, 1931, p. 27 (*Official Journal*, Spec. Sup. 92).

sized the creation of methods capable of handling all disputes whatsoever, so as to leave no scope for the operation of the war system. Steady and remarkable success has resulted from the efforts in this direction, and a tremendous body of agreement has come into force. It will be sufficient here to summarize the existing elements of this system with a particular view to its relationship with the armament problem.[1] The system is both multilateral and bilateral and may be briefly described as follows:

I. Multilateral.

A. Covenant of the League of Nations, in force since January 10, 1920. Arts. 12–15 lay down obligations to employ arbitration (in the strict sense), judicial settlement or conciliation by the Council before resort to war (55 states Members).

B. Statute of the Permament Court of International Justice. Protocol of Signature of December 16, 1920, creates a judicial forum (46 states ratified, 55 states signed).

C. Optional Clause attached to the Protocol of Signature. Parties bound are suable, by reason of this prior consent, with respect to categories of justiciable disputes defined in the declarations of acceptance (38 states bound, 46 signatories).

D. Treaty for Renunciation of War, Paris, August 27, 1928, embodies agreement never to seek the settlement of any disputes by other than pacific means (60 states ratified or adhered).

E. General Act for Pacific Settlement of International Disputes, Geneva, September 28, 1928. Establishes general system for settlement of all disputes by conciliation, judicial settlement or arbitration enabling adherents to consolidate their engagements (18 adherents).

F. Multilateral conventions. The numerous conventions on all sorts of international questions made since the war embody clauses providing that the interpretation or

[1] For a summary account of the system, see Myers, *Origin and Conclusion of the Paris Pact*, p. 1–33.

application of the specific convention shall be submitted to some form of pacific settlement. This standard provision removes whole categories of international relations from the possible likelihood of warlike disputes. The significance of the habit is great, but no detailed analysis of its actual scope can here be given.

II. *Bilateral Conventions.*

A. Four hundred of these are in force between pairs of states. The great majority of them provide for the settlement of all disputes by some method of pacific settlement.

B. Bilateral treaties on all sorts of subjects containing the clause referring disputes over interpretation or application to some form of pacific settlement. This has the same effect, as mentioned under multilateral conventions above, of taking whole categories of relations out of the range of warlike possibilities.

In connection with the treaty for the renunciation of war, two circumstances are worth mentioning, since they indicate trends that will undoubtedly become more important in the immediate future. The first is that arbitration is incorporated in a number of national constitutions as a method to be exhausted before recourse to war is legally permissible to the state in question. The Venezuelan constitution has embodied such a provision since 1874; that of the United States of Brazil since 1891; that of Portugal since 1908; that of Uruguay since 1918; that of the Dominican Republic since 1924. In the constitution of the Spanish Republic a further provision appears. By an article adopted November 3, 1931, the President is authorized to declare only war that is in accord with the Covenant of the League of Nations, is beyond question defensive and after the dispute representing the *casus belli* has been submitted to the pacific settlement of the League. No treaty relating to war can be made unless it conforms to the general laws laid down by the League.[1] The majority of present constitutions repeat or reflect the purpose of the oldest consti-

[1] *New York Times*, November 4, 1931.

tution in the world, that of the United States, which was established, among other purposes, to "provide for the common defense."

The second development is emanating more directly from the treaty for renunciation of war and expresses the conception that, recourse to war being condemned and its employment as an instrument of policy foresworn, the individual citizen offends if he acts contrary to those ideas. Three countries, Brazil, Poland and Rumania, have embodied such provisions in their draft penal codes.[1] Art. 229 of the new Rumanian penal code was adopted unanimously in the following terms:[2]

> Those who, with the purpose of bringing the Rumanian state to declare war of aggression shall incite public opinion to such a war by any direct propaganda by means of the methods indicated in Art. 136 (speech, addresses, statements, petitions, outcries, song, etc.) shall be punished by simple imprisonment from two months to one year and by a fine of from 5,000 to 20,000 lei. Prosecution shall be undertaken only if it is established that reciprocity is assured by the laws of the foreign state against which the propaganda has been directed.

The engagements mentioned above have the collective effect of putting a high premium upon the employment of methods of pacific settlement and of throwing a burden of proof upon a government which shows a tendency not to resort to such methods. By reason of their multilateral obligations, it is scarcely too much to say that not only are the great majority of all nations obligated to resort to pacific settlement for the settlement of treaty disputes, but that their multilateral and bilateral treaties of pacific settlement cover the very widest range of all their relations, whether or not determined by treaty. The record of an examination of the precise scope of the international relations covered by these engagements would be tedious, but it should be clear that the present-day world is thoroughly committed to a maximum use of methods of pacific settlement.

---

[1] See memorandum of the Polish Government, G. 602. M. 240. 1931. IX. IX.
[2] Académie de Droit International. Recueil des Cours, 1930. Vespasian V. Pella, "La répression des crimes contre la personnalité de l'Etat."

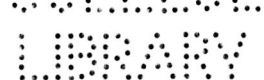

It is frequently said that occasions may arise when treaties are not kept, and it is concluded from that statement, which is supposed to be supported by the verdict of history, that in consequence treaties do not constitute a firm reliance. It is pertinent to leave past conditions aside, since all the documents under discussion are of recent origin and, without exception, have been ratified by the parties after a full appraisal of the obligations undertaken and with complete deliberation by their representative governments. Within their scope, they must be considered as serious engagements. The violation of such engagements would not be a light matter, and in discussing the subject it is not appropriate lightly to suggest violation. Any modern state will make sacrifices not to get into the position of appearing to violate treaties, and very many instances of long delays and extensive parliamentary debates upon the engagements referred to above are ample evidence of the serious attitude which is taken toward them. It can not be assumed that the intention to violate these or any international treaties exists; and if it should, it must be remembered that grave responsibility would attach to the act.

War Possible Only by Treaty Violation

Assuming that violation will not take place, except as an unlikely and completely desperate resort, the present status of pacific settlement may be broadly indicated by observing that no state in the world to-day can embark on a war — the eventual purpose of armament — without violating at least one multilateral treaty. Afghanistan, Costa Rica, Ecuador, Egypt, Iceland, the Soviet Union, Turkey and the United States could go to war by violating only the treaty for the renunciation of war; Argentina could enter that state only by violating the Covenant of the League of Nations. Bolivia, the Dominican Republic, Guatemala, Honduras, Mexico, Nicaragua, Paraguay and Peru could embark on war by violating two multilateral treaties, the Covenant of the League of Nations and the treaty for renunciation of war; and Brazil could do so against the Statute of the Permanent Court and the Optional Clause. Every other state in the world can get into war only across the hurdles of the obligations involved in from three to five of the great multilateral conventions: the Covenant of the League of Nations, the Statute of the Court, the Optional Clause, the treaty for renunciation of war and the General Act of Geneva.

This evidence of the effect of international solidarity merits another remark. Each of the five treaties mentioned is of the type known as open multilateral. The engagements of their texts are taken by each state individually and by each state toward every other party. Each government is, therefore, bound not only to itself by reason of its national ratification of the document, but it is bound toward every other party, for each of which any deviation from a right line of conduct would create either an affront or a duty to oppose the divagation. That is a new and fundamental factor in international relations and is a full justification for considering the world which will struggle with the solution of the armament problem in 1932 as a reciprocally interlocked unity.

One other phase of pacific settlement may be mentioned. A frequent depreciation of the method is to call attention to the fact that certain states, whose relations are tense, are not fully bound by such engagements. The suggestion is usually made in a general rather than a precise sense. It is obvious that much of the body of multilateral engagements must be between states whose relations are very unlikely to become tense. Switzerland and Uruguay, for instance, are not likely to have serious differences. The whole body of engagement to which such parties contribute, nevertheless, creates a world standard to which fashion dictates conformity.

The real possibilities of conflict are between states whose relations are close and which can consequently develop many points of friction. Roughly speaking, wars must occur between neighbors, for it is very difficult in the case of states lying in the relation of A B C for A to get into war with C. With a view, therefore, to presenting the situation precisely, the following table of pacific settlement treaties with relation to geographical contiguity is presented. The signs attached to the state names indicate obligation under the great multilateral treaties. Opposite them are the neighbor states. One of the best indications of peaceful intentions of neighboring states is their willingness to make all-in bilateral pacific settlement treaties.[1] The neighbors are, therefore, divided into two columns. The first column shows those which have all-in bilateral pacific settlement treaties with a country, and those in the second column are without such engagements. It may safely be assumed that any real crisis, involving a possibility of the use of armament can originate only between the states of the third column in relation to the first, or vice versa. The table as a whole shows the extent to which neighbors have foregone the expectation of relying on armament in their relations with one another.

PACIFIC SETTLEMENT AND WAR POSSIBILITIES[2]

Geographical contiguity with relation to bilateral all-in engagements

* Member of the League of Nations.
§ Party to the treaty for renunciation of war.
† Contracting party to the Statute of the Permanent Court of International Justice.

‡ Contracting party to the Statute of the Permanent Court of International Justice and to the Optional Clause.
‖ Adherent to general act for pacific settlement of international disputes.

	Treaty	Non-Treaty
§ AFGHANISTAN	*§† Persia (1921, 1927) § U.S.S.R. (Turkmenistan) (1931)	*§‡ Gr. Britain (India)
*§‡ ALBANIA	*§‡‖ Italy (1926)	*§‡ Greece *§‡ Yugoslavia

[1] In the subjoined list the "all-in" treaty is held to exist if no dispute is exempted from judicial, arbitral or conciliatory procedure, regardless of exemptions from any particular method.

[2] The data below respecting bilateral treaties of pacific settlement is taken from a manuscript revision and continuation of the "Index of Bipartite Pacific Settlement Treaties" published in Myers, *Origin and Conclusion of the Paris Pact*, p. 197–218.

ARBITRATIONS AND NATIONAL SAFETY

* Argentina	* Bolivia (1902, 1921) ‡ Brazil (1828, 1905) *§† Chile (1902) *§ Paraguay (1876, 1899) *§‡ Uruguay (1899)	
*§‡‖ Australia	*§‡‖ Netherlands (Dutch E. Indies) (1905)	*§‡ Portugal (Timor-E. Indies)
*§‡ Austria	*§† Czechoslovakia (1926) *§‡ Hungary (1923, 1931) *§†‖ Italy (1930) *§‡ Switzerland (1924) *§‡ Yugoslavia (1926)	*§‡ Germany
*§‡‖ Belgium	*§‡‖ France *§‡ Germany (1925) *§†‖ Gr. Britain *§†‖ Luxemburg (1927)	*§‡‖ Netherlands
* Bolivia	* Argentina (1902, 1921) ‡ Brazil (1909) *§‖ Peru (1863, 1873, 1901, 1918)	*§† Chile *§ Paraguay
‡ Brazil	* Argentina (1828, 1905) * Bolivia (1909) *§‡ Colombia (1918) *§‡‖ France (1909) (Fr. Guiana) *§‡‖ Gr. Britain (1909, 1919) (Br. Guiana) *§ Paraguay (1911) *§‖ Peru (1909, 1918) *§‡ Uruguay (1916) *§† Venezuela (1909)	*§‡‖ Netherlands (Dutch Guiana)
*§‡ Bulgaria	*§‡‖ Greece (1929) § Turkey (1929)	*§‡ Rumania *§‡ Yugoslavia
*§‡‖ Canada	*§‡‖ Denmark (Greenland)	§ United States
*§† Chile	* Argentina (1902)	* Bolivia *‖ Peru
*§ China		*§‡‖ France (Indo-China) *§‡‖ Gr. Britain (India) § U. S. S. R. *§† Japan
*§‡ Colombia	§ Ecuador (1856, 1905) *§‖ Peru (1829, 1870, 1905) *§† Venezuela (1842)	‡ Brazil *§‡ Panama
§ Costa Rica	*§ Nicaragua (1868)	*§‡ Panama

*§† Cuba		*§‡‖ Gr. Britain (Bahamas) (Jamaica)
		*§‡ Haiti
		§ United States
*§† Czecho-slovakia	*§‡ Austria (1926) *§‡ Germany (1925) *§† Poland (1925) *§‡ Rumania (1929)	*§‡ Hungary
*§‡‖ Denmark	*§‡ Germany (1926) *§‡‖ Gr. Britain (1905) (Greenland-Canada) § Iceland (1930) *§‡‖ Norway (1924, 1926) *§‡‖ Sweden (1924, 1926)	
*§ Dominican Republic	*§‡ Haiti (1929)	§ United States (Porto Rico)
§ Ecuador	*§‡ Colombia (1856, 1905)	*§‖ Peru
§ Egypt		*§‡‖ Belgium (Belgian Congo) *§‡ Ethiopia *§‡‖ France (Fr. West Africa) *§‡‖ Gr. Britain (Anglo-Egyptian Sudan) *§‡‖ Italy (Libya, Eritrea)
*§‡‖ Estonia	*§‡‖ Finland (1925) *§‡ Latvia (1923, 1925)	§ Soviet Union
*§‡ Ethiopia	*§‡‖ Italy (1928) (Eritrea, Italian Somaliland)	*§‡‖ Gr. Britain (Br. Somaliland, Kenya, Uganda, Anglo-Egyptian Sudan)
*§‡‖ Finland	*§‡‖ Estonia (1925) *§‡‖ Norway (1924, 1926) *§‡‖ Sweden (1924, 1926)	§ Soviet Union
*§‡‖ France	*§‡‖ Belgium ‡ Brazil (1909) (Fr. Guiana) *§‡ Germany (1925) *§‡‖ Gr. Britain *§‡‖ Luxemburg (1927) *§‡ Portugal (1928) (Portuguese Guinea) *§‡ Siam (1925) (Indo-China) *§‡‖ Spain (1929) *§‡ Switzerland (1925) § Turkey (1926) (Syria)	*§‡‖ Italy

ARBITRATIONS AND NATIONAL SAFETY

*§‡ GERMANY
 *§‡‖ Belgium (1925)   *§‡ Austria
 *§† Czechoslovakia (1925)
 *§‡‖ Denmark (1926)
 *§‡‖ France (1925)
 *§‡ Lithuania (1928)
 *§‡‖ Luxemburg (1929)
 *§‡‖ Netherlands (1926)
 *§† Poland (1925)
 *§‡ Switzerland (1921)

*§‡‖ GR. BRITAIN
 *§‡‖ Belgium   *§† China
   ‡ Brazil (1909, 1919)   *§† Venezuela (Br.
    (Br. Guiana)   Guiana)
 *§‡‖ Denmark (1905)
    (Greenland-Canada)
 *§‡‖ France
 *§‡‖ Netherlands (1905)
    (Dutch Guiana-Br.
    Guiana, E. Indies)
  *§‡ Portugal (1904) (An-
    gola, Mozambique-
    Union of S. Africa,
    Tanganyika, Nya-
    saland Protectorate)
 *§‡ Siam (1925) (India)
  § United States (1914)
    Iraq (1930)

*§‡‖ GREECE
 *§‡ Bulgaria (1929)   *§‡ Albania
  § Turkey (1930)
 *§‡ Yugoslavia (1929)

*§ GUATEMALA
 *§ Honduras (1895)   *§‡‖ Gr. Britain (Br.
              Honduras)
 *‡ Salvador (1890)   *§ Mexico

*§‡ HAITI
 *§† Dominican Republic   § United States
   (1929)   (Porto Rico)

*§ HONDURAS
 *§ Guatemala (1895)   *§‡‖ Gr. Britain (Br.
              Honduras)
             *§† Nicaragua
             *§‡ Salvador

*§‡ HUNGARY
 *§‡ Austria (1923, 1931)   *§† Czechoslovakia
              *§‡ Rumania
              *§‡ Yugoslavia

§ ICELAND
 *§‡‖ Denmark (1930)

*§‡‖ INDIA
               § Afghanistan
              *§† China
              *§† Persia
              *§‡ Siam
              § Soviet Union

*§‡‖ IRISH FREE
   STATE

*§‡‖ Italy	*§‡ Albania (1926)
	*§‡ Austria (1930)
	*§‡ Ethiopia (1928)
	  (Eritrea, Italian
	  Somaliland)
	*§‡ Switzerland (1924)
		*§‡‖ France
		*§‡ Yugoslavia

*§† Japan		*§† China § United States (Formosa-Philippines)
*§‡ Latvia	*§‡‖ Estonia (1923, 1925) *§‡ Lithuania (1925, 1930)	§ Soviet Union
*§† Liberia		*§‡‖ France (Fr. West Africa) *§‡‖ Gr. Britain (Sierra Leone)
*§‡ Lithuania	*§‡ Germany (1928) *§‡ Latvia (1925, 1930) § Soviet Union (1926)	*§† Poland
*§‡‖ Luxemburg	*§‡‖ Belgium (1927) *§‡‖ France (1927) *§‡ Germany (1929)	
*§ Mexico	§ United States (1848)	*§‡‖ Gr. Britain (Br. Honduras) *§ Guatemala
*§‡‖ Netherlands	*§‡ Germany (1926) *§‡‖ Gr. Britain (1905) (E. Indies, Br. Guiana)	*§‡‖ Belgium
*§‡‖ New Zealand		
*§ Nicaragua	§ Costa Rica (1868)	*§ Honduras § United States
*§‡‖ Norway	*§‡‖ Denmark (1924, 1926) *§‡‖ Finland (1924, 1926) *§‡‖ Sweden (1924, 1925)	
*§‡ Panama		*§‡ Colombia *† Costa Rica § United States
*§ Paraguay	* Argentina (1876, 1899) ‡ Brazil (1911)	*§ Bolivia
*§† Persia	§ Afghanistan (1921, 1927) § Turkey (1926)	*§‡‖ Gr. Britain (India, Iraq) § Soviet Union
*§‖ Peru	* Bolivia (1863, 1873, 1901, 1918) ‡ Brazil (1909, 1918) *§‡ Colombia (1829, 1870, 1905)	*§† Chile § Ecuador

ARBITRATIONS AND NATIONAL SAFETY

*§† Poland   *§† Czechoslovakia (1925)   *§‡ Lithuania
                 *§‡ Germany (1925)   § Soviet Union
                 *§‡ Latvia (1925)
                 *§‡ Rumania (1926, 1929)

*§‡ Portugal   *§‡‖ France (1928) (Fr. Guinea-Portuguese Guinea)
                 *§‡‖ Gr. Britain (1904) (Angola, Mozambique)
                 *§‡‖ Spain (1928)

*§‡ Rumania   *§† Czechoslovakia (1929)   *§‡ Bulgaria
                 *§† Poland (1926, 1929)   *§‡ Hungary
                 *§‡ Yugoslavia (1929)   § Soviet Union

*‡ Salvador   *§ Guatemala (1890)   *§ Honduras

*§‡ Siam   *§‡‖ France (1925) (Fr. Indo-China)
                 *§‡‖ Gr. Britain (1925) (India)

*§‡‖ South Africa   *§‡‖ Belgium (Belgian Congo)   *§‡ Portugal (Angola, Portuguese E. Africa)

§ Soviet Union   § Afghanistan (1931)   *§† China
                 *§‡ Lithuania (1926)   *§‡‖ Estonia
                                           *§‡‖ Finland
                                           *§‡‖ Gr. Britain (India)
                                           *§‡ Latvia
                                           *§† Persia
                                           *§† Poland
                                           *§‡ Rumania
                                           § United States (Siberia-Alaska)

*§‡‖ Spain   *§‡‖ France (1929)
                 *§‡ Portugal (1928)

*§‡‖ Sweden   *§‡‖ Denmark (1924, 1926)
                 *§‡‖ Finland (1924, 1926)
                 *§‡‖ Norway (1924, 1925)

*§‡ Switzerland   *§‡ Austria (1924)
                 *§‡‖ France (1925)
                 *§‡ Germany (1921)
                 *§‡‖ Italy (1924)

§ Turkey   *§‡ Bulgaria (1929)
                 *§‡‖ France (1926) (Syria)   *§‡‖ Gr. Britain (Iraq)
                 *§‡ Greece (1930)   § Soviet Union
                 *§† Persia (1926)

§ UNITED STATES	*§‖ Gr. Britain (1914) (Canada) *§ Mexico (1848)	*§† Cuba *§† Dominican Republica (Porto Rico) *§‡ Haiti (Porto Rico) *§† Japan (Formosa-Philippines) *§† Nicaragua *§‡ Panama § Soviet Union (Siberia-Alaska)
*§‡ URUGUAY	* Argentina (1899) ‡ Brazil (1916)	
*§† VENEZUELA	‡ Brazil (1909) *§‡ Colombia (1842)	*§‖ Gr. Britain (Br. Guiana)
*§‡ YUGOSLAVIA	*§‡ Austria (1926) *§‡ Greece (1929) *§‡ Rumania (1929)	*§‡ Albania *§‡ Bulgaria *§‡ Hungary *§‡‖ Italy

PART TWO

THE MEETING OF THE WORLD'S MINDS

CHAPTER V

THE GROWTH OF THE DRAFT CONVENTION

The Draft Convention of the Preparatory Commission for the Disarmament Conference was the agreed basis on which the first General Disarmament Conference started its work. As drawn up on December 9, 1930, it set down the decisions reached by the 27 governments which in the previous five years had had special interests to be taken into account or special considerations to offer. The 37 other governments participating in the conference possess less absolute armament and are naturally desirous to see others reduce theirs. While it represents no firm agreement of the 27 states for which the limitation or reduction of armament is a genuine problem, it does represent the elimination from the international scene of a vast amount of prior disagreement and the narrowing of the area in which disagreement still exists.

The Draft Convention embodies a distinct step in the advance toward disarmament and the realization of Art. 8 of the Covenant. It enunciates a series of principles, most of which have taken shape from debates so extensive that they can reasonably be regarded as net results. Proceeding from the terms of the Draft Convention, the states in the conference will reanalyze their own positions and develop a new structure, based for the most part upon its principles. It is a characteristic of the armament problem that the introduction of a new factor has far-reaching effects upon others. The existence of the Draft Convention for 14 months prior to the conference gave states the opportunity to reexamine their positions in the light of the principles it embodies, and the conference will divulge the results.

In addition, the lack of agreement expressed by the reservations to the Draft Convention has called attention to matters or points of view which have been given serious attention in the interval by some governments. It is notable that the 46 reservations attached to the Draft Convention are almost exclusively aimed at going farther than the accepted text. They do not include those of the Soviet Union,[1] which were spread on the record in the final session of the Preparatory Commission and which were exclusively objections that the Draft Convention did not go far enough or deal with some fundamental points.

The Draft Convention is incomplete so far as the limitation or reduction of personnel or material by numbers. All attempts at decision as to those figures were avoided in the Preparatory Commission. The Draft Convention may, however, be defined as a carefully constructed statement of the means and methodology for limiting or reducing armament. It is the purpose of the succeeding pages to define the means and methodology thus determined as the basis for the actual decisions of the conference, which will apply them to limitation or reduction of armament by number in all categories.

In order to appreciate the advance already made, it is appropriate to record the substance of the developments in 11 years.

(1) *A Practical Task.* While reduction of armament was for many years discussed as an aspiration, it has only been in the postwar period that it can be said to have become part of a practical program of international action. This development was due to the incorporation of Art. 8 in the Covenant of the League of Nations which provides:

> The Members of the League recognize that the maintenance of peace requires the reduction of national armaments to the lowest point consistent with national safety and the enforcement by common action of international obligations.
>
> The Council, taking account of the geographical situation and circumstances of each state, shall formulate plans for such reduction for the consideration and action of the several governments.
>
> Such plans shall be subject to reconsideration and revision at least every 10 years.

[1] *Documents of the Preparatory Commission*, Series X, p. 400.

After these plans shall have been adopted by the several governments, the limits of armaments therein fixed shall not be exceeded without the concurrence of the Council.

The Members of the League undertake to interchange full and frank information as to the scale of their armaments, their military, naval and air programs and the condition of such of their industries as are adaptable to warlike purposes.

All states Members of the League thus have a common and somewhat detailed objective and, as a matter of fact, all non-Member states have associated and cooperated in realizing the general object. In addition to the impulse given by this obligation, a considerable number of states in the preamble of the military, naval and air clauses of the peace treaties recorded that the conditions imposed by those clauses were for the purpose of rendering "possible the initiation of a general limitation of the armaments of all nations."

(2) *Mechanism.* In 10 years a well-tried and apparently satisfactory mechanism for realizing this objective has been created in a series of diplomatic and expert committees, the conference and a trained secretariat.[1] The development of this mechanism has resulted from experience with many trials and mistakes. In other words, the world possesses instruments appropriate to its purpose. As it were, a well-equipped factory has been brought into existence for turning out the product.

(3) *Coordination of policy.* Ten years ago there was no obvious similarity in the attitudes held by the various states respecting the need, amount or use of armament in general or of its types in particular. Strategy in the military sense

[1] The Third Committee of the Assembly, 1920– ; the Temporary Mixed Committee for the Reduction of Armaments, 1920–24; the Coordination Commission, 1924–25; the Committee of the Council, 1924– ; the Preparatory Commission for the Disarmament Conference, 1925–30; the Committee on Arbitration and Security, 1927–30; the Conference on Trade in Arms, etc., 1925; the Joint Commission on Disarmament, 1926; the International Blockade Commission, 1921; committees of experts on civil aviation, on chemical and bacteriological warfare, national defense budgets, etc., besides numerous subsidiary committees and subcommittees. All this machinery culminated in the Preparatory Commission. The Disarmament Section of the Secretariat has served them all. For complete list and references to reports see Marie J. Carroll, *Key to League of Nations Documents placed on Public Sale 1920–1929*, p. 293–302, and *Supplement*, p. 51.

was the controlling factor. To-day, much of the confusion of thought has disappeared from governmental expressions, and military strategy more and more gives place to the strategy of politics, which is again clearly recognized for what it is, namely, a national interested attitude of mind. While states do not talk in the same terms respecting armament, they are, at least and for the first time, talking relatively in the same language.

(4) *Change of View.* In 10 years the views of states and peoples have altered a number of times respecting armament. In the early days attention was concentrated upon a mere shift of the weight of armament from the national field to an international pool, which might be called upon in case of defined needs. Now it is recognized that armament is a physical expression of national dangers or suspicions and that its real reduction depends upon the elimination of dangers felt or anticipated by the individual state and the enlargement of its subjective sense of security.

(5) *Increase of International Order.* Conscious and steady application of the pacific settlement of international disputes has brought into existence a growing system of mechanisms for the appropriate treatment of all disputes likely to lead to a rupture. In consequence, the recognized transfer of disputes from the category in which armament would be applicable to that in which pacific settlement is applied reduces the absolute and essential character of armament.

(6) *Technical Homologation.* Discussions of the actual substance of the armament problem have resulted in a large amount of technical agreement. Reconciliation of views, for instance, as to whether a rule of reduction by global or category tonnage in naval craft has occurred, and the present status of the entire question exemplifies numerous other agreements or approaches to a single point of view.

(7) *"Security" an International Problem.* The position of the world respecting armament is no longer confined to the mere study of the problem of limiting effectives and material, and of expenditure in connection with them.

They are the outward evidences of that lack of inward and spiritual grace upon which their disappearance depends. That lack has been concentrated for purposes of official discussion into the word "security" and has taken the form of a presentation of national defense requirements. Very early in the Geneva debates it became crystal clear that national defense, and the satisfaction with it which inspires a feeling of security, was an international and not a national matter.

In the prewar period, a nation's armament was regarded as exclusively its own business and the actual equipment was determined by national ability to provide men and mechanism. The inevitable result was unrestrained rivalry. In those days, it was not only the dangers that a state could perceive, but the frustration of its actual or possible desires, legitimate or illegitimate, which added, and gave essential character, to the rivalry that existed. It is a fundamental mistake ever to assume that a state acts from what it regards as bad or unworthy motives. The true understanding of international affairs consists very largely in penetrating to the explanation of how a people can get into a state of mind where it regards a particular objective as good and desirable, though disinterested outsiders can only view it as reprehensible, short-sighted, or worse. The only way yet found to reconcile such antagonistic views is the shopping of ideas in conference of some kind.[1] Any

[1] When national security has to stand international scrutiny, it necessarily becomes less subjective and more objective. Interpretations that a national public accept may be just jokes to a foreigner. The demagogic line of argument loses its efficacy when the national security has to be explained to the representatives of other states, and wise governments will not try to retail abroad what sounds good at home.

An instance of a government attempting to put its sense of insecurity into terms suitable for foreign consumption is Poland. The Warsaw Government states that its political situation is such that it must reckon with the eventuality of being attacked from several sides. The length of her frontiers liable to attack is 3,986 kilometers (2,470 miles). Considering that the League of Nations does not dispose of an international armed force, the military situation of Poland depends on the following factors: military power of neighboring countries; lack of fortified defenses; lack of navy; faulty communication system; unfavorable geographic conditions. Geographical considerations are: total length of borders 5,536 kilometers (about 3,432 miles); unfavorable state of border; unfavorable situation of industrial centers, all of which are close to the frontiers; absence of natural defenses; lack of high roads and means of communication. (*Particulars*, p. 4, C.643. M.257.1931.IX.21.)

meeting is certain to clarify attitudes, even though it reaches no decision. Continuous meetings eventually reconcile apparently irreconcilable views and open avenues of accomplishment not previously thought of.

Steps of Progress

This process of development has been proceeding for more than 10 years and has produced a state of mind substantially different from that which existed at the close of the Great War. It has also resulted in new standards to be aimed at, in new decisions and in the real comprehension of essential phases of the disarmament problem. To recount the course of development would be entirely too tedious and complicated a prelude to the description of the present status of agreement. Nevertheless, much of the significance of the existing decisions — not to mention the prospect of better ones — depends upon appreciating the steady evolution of an inextricable mass of convictions and ideas into a fairly definite body of agreement, plentifully interspersed with very definite disagreements. On its technical side the General Disarmament Conference will have the duty to confirm or improve the agreements and to resolve the disagreements so far as possible. The specific stages which have been surmounted must serve as the summary prologue to the account of the actual content of the Draft Convention:

Military Approach, 1920. In the League of Nations, the first important decision on armament was the establishment by the Council on May 9, 1920, of the Permanent Advisory Commission on Armaments provided for in Art. 9 of the Covenant. The Council at the time quite properly analyzed the duty of that commission as one calculated to give the League organ the authoritative views of governments respecting armament problems, since obviously no decision on armament could be arrived at without taking official opinion into account.[1] That commission was, there-

[1] The study of Art. 8 of the Covenant was first assigned to the Permanent Advisory Committee on Military, Naval and Air Questions by reference of the Council on October 20, 1920 (*Minutes of the Tenth Session*, p. 7, 99, 115).

fore, made up of military, naval and air officers representing the governments members of the Council. It has long since disappeared from the disarmament scene, though still available.

Civilian Inquiry, 1921. The first session of the League Assembly in November-December, 1920, brought all Member states together. Representatives of the whole world, they decided that the armament question was not advisably left to military experts. That was the second important decision. In accordance with that idea, the Council appointed the Temporary Mixed Commission for the Reduction of Armaments, "composed of persons possessing the requisite competence in matters of a political, social and economic nature, to prepare for submission to the Council in the near future reports and proposals for the reduction of armaments as provided for by Art. 8 of the Covenant."[1]

Guaranty Approach, 1922. The following year, the plenary Assembly urged that this commission should make its proposals in the form of a treaty, the commission itself having discovered that the feeling of insecurity was the chief deterrent to making definite progress. The year 1922 was mostly taken up with discovering how many angles the thorny problem of armament had, with technical cooperation between the two existent committees and with estimating the current situation, formal, informal and psychological.

The 1922 Assembly, from consideration of the report of the commission, laid down the principles that reduction of armament could not "be fully successful unless it is general;" that there was a relation between reduction and "a satisfactory guaranty of the safety" of many governments; and that such a guaranty might be found in a defensive agreement open to all countries providing "immediate and effective assistance in accordance with a prearranged plan in the event of one of them being attacked."

---

[1] *Resolutions adopted by the Assembly . . . 1920*, p. 31. The commission was the main organ of the League on the subject until 1925. It held 10 meetings and made a considerable exploration of the field of work, producing the draft treaty of mutual assistance, which was a lineal forerunner of the Geneva protocol. Reports on its meetings may be consulted in *Minutes of the Fourteenth Session of the Council*, p. 131; *Official Journal*, III, p. 403, 982, 1432; IV, p. 426, 719, 1423; V, p. 1605.

The United States in 1921 invited the five naval states and the four other states with Far Eastern interests to a conference at Washington where naval armament was first brought under control by establishing ratios between the capital ship and aircraft carriers. The Washington conference also established new relations with China and adjusted the political relations of the states having possessions in the region of the Pacific Ocean. Retrospectively, aside from the solution of the physical problem of naval control, the conference exemplified the thesis of the concurrent solution of "political" and armament relations.

Lastly, the 1922 Assembly in Resolution XVI called attention to the desirability of settling such outstanding controversial questions as those of reparation and interallied debts, basing the advice upon the consideration "that moral disarmament is an essential preliminary condition of material disarmament, and that this moral disarmament can only be achieved in an atmosphere of mutual confidence and security."[1] The objective of moral disarmament as a condition of material disarmament may be said to be the third important development. Though only an idea and not a binding obligation, the phrase "moral disarmament" maintains its vigor and effectiveness as an objective of postwar policy.

"*Aggression a Crime*," *1923*. The fourth important development came from the Temporary Mixed Commission in fulfillment of a desire of the Assembly. The Draft Treaty of Mutual Assistance was presented to the session of the Assembly in 1923, where the Third Committee attempted to put it into shape for signing. In the commission itself a cleavage had taken place between the point of view of states which were nervous about their security and those which were not. The difference was still more marked in the Assembly committee. States which felt reasonably secure differed in their disposition toward rendering assistance. Some felt that such aid was a duty of solidarity and were willing to agree to it, provided a satisfactory definition

---

[1] *Resolutions and Recommendations adopted by the Assembly . . . 1922*, p. 24–27.

of the proper conditions could be found. None of them was, of course, willing to come to others' aid on the applicants' mere request. The states that felt insecure, and consequently set store on assistance, were at first somewhat disturbed by the demand for assurance that their own hands would be clean. The tendency for the negotiators to pull apart was speedily dispelled by a general consensus that aggressive war was the thing to be prevented. The commission and the Assembly committee proceeded to elaborate texts on the basis "that aggressive war is an international crime" and that no one of the contracting parties "will be guilty of its commission." An attempt to define aggression was made, including efforts to analyze the phases of mobilization so as to fix the significance of violation of frontiers, etc.[1] The Draft Treaty of Mutual Assistance was not opened for signature by the 1923 Assembly, and in the course of the next year, circulation of its text to states resulted in a support insufficient to justify proceeding along the lines it laid down.

Pacific Settlement. The fifth important development was the bringing of pacific settlement into the picture. The Draft Treaty of Mutual Assistance of 1923 negatively stated that a war would not be considered aggressive if a state had complied with a unanimous recommendation of the Council, a verdict of the Permanent Court of International Justice or an arbitral award against a high contracting party which had not accepted such decisions, provided the first state "does not intend to violate the political independence or the territorial integrity" of the state which had not accepted the decision. In the debate in the Third Committee in 1923, Christian L. Lange, the delegate of Norway, made what proved to be the fundamental objection to the Treaty of Mutual Guaranty:[2]

The draft treaty therefore which they had before them sought to solve the problem solely as it affected guaranties of a military

[1] *Records of the Fourth Assembly, Plenary Meetings,* p. 403, 406 (*Official Journal*, Spec. Sup. No. 13).
[2] *Ibid., Meetings of the Committees. Minutes of the Third Committee,* p. 16 (*Official Journal*, Spec. Sup. No. 16).

character. It continued to apply the old maxim: *Si vis pacem para bellum.*

He wondered whether this were not a survival of the superstition that force was effective.

Militarism would perhaps assume as dangerous a character in the international domain as it had in the national.

At the same time, the speaker did not deny that it might appear necessary to set up guaranties of security for certain states, which would be supplementary to the provisions of the Covenant, in order to induce them to disarm. But the draft appeared to be unilateral.

The Covenant did not merely require the abolition of material force. It set up a legal system of arbitration and conciliation. It established international cooperation. Ought they to add to this noble edifice a new building which would be out of keeping with the original architecture?

They should add moral and legal guaranties to material guaranties and should require states to respect the idea of law.

"Arbitration, Security, Disarmament." The sixth important development, which still maintains its force, was the appearance of the formula arbitration, security, disarmament. The Draft Treaty of Mutual Assistance was circulated to states, of which 29 returned formal replies to Geneva.[1] The United States Government contented itself with stating that it could not adhere "in view of the constitutional organization of the government and of the fact that the United States is not a Member of the League."[2] The majority of the other replies were favorable, but serious criticisms were made in some. One objection concerned the failure to define aggression in a manner that would prevent misuse of the defining formula, which was objected to as a purely negative one. It was not regarded as providing a sufficient basis for reduction of armament. Before the 1924 session of the Assembly, the Dawes (Experts') Plan had been implemented at a London conference, which had resulted in a successful agreement by reason of the fact that provision for the settlement of foreseeable differences by arbitration had been made. In the

[1] *Records of the Fifth Assembly. Meetings of the Committees. Minutes of the Third Committee*, p. 129–168.
[2] *Ibid.*, p. 142.

THE GROWTH OF THE DRAFT CONVENTION   113

whole body of documents, 19 separate arbitral jurisdictions had been created, so that the delegations of the principal states appeared at Geneva in September with a lively sense of the value of pacific settlement. Use of the arbitral principle had been due to Premiers Edouard Herriot of France and J. Ramsay MacDonald of Great Britain, both of whom addressed the Assembly and spoke eloquently in favor of adopting arbitration as a means of obtaining that degree of security which would warrant disarmament. It was Premier Herriot who actually associated the words in the now memorable formula.[1] As a consequence of the debate, the Assembly adopted a resolution which virtually constituted its first and third committees into an international conference to realize the idea.[2]

All-in Guaranty, 1924. The seventh immediate development was the resulting protocol for the pacific settlement of international disputes done at Geneva, October 2, 1924. Produced by an enthusiastic loyalty to ideals seldom encountered in practical affairs, the Geneva protocol aimed to solve the multifarious problems of the rule of law on earth and of security at one and the same time. Its terms contemplated that its signature would be followed by an international conference for the reduction of armaments. It provided for the amendment of the Covenant so as to render impossible a legal resort to war, because either a formula or jurisdiction for the solution of every type of international dispute was provided in the protocol. Each signatory was to accept the compulsory jurisdiction of the Permanent Court of International Justice, which involves liability to suit without specific consent for a particular issue. The points in the Covenant where a dispute is not completely settled were filled in by special provisions. During the submission of a dispute, no increases of military strength were to take place. Threats of aggression were to be abstained from, and criteria for their identification laid down. Demilitarized zones were contemplated. Presumptions of aggression of an objective nature were set forth.

[1] *Records of the Fifth Assembly. Plenary Meetings*, p. 52.
[2] *Ibid.*, p. 77.

Additional stipulations as to applying the sanctions contemplated in Art. 16 of the Covenant were dealt with in some detail.[1]

The protocol did not come into force. While preparations for the contemplated conference on reduction of armament were delayed, the British Government was studying the proposal. On March 12, 1925, its representative in the Council made a statement[2] which prevented further progress in realizing it. Speaking for the British dominions as well, the London representative expressed also the general view of those states which did not feel themselves to be insecure. The purpose of the protocol, he said, was to facilitate disarmament by closing certain gaps in the scheme of the Covenant for peaceably settling international disputes and by sharpening the sanctions, especially the economic sanctions. Aside from technical criticisms, the British representative expressed the view that the protocol made in the Covenant changes that were "formal rather than substantial; they aim at theoretical completeness rather than practical effect." It was the sanctions that concerned him most, and concerned him particularly because the United States remained outside the obligation. With it remaining aloof and perhaps trading with the offender, there was no certainty either that sanctions would stop trade or that the offending state "would be crushed or even that it would suffer most." He suggested that the protocol was calculated to meet the wishes of those states which felt themselves insecure and that the real solution of their problems was to be found in a bold facing of the "extreme cases" which concerned them. In other words, he suggested that the deep-lying causes of hostility "which for historic or other reasons divide great and powerful states" be solved directly by those concerned rather than be affected indirectly by a general system of pacificatory machinery.

Regional Guaranty, 1925. The eighth important development was the Locarno settlement. It exactly met the recommendation of the British representative who had the

[1] *Records of the Fifth Assembly. Plenary Meetings*, p. 498.
[2] *Official Journal*, VI, p. 446.

original German proposal from Herr Stresemann the month before he made his statement. The Locarno treaties of October 16, 1925, were a great event in political sanitation.[1] The Franco-German tension on the Rhine boundary was precisely one of the extreme cases of subjective security that disturbed relations. The Locarno treaty of mutual guaranty demilitarized the bridge-head zones which were occupied as a consequence of Arts. 42–44 of the treaty of Versailles, and further pledged Belgium, France and Germany to solve all disputes between them by pacific methods. The demilitarization was placed under the guaranty of the three states immediately concerned and of Great Britain and Italy. Arbitration conventions between Germany on the one side and Belgium, France, Czechoslovakia and Poland on the other side provided for the pacific settlement of all questions between the respective parties on which they were unable to reach an amicable solution by the normal methods of diplomacy. If such questions are not submitted to a judicial decision, a permanent conciliation commission shall propose an acceptable solution and present a report. If within a month an agreement is not reached between the parties, either may bring the matter before the Council of the League. All disputes "with regard to which the parties are in conflict as to their respective rights," including specifically the recognized categories of justiciable disputes, shall be submitted to arbitration or the Permanent Court of International Justice. Before resort to such a tribunal, however, the permanent conciliation commission may be asked to examine such disputes. In the event that its examination results in no amicable agreement, the matter goes to an arbitral tribunal or the Court. The Locarno agreements entered into force September 14, 1926, on the admission of Germany into the League of Nations.

Security by Arbitration, 1927. The ninth important development has been the exploration of the arbitration and security factors of the formula "arbitration, security and reduction of armament." With a view to exploring the

[1] See Myers, *The Locarno Conference* (World Peace Foundation Pamphlets, IX, No. 1).

facts, the Secretariat of the League published in 1926 a collection of the treaties devoted to those factors. In 1927, the Assembly in a resolution declared that states Members of the League were under an obligation to conform to the principles, "that all wars of aggression are, and shall always be, prohibited" and "that every pacific means must be employed to settle disputes of every description which may arise between states."[1] This resolution in effect was regarded as the essence of the Locarno experience. The 1927 session of the Assembly, convinced that arbitration and security merited more attention, called for the establishment of a committee to consider "the measures capable of giving all states the guaranties of arbitration and security necessary to enable them to fix the level of their armaments at the lowest possible figures in an international disarmament agreement." This Committee on Arbitration and Security in 1928 prepared six model conventions dealing with the pacific settlement of international disputes, mutual assistance and nonaggression.[2] Respecting pacific settlement, the feature of the six documents was that all their equivalent clauses were identic. The distinctive articles of the conventions on mutual assistance and nonaggression were borrowed from the Locarno treaty of mutual guaranty. When the ninth session of the Assembly received these documents, it felt that each of them might doubly serve the convenience of states desiring to contract under their provisions and provide the most valuable feature of making available standard forms of procedure for the types of pacific settlement contained in them. The Assembly felt that the time was ripe for affording an opportunity to consolidate the practices of pacific settlement in a standard form. Accordingly, in its committees it developed the General Act for the Pacific Settlement of International Disputes which, with the others, it opened for adoption. The

[1] *Resolutions and Recommendations adopted by the Assembly 1927*, p. 22 (*Official Journal*, Spec. Sup. No. 53). The resolution was proposed by Poland and anticipated the signing of the Briand-Kellogg pact by a year, being adopted while those negotiations were still bilateral between France and the United States.

[2] *Ibid., 1928*, p. 26–57 (*Official Journal*, Spec. Sup. No. 63) for final form.

General Act in form consists of three chapters devoted to conciliation, judicial settlement and arbitration and a Chapter IV embodying valuable general provisions. The scope of the three forms of pacific settlement is defined in the first article of each chapter, and procedural provisions follow the defining clause. The chapter devoted to general provisions deals with further procedural matters, but contains two articles which enable full or qualified accession to be made and which provide a standard form for the expression of reservations. The General Act enters into force 90 days after the accession of each contracting state. It thus started its career as a bilateral treaty between Belgium and Sweden on August 16, 1929, and continues as a multilateral engagement of constantly widening effect.[1]

In the same Assembly, a resolution of the Member states recommended to themselves that they should consider subscribing to the Optional Clause of Art. 36 of the Statute of the Permanent Court of International Justice conferring on the Court compulsory jurisdiction with respect to justiciable disputes, with the consequent reciprocal liability to suit within those limits.[2]

Renunciation of War, 1928. The tenth important development was the general treaty for the renunciation of war signed at Paris, August 27, 1928, and in force since July 24, 1929, binding without limit of time upon 61 states.[3] This treaty, originally proposed as a bilateral engagement between France and the United States by Aristide Briand, the French Minister of Foreign Affairs, was negotiated by the skill and devotion of Frank B. Kellogg, Secretary of State of the United States, as a multilateral

[1] For the text and status see Appendix II, p. 324.

[2] By February 1, 1932, the Member states had taken their own advice to the following extent: Albania, Australia, Austria, Belgium, Brazil, Bulgaria, Canada, Colombia, Denmark, Estonia, Ethiopia, Finland, France, Germany, Great Britain, Greece, Haiti, Hungary, India, Irish Free State, Italy, Latvia, Lithuania, Luxembourg, Netherlands, New Zealand, Norway, Panama, Portugal, Rumania, Salvador, Siam, South Africa, Spain, Sweden, Switzerland, Uruguay, Yugoslavia.

[3] Bolivia, Salvador and Uruguay have signified their intention to adhere, but by January 1, 1932, had not deposited the necessary instrument. Argentina and Brazil have not adhered, apparently because they were not invited into the group of 15 original signatories.

treaty. There is debate among technicians as to what it means in a legal sense. Its three provisions, however, put a burden of proof in the public mind against a state's using warlike methods. That is of primary importance in creating a new outlook toward armament and war. The three principles it enacts between states are:

1. The high contracting parties solemnly declare in the names of their respective peoples that they condemn recourse to war for the solution of international controversies.

2. The high contracting parties solemnly declare in the names of their respective peoples that they . . . renounce [war] as an instrument of national policy in their relations with one another.

3. The settlement or solution of all disputes or conflicts of whatever nature or of whatever origin they may be, which may arise among them, shall never be sought except by pacific means.

Resistance Lessens, 1929–1930. The eleventh important development was what may be called the breaking of the technical log jam. Each of the foregoing decisions and shifts of attitude had in some way advanced the work, though not necessarily in an obvious manner. By 1927, the Preparatory Commission had given a first reading to a text which was intended to do little more than stop increase and to establish agreeable relations between the national defense structures of the parties. All the particular and particularistic considerations of the states represented in the commission were being aired and the debates to a considerable extent were a presentation of what states were not willing to do. At the fourth session of the commission in November, 1927, the Soviet Union was represented for the first time and signalized its entrance into the discussion by submitting for immediate debate a project for complete and immediate disarmament.[1] That precipitated an argument on the fundamental question as to whether the work of the commission was going to cut armament out of the body politic or only going to prune it. The decision in March, 1928, was against taking the radical

[1] C.46.M.23.1928.IX.5, *Documents of the Preparatory Commission,* Series VI, p. 324.

step,[1] and the commission continued by going as far as it could in adopting a draft convention on first reading. It did not get beyond that point, since on various questions the states most concerned were unwilling to shift their angle of vision sufficiently to allow an agreement to be reached. The principal deadlock at that time lay in the field of naval material, where controversy had been heightened rather than allayed by the failure of the conference for the limitation of naval armaments, called at Geneva by President Coolidge June 20-August 24, 1927.

A year passed in which technical armament discussion was left aside, but attention was concentrated upon developing pacific settlement. The Briand-Kellogg pact, the General Act for the pacific settlement of international disputes and a notable increase in acceptances of the Optional Clause to the Statute of the Permanent Court of International Justice took place in the multilateral field; bilaterally many states contracted treaties of general pacific settlement. Various matters causing political tension came to the surface for definite discussion and were eliminated from the scene. Public discussion of all phases of the question — political, pacificatory and technical — took place, and both official and unofficial opinion underwent change. The result was a measurable revaluation of the position when the sixth session (first part) of the Preparatory Commission was held at Geneva, April 15-May 6, 1929. That session encountered the influence of public opinion in a more marked degree than previously — continuity of meeting had advertising value — and the delegates uniformly exhibited a disposition to see how far they could go, instead of how much they could keep from doing. For a week they ran along that way, and then on April 22, Hugh S. Gibson, the United States delegate, assumed the lead in establishing the tendency to accommodate views. Essentially he said:[2]

During the first reading of the Draft Convention, it was the duty

[1] See the resolution of March 24, *Documents of the Preparatory Commission*, Series VI, p. 307.
[2] *Documents of the Preparatory Commission*, Series VIII, p. 56–58.

of each one of us to put forward the views of his government on the various problems before the commission, to urge them upon his colleagues and endeavor to persuade them that those views should be adopted. It was only in this way that we were able to throw full light upon the complicated questions the solutions of which we seek. When we come to the second reading, however, a renewal of the old discussions is no longer in order. Our first duty is for each one of us to examine all phases of the problem before us with a view to discovering what measures of concession can be offered by each delegation. Agreement upon a single text can be achieved only by a maximum of such concession . . .

I feel that we are able to deal to best advantage with the specific questions on our agenda only if we bear clearly in mind the recent important changes in world conditions.

Since our last meeting, the nations of the world have bound themselves by solemn undertaking to renounce war as an instrument of national policy. We believe (and we hope that our belief is shared by other nations) that this agreement affirming humanity's will to peace will advance the cause of disarmament by removing doubts and fears which in the past have constituted our principal obstacle . . .

Any approach to the disarmament problem on purely technical grounds is bound to be inconclusive. The technical justification of armaments is based upon the experience of past wars and upon the anticipation of future wars. So long as the approach to the problem is based upon old fears and old suspicions, there is little hope of disarmament. The lessons of the old strategies must be unlearned. If we are honest, if our solemn promise in the Pact means anything, there is no justification for the continuation of a war-taxed peace. Great armaments are the relic of another age, but they will remain a necessary relic until the present deadlock is broken and that can be accomplished only by the decision of the powers possessing the greatest armaments to initiate measures of reduction . . .

My Government has never believed that an effective approach to the problem of disarmament could be made by methods of reduction of armaments alone. It feels that genuine disarmament will follow only from a change of attitude toward the use of force in the settlement of international disputes. It is for that reason that I venture to make this appeal that the countries here represented examine the whole problem afresh in the hope that they will find in general world conditions, and in the solemn obligation they have taken among themselves, a reassurance as to their security, and that

THE GROWTH OF THE DRAFT CONVENTION

they will find in this the confidence to enable them to dispense with the armaments which hitherto have seemed so essential.

Mr. Gibson in the course of his remarks specified various concessions which he was willing to make, and he was followed by other delegates who yielded points of view that they had persistently advocated. The discussions continued for two weeks; considerable ground was covered, but there ensued a further deadlock, with the problem of naval material still untouched.

The urge to get forward resulted in the adjournment of the session until the naval states could reach agreement, and the London Naval Conference of January 22-April 22, 1930, was their contribution to the breaking of the jam. The failure of France and Italy to agree at London and the new influences to be added from the Assembly of the League in September, 1930, led to the adjournment being prolonged until November 9 of that year. In that second part of the sixth session of the Preparatory Commission the same spirit of concession and of seeking means to agree that characterized the first part of the session 18 months before were markedly present. Once more there was a collapse of the log jam, with the net result that the Draft Convention as adopted on December 9, 1930, came into being.

Data for the Conference

The Preparatory Commission emphasized in its report that the practical scope of a convention would be determined by fixing in figures the extent of the undertakings it involved, a task which was called delicate and complicated. The first and foremost condition for the successful discharge of that task, said the commission, was "a thorough and systematic preparation of the conference itself." The history of this preparation shows the manner in which multilateral negotiation works out constantly to more satisfactory ends.

The German delegation, seconded by the Italian, proposed that the Preparatory Commission should ask the various governments for detailed particulars of their present armaments.[1] The commission regarded the German proposal as too restricted and held that the Council of the League should take the necessary steps. The Council on January 24, 1931, accordingly adopted a resolution instructing the Secretary-General to take measures to obtain particulars "from the different governments with regard to the position of their armaments and all data, technical or otherwise, which might help to inform the conference and to justify such concrete proposals as the governments may lay before it." A circular letter of February 17 called for such information from the governments which, it will be noted, were asked to furnish considerably more data than were contemplated in the original German suggestion.

On March 12, the British Government communicated the suggestion that this preliminary exchange of information "would gain greatly in value if the information to be furnished by each government were to be supplied on a uniform model." Admitting that the Draft Convention was only tentative, it "may be taken as representing the largest common measure of agreement possible at the present stage on the elements which will have to be subject to limitation and reduction." Therefore, the London Government suggested "that the information now required might be most conveniently given on the lines of the tables annexed to the Draft Convention." The British Government requested the Secretary-General to learn whether this suggestion of procedure was generally acceptable.[2]

On March 27, the German Government forwarded a note in which it defined the purpose of the Council as being "to supply the future Disarmament Conference with a complete table of the factors with which it must be acquainted in order to determine the methods and extent of the reduction and limitation of armaments." Germany also regarded it essential that all particulars be supplied on a single model and, therefore, suggested for the agenda of the May session

[1] *Report*, par. 303; *Documents of the Preparatory Commission*, Series X, p. 267.
[2] C.198.M.80.1931.IX (C.P.D.299), *Official Journal*, XII, p. 1238.

of the Council the question of the distribution of an appropriate questionnaire.[1]

On April 25, the Soviet Union replied, holding that the collection of the information in question was a step which went beyond a purely technical preparation for the conference, since the determination of the amount and form of information might have a considerable bearing on the work of the conference and be of special political importance. While not recognizing the competence of the Council, it forwarded its own information for the president of the conference and asked to be supplied with that of other governments.[2]

Meanwhile, on April 20, the British Government had inquired whether the German proposal had simply crossed the British request for uniform information or was an alternative to it. The German reply to this was that the detailed proposal submitted by Berlin was a better means of achieving the end in view.[3] Forwarded to Geneva under date of April 25, the detailed proposal transmitted model tables much more complete than those included in the Draft Convention.

Meantime, the French Government on April 28 had called attention to the terms of the Council resolution and emphasized that its essential principle was that the mere figures would be of value "only in so far as they are accompanied by explanations or justifications which allow of their being interpreted." M. Briand agreed with the British proposal on the whole, and regarded it as more calculated to realize the terms of the Council resolution than the original suggestion of the Preparatory Commission.[4]

[1] C.214.M.89.1931.IX (C.P.D.300), *Official Journal*, XII, p. 1240.

[2] C.276.M.128.1931.IX (C.P.D. 301), *Official Journal*, XII, p. 1251. The Soviet Union has held to this attitude, and its *Particulars* have accordingly not been circulated by the Secretary-General to governments. However, special exchanges have been effected by the Soviet Union by direct agreement with certain other governments, notably those of France, Italy, Latvia and Poland

[3] C.292.M.136.1931.IX. (C.P.D.303).

[4] C.287.M.135.1931.IX. (C.P.D.304), *Official Journal*, XII, p. 1250.

Amount of Data to be Furnished

The various matters raised by these exchanges came before the Council on May 20 in a report by the Spanish representative. He called attention to the fact that the British and German letters were based on the same principle, but differed as regards the methods of putting that principle into practice. The Soviet Union letter raised the question of the procedure to be followed for communicating to governments the information furnished by the different states.[1]

The main question was whether the tables attached to Art. 30 of the Draft Convention or the more complete tables of the German proposal were to be adopted. Mr. Henderson for Great Britain recalled the laborious development of the Draft Convention tables and advocated their adoption because he thought it was better not to reopen the discussion. The great care and thoroughness with which the German tables had been worked out might make them ideal, "but that might be their chief defect from the practical point of view."[2]

Julius Curtius, the German representative, did not see how the conference could obtain a clear idea of the reduction necessary without information concerning existing material in actual use and in depot, or a correct view of effectives without taking account of trained reserves. The tables proposed by the British Government for use did not include such important factors and, therefore, he regarded the German proposal as the preferable one.

M. Briand for France supported the British proposal to use the Draft Convention models, since it might be dangerous "to touch the result of so much thought and labor." Difficulties had arisen on so many occasions and there had been so many doubts as to whether any results were obtainable that it would be too great a risk to reopen the question of models after an agreement had been reached. Since the German proposal raised these questions anew, he believed that it would certainly cause further delay which would itself be disappointing to the German Government

[1] *Official Journal*, XII, p. 1097. [2] *Official Journal*, XII, p. 1101.

which, comprehensibly, "had never missed an opportunity to protest against the slowness with which the Conference for the Reduction of Armaments mentioned in Art. 8 of the Covenant was being prepared."

The Polish Government rallied to the British proposal, calling attention to the fact that in the *Armaments Year-Book* the data of certain states were incomplete, which put their neighbors in an unequal situation if the latter furnished precise information. Kenkichi Yoshizawa of Japan diverted the discussion from the relative merits of the two sets of tables to the principles involved. He thought that rigidity of detail was relatively less important than (1) uniformity of information, (2) its universality in the sense that all states furnished it, and (3) simultaneity of its supply.

Uniform but Limited Reports

The debate was resumed on May 23, when Señor Lerroux presented a report in which he recorded that the previous debate had indicated acceptance in principle of the British proposal. He called attention to the long debates in the Preparatory Commission which, though not decisive for the Council, must carry great weight with it. Though the British proposals were not ideal, he felt that the Council must for the present "concentrate on what is practicable rather than on perfection." The Council was only in a position to make recommendations, but he felt that the rules of uniformity, universality and simultaneity of his Japanese colleague should be its aim. As to simultaneity, he suggested that the information should be received on September 15 and would then "be exchanged among those governments which have themselves supplied it." The British proposal should be supplemented by adding the expenditure tables provided by the Committee of Budgetary Experts. He called attention to the fact that if the request of the Council did not bring all requisite information, the conference "which has, of course, full powers of decision," would be able to ask for anything it needed. After some discussion, the Council adopted the report.

On June 5, the Secretary of State of the United States through diplomatic channels delivered the first *Particulars with Regard to Armaments* to the Secretary-General, embodying a recasting of the information called for in the tables of the Draft Convention and the Report of the Committee of Experts on Budgetary Questions. The Secretary of State requested "that full and immediate distribution and publicity be given to the American figures." He added: "The Secretary of State entertains the hope that other nations may thus be encouraged to lay their figures before the public without delay. The Secretary-General may find it convenient to bring this communication to the attention of other interested governments."

By December 31, 1931, the *Particulars* of 38 states had been received, printed and circulated,[1] while those of 10 others had been received and circulated[2] to those governments which had themselves submitted *Particulars*. In addition, the Soviet Union's report was on file for submission to the conference itself. Only 15 states[3]— in Africa, Asia and America, but none in Europe — had made no reports, but with the exception of China's so-called army and Brazil's and Turkey's fleets, practically all the returns were nevertheless in.

The publication of these and subsequent reports[4] provided for the first time in history official records of armed strengths on a comparable basis. The prior notices in the *Armaments Year-Book* had been furnished by the governments, but not in accordance with any master scheme. The *Particulars with Regard to Armaments*, though all re-

[1] Albania, Argentine Republic, Austria, Belgium, Bulgaria, Canada, Cuba, Czechoslovakia, Denmark, Dominican Republic, Estonia, Finland, France, Germany, Great Britain, Hungary, India, Irish Free State, Italy, Japan, Latvia, Liberia, Luxemburg, Netherlands, New Zealand, Nicaragua, Norway, Panama, Poland, Portugal, Rumania, South Africa, Spain, Sweden, Switzerland, United States, Uruguay and Yugoslavia.

[2] Australia, Costa Rica, Ecuador, Egypt, Greece, Haiti, Lithuania, Persia, Siam, Venezuela.

[3] Afghanistan, Bolivia, Brazil, Chile, China, Colombia, Ethiopia, Guatemala, Hejaz and Nejd, Honduras, Mexico, Paraguay, Peru, Salvador and Turkey.

[4] These *Particulars* have been printed separately as documents circulated to states and as a Publication Sales series 1931.IX.7 *ff*.

sponding to the same set of rules, did not always give easily comparable results. The legal and administrative bases of the military, naval and air services in the various countries frequently created difficulties. Italy, despite very full statistics, did not translate military service into average daily effectives, and these were figured in various ways by others. Japan did not give the budgetary details called for. There were many other discrepancies; but the foundations for comparability are not only laid but well advanced, and the conference will undoubtedly further consolidate and coordinate this statistical work, in addition to establishing uniform rules for limitation or reduction. Moreover, with the model statement at hand and eventually an integral annex to the convention, national administrations will find it increasingly convenient to keep or prepare their records in such a way as to facilitate making the requisite annual reports in accordance with their international obligations.

The importance of the statistical basis provided by the *Particulars* is considerable. A great deal of controversy on armament has arisen in the past because of different national methods of keeping accounts, reporting effectives, etc. As in all statistics, the method employed has a fundamental effect on the result obtained. The *Particulars*, based on common standards, exhibit differences with the memoranda in the *Armaments Year-Book*, which were also made by governments but on their own specifications. With armament statistics thus undergoing a basic change, it has not been deemed advisable to give elaborate tables in these pages. For the sake of emphasizing the changing condition, however, some contrasting statistics from the *Year-Book* and the *Particulars* are given in the Appendix. Future editions of the *Year-Book* will, of course, be built on the new models.

The Armament Truce

The twelfth session of the Assembly of the League of Nations, representing 55 Member states and Brazil, Costa

Rica, Egypt, Turkey and the United States in addition,[1] gave expression to the conviction that a tangible gesture should be made to create an atmosphere favorable to the success of the conference. The Assembly accordingly adopted on September 29, 1931, the following self-explanatory resolution calling for an armament truce:[2]

> Convinced that the crisis which at the present time is creating such profound disturbance among the nations of the world is due to a number of economic and political causes originating principally in the lack of mutual confidence between the nations, and
> Convinced that a renewal of the competition in armaments would necessarily lead to an international and social catastrophe:
> The Assembly addresses a solemn appeal to all those who are desirous that practical effect should be given to the principles of peace and justice upon which the Covenant is based and urges them to devote all their efforts toward creating a world opinion strong enough to enable the General Disarmament Conference to achieve positive results, including in particular a gradual reduction of armaments to be continued until such time as the object laid down in Art. 8 of the Covenant is attained.
> In view of the fact that an undertaking on the part of all states not to increase their armaments would help to create an atmosphere of confidence, to prevent competition in armaments and to prepare the ground for the success of the forthcoming conference:
> The Assembly,
> Requests the governments invited to the Disarmament Conference to prepare for this event by means of an armaments truce and, accordingly,
> Requests the Council to urge the governments convened to the said conference to give proof of their earnest desire for the successful issue of the efforts to insure and organize peace, and, without prejudging the decisions of the conference or the programs or proposals submitted to it by each government, to refrain from any measure involving an increase in their armaments.
> Likewise requests the Council to ask the governments to state before November 1, 1931, whether they are prepared for a period of one year as from that date to accept this truce in armaments.

By January 1, 1932, the armaments truce was in effect

---

[1] Participating in the Assembly Committee's work by special invitation.
[2] *Resolutions and Recommendations adopted by the Assembly . . . 1931*, p. 23 (*Official Journal*, Spec. Sup. No. 92).

THE GROWTH OF THE DRAFT CONVENTION

for 54 governments, including the Soviet Union and the United States and a new participant in the disarmament program, the Kingdom of Hejaz and Nejd.[1] The armaments truce is not a formal agreement, but a moral expression of policy. The replies were in several forms, ranging from a naked assent, through acceptance within the scope of the resolution or accompanying report, to others noting special understandings of its significance. The replies were analyzed, and the president of the Council for the time being concluded from them:

(1) That no government was opposed but, on the contrary, all of them declared their willingness to accept the truce;

(2) That reciprocity had in fact been achieved so far as governments had made that a condition of acceptance;

(3) That interpretations and observations contained in replies appeared "to be in keeping with the spirit and the letter of the resolution and the report."

The Secretary-General of the League in consequence informed states on November 14 that the armament truce, under the conditions of the resolution and report, was "accepted for one year as from November 1, 1931, by the governments invited to the Disarmament Conference."

[1] The list of accepting states is as follows: Albania, Argentine Republic, Australia, Austria, Belgium, Bulgaria, Canada, Chile, China, Colombia, Costa Rica, Cuba, Czechoslovakia, Denmark, Ecuador, Egypt, Estonia, Finland, France, Germany, Great Britain and Northern Ireland, Greece, Haiti, Hejaz and Nejd, Hungary, India, Irish Free State, Italy, Japan, Latvia, Liberia, Lithuania, Luxemburg, Netherlands, New Zealand, Nicaragua, Norway, Panama, Persia, Peru, Poland, Portugal, Rumania, Siam, South Africa, Soviet Union, Spain, Sweden, Switzerland, Turkey, United States, Uruguay, Venezuela, Yugoslavia.

All the correspondence is collected in C.919,M.484.1931.IX.40. (*Official Journal*, XIII, p. 135).

Guatemala adhered on January 19, 1932, bringing the number to 55.

CHAPTER VI

EFFECTIVES FOR ALL FORCES

The text of the Draft Convention may be studied in any degree of detail, so extensive are the records dealing with its elaboration. It is almost literally true that every word of it has been debated in various aspects, and it is certainly true that each word of it not only has the significance of its meaning but an additional significance on account of its position in the sentence structure, which reflects extensive and some times tense debates. One could, therefore, present the contents of the Draft Convention by tracing each of the ideas it contains in its evolution through the six sessions of the Preparatory Commission from 1926 to 1930; to do so would impressively demonstrate the extent to which both ideas and points of view have been eliminated in attaining the present stage of agreement, but beyond that it would be a tiresome, detailed and technical procedure.

With the object of stating precisely the subject matter on which the General Disarmament Conference began its work, it will be sufficient here to report the reconciliation of views expressed in the terms of the Draft Convention itself, to call attention to those points on which several views were maintained, to record reservations of principle or policy which are being carried forward and to note for somewhat full discussion those matters on which disagreement persisted.

The armament question is so wide and diverse that any reader will perceive factors which do not fall under any of these heads. It may be presumed — and this will invariably be found on detailed investigation — that such factors were consciously eliminated in the discussions of the Preparatory Commission as irrelevant to the purposes of a first conference on limitation and reduction of armament.

In discussing the substance of the Draft Convention, the antecedent texts will be occasionally referred to. Those texts in themselves embodied the general conclusions believed to result from prior discussions and may thus be regarded as summaries of opinion in the Preparatory Commission at their dates. The texts referred to are:

1. Preliminary drafts of the British and French delegations[1] in the Preparatory Commission, Third Session, March 21-26, 1927, from which was developed the text of the Draft Convention drawn up at first reading, dated April 26, 1927.

2. Text of the Draft Convention drawn up at second reading in the course of the First Part of the Sixth Session of the Preparatory Commission, April 15-May 6, 1929.[2]

3. Full texts of the Draft Convention drawn up at second reading as completed in the Sixth Session, Second Part, dated November 26, and December 1, 1930.[3]

4. Draft Convention from the Drafting Committee, Sixth Session, Second Part, dated December 3, 1930.[4]

5. Draft Convention on third reading and Report, adopted December 9, 1930 (document under review, reprinted in Appendix, *infra*, p. 265).

The subject was first submitted to any League body on October 20, 1920. The questionnaire was not determined until December 12, 1925.[5] A text on first reading was not adopted until April 26, 1927. The text on second reading was not completed until December 1, 1930. The Draft Convention was not ready for conference until December 9, 1930, and the preparations for the conference itself occupied the time until February 2, 1932 — over 11 years of unremitting preparation.

---

[1] Series IV, p. 358 and 361 and synoptic analysis, p. 370.
A table of the draft texts showing the evolution of the Draft Convention is in Series XI, p. 51 (C.428.M.178.1931.IX.5).

[2] The two foregoing texts are conveniently printed in parallel column in the C.P.D. 211 published in *Documents of the Preparatory Commission*, Series X, p. 423.

[3] C.P.D. 280 and 280 (a), *ibid.*, p. 485, 500.

[4] This is a drafting revision of the second reading and is published in C.P.D. 292, *ibid.*, p. 509.

[5] See the report accompanying it, *Official Journal*, VII, p. 167.

Purpose — Reduction, so Far as Possible

The purpose of the Draft Convention was stated in preambles to the original preliminary drafts and was expressed in three alternative forms in the first reading. The Preparatory Commission decided, however, that, inasmuch as the purposes should correspond with the significance of the convention itself and as that would not be evident until the conference inserted figures, the Draft Convention should appear without any preamble.

The purpose of the Draft Convention is, however, stated in its Art. 1, which stands by itself at the head of the text. By it, "the high contracting parties agree to limit and, so far as possible, to reduce their respective armaments as provided in the present convention." The idea of this article was proposed in second reading with respect to expenditure and was given a general application by the Drafting Committee. It adds the object of reduction to that of limitation of armament, upon which most of the discussion in the Preparatory Commission proceeded. The qualification of reduction "so far as possible" was due to the claim of a number of governments that their present armaments in some or all categories were insufficient to guarantee national safety. The report states that "this reservation was made in precise form, particularly in relation to naval and air armaments, the latter being scarcely developed in the majority of states."[1] The Soviet delegation objected to the qualification on the ground that "the formula adopted allows full latitude for the maintenance and even expansion of armaments."[2]

Respecting the Draft Convention as a whole, the Norwegian and Irish Free State delegates, while accepting it, reserved the freedom of their governments at the conference, in view of the fact that neither had participated in all the work of the commission. The German and Turkish delegations in accepting the Draft Convention as a whole reserved their governments' rights to submit to the conference proposals likely to promote both reduction and lim-

[1] Par. 40.
[2] *Documents of the Preparatory Commission*, Series X, p. 401.

itation.[1] Thus five[2] governments at least are on record as desiring to strengthen the Draft Convention as a whole.

"Average Daily Effectives"

Part I deals with personnel and is divided into two chapters, A, Effectives, and B, Period of Service. The question of effectives concerns land forces more than it does naval and air forces, whose personnel is limited by the character of material. Conscript armies were the principal subject of debate, and trained reserves are not included in the framework. Agreement to the extent reached created little essential difficulty, though technical points were numerous.

The chief of these was the determination of a method to compute service with the forces in terms that would be comparable. It is customary for the public to think of armed forces in terms of enlisted men, but when 64 governments are to produce comparable figures that is not a satisfactory basis for computation. Terms of service vary, while reserves and other subsidiary forces are with the colors for limited times. In order to get a basis that would apply equitably to all types of armed forces it was decided to define them in terms of "average daily effectives," which are reckoned by dividing the total number of days' duty performed in each year by the number of days in such year. Thus, the tables annexed will give information in terms of military service performed rather than of individuals involved. The basic army service of conscripts in France is for one year and of recruits on original voluntary enlistment in the United States for one or three years. Those forces are roughly comparable either on the basis of average daily effectives or on the basis of individuals, but the regular term of conscript service in Belgium is 14 months, while that in Brazil for volunteers under intensive training is four, six or 16 months. The introduction of a common

[1] The indications of their policy are given in C.P.D. 138 and C.P.D. 142 (1), *Documents of the Preparatory Commission*, Series VIII, p. 203, 206.
[2] The Soviet Union declined to accept the Report because the Draft Convention did not go far enough.

denominator of time affords a practical method of putting different recruiting systems into equivalent terms.

The use of the "average daily effectives" formula also avoids an argument which was long continued in the Preparatory Commission concerning conscription. Countries which adopt this system of recruiting maintain strenuously that it fairly equalizes an obligation of service which is technically imposed by the laws of most countries, including those that actually recruit on a voluntary basis.[1] In this connection, there were long debates as to the relative comparability of militia organizations and trained reserves resulting from the conscription system. On the one hand, states using the conscription method objected to having their figures padded by the inclusion of reserves technically subject to duty, but not actually called to the colors; while on the other hand states with militias found it objectionable to have the civilian soldier compared, without some modifying formula, with conscript reserves.

The adoption of the "average daily effectives" formula resolved the principal difficulties involved in such various points of view. Several reservations to the principle, notably by the British Empire and the United States, were withdrawn. Germany found it objectionable that no provision for the limitation of trained reserves was included and Poland, while accepting the method, expressed doubts as to its practical value.

Formations Organized on Military Basis

Among effectives are to be included "formations organized on a military basis." By Art. 4 of the Draft Convention these are to be understood as comprising "police forces of all kinds, gendarmerie, customs officials, forest guards, which, whatever their legal purpose, are, in time of peace, by reason of their staff of officers, establishment, training,

---

[1] The law of the United States reads:
"The militia of the United States shall consist of all able-bodied male citizens of the United States . . . who shall be more than 18 years of age and . . . not more than 45 years of age, and said militia shall be divided into three classes, the National Guard, the Naval Militia and the Unorganized Militia" (*Code of Laws of the United States*, Title 32, Sec. 1, p. 1033).

armament, equipment, capable of being employed for military purposes without measures of mobilization, as well as any other organization complying with the above condition." It is left to the conference "to decide the condition or conditions to be taken into account in determining whether a particular" formation is organized on a military basis.[1] Thus the full answer can not be known until the conference decides, though many organizations in many countries will certainly be included in the formations indicated.[2]

The definition was fully agreed to by the Preparatory Commission so that it may be regarded as expressing a fundamental principle. It has a far-reaching consequence. Hitherto, there has been a general practice in governments to restrict their computations of military effectives to those in certain categories, but to disregard immediately available or potential man power. On the other hand, other governments have tended to reach conclusions as to their own requirements by comparison with what they assume to be the potential strength of their putative rivals. It, therefore, happened that a state's effectives were discussed at home in one set of numerical terms and abroad in other and larger terms. Neither corresponded with comparable realities. The principle under review approaches practical reality. It will provide an agreed formula for determining what addition should be made to the regular services in order to determine the formal and immediate military strength of a given state. The general potential of man power has, of course, always been provided by the detailed population figures and the character of industrial development.

In each state formations organized on a military basis differ widely according to national organization, conceptions of government and administrative requirements. The coordination of the formations to be reported under the Draft Convention is, therefore, a large contribution to the sci-

[1] *Report*, par. 56.
[2] Poland, for instance, reports the frontier Zone Protection Corps of 26,611 effectives, the Frontier Guard of 5,985 effectives and 31,675 Police.

entific analysis of international military structure. In preparation for the conference each state has reported its own formations deemed to fall within the definition. In most cases, it is their establishment by law which controls national interpretation, and it is likely that in many cases national judgments respecting essentially the same formation will differ at the outset and require reconciliation during the conference.

In some states there are national police systems and gendarmerie which would clearly be included; in others, the same formations are organized by municipalities or local administrative units, and they might or might not be included. Further, the incidence of the legislative establishment of police will require consideration. Police established directly by a national law raise no question, but police authorized by a national law and actually appointed and remunerated by a department, province or lesser unit might be regarded as debatable. Police as they exist in the United States, where the national government has no control or even cognizance of them and where these forces frequently depend entirely upon the local municipality, present a question of a different character.

The relation of police and gendarmerie forces to military effectives has another aspect. Their existence under any form of legislation makes it possible to regard them as contributing to release other men for more formal duty.

Such questions may be debated in great detail during the conference, and it will not be until its decisions have been taken that the exact scope of the new principle will be known. The formations referred to are confined to those "capable of being employed for military purposes without measures of mobilization." By mobilization,[1] the Prepara-

[1] It may be expected that the definition of mobilization will be further examined. The full value of methods of pacific settlement is largely conditioned in many minds upon its effectiveness in the case of a sudden attack rather than its ability to handle a problem with the aid of time; and not a few persons tend to discount the actual values of anything but force to allay that fear. The definition of mobilization of the Draft Convention covers measures involving provision for personnel and material to pass as a unit from a peace-time to a war-time footing.

On the record of the Great War, the definition is a limited one. It, of course, covers partial mobilization and a notice by consuls to subjects liable

tory Commission understood "all the measures for the purpose of providing the whole or part of the various corps, services and units with the personnel and material required to pass from a peace-time footing to a war-time footing."

The United States has the following formations:

The Coast Guard, which constitutes "a part of the military forces of the United States and shall operate under the Treasury Department in time of peace and operate as a part of the navy . . . in time of war or when the President shall so direct."[1]

The National Guard, which is included in the "organized peace establishment"[2] of the army.

The organized military reserves, which are included in the organized peace establishment of the army and which consist of the Officers' Reserve Corps, the Reserve Officers' Training Corps, the Enlisted Reserve Corps and the attendants at military training camps.[3]

The Naval Reserve, which consists of the Fleet Naval Reserve, the Merchant Marine Naval Reserve and the Volunteer Naval Reserve, for which there exists the Naval Reserve Officers' Training Corps.[4] In addition some states possess a naval militia.[5]

The Marine Corps Reserve, which consists of the Fleet Marine Corps Reserve and the Volunteer Marine Corps

to military service to join the colors (*British Blue Book*, Nos. 76, 78, 86). On July 31, 1914, Germany proclaimed *Kriegsgefahr* (danger of war), which was described as "the taking of certain precautionary measures consequent upon strained relations with a foreign country" (*Ibid.*, No. 112). The writer has never been able to get any authentic technical definition of the precise action called for, but has been told that it involved notices to be ready to be called, in other words, an insurance against delay in responding owing to a misplacement of a *Pickelhaube*, etc. On August 1, the system of *Kriegszustand* (war footing) was proclaimed (*Ibid.*, No. 136). This involved the actual calling of six classes, sufficient to bring covering troops up to war strength and furnish them a reserve. The French Minister of War, regarding this condition as tantamount to mobilization, decided it was mobilization under another name and ordered a general mobilization of the French army for 3 p.m. of that day, ordering the French troops to remain 10 kilometers back of the German frontier. Later, on August 1, Germany issued orders for "general mobilization," effective the following day.

[1] *Code of Laws of the United States*, Title 14, Sec. 1, p. 339.

[2] *Ibid.*, Title 10, Sec. 5, p. 169.

[3] *Ibid.*, Title 10, Sec. 341–445, p. 182–185.

Ibid., Title 34, Sec. 751, 753–821, p. 1133–1137.

[5] *Ibid.*, Sec. 841–2 p. 1138.

Reserve, in addition to which there are Marine Corps Training Camps.[1]

The *Particulars with Regard to the Armaments of the United States* of June 5, 1931,[2] reports "none" in each of the tables respecting formations organized on a military basis because the existing formations are stated not to be "within the meaning of the definition contained in Art. 4." On this account the sea formation table is blank, and a note conveys the information that total strength of the Coast Guard is 11,866, of whom 1,289 are officers. The same method of reporting facts without assuming responsibility for their military implication is adopted in the case of the National Guard (10,774 average daily effectives), and of 46 air officers and men on duty with the Coast Guard. On the other hand, the tables for land home forces include 1,075 average daily officer effectives representing 22,393 reserve officers called into service for an average of 17½ days each (Tables I and III), and the naval forces 1,402.2 average daily effectives of Naval and Marine Corps Reserves (Table VI).

The British *Particulars*[3] include in land forces Supplementary Reserve, Territorial Army and Officers Training Corps actual strength reduced to average daily effectives; describe four formations not included, and state that there are no formations organized on a military basis. Average monthly strength is the underlying basis of computation. In the British navy the Royal Fleet Reserve, Royal Naval Reserve, Royal Volunteer Reserve, Royal Naval Auxiliary Sick Berth Reserve, Special Reserve of Royal Marine Officers and Retired Officers Courses are included as average daily effectives, but the Coast Guard is excluded. Belgium reports gendarmes, but states they do not fall within the definition.

In France, the gendarmerie, custom guards and forest guards are all organized on a military basis by national law and may be mobilized by decree. Reserves are maintained in *cadres* and are regarded as part of the army structure.

[1] *Ibid.*, Sec. 752, 832, p. 1133, 1138.
[2] *Official Journal*, XII, p. 1552; Publications of the Department of State, No. 204.
[3] C.476.M.203.1931.IX; *Official Journal*, XII, p. 1702.

So the definitions of the Draft Convention and of national law make distinctions between formations that open a new vista of complication. From these details it can be seen how far from simple is the mere effort to establish a basic method for tabulating personnel strength. The reports in model tables to the conference will doubtless suggest many perfecting details to render the scheme more comparable.

It can be seen that the additional personnel factors which will be added to the statistics ordinarily cited will be considerable. All the formations included will be reported upon in accordance with the formula of average daily effectives, and the total figures will, therefore, by no means correspond with the number of individuals concerned, since many of the formations perform military service for only a small portion of the year.

United States reserve officers to the number of 22,393 were called into service for an average of 17½ days and are recorded as 1,075 average daily effectives. Great Britain's Territorial Army of 135,649 becomes 135,730 on average monthly strength performing an average of 19.8 days' service (six drills equal one day's duty), reporting as 7,388 daily effectives. Belgium as a conscript country gives no details as to numerical differences between actual and average daily effectives, though the periods of conscript service vary from 8 to 14 months for the branches of the army.[1]

The Soviet Union has a system of premilitary training (age 19–20), two years in the first and second armies (age 21–22); during these age limits active service is from two to four months according to the arm, with recall periods of one to two months during the succeeding one to three years. The citizen is in the third, fourth and fifth armies from age 23 to 25, subject to one month of recall service per year. Age 26–34 he is in the first reserve and in age 35–40 in the second reserve, not being subject to annual recall.

Significance of the Tables

With these principles to go upon, the Preparatory Commission worked out 12 skeleton tables for reporting average

[1] *Cf. Official Journal*, XII, p. 1551, 1569 and C.476.M.203.1931.IX 8.

daily effectives in the land, sea and air forces. These tables constitute the framework by which it is intended that states shall limit or reduce personnel and afford each other a basis of comparison for their forces in as full and accurate a manner as possible. The tables call for reporting "the average daily effectives which are to not be exceeded" in the land, sea and air armed forces. This general title has been the subject of debate by those who desired it to record figures to which the forces were to be reduced. In accordance, however, with the policy of the commission to leave all questions of figures to the plenary conference, it was decided not to take a decision between limitation and reduction; but it was pointed out that figures which are not to be exceeded might be fixed by the conference below present levels, if public opinion so demanded.

In accordance with this decision, the tables call for a statement of maximum forces, those dealing with land effectives being five in number. Two distinguish between forces stationed in the home country and those stationed overseas. An additional table calls for the total of the two. The maximum formations organized on a military basis are also to be reported for those stationed in the home country and those stationed overseas, without a totaling table.

The table for maximum land armed forces stationed overseas is optional. Those figures ought to be included in the total table, the difference between the total and the home forces presumably representing the figures omitted, if the option were exercised. The German and Italian delegations made a reservation respecting this option on the ground that "the importance of the forces and materials which one contracting party assigns to its oversea territories may vary, in relation to another contracting party, by reason of the geographical situation of its territory in relation to the home territories of the two contracting parties." They thought that one contracting party "will have every reason to regard the oversea forces of another contracting party as forming part of the latter's home forces," if their relative geographic position was close enough to justify such an assumption.[1]

[1] *Report*, par. 73.

The Turkish delegation thought tables ought to be given for each overseas territory. Evidently in mind was the idea that such instances of geographical proximity as that of Algeria and Tunis to France and of Tripoli and Cyrenaica to Italy offered opportunities for interchange of troops that had a bearing on the sense of security of third countries.

The tables for land forces call for the total of the average daily effectives who are subject to service in the period under control. As land forces are very largely dependent for their potential value upon officers and as some states, such as the United States, make special provision for the training of officer personnel beyond the requirements of their effectives, a column for the number of officers in service is given. It is assumed that the two figures in a table covering all states will afford indications of the extent to which states are depending upon the *cadre* system to increase their potential strength without creating full units.[1]

A third column in each table provides for reporting the effectives "who have completed at least x months of service," the period being defined as "the longest period of service which is in force in the conscript land army of any high contracting party at the time of signature of the convention," which is now three years. It is intended thereby to bring out the proportion of an army which consists of seasoned or professional troops, and thus give the figures a further measure of comparability. For land formations organized on a military basis two tables, for those stationed in the home country and those stationed overseas, are given, the columns being the same as for the land armed forces.

Tables VI and VII are those for "the average daily effectives which are not to be exceeded in the sea armed forces." The first deals with sea armed forces proper, and Table VII with sea formations organized on a military basis. In these two tables there are single columns only for the number of total effectives, officers, petty officers and men. This simpler form was justified by the fact that the sea forces depend

[1] United States officers reported are 9.3% of the total personnel, for instance, while French officers are 6% of personnel, British 6.5%, Belgian 7%, and Dutch 4.9%.

upon material and that consequently man power is essentially controlled by the number and size of the units in the navy, there being no general system of *cadre* formations in naval organization. The current figures range from 109,886 men and 10,429 officers (9.5%) for the United States and 96,042.6 men and 8,390.6 officers (8.7%) for Great Britain down to none in Belgium and 20 others.

Tables VIII to XII deal with the average daily effectives which are not to be exceeded in the air armed forces and air formations organized on a military basis. The tables essentially duplicate those given for land forces, except that officers are not to be specially reported. Each table consists of two columns, the first for total effectives and the second for those effectives of all grades who have completed at least z months of service, defined as "the longest period of service which is in force in the conscript air army of any high contracting party at the time of the signature of the convention," which is now three years.

The Preparatory Commission felt keenly that the framework of the tables was of primary importance, since their structure was destined to control the limitation and reduction of personnel which will be arrived at. The tables discussed are intended to provide the basic control of personnel numbers and, therefore, have an intimate relation with a similar set of tables annexed to Art. 30 of the Draft Convention, which provide a more detailed scheme for the exchange of information as to the annual status of all forces.[1]

Problems of Conscription

Chapter B of Part I (Personnel) deals with the period of service of effectives recruited by conscription. Conscription systems differ considerably in detail, but they all recognize a first period of active service and subsequent periods of discontinuous service. Different applications of the idea result in various total periods of liability to service. It was felt to be important to limit the total period of service to which the individual was liable, and this is provided for, the number of months being left for the decision of the confer-

[1] See p. 199 *ff*.

ence. Each contracting party will record in the table the "maximum total periods of service to which the effectives recruited by conscription are liable in the land, sea or air armed forces or formations organized on a military basis," the period being that of the present law for limitation or a lesser period if reduction is agreed to.[1]

As the essential object of the chapter is to register agreement among the states that their armed forces can not exceed a certain maximum of training, an exception for a falling birth rate in any country is provided. According to this (Art. 8), the period of service for an individual may be exceeded to the extent that reduction in the number of recruits brings the total service rendered below the maximum agreed to. The periods of service for different types of forces may vary, but if any state desires to exceed the maximum because of a falling birth rate,[2] it is to notify the fact and the reasons justifying it to the other contracting parties and to the Permanent Disarmament Commission, which has the duty of following the execution of the convention.

Germany proposed that, in states having the conscription system both "the annual contingent and the total period of service which the annual contingent is compelled to serve shall not exceed the figure accepted."[3] This proposal was directed at limiting trained reserves. It was rejected by a vote of 12 to 6 (China, Germany, Netherlands, Norway, the Soviet Union, Sweden).[4] Wherefore, Germany made a reservation because of the lack of a provision for a reduction or limitation of trained reserves and because of failure to provide a method "whereby the effectives of conscript armies serving with the colors and in reserve, and professional

[1] Since the Great War, periods of liability have been reduced in many countries, the French period of active service, for instance, having been cut from three years to one year. Such reduction does not necessarily reduce the absolute number of men performing service.

[2] The article was proposed by Belgium, which called attention to the fact that its 1910 male births (providing the 1930 contingent) were 90,149, while those of 1918 (contingent of 1938) were only 43,654 (*Documents of the Preparatory Commission*, Series X, p. 252).

[3] *Documents of the Preparatory Commission*, Series X, p. 35.

[4] *Ibid.*, Series X, p. 41.

effectives . . . could be reduced to comparable units of calculation."[1]

On this matter of trained reserves there was considerable difference of view, though the general opinion seemed to be that the length of conscript service had an automatic and readily traceable relation to the number of reserves available at any time and the amount of training they possess.

The distinctions made between the periods of service are to be annually reported under Art. 32. From those details, it is evident that the conscription systems differ so widely that a set of formulas will be required to make up the figures for limitation, and that their reapplication to experience (that is, conventional execution) will be very complicated. For instance, the Belgian conscript army in 19 categories of service performs duty from 8 to 14 months with periods of recall, usually of 42 days. All categories average a service of 10 months and 10 days without recall and 12 months with recall, per man.[2] Applying the average to the army as a whole would yield a basis for determining the average daily effectives agreed to. Other factors enter into other systems, for instance, gradations of reserve duty. In any case, once limitation or reduction is established, every administration will have to check its records constantly to keep within safe bounds, unless it deliberately recruits well below the treaty maximum.

As a whole Part I (Personnel) of the Draft Convention provides for the first time in history for definite undertakings respecting the number and character of men used for military purposes. The mere establishment of figures, drawn to a single standard and therefore comparable, will produce a new basis for further advance. Unless the conference registers heavy reductions in personnel, the definiteness of the figures will make them a ready target for all others except their sponsors. There are very few states in the world whose military personnel is not more numerous than other governments believe is justified. Foreign peoples are still more critical. All now have precise data.

[1] *Report*, par. 79.
[2] Belgian *Particulars*, C.436.M.183.1931.IX.8.

CHAPTER VII

THE CONTROL OF MATERIAL

Part II of the Draft Convention deals with material and relates to land, naval and air armaments. Beyond question, it deals with that part of the subject on which the most difficult negotiations will take place. General principles are pretty fully elaborated for naval armaments, less so for air armaments, while for land armaments practically the whole question is remitted to the conference. Owing to the considerable amount of agreement respecting naval armaments, which has brought forth principles capable of general application, and owing to the lack of development and of certainty respecting the position of air armaments, the chapters devoted to them are of a very different character, the former being quite detailed and the latter quite general.

Land armaments are regarded as the outstanding problem in the entire field. Their maintenance is intimately bound up with the policy of states, and both their quantity and distribution are interlocked with "political" considerations to a remarkable extent. Owing to geographical situation, the problem which they represent is most acute in the continent of Europe. "Security," territorial relations and other circumstances contribute to the problem.

A. Land Material

The Preparatory Commission adopted a provisional text respecting the limitation of material of land armaments providing for the limitation of annual expenditure by each state on the upkeep, purchase and manufacture of war material to figures left to be determined in an annex, which was not then prepared. This very tentative decision is even less definite because it was subject to much contention, and the preparation of the annex referred to was remitted to the Committee of Experts on Budgetary Questions, whose report was not available until two months after the closing of the Preparatory Commission's sessions.[1]

The principle of limitation by expenditure was adopted by the commission by 16 votes to 3, with 6 abstentions.[2] The principle of direct limitation lost a place in the Draft Convention by a tie vote 9 to 9, with 7 abstentions.[3] A proposal to adopt the principle of combining the methods of direct and indirect (budgetary) limitation of land material was lost by a vote of 9 to 11, with 5 abstentions.[4] It can be seen from this recital that the very principle of the limitation of land material is not yet determined.

Unless there is a general meeting of minds at the outset, the principles from which to proceed will be the subject of one of the most crucial debates in the conference. As in all debates on armament, the great majority of the states represented will either be neutral or with a negligible stake in the outcome. It is not clear which way the small states will vote in their own interest, and it is not entirely certain that the three votes on the two principles and their combination in the Preparatory Commission will represent the final conclusions of the conference. Roughly speaking, however, it may be said that states laying stress upon security, which is presumed to be especially dependent upon land armament, favor budgetary limitation because it affords fluidity in the choice of instruments; while states not actuated by fear, or not feeling that their position is dependent upon land arma-

[1] C.182.M.69.1931.IX.3; *Official Journal*, XII, p. 676.

[2] *Documents of the Preparatory Commission*, Series X, p. 110. The vote *for* the text by delegations was: Belgium, British Empire, Canada, Czechoslovakia, Finland, France, Greece, Irish Free State, Japan, Netherlands, Norway, Persia, Poland, Rumania, Spain, Yugoslavia; *against*, Germany, Italy, Soviet Union; *abstaining*, Bulgaria, China, Sweden, Turkey, United States, Venezuela.

[3] *Ibid.*, p. 108. *For*, United States, Canada, Germany, Italy, Netherlands, Soviet Union, Sweden, Turkey, Venezuela; *against*, Belgium, Czechoslovakia, Finland, France, Japan, Persia, Poland, Rumania, Yugoslavia; *abstaining*, British Empire, Bulgaria, China, Greece, Irish Free State, Norway, Spain.

[4] *Ibid.*, p. 107. *For*, Canada, Germany, Irish Free State, Italy, Netherlands, Soviet Union, Sweden, Turkey, Venezuela; *against*, Belgium, British Empire, Czechoslovakia, Finland, France, Japan, Persia, Poland, Rumania, Spain, Yugoslavia; *abstaining*, Bulgaria, China, Greece, Norway, United States.

ment, favor direct limitation of material. In general also, states with high standards of living and volunteer armies favor direct limitation because their budgetary costs per unit are invariably greater than those of states having conscript armies.

Looking at the matter without taking sides in the controversy, it can be stated that neither direct nor indirect limitation is at all simple, but that direct limitation is the more logical and thoroughgoing. One principle, or the other, or possibly a combination, will emerge from the conference as an immediate world standard. The result will give an indication of the progress of limitation of armament. On the whole, budgetary limitation affords a more immediately comprehensible barometer of accomplishment, though it postpones the argument as to the relative value of different types of material and leaves entirely untouched the introduction of new mechanisms or resort to "industrial procurement." These factors must be considered in debating direct limitation, but after a decision on that principle had been reached, much less debate would remain and much less difference of opinion.

Attitude of United States

The United States regards itself as relatively disinterested in the question of limitation of land material. It maintains proportionately a small regular army, its potential manufacturing strength is disproportionately large[1] and its costs comparatively high. In the Preparatory Commission it has diligently advocated direct limitation in all divisions of armament. The principle of the direct limitation of material was the one which it proposed, and which succeeded, at the Washington conference for the limitation of naval armaments, and which was again followed at the London Naval Conference.

The United States has from the outset stood for the direct principle in the Preparatory Commission. In Subcommission A, which closed its third session on November 5, 1926, its delegation associated itself with those of the British

[1] On the availability of this strength for military purposes see *supra*, p. 26-32.

Empire, Chile, Finland, Germany, Italy, Japan and the Netherlands in the opinion that[1]

the percentage of its total budget expenditure which a given country devotes to its national defense could not be regarded as a factor for estimating the military effort made by that country without inducing comparisons, which would be both misleading and unfair, between the different countries. The total budgets are framed on principles which are peculiar to the respective states, and military expenditure must be estimated with reference to the requirements of national security and not to the financial situation of the country as shown by budgets.

Mr. Gibson in the third session of the Preparatory Commission stated on April 26, 1927, that "my Government is strongly of the opinion that monetary expenditure for the creation and maintenance of armaments does not afford either a true measure of armaments or a fair basis for the limitation of armaments." He gave three reasons:

(1) Direct and indirect costs under the conscription and voluntary systems are so variable that it is practically impossible to reduce them to a common basis.

(2) Differences in pay, production charges, maintenance charges, costs of labor and material, standards of living, rates of exchange and lack of uniformity in budgets would make the method unfair and inequitable.

(3) "Limitation of expenditure is an indirect method of obtaining limitation or reduction of armaments."

His next sentence may be regarded as the positive attitude of the United States: "My Government is of the opinion that armaments may be limited effectively by direct methods and, in consequence, the application of an indirect method seems highly undesirable as a means of accomplishing what might better be accomplished by direct methods."[2]

Two years later in the first part of the sixth session of the Preparatory Commission, Mr. Gibson on April 22, 1929, made a general statement[3] in which he receded from several

Preparatory Commission for the Disarmament Conference. Report of Subcommission A, p. 61 (C.739.M.278.1926.IX.16).

[2] *Documents of the Preparatory Commission*, Series IV, p. 178.

[3] See *infra*, p. 199 *ff*, for quotations from this statement.

points of view previously held because "the pact for the renunciation of war opens to us an unprecedented opportunity for advancing the cause of disarmament." He recognized that agreement upon a single text could be realized only by a maximum of concessions. "The essential thing," he said, "is the achievement of substantial results. Methods are of secondary importance." His concessions were mostly confined to naval armaments and consisted of yielding on contentious points relating to material; but one of them was the resolution of May 4 admitting land limitation by expenditure as the basis of discussion.[1]

It will be noted that the direct method which was advocated by the United States for application to all forms of armament reduction has been accepted in the Draft Convention for effectives, for naval armaments and for air armaments. No objection has prevailed as to the reporting of budgetary expenditures on armament as a whole, and it may be remarked that in the fiscal sense[2] expenditure is itself a direct method of control. In consequence, the remaining issue is whether the principle adopted for limiting or reducing land armament shall be one which applies to the material involved or, more remotely, to the cost of the material involved. The Government of the United States regards the problem of land armament as of secondary concern to itself and, therefore, is in a good position to take a disinterested attitude in seeking the best possible results.

Before the last decision of the Preparatory Commission was adopted, Mr. Gibson on November 11, 1930, made an extensive summary statement of the position of the United States in which he told his colleagues that his Government was unable for practical reasons to apply a convention providing for budgetary limitation. He called attention to the fact that the remaining question was the limitation of material for land and air forces, for which the United States was ready to accept "the strictest method of limitation —

[1] *Documents of the Preparatory Commission*, Series VIII, p. 179; *cf. infra*, p. 176.
[2] This, for instance, is the form of control exercised by the Congress of the United States through appropriations.

namely, direct limitation with full publicity as to expenditure, weights and numbers," and he added:[1]

> If it gives satisfaction to those states which might be reluctant to see us exempted from any limitation, we are willing, provided that some practical budgetary method is generally agreed upon which is sufficiently detailed and precise to constitute a real method of limitation, to apply to ourselves a direct limitation of material along the lines which we have consistently urged for general adoption here. We honestly believe that this is the most effective method of limitation that has yet been suggested; and, with all deference to the views of others, we still feel that this affords a more scientific knowledge of military forces and material than can be obtained through budgetary limitation. In other words, we feel that it is easier to conceal the application of a dollar than it is the existence of a rifle.

In view of the progress already made in dealing directly with material and also in view of the divided opinion on the proper principle applicable to land armament, the Washington Government has thought it advisable to advocate once more in the conference the adoption of the principle of direct limitation and reduction of land armament as a basic method.

The Course of the Debate

The problem of land armaments in the conference will probably reflect the points of view already expressed. On the first reading of the Draft Convention, the Preparatory Commission had advanced only to the point where the direct and indirect methods of controlling land armament were in juxtaposition on the basis of German and French proposals respectively. The German proposal took the form of a table showing the maximum number of arms and the quantity of ammunition therefor under the following categories:[2]

(1) Rifles or carbines;
(2) Machine guns and automatic rifles;
(3) Guns, long and short, and howitzers of a caliber below 5.9 inches (15 cms.);

[1] *Documents of the Preparatory Commission*, Series X, p. 72.
[2] *Documents of the Preparatory Commission*, Series X, p. 432. A more detailed list was prepared for the German proposals for reporting "particulars" (*Official Journal*, XII, p. 1240, Table II).

(4) Guns, long and short, and howitzers of a caliber of 5.9 inches (15 cms.) or above;

(5) Mortars of all kinds;

(6) Tanks;

(7) Armored cars.

The report of number and ammunition was to cover material in service and in reserve, reserve stocks being a point on which Germany and other states sharing the disarmament mood have been very insistent.

Precise reasons for this insistence have not been stated in words, but the consideration involved is evident. Stocks of material are immediately available for use, and their quantity gives an indication of military possibilities at any given time. A state will explain its stocks in terms of national defense requirements, but a foreign state is fairly certain to interpret them in terms of potential attack. Uncertainty respecting quantities in reserve are sure to be interpreted abroad as implying a possibility of use by the possessor. Certainty respecting them is regarded abroad as a hostage to good faith.

The French preliminary draft provided for the limitation of total expenditure. The Italian and Japanese representatives formally opposed that method, and there followed a series of proposals including (1) full publicity of expenditure, (2) limitation of expenditure, (3) limitation of material by categories, (4) limitation of expenditure and material by categories separately or in combination, and (5) the option to apply any of these methods at the election of the parties.[1]

The commission unanimously approved the fullest possible interchange of information respecting armament and decided that a more precise method than publicity alone should be provided for limitation of war material. It also determined that the optional application of several methods was undesirable. It thus accepted method No. 1 as a preliminary basis and eliminated method No. 5.

The commission, therefore, remitted to the conference the question of determining the principle on which land arm-

[1] See the discussion *Documents of the Preparatory Commission*, Series X, p. 85 *ff.*, and *Report*, pars. 86-92.

ament material should be limited, with the preponderance of tentative agreement in favor of limitation by budgetary expenditure. With the certainty that budgetary limitation would appear in the final convention whether direct limitation was applied or not, the commission made preparation for the determination of the means to carry out the principle. The Committee of Experts on Budgetary Questions was instructed to render an early report, paying special attention to:[1]

(a) The necessity of limiting all the expenditure in question;

(b) The variety of ways in which budgets are presented and discussed in different countries;

(c) The adjustment of the proposed method of limitation to possible fluctuations in the purchasing power of different currencies, especially with regard to the cost of war material;

(d) The conditions in which credits for one financial year might be carried over to the following year or years.

Though the question of direct or indirect reduction on land was very extensively discussed in the Preparatory Commission from most angles, it was only since the commission ceased to function that governments had in front of them any detailed evidence as to the amount of information and control that budgetary limitation or reduction would afford. As the Draft Convention stands, it provides for a statement of the limitation of the annual expenditure of each contracting party for land and naval, but not air, armaments; for the total annual expenditure of each on its land, sea and air forces, and for a report after the end of each budgetary year of the total amounts actually expended in that year on the land, sea and air armaments.[2] The Committee of Experts on Budgetary Questions rendered its report on February 28, 1931, consisting of a most informative analysis of the accounting problems involved for all of these purposes. The draft annex which it prepared and the statements and tables annexed are very valuable contributions to the effort to reduce armament.

Great diversity exists in the accounting methods of various governments, and the recapitulation which is called for

[1] *Official Journal*, XII, p. 322, 676. [2] Arts. 10, 24, 29, 38.

in the draft annex and its statements will undoubtedly offer a new basis for negotiation on the uncompleted land armament problem. Each government in the *Particulars* reported its expenditures in the form prescribed by the committee before the conference, and the circulation of figures, comparable under the same headings, beyond question affected the views of many governments. It is the first time in history that armament expenditures have in any detail been put into officially comparable terms and, in consequence, the comparative facts are certain to open the way for new avenues of negotiation respecting the relation between war materials in the various armies. That in itself is likely to point to agreements on some phases of the problem of land material.

Despite the vote in the Preparatory Commission, the agreement of the states represented in it as evidenced by the Draft Convention provides for both direct and indirect limitation or reduction in all divisions of the subject except land armament. Where both methods are applied to a type of armament, they complement each other. This will undoubtedly have a general effect of encouraging reduction, in addition to a potent effect of giving evidence of good faith.

The report of the budgetary experts demonstrated that a more precise limitation through control of expenditure could be effected than had previously been realized.[1]

Budgetary limitation of land armament, according to the tables of the budgetary experts, will concern means and supplies for transport, buildings and war material, all under general heads. Under war material, the skeleton table calls for reports under "arms, ammunition and fighting material" and under "manufacture of war material in nonautonomous state establishments." Obviously a more effective means of comparison of the material possessed by different armies would be obtained if those headings were greatly elaborated. It may be expected that, if budgetary limitation becomes the principle for this kind of limitation, many proposals for such elaboration will be considered by the conference. With a view to seeking more definite results in this direction,

[1] See Chap. VIII, generally.

the German delegation in the Preparatory Commission reserved the right to reconsider the question after examining the report of the Committee of Budgetary Experts.

The problem of an agreed alteration of the scale of armaments on its physical, in distinction from its psychological, side admittedly depends upon reconciling differences in the situations of the countries concerned. While all those thorny points remain untouched in adopting the principle of budgetary limitation, this principle adds another series of differentials to be taken into account.

Several delegations[1] insisted in the Preparatory Commission that account must be taken of the circumstances peculiar to each state, and adduced a claim to preferential treatment for nonindustrial countries or countries whose budgets were less than a figure to be fixed by the conference. The Greek delegate thought it essential that the economic circumstances, standard of living, cost of labor and stock of material in each country at the signing of the convention should be taken into consideration in striking a balance on the principle of budgetary limitation. "Obviously," said M. Politis, "if the material a country possessed at that time were worn out or incomplete[2]; if, consequently, it were in a clear position of inferiority as compared with the other signatory states, that would constitute a factor to be taken into account in fixing the budgetary limit binding upon that country." As the speaker offered no suggestion as to how budgetary limitation would afford a standard for determining the condition of usefulness or the completeness of material, it can be seen at a glance that the budgetary approach to the subject is certain to lead into an evaluation of material. The Turkish delegation made a reservation respecting budgetary limitation with reference to the special position of countries in which industry is not adequately developed, the ground, of course, being that purchases abroad were subject to greater price fluctuations than purchases made within national boundaries.

[1] *Report*, par. 97.
[2] As quoted in par. 98 of the *Report;* but the word is "defective" as reported in the speech of November 13, 1930 (*Documents of the Preparatory Commission*, Series X, p. 88).

The British delegation perhaps represented the most typical view in the Preparatory Commission's session of 1930. Viscount Cecil, who had previously advocated direct limitation of land armament, was ready to admit that it was in theory the most effective and obvious system to adopt, but was afraid that the direct method was impossible of realization either with respect to all armament or only the larger weapons. While prepared to accept any practical scheme for direct limitation of the important weapons that would command general approval at the conference, the British Government in the commission advocated the adoption of the indirect method of budgetary limitation. In doing so, the delegation recognized that "such a method is not so complete; but, so far as it goes, it is, they feel, more effective and more reliable." The British believed that the checks and controls to which it was subject would prevent its being evaded to any considerable extent. They also asserted that "it has the additional advantage that it may serve to arrest competition in the development and perfection of weapons."

One delegation, the Norwegian, noted that a combination of direct and indirect limitation had not been precluded to the conference, while the Japanese delegation observed that its own support of indirect limitation did not exclude recourse to the direct method by a limited number of states which were unable to accept that principle.

The United States delegation reiterated that it was unable to accept budgetary limitation so far as it was concerned, but did not wish that attitude to constitute an obstacle to others accepting the method. The exact position of the United States is not clear. If a practical budgetary method were generally agreed upon to constitute an effective means of limitation, the United States were, says the *Report*, "prepared to apply, as far as they were themselves concerned, direct limitation instead of indirect limitation." This apparently amounts to saying that, if everybody else will effectively limit contractually on a budget basis, the United States will effect a limitation satisfactory to itself and which it unilaterally holds to be fair to the other parties.

The Spanish delegation was of the same mind as the United States, but held that direct limitation would have to be confined to material in service. On the other hand, the German delegation objected to budgetary limitation of material in service and in reserve because it wished to see the limitation and reduction of both categories on the basis of specific articles and numbers.[1]

It can be seen that there is no real agreement even upon the basis of budgetary limitation, which has from the outset been advocated principally by France. It is also apparent from the reservations that no agreement on budgetary limitation can be reached in the conference without taking into account, to a greater or lesser extent, the characteristics of the actual materials for which budgetary funds would be expended. The position in advance of the conference, therefore, was that the limitation or reduction of land material had not advanced beyond a degree of progress toward an agreement on the basis of budgetary limitation.

The United States Government in observing this posture of affairs did not deem it wise to alter its position in advance of the conference. Its position called forth some comment on the assumption that it was hindering agreement. The facts and the governmental policy seem to be quite otherwise.

No one in the Preparatory Commission or in the conference, and no informed person outside of either, is likely to hold that indirect limitation of land material is both the ideal and final method. The expense of maintaining armament has in the last generation attracted an extraordinary amount of attention, but it is impossible to argue that the serious amounts of money involved are in reality the fundamental question. Before officially organized international attention was given to the subject of armament, its cost was the element of it which was best adapted to bring the underlying problem to public attention. To direct the thought of the world to the disproportionate amount of public funds absorbed by armament was perhaps an essential first step in raising the issue; at any rate, it was historically the first

[1] The summaries from *Report*, pars. 94–102.

step taken. Public opinion developed in favor of the Washington naval conference almost exclusively because of the persuasive fact that the cost of past and future war was at that time (1921) absorbing something like 90% of the annual expenditures of the United States; and the monetary figures continue to retain their hold on the public mind as an incentive to obtain reduction of armament.[1]

While the cost and quantity will never be separated in the armament problem, the historical accomplishments of the Washington and London naval conferences were due to dealing with the problem of quantity rather than its monetary value. If the problem is examined from the theoretical point of view, it can readily be seen that a solution of the question of relative material both determines the element of expenditure and stabilizes the relations between the states affected. Consequently, the experience of the two postwar naval conferences naturally led to the conclusion that dealing with the material of armament was the fundamental approach. While its quantity and quality register the barometric pressure of the subjective feeling of insecurity, the cost has come to be regarded in the United States Government as a subsidiary factor.

In the world in general it may be said that three considerations lie back of official advocacy of budgetary limitation:

(1) The accomplishment of something in the direction of disarmament with a minimum disturbance of the present status of armed forces;

(2) The empirical acceptance of a method on which it is believed some sort of agreement can be reached;

(3) The use of a method whose effect is immediately apparent in terms familiar to all.

No person in responsible position argues that budgetary limitation is superior to direct limitation, but only that it is more feasible.

The United States has steadfastly held that it is desirable to exhaust every effort and influence to attain results by the

[1] The United States Treasury regards public debt service, pensions and War and Navy Department expenditures as due to war, past or prospective. These items in all great states represent from two-thirds to three-fourths of total annual budgets.

final method before transferring its support to the application of a subsidiary method. It has been said that the acceptance of a principle in the first General Disarmament Conference will make it more difficult to change to a better principle later. Such a shift might occur, but it would obviously be more difficult to make it after a considerable body of agreement based on the inferior plan had come into existence. The conference debate on reduction of land armament by direct or indirect methods is, therefore, going to be a test of how fundamentally the question is to be examined. The United States Government indicates that it will strive for the adoption of the best method at the outset.

It has been suggested that the attitude of the United States has been affected by the Constitution of the country. By Art. I, Sec. 8, of the Constitution, the Congress has power to provide financially for the common defense, to raise and support armies, to provide and maintain a navy and to make appropriations for these purposes. It has been suggested that, in view of these exclusive functions of Congress, the Executive would not have the power to make, and the Senate alone to advise and consent, to a treaty which stipulates that Congress as a whole should not appropriate above certain amounts for purposes of defense. In the past similar argument has been used against the making of treaties for the pacific settlement of international disputes on the score that they infringed the power of Congress to declare war.

But it is obvious that neither argument is in practice really substantial, except as a mere matching of technical words. It is true that the power of Congress to declare war is to be exercised in its discretion and, therefore, can not be abridged. But it is more importantly true that war as a status is not a desirable condition, while the avoidance of its possibility exactly corresponds with the fundamental idea of the general welfare. The power is, therefore, one which is in no way violated if conditions can be set up which reduce the incentive to exercise it. Similarly, the maintenance of the means of national defense is not a desirable

THE CONTROL OF MATERIAL

end itself, but is responsive to existing conditions. It is neither a violation of the letter or the spirit of the Constitution to seek to curtail the exercise of an undesirable function by foregoing a power to provide for it. This is especially true when the self-restraint involved is part of the consideration which makes it possible to reduce the burden upon the country. Difference of opinion might, of course, exist as to the advisability of a given limitation of appropriations for the defense force, but responsible men in public affairs hold that no constitutional objection exists as to budgetary limitation *per se*.

The United States is in a good position to stand staunchly for the best method of limitation of land armament at the present juncture. Its spokesmen on a number of occasions have stated that its own forces were already reduced and that the present phase of the problem did not concern them. It is true that the regular army and its material are proportionately at a low level and the legal provisions which control the federal relationship to the state militia and other subsidiary military organizations are of a character not to bring them within the definitions of effectives laid down in the Draft Convention.

If the conference should base its agreement respecting land armament upon budgetary limitation, the differentials in American and foreign costs would create a contrast which would attract attention, but which would doubtless come to be readily understood as essentially due to higher and more elaborate maintenance costs. The United States would naturally prefer a basic principle which would not entail such a contrast.

The present question is to arrive at a definite basis of agreement on armament founded upon existing effectives. The immediate problem is to determine relationships among the formally trained portions of the male populations. When that general question is settled, there will be a tendency to examine man power potential, essentially based upon the whole population, which is certain to bring under examination the various formations mentioned above. If the conference should confine itself to budgetary limitation, the question of war potential in man or industrial power would scarcely arise. If it should advance to consideration of direct limitation and there fix limits or reductions in land arms and munitions in service, the extent of manufacturing facilities would scarcely arise. If either direct or indirect limitation should deal with reserve stocks, that question would arise only to a certain degree. But in these days of mechanized armies, the potential production of munitions may eventually be the point around which the land armament argument revolves.[1]

B. Naval Material

Chapter B of Part II (Material) of the Draft Convention relates to naval armament which, as a serious international problem, is controlled by the treaties of Washington of February 6, 1922, and of London of April 22, 1930.[2] Those two treaties concern the material of the United States, the British Empire, France, Italy and Japan, five states which together possess 80% of the existing tonnage and which have no near rivals. The decisions of the five are, therefore, compelling in the naval field, and their failure to agree actually held up the preparations for the conference some three years.

Between 1927 and 1930, other states frankly took the attitude that the naval problem lay with those five, and in two sessions of the League Assembly, those governments were urged to "seek without delay, in the most liberal spirit of conciliation and international solidarity, agreed solutions which will enable the work of the Preparatory Commission to be brought to a successful issue."[3] Under that impulse and their own desire to make headway, those states supplemented the Washington treaty with the London treaty and so were enabled to present to the second part of the sixth session of the Preparatory Commission a solution of a

[1] "Industrial procurement" is discussed *supra*, p. 26-32.

[2] For texts see *Armaments Year-Book; Treaty Series*, XXV, p. 202, and CXII, p. 65, Reg. No. 609 and Reg. No. 2608; United States *Treaty Series* Nos. 671 and 830.

[3] *Resolutions and Recommendations adopted by the Assembly* . . . 1928, p. 57–58 (*Official Journal*, Spec. Sup. No. 63).

problem which had necessitated the adjournment of the first part of that session a year and a half before.

The purpose of the London naval treaty was to apply the principles of the Washington treaty to all categories of naval craft. The treaty was divided into five parts, all of which were signed and ratified for the United States, Great Britain, the British dominions and India and Japan, and which entered into force for them on December 31, 1930.[1] Parts I, II, IV and V of the treaty were signed by, and apply on ratification to, France and Italy. Part III specifically limits the tonnage in cruisers, destroyers and submarines of the British group, Japan and the United States. On March 1, 1931, France and Italy announced an agreement through the intervention of Great Britain for the corresponding limitation of their own similar categories,[2] but its consummation was delayed.

When the Preparatory Commission met in November, 1930, the Washington and London treaties were together regarded as having solved in principle the limitation and reduction of naval material. Accordingly, the American, British, Canadian, French, Irish Free State, Italian and Japanese delegations presented to the commission a draft basis of discussion[3] for the chapter on that subject. This was based upon the principles accepted by those governments in the Washington and London treaties, which were adopted without noteworthy change by the commission as Chapter B of the Draft Convention. In this way, the long controversy in the Preparatory Commission between limitation of tonnage by categories and limitation of total tonnage, with freedom to allocate among the categories of vessels, was finally obviated. The Washington and London conferences thus enabled the commission to adopt the most direct form of limitation to seagoing armament.

It can be seen that the problem of naval material is a comparatively narrow one so far as the agenda of the

[1] United States *Treaty Series* No. 830.

[2] On the problem and the development of the tripartite agreement of March 1, 1931, see William T. Stone, *The Franco-Italian Naval Dispute* (Foreign Policy Reports, VII, No. 8).

[3] *Documents of the Preparatory Commission*, Series X, p. 462.

General Disarmament Conference is concerned. Four-fifths of the existing material is already controlled through the direct method by existing agreements between its owners. The Draft Convention provides for the application of the principles, already adopted by the navally capable states, to all naval armament. As the 27 states in the Preparatory Commission represent 5,115,000 out of 5,386,000 tons, or 95%, of the existing material, it may be assumed that Chapter B will at least be accepted as a minimum.

Whether the conference will go beyond it will depend primarily upon the five chief states already obligated. The only reservation, of the 13 attached to the chapter, likely to result in debate is one of the German delegation in favor of direct limitation by specific articles and by numbers of non-floating naval material.[1]

In the provisions adopted, however, the tonnage limits of categories as given in the London treaty were quoted, covered by an annotation that the figures were given "only as an illustration." In the world there is considerable popular feeling that the capital ship of 35,000 tons is too big for any modern naval use and too expensive to build and maintain for any parliament to be able to justify an appropriation for any future construction.[2] France, Italy and Japan do not wish them, Germany is limited by treaty to 10,000 tons, and no lesser fleet could find a tactical place for a craft of that size. Great Britain favors the 25,000 ton limit, but the United States navy holds that the 35,000 ton capital ship continues to play a part in its scheme of things. As the largest capital ship in the world is the British *Hood* of 42,100 tons and the largest of the United States 32,600 tons, it is probable that Great Britain and the United States will be able to agree on a figure less than 35,000.

The Draft Convention provisions are to apply "through-

---

[1] *Report*, par. 109.

[2] The 32,600-ton battleships last built by the United States represented an expenditure averaging $27,500,000 as compared with 10,000-ton first-line cruisers *Salt Lake City*, 1929, costing $12,860,000 and the government-built *Pensacola*, 1930, costing $14,136,000. Aircraft carriers run about $45,000,000.

out the duration of the present convention." The Washington and London treaties run until December 31, 1936, and further provide for a conference of revision in 1935. There is consequently a pertinent question as to whether the five great naval states will wish to insist that this circumstance should control the duration of the convention of the Disarmament Conference as a whole, or whether some scheme will be devised in negotiation to leave their armament under its own treaty status, while establishing general rules for all the world, including themselves. Solution of this apparently technical question may very well determine whether a second general disarmament conference will be convened within five years or whether a different lapse of time will be decided upon.[1]

The scope of agreement on naval armament before the meeting of the conference was as follows:

The global tonnage of war vessels is not to exceed a figure to be fixed for each contracting party in Table I.[2]

Vessels exempt from limitation are:

(*a*) Naval surface combatant vessels under 600 tons;

(*b*) Naval surface combatant vessels of 600 to 2,000 tons, mounting no gun above 6.1 inches caliber and not more than four 3-inch guns, not fitted to launch torpedoes, and with less than 20 knots speed;

(*c*) Naval surface vessels not built as fighting ships, without the foregoing characteristics, and also unprotected by armor plate, not fitted to launch mines or to receive aircraft and not designed to launch more than three aircraft.

A list of special vessels, to be determined, will also be exempt.

These provisions, Art. 11, Table I and Annexes I and II, will have the effect of determining the group of states for which naval limitation and reduction will apply. Of the 64 states invited to the General Disarmament Conference, 21 have no naval vessels at all and are, therefore, uncon-

[1] The duration of the convention is discussed below under Arts. 57-59.
[2] The Soviet delegation in the Preparatory Commission insisted that the global tonnage figure should be reduced from the present tonnage.

cerned.[1] The exemptions indicated will clearly have the effect of eliminating Albania, Bulgaria, Canada, Colombia, Cuba (probably), Ecuador, Egypt, Finland, India, Latvia, Mexico (probably), Persia, Siam, South Africa, Uruguay and Venezuela, while Peru and Yugoslavia are on the line. Some 39 states, therefore, will not be affected at all.

Table II provides for the distribution into categories of the tonnage of the two dozen states subject to naval limitation and reduction. It was hoped that before the conference France and Italy would have reached an agreement limiting their tonnage under Part III of the London treaty and would, therefore, be bound by the whole of that treaty.[2] As they are not within the scope of that agreement, they will fall under Art. 12. By this article, Table II will show "the way in which each high contracting party intends to distribute" its limited global tonnage by categories.[3]

The table once more serves to narrow down the incidence of naval limitation. Though based in its titling on the table of the London naval treaty, it draws a distinction between categories of capital ships and blesses internationally an important change of nomenclature to which the naval experts resorted in reconciling themselves to the Washington naval treaty. Before that treaty, and for some time afterward, the naval experts regarded capital ship as synonomous with battleship or battle cruiser, and declared it axiomatic that "the battleship was the backbone of the fleet."[4] Then

[1] That is, Afghanistan, Austria, Belgium, Bolivia, Costa Rica, Czechoslovakia, Dominican Republic, Guatemala, Haiti, Hejaz and Nejd, Honduras, Hungary, Irish Free State, Liberia, Lithuania, Luxemburg, Nicaragua, Panama, Paraguay, Salvador and Switzerland.

[2] The French Government in its memorandum of July 15, 1931, stated that it hoped by that time that "a suitable arrangement will enable France and Italy, in full agreement with the British Commonwealth of Nations to set forth their intentions in the matter of construction for the next few years in a temporary *modus vivendi* of a nature to facilitate the work of that conference" (C.440.M.187.1931.IX, p. 5.). Negotiations were resumed in August, and continued at Geneva in February, 1932.

[3] It is interesting to observe that in 1926 there were 1,938 naval combatant vessels of all kinds; on February 1, 1931, the total was 1,882 and on January 1, 1932, the British *Return of Fleets* showed 1,741, an 8% drop in 11 months.

[4] The *Report of the Secretary of the Navy for 1920*, p. 7, says:
"The capital ship of the present day is the lineal descendent of and development from the 'ship of the line' of a century ago. New types have arisen, as when the armor-clad came into existence, but the battleship or its equiva-

they discovered that, while capital ships were necessary for national defense, a capital ship was not necessarily synonomous with any particular type, but was the heaviest category actually in the fleet. This evidence of thought has now been internationalized in the Draft Convention by dividing capital ships into two subcategories, the second of which is "for parties who do not possess any capital ship of a standard displacement exceeding 8,000 tons."

On this basis, what may be called first-class capital ships are found to be possessed only by the five dominant states and these eight additional ones:[1] Argentina, Brazil, Chile, Germany, Greece, the Soviet Union, Spain and Turkey. Really only Germany and the Soviet Union of these eight count.

Aircraft carriers form a category by themselves, and the cruiser category is distinguished between those mounting guns more than 6.1 inches and those with guns of less than that caliber. Destroyers are bracketed with cruisers as light surface vessels, and the fifth category is submarines, it being assumed that miscellaneous craft are subsidiary and have no intrinsic fighting value.

The allocation of tonnage by categories is contemplated in the Draft Convention as being optional at the outset, but obligatory after the choice has been made.

The London naval treaty laid down the possibility of a 10% transfer between the categories of cruisers with guns less than 6.1 inches and of destroyers. In the Draft Convention, transfers from category to category are contemplated, and a table is to be developed stipulating what

---

lent has always survived. There have always been those searching for something simpler, and more especially cheaper, and with the development of every new weapon enthusiasts have claimed that the battleship has been rendered obsolete . . . Developments of the past year have confirmed the conclusions of the department that battleships were still the backbone of the fighting fleet, and this is no time for their abandonment."

[1] The list is formal only. Six of these states have big ships as souvenirs of the past. Argentina's two 27,940-ton battleships are 17 and 18 years old (reconstructed in 1924–25); Brazil's two 19,200-ton battleships are over-age (completed in 1910, one reconstructed 1917–19); Chile's 28,000-ton battleship dates from 1915; Greece's 9,960-ton battle cruiser of 1910 was reconstructed in 1927; Spain's two 15,452-ton battleships are 17 and 10 years old; Turkey's 22,640-ton battle cruiser is second hand from Germany and was built in 1912, and its 9,900-ton battleship dates from 1891.

transfers are permissible. The rules state that there shall be full freedom of transfer as regards surface ships in fleets with total tonnage under 100,000 tons. If this figure is maintained, the control of transfer will apply only to Argentina,[1] France, Germany,[1] Great Britain, Italy, Japan, the Soviet Union, Spain[1] and the United States. As regards the lesser of these, the amount of transfer will vary in inverse ratio to the amount of their global tonnage. These provisions indicate an accepted principle that, except for submarines, a state with 100,000 naval tons could transfer all of its surface tonnage from one category to another in effecting new construction, while Great Britain and the United States would not possess that privilege to an extent above 10% and applicable only in the smaller categories, the intermediate navies having intermediate ratios. No transfer, however, is to take place except after notification to all others and to the Permanent Disarmament Commission, which is assigned the duty of following the execution of the convention. This transfer privilege is calculated to have an important bearing upon the future of naval strategy since in essentials it draws a graduated line between those fleets recognized as having obviously and solely a defensive purpose and those which are regarded as defensive as a form of international politeness.

Moreover, the right of transfer will put a premium upon selection of a tonnage limit which will give elasticity of choice corresponding to the technical interests of the state, a new element. Argentina, for instance, has a nominal naval tonnage of 113,415, reduced to 94,162 by allowing for depreciated tonnage, thus avoiding the control. Germany has commissioned tonnage of 128,510 and depreciated allowance of 26,906, a net of 101,604; by readjustment its fleet can be put below 100,000 tons.[2] Spain with 117,432 tons nominal shows 50,459 depreciated tonnage, or a net of

[1] That is, without allowance for depreciated tonnage.

[2] The seventh *Armaments Year-Book* figures are employed; the *Particulars* (C.524.M.219.1931.IX.) would give a different result. The German fleet in commission consists of 79,200 tons of first-class capital ships (according to the categories of Table II); 31,300 tons of second-class cruisers and 18,010 of destroyers. When one 13,200-ton capital ship is replaced by the 10,000-ton *Ersatz Preussen*, the total will drop to 98,400 for ships in commission.

66,973. Obviously, an encouragement to claim depreciation for attaining the increased freedom of ratio at a lower level will be a future factor.

Arts. 14 to 16 deal with the displacement and guns of various categories. No capital ship exceeding 35,000 tons standard displacement or carrying guns exceeding 16 inches is to exist. This is the provision of the Washington treaty and applies primarily only to the five great naval states. Both limits are excessive, since only one ship, the battle cruiser *Hood*, 1920, of Great Britain exceeds that figure, and the average size of capital ships now in existence is more than 5,000 tons below it.[1] There are only 58 16-inch guns in the world on 7 ships, though there are 100 15-inch guns on 13 others. Since the Draft Convention relates to capital ships rather than to battleships or battle cruisers as types, both the tonnage and gun-size limit might be reduced to figures that correspond to what Japan, Great Britain or the United States will find it possible to build; for the Draft Convention applies only to future construction, not that which is already in existence.

The Washington treaty figure of 27,000 tons for aircraft carriers is repeated, but here again recent practice has resulted in construction far below that figure. Aircraft carriers above 10,000 tons may carry 8-inch guns, while those below are restricted to 6.1-inch guns. As the smaller carrier has become more popular, it is possible that the higher tonnage figure may be considerably reduced. The armament of aircraft carriers is limited to 10 guns above 6.1 inches and is unlimited below that caliber, which may prove to be a definite encouragement to the building of smaller vessels.

Submarines are restricted to a tonnage of 2,000, which is a displacement to which very few of the craft have yet attained.[2]

It will thus be seen that nearly all the tonnage limits per vessel may be subject to reduction in the conference. It

[1] The average for Great Britain is 28,715 tons; United States, 29,800 tons; Japan, 30,440 tons, with other capital ships less than 25,000 tons.

[2] Out of 110 United States submarines, three are above 2,700 tons and three at 2,000, while nothing building is above 1,500 tons.

may be assumed that all the navally important states will favor such reductions in some category or other.

The Draft Convention binds the parties neither to acquire nor to construct for others either ships or armament exceeding the prescriptions to be arrived at in the convention. In the case of vessels to be replaced, definitions of over-age are adopted from the London treaty. The age of capital ships and aircraft carriers is 20 years, as is that of other surface vessels exceeding 3,000 tons and laid down after December 31, 1919. Surface vessels under 3,000 tons are given a life of 16 years, and submarines of 13. The idea of fixing age limits for naval craft was put into the treaty of Versailles where Art. 190 operates as a control in this respect of the German navy. In the Washington and London treaties age limits were assigned to the various categories in order to afford a basis for computing strengths and to prevent competitive acceleration in fleet turnover.

This schedule of the life of various categories of war vessels opens the way to the refinement of naval tonnage for comparison. It is quite likely that the conference will add an additional column to the tonnage tables in order to take depreciation into account, for governments have during the past few years been reporting their depreciated tonnage for the *Armaments Year-Book*. No attempt has yet been made to revalue fleets on this basis, though the principle of the computation has been accepted since the Washington treaty. If the conference decides to make a showing of reduction, in addition to limitation, the principle will certainly be employed at Geneva in 1932.

The great navies have in the last 10 years been so continuously subjected to restriction in fundamental respects that even yet the depreciation factor has not been put to full use as an argument for new construction. Yet at the conference, or subsequently, it is certain to be used as a means of comparison. The principle is a simple one. A capital ship has an assigned age of 20 years; therefore, a 10,000-ton capital ship five years old has depreciated one-fourth and would rate as 7,500 capital tons. It is, however, obvious that such a computation would be unimpeachable only in case the ship had not been modernized or otherwise rejuvenated. Some time the whole problem of the amortization of naval vessels will start an international argument. The first debate on it may or may not take place at the General Disarmament Conference.

The seventh *Armaments Year-Book* shows that the conference can make a fine showing by writing off this depreciated tonnage. Out of 5,312,000 tons in the world reported as of 1929 the returns show 2,000,000 as depreciated, while there is also a considerable amount that is over-age and therefore rates as zero instead of its nominal displacement. When the naval experts figure their own strength they depreciate, but have used the nominal strength of other nations when they figured for the information of appropriating parliaments. The naval situation would be much clarified if this over-age material were scrapped and taken out of all accounts. It will be made additionally clear when all tonnage is figured and regularly reported on the depreciation basis. Modernization or rejuvenation[1] have taken place as devices to maintain construction appropriation levels and to correct construction errors. Such devices have the effect of complicating the operation of the depreciation and over-age formula. The conference may take them into consideration in this connection, especially with respect to the minor categories, which interest a considerable number of states whose relative strengths are mutually reactive.

The relation of merchant shipping to naval strength is dealt with in Art. 19. The great naval states have made considerable use of their merchant fleets as subsidiaries to their navies. This has been done in the past by granting of subsidies, by passing upon plans, by the stiffening of decks to support guns, by the carrying of ordnance in storage aboard ship, by organizing seamen into naval reserves and by other means. Art. 19 deals with this situation and permits "the necessary stiffening of decks for the mounting of guns not exceeding 6.1 inches in caliber." Otherwise "no preparation shall be made in merchant ships in time of

---

[1] Argentina has rejuvenated two and the United States modernized eight battleships.

peace for the installation of warlike armaments for the purpose of converting such ships into vessels of war." The Japanese delegation did not regard the word "preparation" as clearly prohibiting aircraft equipment on merchant vessels and reserved the right to raise that question at the conference. It is possible that fuller precision of the word will be attempted at Geneva, to determine, for instance, whether the granting of a subsidy to a shipping company in order to facilitate the transfer of its vessels to a government would be regarded as a preliminary step for installing warlike armament.

Of the two dozen states with naval armament to be limited, only about half are presently equipped for naval construction. In consequence, war vessels are in many instances built in one country for the account of another. A provision of the Washington treaty, carried over into the London treaty and thence to the Draft Convention, stipulates that no party shall use as its own any vessel of war constructed or under construction in its jurisdiction for another state. The Washington and London treaties thus abolish the secondhand business in naval craft, and the Draft Convention also provides that the parties are not to dispose, "by gift, sale, or any mode of transfer," of any war vessel in such a manner that it may become a war vessel of any foreign navy.

Disposal of surplus tonnage is to take place in accordance with rules incorporated from the London treaty, which provide five methods:

(1) By scrapping (sinking or breaking up);

(2) By converting the vessel to a hulk;

(3) By converting the vessel to target use exclusively;

(4) By retaining the vessel exclusively for experimental purposes;

(5) By retaining the vessel exclusively for training purposes.

Vessels retained for target, experimental or training purposes are eventually to be scrapped or converted to hulks. Full details for each form of disposal are given.

The last article of the chapter is the provision for limiting the annual expenditure of each state "on the upkeep, purchase and manufacture of war material for naval armaments." Here the indirect method supplements the direct method, of which the details have been described. As in other parts of the Draft Convention relating to expenditures, only the main principle could be set down, since the practical and detailed conditions to be met were developed by the Committee of Budgetary Experts after the adjournment of the Preparatory Commission. From that committee's report, it is evident that the same rules will, so far as possible, apply to the return for total limitation of expenditures. They will be discussed in the next chapter.

Respecting the provision for limiting naval expenditures, the delegation of the United States made its general reservation, calling particular attention in the debates to the fact that costs in its industrial system were likely to be higher than elsewhere. The Japanese and French delegations did not see their way to accept the special limitation of expenditure for naval armament on account of its being limited directly and also indirectly by the limitation of the aggregate expenditure on armament as a whole. The British and Italian delegations announced that their acceptance of the article would depend upon the attitude finally adopted by other maritime states. Thus, this provision in the Draft Convention stands on an indefinite footing, not having been actually accepted by the five states possessing 80% of the material to which the limitation would apply. The German delegation reserved its opinion until it had studied the report of the Committee of Budgetary Experts.

C. Air Material

Chapter C of Part II relates to the material of air armament. A few countries have organized their aerial defense into a separate department, but the great majority attach their air forces to their armies, or their navies if they have them. There are 43 states reporting air forces. In only nine — Australia, Canada, Great Britain, Italy, New Zealand, Portugal, the Soviet Union and Sweden — are the air forces independent of the other services. Aside from one or two instances of a combined ministry for all defense services, all the other states attach their air troops to the army or army and navy.

The first question which the Preparatory Commission encountered respecting air armament was the relation between military and civil aviation. A special committee of experts studied the subject, and it transpired that there was not now a great likelihood of transfer from one type to the other, owing to the rapid technological advance that was taking place. Yet it remained true that civil aviation material might more easily be transformed for military use than almost any other type of material of warlike utility.

The Committee of Experts on Civil Aviation was unanimously of the opinion in 1927 that "in any limitation of air armaments it is essential to avoid hampering the development of civil aviation." Recognizing that it was impossible to forecast developments in civil aviation, which were dependent upon a large body of "interdependent scientific, economic, industrial and other factors," they were of opinion that any attempt to limit both military and civil aviation was, if possible at all, feasible only in agreements of very short duration. Assuming that the difference in requirements between the two types of aircraft would increase, the committee of experts[1] recommended their complete divorce. This decision was approved in principle by the Preparatory Commission and was confirmed by the Assembly. The eighth session of the Assembly on September 24, 1927, noted that there was then a close connection between the requirements and development of civil and military aviation which led to difficulties in limiting air armaments without hampering civil aviation, and declared "that it is desirable, for this purpose, that the development of civil aviation should be directed solely toward economic ends to the exclusion of military interests." Governments were invited to act upon this principle.[2] This recom-

[1] *Preparatory Commission for the Disarmament Conference. Subcommission B. Report No. II* (C.P.D.39.1927.IX.3).

[2] *Resolutions and Recommendations adopted by the Assembly . . . 1927*, p. 22.

mendation of the Assembly, representative of the entire membership of the League, is embodied in Art. 28 of the Draft Convention.

The parties are to refrain from prescribing military features in the construction of material to the end that it may be built for purely civil purposes, and no civil aircraft shall be prepared for conversion into military aircraft in time of peace. Civil enterprises are not to be required to employ personnel especially trained for military purposes. Such trained personnel is to be employed in civil undertakings only provisionally and temporarily, and is to be included in the limitations applicable to the military personnel of each party. The direct or indirect subsidizing of air lines for military purposes is not to take place. While military aviation depends upon the exclusive efforts of each state, the contracting parties undertake to encourage the conclusion of economic agreements between civil aviation undertakings and to confer with that object in view.

Military aviation was but slightly developed before the Great War, during which it acquired an important position. Strategists have not yet digested the possibilities of aircraft. Opinion differs all the way from regarding aëroplanes as superior scouts to regarding them as providing military combat with a third dimensional function which subordinates land and naval forces. The agreement to separate the development of civil and military aviation is, therefore, an important principle. It probably represents the first instance in history where military and civil requirements have been consciously rent asunder.[1] However, the strategical uncertainty of aviation's value remains and is reflected in the other provisions agreed upon.

Arts. 25 and 26 attempt to lay down only principles of limitation. Two standards were adopted, number and total horse power. Numbers of aëroplanes are, of course,

[1] The "Fundamental Naval Policy of the United States," edition of August 4, 1931, contains this general paragraph:
"To give every encouragement to civil aviation with a view to advancing the art and to providing aviators and aircraft production facilities available for war."
If that policy is consonant with Art. 28 of the Draft Convention, no full divorce of civil and military aviation would seem to be realized.

readily reported, but it was not so easy to determine an additional standard for closer evaluation. The Preparatory Commission left the determination of rules for the adoption of a standard horse power measurement to a committee to be appointed. The Council of the League appointed such a committee on January 24, 1931, and the committee met at Geneva, April 20–24.

The committee, after discussing at length the factors involved, decided upon a formula which is a function of the volume swept, multiplied by the weight of the power unit. The committee concluded (1) that a formula for horse power rating must be one that would not require verification by a dynamometer, and (2) that a simple formula, which would not affect construction and distort design from its natural development, was desirable. The two factors decided upon were the result. Rating by volume swept is based upon the maximum rate of consumption of oxygen and is determined from the dimensions of certain significant parts of the engine, notably the bore and stroke of the piston. The relation between the total weight of the aerial engine and its total horse power accounts for employing the factor of rating by weight. Neither rating alone was found to be without both defects and advantages.

The power index in horse power, according to the formula adopted, is the square root of the total cubic decimeter volume of cylinders of the engine multiplied by the weight in kilograms of the engine and its primary accessories in running order, but empty of oil and water, multiplied by the constant 20. The same formula is to be used for dirigibles, except that the volume and weight are to be multiplied by the constant 8.[1]

With this formula, if accepted, Art. 27 will be filled in with rules for measuring horse power. Arts. 25 and 26, in connection with tables attached, will then enable a presentation of the number and total horse power of both aëroplanes and dirigibles "in commission and in immediate reserve" in the land, sea and armed forces of each of the contracting parties.

[1] C.259.M.115.1931.VIII; *Official Journal*, XII, p. 1252.

Notwithstanding the general engagement to keep civil and military aviation separate, the Draft Convention provides for the reporting of aëroplanes and dirigibles "capable of use in war, organized on a military basis." Such aëroplanes "in commission and immediate reserve" are not to exceed the figures to be agreed upon and set down in the table. The dirigibles organized on a military basis are limited to those "in commission."

No specific provision is made for the limitation of the annual expenditure on the upkeep, purchase and manufacture of air armaments as is provided for the land and naval material. Expenditure on aircraft is still a minor part of total military expenditure. Aviation is still in its infancy, and its strategical values are not yet determined. They are closely related to technical improvements, and apparently no state thought it was advisable, in the interest of its "national defense," to attempt to limit expenditure on that arm.

It will be noted that aëroplanes "in immediate reserve" are to be included in the limitation. This was decided on a British proposal and was accepted by the close vote of 9 to 8, with various abstentions, to apply only to complete machines in immediate reserve belonging to the state. No limitation of machines in parts, unassembled, is provided for.

The struggle between disarmament and the retention of tactical advantages is apparent in the total lack of any provisions respecting turnover of material. Naval vessels have very carefully been given prescribed lengths of life. Aëroplane models may succeed each other at any rate of speed which the "national defense" authorities of a country may be able to manage.[1]

[1] See further *infra*, p. 211.

CHAPTER VIII
CONTROL OF EXPENDITURE

Part III of the Draft Convention relates to budgetary expenditure and consists of but one article, Art. 29. It prescribes that "the total annual expenditure of each of the high contracting parties on his land, sea and air forces and formations organized on a military basis shall be limited to the figure laid down for such party" in the annex.

This provision relates both to effectives and material, and its assignment as the whole of Part III of the Draft Convention reflects the extremely difficult problem which it raised. Originally proposed by the French delegation in the third session of the Preparatory Commission, it was opposed by the British, Italian and Japanese delegations on the score that budgetary limitation should be effected solely by publicity for the sake of information instead of as a formal obligation including figures. The delegates of the United States and Germany on the first reading thought that the provision should not be included at all. Thus, states whose interest did not lie in the direction of economy were aligned against the proposal.

The matter was at this juncture when at the final meeting of the first part of the sixth session of the Preparatory Commission the United States delegation presented for adoption the resolution of May 4, 1929. This resolution recorded that, the systems of direct limitation of material in service and in stock being rejected and the system of indirect limitation (limitation of expenditure on material) not meeting with general assent, the Preparatory Commission "decides that the limitation and reduction of material must be sought by means of publicity of expenditure." When the article of the first reading text concerning this matter came up in the second part of the sixth session of the commission,[1] it

[1] *Documents of the Preparatory Commission*, Series X, p. 194–206.

resulted in some discussion in which the general principle of budgetary limitation was adopted by a vote of 19 to 2, and another vote on the principle of the separate limitation of expenditure on the three arms was rejected 8 to 7. A vote was then taken unanimously in favor of the French proposal as it then stood.

It is interesting to note that the article finally adopted simply states that annual expenditure shall be limited to the figure to appear in the annex, while the proposal voted recorded an agreement "to limit and as far as possible to reduce" expenditure. This reference to reduction was accepted as a result of a proposal by the Soviet delegation, In the final preparation of the Draft Convention, however. that provision was repeated as Art. 1 of the entire Draft Convention and in the final revision was omitted from Art. 29 as a repetition. It is, however, to be read into Art. 29 as into every article where it is pertinent.[1]

A note attached to the article says that the report of the Committee of Budgetary Experts is to be taken into account in pronouncing on this article, "particularly as regards the possibility of a distinct limitation on land, sea and air forces." The annex called for in the article is still in the form of a report from these experts, which has been several times referred to above.

The report of the committee relates primarily to developing the annex and relevant procedure for Art. 29, and it will here be convenient to review its contents. The budgetary experts, however, had a more complicated problem than simply laying down the framework within which states were to bind themselves to limit total annual military, naval and air expenditure for the duration of the convention. Their work related to four other articles of the Draft Convention as well. Art. 10 limits annual expenditure on land material; Art. 24 that on naval material; Art. 33 provides for a report for each budgetary year after its completion on total actual expenditures on land and sea armed forces "by categories of material," and Art. 38 provides for a similar report of the total amounts actually expended in the course of each year

[1] *Ibid.*, p. 509, 521.

on land, sea and air armaments. Annexes are called for to Arts. 10, 24, 29 and 38.

Models for Several Purposes

The Committee of Budgetary Experts was consequently called upon to analyze budgetary practices and to produce model forms (1) to limit land and sea material individually (Arts. 10 and 24), (2) to limit expenditure on all land, sea and air forces (effectives and material) as a whole (Art. 29), (3) to furnish expenditure reports on categories of land and sea materials (Art. 33)[1] and (4) to furnish expenditure reports on land, sea and air armaments as a whole (Art. 38). The committee found much in common between these various objects and, as it were, made a combined report upon all of them except Art. 33.

The Committee of Budgetary Experts originally studied the subject in 1927 and had rendered a preliminary report at that time.[2] In beginning its work, the committee examined the problem before it from the point of view of the publicity of expenditures, realizing that in case of a limitation the total would be stabilized, though the allocation in categories would not necessarily be fixed. The committee's work at its sessions in December, 1930, and February, 1931, produced not only standard models, but a report in which the delicate complications of elaborating a standardized international model applicable to many national budgets were analyzed.[3]

One of the questions before the committee was a Soviet proposal for a new article to Part III, excluding from national budgets "secret funds intended in a disguised form for extraordinary expenditure on special preparations for war or an increase in armaments." The committee found that this proposal raised the question of the amount of detail which was to be published, as well as that of classification of expenditure. So far as it related to classification,

[1] This subject is discussed in Chap. IX, *infra*.
[2] The interim report is C.P.D.40.1927.IX.4. For the terms of reference see *supra*, p. 152.
[3] *Official Journal*, XII, p. 660; separately as C.182.M.69.1931.IX.

the committee thought it involved political considerations that it would be difficult for budgetary experts to deal with. But the committee held that it was appropriate that the Draft Convention embody another undertaking to include all expenditure for armament, whether styled secret or not. It was possible that funds voted for one purpose might be used for a different one. The committee consequently suggested an overriding clause to the effect that states should return "all their expenditure on armaments classified according to its true utilization."

The committee found that it was essential that states should understand exactly what they were agreeing to limit and that the significance of the items remain the same from year to year. It, therefore, was suggested that model statements should be made on the basis of the latest closed accounts before the conference so that each state would have opportunity to explain exactly what method had been followed and thus be able to agree readily as to the exact manner in which to handle various items. In this connection it was realized that any model statement was likely to require the use of unpublished or unaudited figures and that states might have to depart from the instructions on account of their administrative practices. The resolution of the Council calling for particulars with regard to the status of armaments substantially carried out this suggestion. This resolution, passed by the Council on May 23, 1931, invited governments to return by September 15 records for the latest complete fiscal year on the basis of the tables annexed to the Draft Convention and the budgetary experts' proposals. The expenditure tables returned could be constructed only by a complete reanalysis of official records in addition to the regularly published national accounts. Legislative convenience or habit and administrative customs have given each national set of figures a distinct individuality, which the reworking under the standard model reduces to a large degree of comparability.

The experts, on examination of the budgetary documents of the various governments, found great divergency in practice as to what was regarded as an expenditure. Military expenses are, of course, appropriated for; they are spent with regard to appropriation accounts. There are five stages. A commitment entered into may be nationally treated as an expenditure. So far as the military department is concerned, an expenditure is effected in its budget when goods are delivered or services are performed. The initiating office regards the transaction as closed only when the invoice is received and accepted. In a disbursing officer's records an expenditure is likely to be regarded as dating only from the time when authority is given to pay the amount. Lastly, the cash disbursement takes place and the expenditure is effective from any point of view. Published accounts of many government departments, which are prepared as information for legislative bodies with a view to establishing the need for future appropriations, frequently include large sums committed, but with reference to which the goods called for are then neither delivered nor deliverable. At any given moment an organization will also have considerable sums involved in accounts payable.

The budgetary experts set out to determine the meaning of the term "expenditure" with respect to the five recognized stages from commitment to actual disbursement. They decided that internationally an expenditure was not to be regarded as made until authority was given to pay the amount involved. In reaching this decision they called attention to the fact that commitments, deliveries and invoicing were always taking place, and that at any given time it could reasonably be assumed that the amounts outstanding under those heads would not vary greatly, while the possibility of change in any case rendered those stages of expenditure tentative.

The committee next examines the question of credit purchases and deferred payments and also the problem of *exercice* accounts. The *exercice* accounts of some states roughly give the effect of what is known in the United States as a deficiency appropriation bill; that is, they enable an administrator to extend beyond a given calendar period the budget requirements of that period. The deferment of purchases, payments and of accounting seemed to the committee to point to differences in practice which the existence of a standard form would normally tend to decrease. As they were all likely to be continuing factors without much change in quantity,[1] the committee thought that accounts for international reporting could properly be prepared to show the payments actually effected during the 12 months of the budget year, without reference to their authorization. The committee proposed an addition to the Draft Convention to avoid its weakening by means of deferred payments. The clause proposed reads:[2]

> The high contracting parties undertake not to employ the system of credit purchases or any other system of deferred payments in such a way as to increase their armaments, and, in particular, their war material beyond the level which the parties would have been able to attain under the convention if the payments had not been deferred.

The committee advocated the reporting of gross expenditure rather than net, and devotes a paragraph of its draft annex to the subject. In many countries it has been a practice to grant state subsidies for armament purposes, to make loans to manufacturing companies or to have an interest in their capital or other shares and profits. In some cases these have an intimate bearing upon the development of a country's resources. The committee did not feel qualified to lay down a controlling rule on a matter so obviously affecting internal policy, but provides that an annexed table state the amount of "loans made to, or participations acquired in, enterprises having among their objects the furnishing of goods or services for armament purposes, where these have been excluded from the return on the ground that they are not regarded as armament expenditure."

The committee foresaw that reduction of armament might entail special expenditure of both a recurring and non-recurring character. The withdrawal of a garrison from a

[1] The "unpaid obligations" of the United States Navy Department for the fiscal year ending June 30, 1929, amounted to $143,627,340; for the year ending June 30, 1930, to $178,086,678; and for that ending June 30, 1931, to $184,690,715. See recapitulation of Statement 26 in the Bureau of Supplies and Accounts, *Report of the Paymaster General*, for the years given.

[2] *Official Journal*, XII, p. 682. The report of the committee is C.182. M.69.1931.IX.3. It is also printed in *Official Journal*, XII, p. 676.

town might, in the governmental system of a country, entail a compensation for loss of trade, etc.; or a reduction of personnel might involve an increase in pensions, which themselves represent a separate problem. The committee felt that such expenditures, except pensions, should show in the return.

To Prevent Shifting of Expense

The armament problem is grounded upon distrust. It is, however, obvious that if a budgetary limitation should be adopted, attention might be diverted to securing funds outside. Interested citizens, for instance, might be disposed to make gifts for purposes not possible of realization under treaty. A certain amount of national defense might be devolved upon local authorities or public institutions not under the control of the central government, which is primarily bound by the treaty. Other departments of a government might assume functions which would contribute to the national defense, though outside of the controlled administrations. In principle, the Committee of Budgetary Experts provides for the inclusion of all such expenditures actually made, regardless of the source of authority. The committee concluded that the difficulties in this connection were not serious, "if the governments in good faith include in the model statement all extra budgetary expenditure which can reasonably be ascertained" and if the rule of "true utilization" in reporting is followed. As to many forms of such expenditure, the committee says:[1]

Occasionally, government departments are allowed to use certain current receipts without limit and without accounting therefor to parliament. Organizations for physical or preparatory military training sometimes receive contributions from private individuals or institutions or local authorities. Reserve personnel or conscripts are expected to provide part of their own equipment, and their employers are occasionally required to contribute to their maintenance during their period of training. Local authorities provide quarters and other facilities for the maintenance of garrisons or for training. Generally, the personnel or material of the

[1] *Official Journal*, XII, p. 686.

armed forces is carried by railways at reduced rates, although it is frequently impossible to assert that these reduced rates are lower than is appropriate in the case of a customer as important as the state.

Without attempting to give a synthetic definition of expenditure on national defense, the committee framed a list of headings under which it believed all forms of expense would fall. In allocating expenses to the three arms, it defined the items to be included under the standard headings and noted that accuracy in allocating accounts to them must depend upon the goodwill of governments in the last analysis.

Fixing limits for expenditure involved a number of questions of a somewhat delicate character. A problem on which the committee offers a solution, though it has not been under discussion by states, relates to the transfer of expenditure from one of the three forces to another. If land, naval and air[1] expenditures are separately limited, it is obvious that a decision to spend more on one force and less on another without increasing the total expenditure would be interfered with. With the policy of whether styles in national defense should change, the committee, of course, had nothing to do but, assuming that the question of such transfer would arise, the committee thought it well to provide what it calls "a restricted *virement.*" Two forms of this transfer proposal are suggested. One is that the aggregate total should be set at a figure higher than the separate limits for the land, naval and air forces, the aggregate difference being available for any of the three forces. The second suggestion was that separate limits for the three forces would be set, but could be modified by permitted percentages of change to be agreed upon at the conference and based on the rules contemplated for transfer of naval tonnage. The principle adopted in these rules is that freedom of transfer varies in inverse ratio to the size of the forces involved. From a technical point of view, the committee thought that this type of suggestion might solve a problem

[1] The Draft Convention does not in fact limit air expenditure separately but only in the total.

for a state which found it difficult to foresee during the period of the convention "the development of expenditure which will follow the technical evolution of the respective forces."

From the point of view of limitation, the carrying forward of credits is not regarded as creating a practical difficulty, but variation in expenditure from one year to another requires special consideration. There are four general reasons why annual expenditure would fluctuate:

(*a*) Inability to effect expenditure in a given year;

(*b*) Delays in manufacture and delivery of goods;

(*c*) Concentration of purchases in a given year, especially by countries purchasing abroad;

(*d*) Grouping of construction orders in certain years.

Noting that the first two reasons for fluctuation are unavoidable and that the last two are capable of control, the committee thought it advisable that percentages of elasticity should be fixed within narrow limits. The committee suggested another article to the Draft Convention as follows:[1]

> Each of the high contracting parties undertakes:
>
> (*a*) To maintain during each consecutive period of four years the average level of its annual expenditure within the limits laid down in Arts. 10, 24 and 29 of the Draft Convention of the Preparatory Commission for the Disarmament Conference;
>
> (*b*) Not to exceed during any given year this average limit by more than a percentage fixed for the high contracting party in Table . . .

In suggesting this new decision, the committee called attention to the possibility of stipulating that in the first one or two years the average should not be exceeded at all. Another reason for which change might be required would be a national catastrophe enforcing a temporary reduction in armament expenditure or an accident such as the loss of a warship. Such conditions might be dealt with in the final decision.

[1] *Official Journal*, XII, p. 689.

Effect of Currency Fluctuation

The committee was requested especially to study the question of fluctuations in the purchasing power of various currencies. After examining such factors as the gold standard and the gold exchange standard, the position of countries under and outside of either system and the evidence afforded by various indices, the committee reached the definite opinion "that no existing index or combination of indices can form a suitable basis for an automatic adjustment of the limits provided for in the convention." The difficulty of devising a special index was complicated by the fact that limitation will put a premium upon quality and that, therefore, the expense per unit of material will tend to rise. That was the current case with respect to air force material. In seeking an index, the committee analyzed total defense expenditures by certain categories and found the following interesting percentages from the analysis of four budgets: Personnel, 40 to 50%; transport, 10%; buildings, 15%; war material, 25 to 35%.

But the committee rejected an automatic index in favor of a living organism with the task of judging the merits of each case of readjustment (the committee contemplated no revision) on the demand of a government. The committee, therefore, suggested a new article to the Draft Convention envisaging the following system:[1]

(a) Whenever a high contracting party proves in the manner provided below that fluctuations in the purchasing power of currency have seriously increased the cost of its armaments and that in fact changes in the cost of certain items have not been compensated by changes in the opposite direction in the cost of other items, that high contracting party may submit a demand for a readjustment of its limits.

(b) Each high contracting party may demand a readjustment of the limits on the ground of an increase in the purchasing power of currency substantially reducing the cost of armaments of one or more high contracting parties.

(c) Any such demand shall be transmitted to the Financial Committee of the League of Nations, which shall give its opinion on this

[1] *Official Journal*, XII, p. 691.

demand and also on the question whether, in the circumstances, a readjustment of the limits of other high contracting parties would also be justified. The demand of the high contracting party, together with the report of the Financial Committee, shall then be considered by a conference of all the high contracting parties.

The committee calls attention to the fact that this possibility for readjustment creates a safety valve without which contracting parties to the convention might play safe and "add to the amounts they demand a margin sufficient to cover the risk, and that therefore the figures in the convention would be higher than they need be." The committee directs attention to the fact that its suggestion puts the burden of proof on the party demanding a readjustment. It further suggests that the possibility of readjustment might be discouraged to a certain extent if it were possible to lay down that gold standard countries, in which stationary conditions were to be expected, should be able to demand a readjustment only after a certain interval.

While disclaiming any intention of laying down the rules for passing upon a demand for readjustment, the committee indicates that the following circumstances might be taken into consideration in examining such a demand:[1]

(1) Inflationary developments in a country which no longer maintains the gold standard. In such a case the readjustment would probably only have to be made in the figures of the country where the inflation has occurred.

(2) A general increase of salaries and wages in a country, for instance, as the result of an increase in the cost of living.

(3) The question whether or not an increase in salaries or wages represents an endeavor to increase the quality of the defense services by granting higher pay to the personnel.

(4) The question whether or not the increase in the pay to the defense personnel is accompanied by an increase in pay in the civil service.

(5) Changes in wage levels, the price of the raw materials needed, and the methods of production, affecting the price of war material.

(6) The question whether economies have been effected as a result of rationalization in the widest sense of the word.

[1] *Official Journal*, XII, p. 692–693.

(7) The question whether an apparent increase in cost is not due to an improvement in "quality," in which case it should not lead to a "readjustment" of the figures.

(8) The question whether, in the case of countries purchasing a portion of their war material abroad, there has been a real increase in prices in the country or countries from which the material is purchased.

Does not Gauge Armed Strength

The Committee of Budgetary Experts devotes a chapter of its report to the impossibility of comparing the strength of armaments of various countries on the basis of figures of defense expenditure. In reaching this conclusion, it contributes to the point of view that direct limitation is desirable so far as comparability of armed strength is concerned, while the conclusion additionally gives point to the contention from the opposite angle that expenditure is not the measure of armed strength. The close examination made by the committee of the administrative circumstances in many states leads it to point out that some departure from classification and definitions will be necessary, though it believes that for most states the deviation from instructions will be very restricted.[1] However, a certain resultant lack of uniformity will diminish comparability.

In this connection, it calls attention to the fact that defense requirements frequently benefit from goods and services not reflected in budget expenditure. "Soldiers recruited voluntarily," it says, "must be paid at rates which bear some relation to the wage level of the country concerned, while recruits under a system of conscription generally receive only a more or less nominal remuneration, the compulsory service being in itself a kind of tax which does not enter into the budget accounts." Maintenance is greatly influenced by the standard of living and statistics show, says the committee, "that there is, in fact, a great variation in the cost of maintaining a soldier as between one country or another." Such differences are not reflected in efficiency.

[1] *Cf.* the discussion of the *Particulars with Regard to Armaments,* Chap. V, *supra,* p. 126.

States obtaining their war material from state factories make no provision for interest on capital invested, while those purchasing from private industries pay prices which include both interest charges and profits. The committee, however, calls attention to the fact that expenditure figures can prove "a useful criterion for appreciating the development of armaments from one year to another, so long as the methods of administration remain the same."[1]

REANALYSIS OF BUDGETS

Ever since budgets have been voted for armament, the technical services and executive governments have secured funds for military purposes in such forms that the actual use of funds could not be traced. The Committee of Budgetary Experts were not only familiar with the national practices of the 11 countries from which they came[2] but had the benefit of studying a large number of budgets. In consequence, in their report as experts they penetrated most of the devices used to disguise the accounts and in the rules and table rubrics they established formulas calculated to bring out the facts. The model statement, filled out by states, automatically makes the national figures highly comparable with each other.

The task assigned to governments is complicated. It involves a complete reanalysis of both published and unpublished accounts in accordance with the rules of the budgetary experts. Many of the countries reporting found that the task of recasting the accounts required much time and labor. The results they obtain, when studied as a whole, will doubtless have a powerful influence upon governmental practices, since they call attention to discrepant expenses for the same or even less results. Particularly they divulge diverse ratios of expenditure under various heads.

The United States spent 45.3% of its total for naval forces

---

[1] *Official Journal*, XII, p. 697, as corrected by C.413.M.169.1931.IX.7. Annex.
[2] France, Turkey, Czechoslovakia, Japan, Sweden, Finland, Yugoslavia, Great Britain, Belgium, Italy and Germany.

on war material as against 46.9% by Great Britain; but under that head the United States spent only 18.5% for the item "new construction and maintenance" while Great Britain devoted 38.7% to that item. For "arms, ammunition and war material" the United States spent in the aggregate for land, naval and air forces 214% of what Great Britain spent, though the total expenditure of the United States was only 137% of that of Great Britain.

The United States, Italy and Japan were the only states reporting expenditures under the annexed Tables C or D, block credits and purchases on credit or deferred payments. The total of the United States under these two items amounted to $181,086,677, more than the total armament expenditure of all but seven countries in the world. Of that total all but $3,000,000 was on account of the navy. Under Table D the United States navy reported purchases on credit and deferred payments[1] of $94,688,569. The table was called for by the budgetary experts in connection with a suggestion that countries undertake "not to employ the system of credit purchases or any other system of deferred payments in such a way as to increase their armaments and, in particular, their war materials." Italy reported a total of 5,207,079,845 lira ($274,056,834) of block credits and 1,705,210,620 lira ($89,747,927) of purchases on credit and deferred payments, or a total under Tables C and D of 6,912,290,465 lira ($363,804,761) or 109.5% of Italy's total expenditures. Japan reported block credits, presumably of the Table C type. The Japanese system is a vote in a considerable sum, of which a part is allotted to a given year. The allotment for the land and naval forces in the year under report amounted to 226,221,435 yen ($113,111,000) of which 52,542,264 yen ($26,272,000) was apparently included in the regular expenditures, leaving 173,679,171 yen ($86,840,000) of block credits allotted to the year outstanding.

[1] Redefined by the United States as "additional obligations incurred under special authorization of Congress and for which no appropriation has been made" (C.413.M.169.1931.IX.7, Annex).

Account of the United States

Though it remains for the conference to determine the exact form in which the model tables will appear under Art. 10 (land material), Art. 24 (naval material), Art. 29 (expenditure limitation) and Art. 38 (expenditure made), the Budgetary Experts prepared a Draft Annex and Model Statement in substantially the same form for all. For the sake of associating the models with the discussion of the subject, the tables are appended as finally filled in by the United States Government, reporting the expenditures of the fiscal year ending June 30, 1930:

TABLE A. TOTAL EXPENDITURE[1]

Land Forces	$324,945,363
Naval Forces	375,291,828
Air Forces	[109,066,495[2]]
	$700,237,191

[1] The United States did not fill in this table, the figures for which are the grand totals of Tables B, C and D.

[2] Air forces are an integral part of the United States land and naval forces, and this amount is therefore already accounted for in the preceding items.

TABLE B. LAND FORCES[1]

Category of Expenditure	Armed forces stationed in the home country (optional)	Armed forces stationed overseas (optional)	Formations organized on a military basis stationed in the home country (optional)	Formations organized on a military basis stationed overseas (optional)	Total[2]
	(1)	(2)	(3)	(4)	(5)
					Fiscal Year Ending June 30, 1930

HEAD I
Effectives

Personnel normally forming part of formations and services:

A	Pay and allowances of all kinds: Officers....................	$63,684,726
B	Ditto: N.C.O.'s and men........	68,509,990
C	Ditto: Civilian personnel.........	17,797,127

Personnel not normally forming part of formations and services:

D	Persons undergoing preparatory military training, reservists and reserve organizations..........	20,502,289
E	*Maintenance of personnel referred to in subheads A to D*............	44,205,838

HEAD II
Transport

F	Horses and other animals, forage, harness and shoeing...........	6,153,812
G	Coal, fuel, oil, petrol, lubricants, etc., and other transport expenses	19,201,371

TOTAL: HEADS I AND II.............	$240,055,153

[1] The air components are an integral part of the U. S. Army and are included in these figures.

[2] Columns 1–4 (optional) were not filled in.

B. LAND FORCES—*Continued*

Category of Expenditure					Total
HEAD III **Buildings**	(1)	(2)	(3)	(4)	(5)
H Construction of new fortifications and defense works					$437,725
K Barracks, other buildings, upkeep, furniture					31,634,049
TOTAL: HEADS I TO III					272,126,927
HEAD IV **War Material**					
M Arms, ammunition and fighting material					43,861,270
M (*a*) Engineer and other warlike stores					8,957,166
N Manufacture of war material in "nonautonomous" state establishments (expenditure not divisible between subheads M and M (*a*)					
TOTAL: HEADS III AND IV					84,890,210
GRAND TOTAL					$324,945,363

C. NAVAL FORCES [1]

Category of Expenditure					Total[2]
HEAD I **Effectives**	(1)	(2)	(3)	(4)	(5)
Personnel normally forming part of formations and services:					
A Pay and allowances of all kinds: Officers					$43,201,180
B Ditto: N.C.O's and men					78,127,618
C Ditto: Civilian personnel					
Personnel not normally forming part of formations and services:					
D Persons undergoing preparatory military training, reservists and reserve organizations					14,933,170
E *Maintenance of personnel referred to in subheads A to D*					45,474,812
TOTAL: HEAD I					$181,736,780

[1] The air components are an integral part of the U. S. Navy and are included in these figures.
[2] Columns 1–4 (optional) were not filled in.

C. NAVAL FORCES—*Continued*

Category of Expenditure	(1)	(2)	(3)	(4)	Total (5)
HEAD II **Transport**					
G Coal, fuel, oil, petrol, lubricants, etc., and other transport expenses					$15,382,564
HEAD III **Buildings**					
H Construction of new fortifications and defense works............					
K Barracks, other buildings, upkeep, furniture.....................					7,913,930
HEAD IV **War Material**					
L Ships: new construction and maintenance.....................					68,492,508
M Arms, ammunition and fighting material.......................					101,766,046
N Manufacture of war material in nonautonomous state establishments (expenditure not divisible between subheads L and M)....					
TOTAL: HEADS II, III AND IV					193,555,048
GRAND TOTAL....................					$375,291,828

D. AIR FORCES[1]

Category of Expenditure	(1)	(2)	(3)	(4)	Total[2] (5)

HEAD I
Effectives

Personnel normally forming part of formations and services:

A	Pay and allowances of all kinds: Officers....................	$10,732,556
B	Ditto: N.C.O.'s and men.........	13,538,642
C	Ditto: Civilian personnel.........	6,361,088

Personnel not normally forming part of formations and services:

D	Persons undergoing preparatory military training, reservists and reserve organizations..........	702,538
E	*Maintenance of personnel referred to in subheads A to D*	6,726,155

HEAD II
Transport

G	Coal, fuel, oil, petrol, lubricants, etc., and other transport expenses	6,619,367

HEAD III
Buildings

K	Barracks, other buildings, upkeep, furniture....................	6,061,976

HEAD IV
War Material

M	Arms, ammunition and fighting material.......................	58,324,173

TOTAL...........................	$109,066,495

[1] These figures are not additional to, but are included in, tables B and C (see footnotes to those tables).

[2] Columns 1–4 (optional) were not filled in.

ANNEXED TABLES

TABLE A. EXPENDITURE ON PAY OF RESERVES FOR THE YEAR ENDING　　　　　　　　JUNE 30, 1930
1. Remuneration outside periods of training of personnel not employed.......................... $9,088,005
2. Remuneration during training of reservists called up..................................... 28,745,719

Note. — The above figures are not additional to, but are included in, tables of land and naval forces.

TABLE B. EXPENDITURE ON SHIPBUILDING FOR THE YEAR ENDING　　　　　　　　JUNE 30, 1930
1. New construction........................... $36,799,942
2. Maintenance and repairs..................... 32,817,954

Note. — The above figures are not additional to, but are included in, tables of land and naval forces ($1,125,388 and $68,492,508, respectively.)

TABLE C.[1] STATEMENT OF THE AMOUNT OUTSTANDING, AT THE END OF THE FINANCIAL YEAR . . . OF BLOCK CREDITS VOTED IN RESPECT OF EXPENDITURES FOR MORE THAN ONE YEAR $86,398,108

Note. — $3,000,000 of this figure is for the army.

TABLE D.[1] STATEMENT OF THE AMOUNT OUTSTANDING ON JUNE 30, 1930, IN RESPECT OF PURCHASES ON CREDIT OR DEFERRED PAYMENTS RELATING TO GOODS DELIVERED OR SERVICES RENDERED, IN CASES WHERE THE DUE DATES OF PAYMENT ARE LATER THAN THOSE CUSTOMARY IN CONTRACTS OF THE SAME KIND WHICH DO NOT PROVIDE ANY SPECIAL CREDIT FACILITIES....................... $94,688,569

Note. — This total is entirely for the navy.

[1] In a communication dated October 27, 1931, the Department of State said that if Table C had been headed "obligations under appropriations already made and outstanding on June 30, 1930," and if Table D had been headed "additional obligations incurred under special authorizations of Congress and for which no appropriations has been made," they would have "more accurately described the figures inserted than the phraseology prepared by the Committee of Experts on Budgetary Questions, whose headings to the model tables were adopted throughout." It is stated that the figures in Tables C and D "are not additive to the grand total of expenditures" for the year, but "are merely obligations entered into for future delivery of goods or future rendering of services, the payment for which will be included in the expenditures for future fiscal years, if and when such goods are received or services rendered."

TABLE E. STATEMENT FOR THE FINANCIAL YEAR 1930 OF LOANS MADE TO, OR PARTICIPATIONS ACQUIRED IN, ENTERPRISES HAVING AMONG THEIR OBJECTS THE FURNISHING OF GOODS OR SERVICES FOR ARMAMENT PURPOSES, WHERE THESE HAVE BEEN EXCLUDED FROM THE RETURN ON THE GROUND THAT THEY ARE NOT REGARDED AS ARMAMENT EXPENDITURE.................................. None

TABLE F. EXPENDITURE WITH RESPECT OF PENSIONS FOR THE YEAR ENDING JUNE 30, 1930 .... $714,005,086
    (a) National homes.................. 12,890,995
    (b) Veterans' Bureau................. 452,150,622
    (c) Pension Bureau.................. 220,475,744
    (d) Retired pay (officers and men):
          Land forces.................... 20,113,145
          Naval forces................... 8,374,580

Note. — Items (a) to (c) are paid from Veterans' Bureau appropriations. Item (d) is not additional to, but included in, tables of land and naval forces.

TABLE G. PRINCIPAL MODIFICATIONS MADE SINCE THE LAST RETURN IN:........................

1. Provisions relating to the grant of pensions of any contributions made by the personnel towards the cost of these pensions............
2. Provisions relating to the taxation of the pay or pensions of the personnel.................
3. Provisions relating to social insurance or analogous benefits of the personnel, and to the contributions made by the personnel for this purpose....................................

No previous return has been made.

CHAPTER IX

CONTROLS BY PUBLICITY

Part IV of the Draft Convention is entitled "Exchange of Information." On several occasions in the work of the Preparatory Commission it looked as if the exchange of information might be about all that could be included in a convention.

It is well to bear in mind that the exchange of information dealt with in the Draft Convention is additional to the exchange which has continued since 1924 in the form of the *Armaments Year-Book* and the *Statistical Year-Book of the Trade in Arms, Ammunition and Implements of War*. The facts printed in those publications are furnished by governments solely in conformity with their consciences. Those notices differ according to the election of the compiling state, and they possess comparability only in a limited degree and to the extent that optional imitation of form of presentation or editorial arrangement have contributed that quality. With all its limitations, however, the *Armaments Year-Book* has been a uniquely valuable manual and a striking bit of evidence of the extent to which the whole structure of an armed world has depended upon secrecies of omission and commission for its continued maintenance. This condition of calculated misrepresentation was so deeply impressed upon the whole area of the problem that throughout the last 10 years there has been a constant emphasis upon bringing to light what states are doing, allegedly in the name of national defense. There were times when even most eager official workers for disarmament were willing to accept the exchange of authentic information as the best attainable step. The Draft Convention, however, shows that enough progress has been made in getting toward the heart of the problem that exchange of information is now to be regarded only as an essential supplementary element in the limitation and reduction of armament.

Disproportionately in the past the need for, and the increase of, national armament have been based upon allegations of changes in other nations. Secrecy down to the most insignificant details was the universal practice and was coupled with the most diverse methods of keeping accounts and making reports. In prewar days, there were numerous controversies on apparently as simple a matter as the analysis of naval tonnage, due to the fact that almost any naval intelligence division would miss, perhaps not with malice prepense, some of the intricacies deemed important by foreign general boards. Some states by law keep the most trivial details of military and naval affairs secret, and in some countries high treason by indiscretion about such things can be committed without intent by carelessly snapping a camera at the wrong time. The part of the Draft Convention devoted to the exchange of information is, therefore, of considerable importance. A large amount of the rivalry and suspicion that has characterized military affairs has in the past been due to the interested interpretation of facts secretly collected by national officials. Military people congenitally read other nations' actions pessimistically, and have had every incentive to arrange their own records for purposes of concealment and for advantages in seeking new appropriations. The furnishing of identic information in standard forms to the Secretary-General of the League of Nations for publication both to governments and to the world's public will materially alter the feeling of suspicion which has been generally felt and the national attitudes of mind resulting therefrom.

Part IV of the Draft Convention consists of nine articles, which provide for 16 tables to be filled in by each state annually, to be sent to the Secretary-General of the League within a few months and to be published each year within a given time. The tables are similar to those which provide for the limitation or reduction of effectives, material and expenditure, and their annual preparation and publication will, therefore, provide a form of public supervision over the

MORE ANNUAL DETAILS ON EFFECTIVES

Arts. 30–32 provide for the annual reporting of information respecting effectives. The reports will be somewhat more extensive than the terms of limitation or reduction under Part I.[1] It was possible to make some further agreement with respect to information, and it remains to be seen to what extent the additional data will in practice yield results equivalent to reduction.

The 12 tables for the annual reports of effectives are more detailed than those given in Part I for their limitation during the treaty period. For land forces, "soldiers whose period of service has exceeded the legal period of service, but is less than" the longest period of service in force in any conscript army are to be annually reported. An optional statement may also be made of "recruits not trained as defined in the national legislation," while in the tables for naval forces there is a column for effectives other than officers who have completed at least that maximum period of service.

In all the tables covering land, naval and air forces, there is place for an optional statement concerning "recruits not trained as defined in the national legislation." When the commission was debating publicity in 1929, the desirability of this rather cryptic heading became evident. Attention to effectives has all along been concentrated upon the conscript army, and the volunteer army, with its complicated concomitants of supplementary institutional and associational training, has been dealt with only incidentally. In the discussion on second reading,[2] there was a lengthy debate about reporting of both the men serving the normal period and those who had completed the longest period of service in force in any conscript army. This distinction in the tables brings out the number of professional soldiers distributed among the conscripts. Where the period of con-

---
[1] See description *supra*, p. 133 *ff*, and tables *infra*, p. 290 *ff*.
[2] *Documents of the Preparatory Commission*, Series VIII, p. 139–151.

scription is one year, and if the longest period in any service is three years, those attaining the latter length of service would be separately noted.

The possessors of the volunteer system had trouble in understanding how this would apply to them, since the period of volunteer service is longer than that for conscripts, and reenlistments under it are of quite a different character. The United States thought the scheme would preclude an enlisted man in the voluntary army from reenlisting, but was assured that that was not at all the intention. On the other hand, the British representative failed to see any sense in distinguishing in a four-year volunteer enlistment between the first three years and the last one. The intention being to establish the rôle played by the essentially professional element in all armies, it was pointed out that with voluntary service regarded as practically synonymous with the professional, it was only the number of such troops among conscripts that it was necessary to take account of. A couple of days later, the commission adopted the phraseology indicated,[1] which consequently is to be understood as affording the opportunity to report the extent of training given to conscript recruits in addition to their regular period of service, while implying that the national legislation of states having the volunteer system gives the essential key to length of individual service in their forces.

The German delegation made a reservation against allowing the option without an obligation to publish simultaneously information respecting trained reserves.

The tabular publicity reports, like the limitation tables for effectives, are based upon the average daily number, which is generally recognized to be the method of computation best adapted for comparison. In some forms of military organization the real effectives may be considerably higher than the average effectives.[2] Art. 30 obligates the parties to attach to the statement explanatory notes showing the elements on which the figures are based and stating for each sort of effectives (recruits, militia men, reservists, ter-

[1] *Documents of the Preparatory Commission*, Series VIII, p. 183.
[2] *Cf. supra*, p. 138.

ritorials, for example) the actual number of each and the number of days' service performed. The German delegation here as elsewhere made a reservation because there was no provision for publicity regarding either trained reserves or the figure of the annual contingent.[1]

Reports on Subsidiary Formations

The German insistence upon this point of view seems to be the result of the obligations devolving upon it by reason of Arts. 173–178 of the treaty of Versailles. These abolish conscription, establish a period of enlistment of 12 years for men and 25 years for officers, prohibit ex-officers from having any military obligations, restrict military education and prohibit military training by educational establishments, veteran societies and other social organizations. In other words, effort was made to abolish the German trained reserve. Germany desires at least to obtain a commitment from other countries as to the number of their reserves and, of course, the contrast between the German condition and the condition of others would prove embarrassing for the latter. Germany intends to raise the question at the conference, and if it does it may be presumed that the Berlin government will take good care to have its own house in order in that respect. From the point of view of the others, the question of trained reserves has not been regarded as of particular importance. Population statistics already show proportions; the great uncertainty is the decreasing value of a man as his training period recedes into the past. Annual contingents are based on population; they are not secret as to full quotas or the actual drawings from them, but are not compiled for international circulation and commitment. Probably the best argument in favor of the German contention is the lack of disposition on the part of those affected to produce the details, which at least creates the impression that they are clinging to a secret supposedly of military value and, therefore, not of a strictly defensive character, accurately speaking.

There was a certain difference of opinion in the Prepara-

[1] But many states in the *Particulars* have given this information.

tory Commission respecting the reporting of forces in overseas territory. From the point of view of publicity, about the same considerations arose as in discussing these effectives with respect to limitation. Forces and formations organized on a military basis are to be given publicity only as to armies, it being regarded that naval and air forces, by reason of their smaller numbers and the character of the arms, are not necessarily significant on account of where they are situated. In the interest of full detail, it was proposed that publicity of the land forces situated overseas be given for each territory. The French and Japanese delegations opposed this idea on the ground that a report by districts was no more necessary for the overseas territory than for the districts of the home country, while the numerous distinctions between categories of troops, constant shifts of forces and local variations of service would make accurate reports difficult to prepare. The British delegation concurred in this attitude. The totals but not the distribution are to be reported.

The commission adopted a provision in Art. 31 for an annual report of the number of youths who had received preparatory military training during the year. This report is to be made by those states having both the conscript and voluntary systems of recruitment, but the report is to be confined to youths who have compulsorily received preparatory training. The extent of voluntary training was deemed by the commission to be a subject upon which governments would not be in a position to supply statistical information, though the German and Italian delegations thought that particulars on voluntary training should also be given. This provision aptly illustrates the complications in the structure of armed forces. In a country where the school system is controlled by the state, the prescription of drill in schools and colleges would require international publicity. In the United States military drill in colleges is conducted under authority of national law to the extent of employing over 1,700 officers for instruction.[1] An institution providing for the training secures aids and allowances from the

[1] *Report of the Secretary of War 1930,* p. 324.

War Department, but the obligation to undergo training is not fixed by that Department, but by the authorities of the institution accepting its conditions. The question would naturally arise whether the training effected under those circumstances is compulsory training which the United States would obligate itself, by the allowance granted, to report upon.

It is interesting to remark that the commission adopted this provision for reporting compulsory preparatory military training on the proposal of France and substantially without debate. It has the effect of throwing light upon the military value of recruits inducted into the army and seems to be a commitment to the principle of divulging information respecting the army it actually maintains.

At first sight, the reporting of preparatory training would seem to furnish an argument for the reporting of subsequent training and military value, that is, the status of trained reserves. The Draft Convention as a whole, however, carefully avoids dealing with the question of war potential, whether in man power or material. There seems to have been a general consensus that the immediate task was to determine what exists rather than what might exist. Determination of the actualities is rather obviously a first step.

In dealing with effectives the closest the Draft Convention came to dealing with trained reserves under the conscript system was Art. 32, by which the contracting parties shall forward annually to the Secretary-General of the League the provisions of their law, relating to effectives in the land, sea and air forces and formations organized on a military basis, embodying information as to:

(1) The total number of days comprised in the first period of service;

(2) The total duration in days of the ensuing periods.

In Arts. 6–9 relating to limitation of effectives, the total number of days of service liability are to be reported, but the total is not there divisible according to the periods of service exacted. The conscript system varies from country to country, but has certain uniform features. Each conscript is subject to an initial period of duty in the active forces; in France, one year. In France, there follows a period of three years in which the citizen is immediately available for military service, though returned to civil life; he is then in the first line of reserve for 16 years and, lastly, in the second line of reserve for eight years. To continue with France for the sake of clarity, men on the available list are liable to annual call for three weeks' training, those in the first reserve for two periods of similar length and those in the second reserve for one week of special exercises.[1]

The Belgian system requires one period of service of from 8 to 14 months for recruits, followed by another amounting to 42 days for most reservists and two such periods for certain categories of reservist troops. Switzerland has a system of 62–92 days' service for recruits and of 13 days for reservists for "refresher training." The Swiss army statistics are kept in terms of service days. Such arrangements constitute the legal liability on which the value of trained reserves depends. The 27 governments in the Preparatory Commission provided formally for reporting the laws in force each year. But there is no provision for reporting how the law is annually applied.

Expenditure by Material Categories Unsolved

The provision for annual publicity of expenditure actually effected on war material is the one matter in the Draft Convention, as it went before the conference, which was undecided in any degree. Art. 33 provides for communication each year of "a statement drawn up in accordance with a standard model, showing by categories of materials the total actual expenditure in the course of the said year on the upkeep, purchase and manufacture of war materials of the land and sea armed forces and formations organized on a military basis." Though publicity on expenditure for air material is not provided for, that is not the nubbin of the difficulty. The trouble revolves around the question of how to show total expenditure by categories of materials. The question is the same one that has kept the Committee on Private

[1] *Armaments Year-Book 1931*, p. 434, 437–438.

Manufacture of Arms from achieving a convention and resulted in postponing its next meeting till after the General Disarmament Conference.[1] The question in its present form did not yield to the technical perspicacity and ingenuity of the Committee of Budgetary Experts, and it, therefore, went to the conference as a conundrum. However, its solution there is likely to be very greatly abetted by the conclusions on other phases of expenditure reached by the budgetary experts.

The unsolved problem has a considerable history, beginning with an initial proposal of the delegation of the Netherlands for an annual report of the number and weight of arms, both in service and reserve, under the 12 categories laid down for the materials defined as subject only to war use in the 1925 convention on trade in arms.[2] That proposal was adopted on first reading simply because no other proposal covering the same ground had been presented, but it was formally opposed by the Japanese delegation on April 21, 1927, and then associated with a comparable alternative draft[3] relating to expenditure on armament, which at the same session was set off against the French proposal that became the forerunner of Arts. 10 and 24 of the Draft Convention. Here cropped up in a slightly different form the important difference, which is still outstanding, between controlling land armament by the direct or indirect methods.[4] When the Dutch proposal came up for second reading on November 22, 1930,[5] a desire for revision of the list led the delegation to propose its study by a committee of experts, which was done. The contest between direct and indirect methods thus had consideration from another angle.

The Subcommittee of Military Experts of the Preparatory Commission dealt solely with the question of material in connection with the Netherlands proposal for publicity. The German, Italian, Spanish, Netherlands, Norwegian and

[1] See Chap. III, D.
[2] See *supra*, p. 64; Art. IB of the first reading.
[3] Art. TA of the first reading.
[4] See discussion *supra*, p. 146 *ff*.
[5] *Documents of the Preparatory Commission*, Series X, p. 217.

Swedish experts were in favor of publicity of material in reserve.[1]

The subcommittee's examination of whether publicity of material in reserve presented drawbacks "from the military point of view" naturally resulted in an affirmative answer. The character of the arguments adduced was eloquent of the state of mind of the military experts. The technical impossibility of supervision was alleged, by which, of course, was meant an indisposition to be supervised. Publicity would reveal the military weak points of certain countries and would not permit arrangements to be made under satisfactory conditions for the conduct of what was called "national defense." Land material not being yet subject to direct limitation, it seemed logical to the prevailing military experts also to establish its publicity on the basis of expenditure. For publicity to be equitable and to provide clear information, it should involve not only numbers, but "the age, the degree of wear, and even the characteristics of the material," so that the complexity of the problem was adduced against it. The possibility of evading publicity by stocking detached parts was the sixth adverse argument. In consequence of these reasons, the question of publicity of reserve stocks did not go beyond the military experts and undergo full examination by the civilian delegates in the final session of the Preparatory Commission.

The experts, from the military point of view, were almost unanimous respecting publicity for material in service. The principal adverse argument was that, as the allowances of units were known, military regulations afforded the evidence on the point and that, therefore, the information was not contributive, while the making known of existing deficiencies would involve the danger of indicating weaknesses to possible enemies or encourage exaggerations.[2] The experts as a group, however, came to the conclusion that, though the figures could be reconstructed from regulation allowances, there was an advantage in having them prepared

[1] *Documents of the Preparatory Commission*, Series X, p. 476.
[2] The argument was adduced by the French, Japanese, Rumanian and Yugoslav experts.

which at least committed the state, while any temptation to exaggerate was not an essential objection to furnishing at all.

The subcommittee reported, with unreserved American approval, a suggestion for an annual statement of the number of weapons in service, differentiated as to age.

The Subcommittee of Military Experts completed its report November 27, and the following day the discussion continued in the commission. The first question posed was whether the commission would accept the table suggested for publicity as to material in service.[1] The proposed table distinguishes three age groups of weapons covering types introduced before January 1, 1890, types introduced between January 1, 1890, and January 1, 1914, and types introduced since January 1, 1914. The land weapons to be reported on under these groupings were:

I. Portable arms:
   (a) Rifles, carbines and muskets (thousands);
   (b) Automatic rifles and other automatic weapons (number);
   (c) Machine guns (number).

II. Pieces of artillery:
   (a) Cannon, howitzers and mortars of a caliber of 15 cms. (5.9 inches) or less (number);
   (b) Cannon, howitzers and mortars of a caliber over 15 cms. (5.9 inches) (number).

III. Tanks of all kinds and armored cars.

Viscount Cecil called attention to the lack of instructions and the indications of lack of agreement among the experts as circumstances making for difficulty in reaching a decision at the time and proposed that the commission adopt an article binding themselves, in reminiscence of Art. 8 of the Covenant, to the interchange of full and frank information according to a table to be prepared by the conference.

René Massigli for France also found himself perplexed by the experts' report and noted the suggestion of the Japanese expert as to the possibility of publicity by value instead of numbers. Referring to the uncompleted work of the Spe-

[1] *Documents of the Preparatory Commission*, Series X, p. 478.

cial Commission on the Private Manufacture of Arms, etc., he thought the adoption of detailed publicity in terms of value would advance agreement all along the line, and introduced a proposal — which was adopted by a vote of 9 to 7 — in substitution for the subcommittee's proposals, and which, with drafting changes only, became Art. 33 of the Draft Convention.[1]

It will be noted that this result left undebated the proposals of the Subcommittee of Military Experts. It should also be remarked that Art. 33 provides for publicity in accordance with a standard model showing, by categories of material, annual expenditure on the upkeep, purchase and manufacture of war materials for both land and sea forces.

BUDGETARY EXPERTS ANALYZE PROBLEM

The commission remitted to the Committee of Budgetary Experts the problem of producing the model called for and that committee in its report dated February 28, 1931, reluctantly came "to the conclusion that it can not recommend any method of detailed publicity by categories of material." This was the only question on its terms of reference on which it did not offer conclusions. Its model statements and draft annex, however, go into considerable detail, and the master lists of items included under the schedules of war material, if accepted by the conference, may go a long way toward facilitating the solution of a baffling question.

The committee in its analysis of the problem stated that the ability to provide figures depended largely on the proportion between war material obtained (1) "by purchase from private manufacturers or autonomous state establishments, or (2) by manufacture in nonautonomous state establishments," which are defined by the committee as establishments "whose expenditure on raw material, salaries and wages, buildings, etc., is entered direct in the budget accounts."[2]

Purchase. As to purchase, many budgets were found to

[1] *Documents of the Preparatory Commission*, Series X, p. 277.
[2] *Official Journal*, XII, p. 693; the definition at p. 685, note.

contain subheads classified according to weapons in a manner suitable for Art. 33. For the most part, these subheads relate to complete and finished weapons and vary, usually without distinction, in the inclusion of repairs and the purchase of raw materials, semifinished parts and separate parts. In this connection the committee found that the distribution of contracts to private establishments, autonomous or nonautonomous state establishments and even regimental workshops presented a great complication in current practice and in the available records.

Manufacture. Reports respecting manufacture were found to raise many questions. Fabrication in nonautonomous state factories would seem to be the most available for Art. 33. But while expenditure on salaries and wages, raw material and buildings are frequently given, accounts seldom are classified according to the types of weapon produced. Such establishments frequently, however, maintain cost accounts showing the cost of each weapon. But these calculations were found irreconcilable with annual budget accounts. There are a number of reasons for this discrepancy. The raw material used in the product was frequently paid for in a different budget year; the labor involved normally comprises expenses chargeable to more than one year; and various overhead expenses have no direct relation to any budget year. The committee pointed out ways by which a reconciliation might be effected between the cost accounts and the budget with respect to a single year's output, but characterized such procedure as unreal unless the production was practically stable from year to year. Among these suggestions was the exclusion of constructive expenditure, such as interest on capital based on a comparison over a period of years. Cost accounts might theoretically be used to establish percentage of expenditure devoted to the output of each category of arms, and it would be possible to use cost account figures directly to indicate expenditure. The combination of these methods would involve mixing budget figures with cost figures drawn up on a different basis, a basis which rarely approximates in a state factory the accounting of a commercial establishment.

Therefore, the resulting figures "would be unlikely to represent with any closeness the expenditure on the war material of the various categories during the year."

Upkeep. As to the upkeep of war material, the committee found it was probably impossible to obtain any complete or consistent account. The cost accounts available present the difficulties referred to, but in many cases even such data are not available, and, as budgets are kept, the upkeep of war material is confused in some cases with the upkeep of stores. Upkeep, in fact, is given different meanings in various states, and in some instances includes repairs and renovation which may amount to complete transformation. The committee believed that the value of any publicity under Art. 33 which did not comprise the cost of upkeep would be small and concluded on this phase of the subject that "it is in practice impossible to classify the cost of upkeep by categories of weapons."

Lastly, the committee called attention to the great difficulty which arises from attempting to go into detail. In the committee's model statement, one of the four heads is war material, and its draft annex shows the items which fall under that schedule.[1] But in facing the question of dividing the items into categories and attempting definitions which would render reports from the different states uniform, the committee was forced to the conclusion that very wide variations would be inevitable. It was further of the opinion that no degree of uniformity could be attained, under present conditions, which would facilitate public comprehension of the system, and which in any case might not operate to the disadvantage of countries acquiring their war material from private manufacturers or autonomous state establishments.

It is pertinent to point out that the report of the committee is not the final word on the matter. The discrepancy between existing accounting systems and the lack of definitions of what falls into various categories defeated the committee's effort to produce practical and equitable formulas. The states in conference could agree to alter their systems

[1] See its text in the Appendix, p. 313.

so as to yield comparable results, and the committee's report in general advanced that possibility. The conference might also solve the question of definitions by laying them down. As the matter stands, the question of publicity of expenditure of categories of material is unsolved.

Other Publicity — Civil Aviation

Arts. 34 and 35 relate to information concerning war vessels. For all vessels not exempt, essential details of the laying down and completion of those built by or for each of the contracting parties, or within their jurisdiction, shall be communicated to the Secretary-General of the League within one month, and the Secretary-General shall communicate the facts immediately to all contracting parties and publish them annually. The names of all vessels shall likewise be communicated.[1]

Arts. 36 and 37 deal with aircraft, on which annual reports of material are to be made. No report is called for upon expenditure. The maximum figures attained in each year are to be the basis of the report. The tables are identical with those under which the material is to be limited and apply for both aëroplanes and dirigibles to the land, sea and air forces. The German delegation here made its customary reservation in favor of the inclusion of material in reserve.

Art. 37 deals with the question of insuring publicity as regards civil aviation. Members of the commission emphasized the importance of its development with relation to armament, and the body decided that regular and official publication of information regarding it would be useful. Not all were convinced that the article belonged in a disarmament convention, holding that the states might more properly provide for the circulation of such data in a convention relating to air navigation. The German delegation made a reservation to this effect. The information to be returned and published is the number and total horse power of civil aëroplanes and dirigibles registered within the juris-

[1] Such reports are made under the Washington and London treaties; for examples, see Department of State, *Treaty Information Bulletin* No. 22, p. 4, and later numbers.

diction of each party and the amounts expended on civil aviation by the government and by local authorities. The United States Government was doubtful whether it would be in a position to furnish data of either type.[1]

The doubt as to the propriety of including such information in a disarmament convention was called to the attention of the Council of the League by the Preparatory Commission, and the point was on the agenda of its 63d session. Therefore, the League Council on May 22, 1931,[2] asked the Communications and Transit Organization to proceed "to an inquiry among all the governments invited to the Disarmament Conference and to a methodical study of the present situation concerning the publication of information on civil aviation whether as regards national regulations, multilateral conventions or special obligations." On this basis, it prepared for the conference a collection of all the provisions in force relating to the exchange or publication of information regarding nonmilitary aviation.[3]

The last form of information to be reported annually and exchanged is the total amount actually expended each year on all armament, land, sea and air, drawn up in accordance with the standard model to be annexed to the article from the report of the Committee of Budgetary Experts.

[1] Respecting the effectives of nonmilitary aviation, the United States Department of Commerce, Aëronautics Branch, was unable to supply detailed information as to commercial and private aviation and to nonmilitary aviation at the disposal of the state or official services. Respecting expenditure of public funds upon nonmilitary commercial aviation, information on direct assistance is available respecting all governmental appropriations and contracts, especially those for air mail; indirect assistance is extended by the establishment of airways, intermediate landing fields and meteorological services. No aids are given to private aviation. Expenditures on "nonmilitary aviation at the disposal of the state or of official services" could be compiled (File 19 of October 31, 1931, addressed to the writer).

[2] *Official Journal*, XII, p. 1128.

[3] See *Study concerning the Present Situation in regard to Publicity of Civil Aviation* . . . (C.95.M.47.1932.VIII.1). The provisional questionnaire is at p. 8.

CHAPTER X

CHEMICALS AND WARFARE

Part V of the Draft Convention consists of the single Art. 39 devoted to chemical arms. By it the contractants, subject to reciprocity, undertake "to abstain from the use in war of asphyxiating, poisonous or similar gases, and of all analogous liquids, substances or processes." They further undertake "unreservedly to abstain from the use of all bacteriological methods of warfare." It will be noted that abstention from the use of bacteria is not subject to reciprocity.

These forms of warfare came into use in 1914–18 and excited a great deal of attention. Part V of the treaty of Versailles imposes the limitations and restrictions upon Germany in order to render possible the initiation of a general limitation of all armaments. Following that preamble, the articles continue as direct obligations upon Germany, with the exception of Art. 171. Its form is distinctive and implies the acceptance of a general policy. "The use of asphyxiating, poisonous or other gases and all analogous liquids, materials or devices *being prohibited*," it says, "their manufacture and importation are strictly forbidden in Germany." At the Washington naval conference, a treaty on prohibited methods of warfare was drawn up in which this provision was quoted and the methods described characterized as "having been justly condemned by the general opinion of the civilized world and a prohibition of such use having been declared in treaties to which a majority of the civilized powers are parties." The states concerned — the United States, the British Empire, France, Italy and Japan — "to the end that this prohibition shall be universally accepted as a part of international law binding alike the conscience and practice of nations declare their assent to such prohibition, agree to be bound thereby as between themselves and invite all other civilized nations to adhere thereto."[1] The other articles of the treaty were similarly declaratory of rules, intended to be international law, respecting protection of lives of neutrals and noncombatants at sea and the prohibition of the use of submarines as commerce destroyers. The treaty as a whole represented an idea, to which the United States was partial, of manufacturing international law on the conduct of warfare. The validity of the treaty depended upon its acceptance by all the signatory parties. France did not ratify, in part because of the provisions respecting submarines, and, though all the other parties were ready to ratify, the document failed to enter into force.

The United States delegation at the Geneva conference on trade in arms in 1925 raised the question a second time. The protocol of June 17,[2] recites the substantive provisions of 1922 in the preamble and declares:

That the high contracting parties, so far as they are not already parties to treaties prohibiting such use, accept this prohibition, agree to extend this prohibition to the use of bacteriological methods of warfare and agree to be bound as between themselves according to the terms of this declaration.

They further pledge the exertion of every effort to induce other states to accede to the protocol.

It is now in force for Australia, Austria, Belgium, the British Empire, Canada, China, Denmark, Egypt, Estonia, Finland, France, Germany, Greece, India, the Irish Free State, Italy, Latvia, Liberia, Mexico, the Netherlands, New Zealand, Persia, Poland, Portugal, Rumania, Siam, South Africa, the Soviet Union, Spain, Sweden, Turkey, Venezuela and Yugoslavia, with the condition of reciprocity expressed in most instances.[3]

[1] William M. Malloy, *Treaties, Conventions*, etc., Vol. III, p. 3118.

[2] League of Nations *Treaty Series*, XCIV, p. 65; Reg. No. 2138.

[3] On September 9, 1931, the status of the protocol in other states was as follows: Brazil, ratification not intended; Czechoslovakia, ratification postponed for consideration with Art. 39 of the Draft Convention after the conference; Japan, ratification processes in course; Luxemburg, ratification processes in course; Norway, under consideration; Switzerland, approval expected at early date; United States, pending in Senate; Uruguay, before Parliament (Document A.30.1931.V, p. 13).

The United States Government transmitted the protocol to the Senate for its advice and consent on January 12, 1926. On June 26, open hearings were held. The burden of these as it reached the public was that relinquishing the chemical arm would be a serious reduction of a form of military strength which was both cheap and easily mobilizable from the United States industrial system. On the following December 9, the protocol was made public and an attacking debate conducted on it in the Senate. On the 13th, it was referred back to the committee, where its continued repose interferes in no wise with the activities of the Chemical Warfare Service of the War Department, which for the fiscal year ended June 30, 1930, spent $979,000 on what were described as "laboratory investigations into chemical developments" and the training of troops "in protective measures against gas attack." The Annual Report of the Secretary of War, 1930, indicates the existence of a contradiction in executive policy. "It has been the aim of our Government," says the chief of staff, "to seek for the international outlawry of the use of toxic gases as a means of combat action."[1] He mentions the 1922 treaty, but not the protocol of 1925, and continues: "In conformity with the general governmental policy, it has been the policy of the War Department to refrain from training troops in the offensive use of chemical weapons." And then the misstatement, characterized as a fact, "that no international agreement restricting the use of chemicals is now in force." The next two sentences read:

It would, moreover, be an extremely hazardous policy to rely on an international agreement as a complete protection against chemical attack. In a death struggle for existence, there would always be the danger that a nation in dire straits would resort to chemical weapons if it saw in that agency the means of escaping defeat and achieving victory.

THE COMMISSION'S DISCUSSIONS

The article in the Draft Convention was due to a joint proposal of Belgium, Czechoslovakia, Poland, Rumania and

[1] *Annual Report of the Secretary of War, 1930*, p. 126.

Yugoslavia.[1] In the discussion, the question arose whether provisions which aimed at codifying rules applicable in war time or prohibiting the use of certain arms belonged in a disarmament convention intended to regulate armament in peace time. The commission adopted the article by a majority vote, thus giving credence to the idea that the Draft Convention should take cognizance of methods of warfare which affected national apprehensions of danger. Another general question discussed was whether such a provision was necessary in the Draft Convention in view of the protocol of 1925 being in force. This question was decided in favor of inclusion on the ground that the parties to the protocol and the convention might be different and, therefore, a larger effect would be gained. The point that inclusion in the Draft Convention would facilitate a wider acceptance of the prohibition was not made, but it is obvious that some states which might not take separate action on an isolated protocol would be quite willing to accept its substance as a part of a treaty whose general purposes they desired to realize.

The 1925 protocol has been generally ratified on the condition of reciprocity. The question arose in the commission whether abstention from the use of chemical arms should not be absolute. Recognizing that the use of gases could only be subject to reciprocity, the commission decided that abstention from the use of bacteriological methods should be absolute. Respecting the deliberate spreading of disease by bacteria, the commission says in its report:

> The use of such methods would, in any case, constitute a crime against international law, in that this arm necessarily strikes the whole population, and no civilized government could possibly wish to be guilty of such a crime even against the armies of a criminal government which had itself resorted to such methods.

The Soviet delegation proposed that all methods and appliances for chemical aggression and bacteriological warfare should be destroyed within three months of the entrance into force of the convention.

[1] *Documents of the Preparatory Commission*, Series IV, p. 332.

In the article as adopted on first reading,[1] there were paragraphs providing for the abstention in peace time from preparation of the prohibited methods and an undertaking not to permit their importation, exportation or manufacture. These paragraphs were reminiscent of the inhibition placed upon Austria, Bulgaria, Germany and Hungary in the peace treaties. In the commission, however, the opinion prevailed respecting both them and the Soviet proposal that such measures created an illusion of action rather than a contribution to solution of the problem. It also raised a query as to responsibility for control and ran into the very difficult scientific field of chemical development. Failure to adopt that provision indicated a disposition to rely upon good will and to bank upon the feeling of responsibility of obligated states.

The German delegation proposed the prohibition of bombing from the air, of large caliber guns and of tanks of every kind on the score that they were essentially offensive in character and intrinsically menaced the civilian population as well as armies. The proposal was rejected. It may be suggested that this decision of the commission tends to draw a line between what might be called normal and abnormal weapons, the prohibition of chemical weapons affecting abnormal military arms.

The German delegation expressed the opinion that the prohibition of chemical weapons should extend to preparation for their use, and the special organization of troops for that branch of instruction in their use.

Poland has suggested that a guaranty in addition to the good faith implied in Art. 39 be sought. Its delegation proposed[2] that the possibility of concluding a convention for affording international aid on as liberal a scale as possible to any country chemically or bacteriologically attacked be considered at some future time. Nothing has been done to realize this suggestion, so that it can not be stated whether the idea would work out as a special extension of humanitarian and sanitary assistance or whether it would involve a

[1] *Documents of the Preparatory Commission*, Series X, p. 442.
[2] *Report*, par. 227.

mobilization of world scientific resources on behalf of the attacked state. Quite possibly both will be examined when the problem comes up for study.

Art. 39 represents complete harmony among the 27 states of the Preparatory Commission. The conference will doubtless accept so much. There is, however, one question which is remitted to the conference for determination. On December 2, 1930, the British delegation in the commission presented a memorandum[1] in which it raised the question whether the phrase "or similar gases" should be interpreted to prohibit tear gases. The opinion of the commission was asked on the point. The French delegation stated that their military regulations prohibited gases causing tears, sneezing, etc., Mr. Gibson for the United States called attention to the fact that the British memorandum raised a question of technical difficulty and wide ramifications. Tear gases were for the most part used in police work for controlling mobs, etc., though they might serve military convenience as harassing agencies. On the other hand, the suggestion raised the question of smokes, which could be either chemical or mechanical, and in that connection involved the whole field of tactical screening. After a short debate of the question, which really embodies a definition of what are prohibited chemical arms, the commission thought it desirable to refer the question to governments and to ask them to make careful studies of the matter so as to be in a position to settle all aspects of the problem at the conference. In this respect an addition to Art. 39 may be expected from the conference.

[1] *Documents of the Preparatory Commission*, Series X, p. 311.

CHAPTER XI

THE PERMANENT DISARMAMENT COMMISSION

There is to be a Permanent Disarmament Commission with "the duty of following the execution of the convention." If the conference does nothing else than create this commission, it will have profoundly altered the position of armament in the modern world. Armament is the most extreme expression of national egoism and to subject it to mutual international supervision is to establish a principle of revolutionary effect. The principle may be regarded as now established, since the Preparatory Commission, which itself included the militarily capable states, adopted Part VI, Chapter A, Arts. 40–49 of the Draft Convention unanimously; no one of the 37 states which came to the fresh consideration of the matter at the conference will have any reason to object at all to the principle.

The provisions relative to the Permanent Disarmament Commission which are to come before the conference are of a thoroughgoing character, calculated to establish a body of marked efficiency for its purpose. They are, in fact, noticeably different in liberal character from most parts of the convention. The difference is probably accounted for by the fact that every interested state was conservative respecting its existing institutions and resisted changes or restrictions which would perceptibly alter its habits of life and particularly its habits of mind; but the establishment of a Permanent Disarmament Commission interfered with no vested interest of material or mentality and, in consequence, the problem was considered with a logic and aloofness absent from the discussions of other phases of the problem.

The establishment of the Permanent Disarmament Commission further calls attention to a factor which makes for development in the current régime of constant negotiation under conference conditions. It was France which first proposed such a commission in its original proposal that, jointly with the British proposal, became the basis for the Draft Convention.[1] The French interest in the organ was due to the preoccupation of the national policy with the idea of guaranties. In the Preparatory Commission it met approval because of its obvious utility, for coordination and the alleviation of possible tensions. The unanimity of the Preparatory Commission was complete in accepting the text agreed upon, and the text itself is complete, except in one respect. The governments which are to appoint the members of the committee were left to the decision of the conference, which once again will have to reconcile the necessity of choosing a limited number of representatives so as to satisfy the principle of the equality of states.

The Permanent Disarmament Commission proposal of the French delegation was voted into the text approved on first reading as part of a chapter dealing with exchange of information and with complaints and derogations. At the sixth session, second part, of the Preparatory Commission these delicate questions, on which sundry additional proposals had been made, were remitted to a subcommittee, of which Nicolas Politis (Greece) was chairman and the representatives of the United States, Belgium, the British Empire, China, Finland, France, Greece, Italy, Japan and Turkey were members.[2] The subcommittee had before it two major texts. One of British origin provided for a commission whose whole function was to review and report upon the information supplied by the contracting parties,[3] and which was to be summoned by the Secretary-General of the League. A French substitute text[4] embodied the ideas of

[1] *Documents of the Preparatory Commission*, Series IV, p. 364. Arts. 22–27 are the provisions, which contain some of the most useful features carried over into the Draft Convention.

[2] *Ibid.*, Series X, p. 210.

[3] *Documents of the Preparatory Commission*, Series X, p. 471, substantially Arts. 40 and 49 of the Draft Convention.

[4] *Ibid.*, p. 472. In the note accompanying it is the following statement: "While putting forward these new proposals, the French delegation continues to think that international supervision is the necessary and natural complement of any convention on the limitation of armaments. But, as it does not appear likely that unanimity can be reached in the commission on provisions involving strict supervision and investigations on the spot, the French delegation is ready to consider a less complete system which would nevertheless make it possible to supervise — and to a large extent insure the execution of—the obligations laid down in the provisions *adopted*."

THE PERMANENT DISARMAMENT COMMISSION

Arts. 46 and 47 among others. A further French amendment reverted to that delegation's concern with violation of the convention. The Chinese and Turkish delegations also made proposals respecting the method of selecting the commission. The text elaborated from these elements was adopted on second reading on December 2, unanimously and without discussion.

The Permanent Disarmament Commission is to be set up at Geneva with the duty of "following the execution" of the convention. It is to consist of a number of members, which is to be fixed by the conference, and the members are to be appointed by the governments to be determined by the conference. Though governments appoint the members, they are not to represent their governments, whose function and influence end with the naming of the person. The members of the commission are to be appointed for a term of years, and during that term of office are irreplaceable unless death, voluntary resignation or serious and permanent illness should create a vacancy. The commissioners are not necessarily technical experts, but may be assisted by such experts.

The commission is to be convened for its initial meeting on summons by the Secretary-General of the League, within three months of the entrance of the convention into force, for the purpose of electing a provisional president and vice-president and of drawing up its rules of procedure. Thereafter, it will act with a very large degree of independence under the rules of procedure, made by itself and subject only to the condition that they must be on the basis of the provisions of the convention. The commission is to meet annually in ordinary session on a date to be fixed in its rules. It may hold an extraordinary session on the summons of its president, in the cases provided for in the convention and whenever an application to that effect is made by any contracting party.

As the Draft Convention stands, the commission is assigned six specific duties under it, in addition to the general review of information to be submitted in accordance with its terms. If any state maintaining the conscription system should increase the period of service owing to a fall in the birth rate, the measures taken and justificatory reasons are to be notified to the commission by Art. 8. By Art. 13 any modification in the distribution of naval tonnage by transfer from one category to another is to be notified to the commission. The commission is to be notified immediately if any state temporarily suspends any provision of the convention for the assigned reason that "a change of circumstances constitutes . . . a menace to its national security," and is to weigh the situation created, simultaneously with a mutual consultation among the other contracting parties (Art. 50). The commission is to receive, grant hearings and report to the contracting parties and the League Council upon any complaint by one party that another has excess armaments, or is violating or endeavoring to violate provisions of the convention (Art. 52). The commission is to render an opinion to enable the League Council to fix the date of the second General Disarmament Conference, a fixation dependent upon numerous delicate and responsible considerations[1] (Art. 58). During the term of the convention it must concur in any request for a fresh examination, with a view to revision, of any provisions of the convention due to changes of condition "as the result of technical transformations or special circumstances" (Art. 59). It is, however, likely that the conference may invest the commission with other functions in putting the Draft Convention into final shape, and its primary duty of reporting upon the data regularly called for by the convention might very likely result in extraordinary sessions.

Two-thirds of the members of the commission are required for a quorum, but all of its decisions are to be taken by a majority vote of the members present, each member having only one vote. The standard provision in postwar international organizations for representation of interests affected is included:

> Any high contracting party not having a member of its nationality on the commission shall be entitled to send a member appointed

[1] *Cf. Report*, par. 286.

THE PERMANENT DISARMAMENT COMMISSION

for the purpose to sit at any meetings of the commission during which a question specially affecting the interests of that party is considered.

This seems at first sight to be a little out of line with the general principle of the commission's organization, since the *ad hoc* member would more definitely represent the national interest than a regular member of the commission. It is the clear intention of the chapter that the commissioners do not represent the state, but an *ad hoc* member would almost certainly do so in some measure. The apparent discrepancy is got around, at least in part, by a further provision that each member of the commission "shall be entitled on his own responsibility to have any person heard or consulted who is in a position to throw any light on the question which is being examined." Realizing that the questions coming before the commission would be very delicate, the Preparatory Commission wished to emphasize that great circumspection should be exercised in selecting sources of information and avoided the temptation to lay down any rules in this regard by granting to the commissioners the right to call persons to be heard or consulted on their individual responsibility. It would then follow that the normal procedure in the case of an *ad hoc* member would be for him not to appear as an advocate, but to exercise the right of having an advocate of the national interest which caused him to be on the commission to be heard by it.[1]

In case the commission has questions concerning derogations from the convention or complaints of one party against another before it, the votes of members appointed by the parties concerned shall not be counted in determining the majority. The commission in this way acquires the faculty of maintaining its decisions upon a neutral basis, since the rule applies both to *ad hoc* and ordinary members. The majority vote provision facilitates decisions, and it is stipulated that a minority report may be drawn up. Moreover, each member is entitled to require that any report of the commission shall take account of his opinions or suggestions, "if necessary in the form of a separate report." Thus

[1] The same practice would naturally be followed by a permament commissioner in case a national interest were involved.

insurance is given that all shades of opinion may be made public.

The normal function of the Permanent Disarmament Commission is to receive all information supplied by the contracting parties to the Secretary-General of the League "in pursuance of their international obligations in this regard." Specifically as things stand at present, that provision would bring to the commission the material supplied for the *Armaments Year-Book* and respecting the international trade in arms under Art. 8 of the Covenant; the annual reports respecting effectives, land and naval material and total expenditure under Part IV of the Draft Convention; any information respecting manufacture of arms to be determined under the incomplete convention on private manufacture; possibly the returns on civil aviation with relation to military aviation; and perhaps other data. The commission is to make at least one annual report on the information submitted to it and on any other information "that may reach it from a responsible source and that it may consider worth attention." The object of the report is to show the situation as regards the fulfillment of the convention. In other words, the data are to be studied by the commission in relation to the tables of limitation or reduction (whichever they prove to be) embodied in Parts I-III of the convention. The annual report, therefore, is indicated as an annual, official and independent check-up on the status of armament. The commission in its rules of procedure will lay down a definition of what sources, in addition to governments, it regards as responsible and as able to furnish information which it may consider worth attention.

The report is to be communicated "forthwith" to the contracting parties and to the Council of the League. It "shall be published" on the date fixed in the rules of procedure of the commission. Apparently in line with its independent character, the commission itself controls both the communication and publication of its reports.

No provision is made for the finances of the commission, either with regard to honoraria or expenses of meetings or of publication. The Preparatory Commission considered the question of salaries, but came to no decision, "especially as the question will readily settle itself in due course."[1] The simplest method is to provide that its expenses be met through a special section of the League budget.

As stated, the only fundamental questions outstanding respecting the commission are that of its composition and the term of service of its members. The period of appointment should create no difficulty and was left open by the Preparatory Commission because the period has an obvious relation to other lapses of time in the convention, including its duration, all of which were remitted to the conference. The problem of composition of the commission is distinctly a political one which, considering the diversity of views expressed in the Preparatory Commission, had to be left to the plenary conference. There was never a question but that the commissioners should be appointed by governments. It is scarcely conceivable that states would intrust judgments concerning the keeping of their engagements on matters regarding which their feelings are so tender to any group of purely private individuals. The fact that the governments have foregone any claim to control or replace their appointees was, surprisingly, determined without debate or difficulty. But the particularism which lies at the bottom of the armament interest manifested itself in the appointment of the commission. Some delegations to the Preparatory Commission[2] favored a commission composed of representatives of all the high contracting parties, but it was decided that an organ of comparatively small size should be established.[3] The British project suggested granting the right of appointment to the Council of the League and to certain non-Member states. The French amendment conferred the right on the states members of the Council, on non-Member states to be designated by the conference and on certain League states not represented on

[1] *Documents of the Preparatory Commission*, Series X, p. 245, 247, 248.

[2] A Turkish amendment to this effect was considered (*Documents of the Preparatory Commission*, Series X, p. 473).

[3] The vote in the subcommittee (*ibid.*, p. 470) was 6 to 3. Belgium, the United States, Great Britain, France, Italy and Japan voted against universal representation, and China, Finland and Turkey for it.

the Council, which were to be designated by the conference. A Chinese proposal recommended that the Council should elect the countries entitled to nominate members. It falls to the conference to decide between these and any other methods of selecting appointing states which may be proposed during its session.

The provisions described were not only unanimously adopted, but were not the subject of any reservation. Only one alternative suggestion was maintained in the report.[1] The commissioners may be assisted by "technical experts." The French delegation favored commissioners who were technical experts, "giving purely technical opinions and not prejudging any political conclusions that the governments might draw from those opinions." The majority of the commission rejected this point of view. The French delegation stated that it still preferred that system.

[1] *Report*, par. 238.

CHAPTER XII

INSURANCE OF GOOD FAITH AND FULFILLMENT

Intimately connected with the establishment of the Permanent Disarmament Commission are two chapters entitled "Derogations" and "Procedure regarding Complaints." Here for the first time the technical control of armament impinges on the underlying political[1] conditions in definite provisions. In addition to the establishment in principle of this inevitable relation, the appearance of the three articles in the Draft Convention by a unanimous vote of the Preparatory Commission represents an important recognition of realities hitherto avoided.

The United States, for instance, until the eleventh hour toyed with the idea that armament control should be kept in its exclusive compartment, settled in its own technical terms, and should involve no commitments beyond tons and guns and dollars. Some other states leaned in the same direction. The general burden of the argument was an over expansion of the fundamental condition underlying any treaty, namely, that it is based on good faith.

---

[1] "Political" is a weasel word of international relations; no one knows what it means. Judge Kellogg in an observation on the case of the Free Zones (second phase) says a political question "is a question which is exclusively within the competence of a sovereign state . . . There is no rule or principle of law, no norm of equity, justice or even good conscience, which the Court can apply; for, unless limited by treaties, the power of a state in this domain is unlimited" (Publications of the Court, Series A, No. 24 (A/B, No. 39), p. 41). But that is to say that "political" and "domestic jurisdiction" are synonymous, which cannot be true. Politics has two meanings, the practice of government and the partisan alignment of citizens for that purpose. A "political" question may be one connected with either meaning, or one reflecting the policy, that is, the individual and interested attitude of a government. In international relations the word should imply the latter meaning and connotes a matter which a state insists on having examined in connection with the interests involved instead of on the basis of recognized rules.

Case A. Notion of Circumstantial Menace

The provisions under review are the "escape" clause and the mechanism for handling violations. In ordinary treaties, the considerations underlying these clauses are taken care of either by a duration clause or by a compromisory clause providing that any dispute between the parties as to the interpretation or application of the treaty's provisions shall be left to pacific settlement. These clauses are included in the Draft Convention (Arts. 54, 57*ff*.), but by common consent are not enough in an armament agreement.

Underlying "political" conditions are in the back of the minds of all negotiators in any gathering to limit or reduce armament. It has always been so at Geneva; it was so at Washington and again at London. In the treaties effected at Washington, the political consideration took the form of a treaty signed December 13, 1921,[1] by which the United States, the British Empire, France and Japan agreed "between themselves to respect their rights in relation to their insular possessions and insular dominions in the region of the Pacific Ocean"; in case of a controversy involving those rights, they provided for a joint conference to consider and adjust the matter; if those rights should be "threatened by the aggressive action of any other power," they agreed to communicate on the joint or separate action to be taken "to meet the exigencies of the particular situation." On the entrance of that treaty into force on August 17, 1923, the Anglo-Japanese alliance of July 13, 1911, was terminated.

The whole arrangement, though a separate document, was a substantial condition making possible the treaty for the limitation of naval armament of February 6, 1922.[2] In Art. XIX of the latter treaty, there was a purely "political" agreement. By it "the United States, the British Empire and Japan agree that the status quo at the time of the

[1] Malloy, *Treaties Conventions*, etc., Vol. III, 3094; United States *Treaty Series* No. 669.

[2] *Ibid.*, p. 3100; United States *Treaty Series* No. 671; League of Nations *Treaty Series*.

signing of the present treaty with regard to fortification and naval bases shall be maintained" in certain specified areas. And the same treaty additionally contains this provision:

Art. XXI. If during the term of the present treaty the requirements of the national security of any contracting power in respect of naval defense are, in the opinion of that power, materially affected by any change of circumstances, the contracting powers will, at the request of such power, meet in conference with a view to the reconsideration of the provisions of the treaty and its amendment by mutual agreement.

In view of possible technical and scientific developments, the United States, after consultation with the other contracting powers, shall arrange for a conference of all the contracting powers which shall convene as soon as possible after the expiration of eight years from the coming into force of the present treaty to consider what changes, if any, in the treaty may be necessary to meet such developments.

The London naval treaty of April 22, 1930, was negotiated by statesmen who recognized even more clearly that the technical problem in front of them was only a manifestation of underlying conflicts of national policy. An extensive effort was made to base the treaty upon what has been called a consultative pact. Again, the United States was the chief resistant. Secretary of State Stimson of the delegation to London on March 26 issued a statement in which he said "that America had no objection to entering into a consultative pact as such," but would not enter into any treaty where there was danger "of its obligation being misunderstood as involving a promise to render military assistance or guaranteeing protection by military force to another nation." He continued:

Such a misunderstanding might arise if the United States entered into such a treaty as a *quid pro quo* for the reduction of the naval forces of another power. That danger has hitherto inhered in the present situation, where France has been demanding mutual security as a condition of naval reduction, as appears from her original statement of her case last December.

If, however, this demand for security could be satisfied in some other way, then the danger of a misunderstanding of a consultative pact would be eliminated, and in such case the question would be approached from an entirely different standpoint. In such case the American delegation would consider the matter with an entirely open mind.

The London treaty as it entered into force on December 31, 1930, contained the following provision:[1]

Art. 21. If, during the term of the present treaty, the requirements of the national security of any high contracting party in respect of vessels of war limited by Part III of the present treaty are in the opinion of that party materially affected by new construction of any power other than those who have joined in Part III of this treaty, that high contracting party will notify the other parties to Part III as to the increase required to be made in its own tonnages within one or more of the categories of such vessels of war, specifying particularly the proposed increases and the reasons therefor, and shall be entitled to make such increase. Thereupon the other parties to Part III of this treaty shall be entitled to make a proportionate increase in the category or categories specified; and the said other parties shall promptly advise with each other through diplomatic channels as to the situation thus presented.

Involves the Aggression Problem

The question involved in providing an escape clause for the Draft Convention ran back into the early debate in the Temporary Mixed Commission respecting the action to be taken in case of a state sustaining an aggression. It will be recalled that the effort to define aggression has failed on several occasions, but that progress has been made in the interval in dealing with that putative condition. Both the convention on financial assistance and the general convention to improve the means of preventing war[2] provide for appraising the conditions of fact which would constitute a recognizable act of aggression, though avoiding definitions in advance.

Both the British and French drafts, from which the Preparatory Commission began work, contained articles dealing with the circumstances under which a contracting state

[1] *Armaments Year-Book, 1931*, p. 1122; League of Nations *Treaty Series*, CXII, p. 87; Reg. No. 2608.
[2] See *supra*, Chap. IV, p. 74 and 83.

would be entitled to increase its own armament. Both drafts contemplated any derogation from the convention as calculated to meet specific conditions and as temporary. Viscount Cecil's text made three exceptions for a state:

(1) If a war in which it is a belligerent has broken out, or
(2) If it is threatened with a rebellion, or
(3) If this increase is effected with the consent of the Council of the League of Nations.

The French draft contemplated only the case when a contractant might be "compelled by the unjustified aggression of another power to resort to measures of mobilization" as defined in the draft. In that case, the state would be released for the duration of the conflict, but the pacificatory machinery of the League of Nations would be immediately brought into action.[1]

On the first reading, no decision was taken between these proposed systems. In the sixth session (first part) of the Preparatory Commission, the subcommittee appointed on November 21, 1930, was assigned to consider the problem. In it the United States delegation proposed that the system of derogations should be limited to the case of a change of circumstances constituting a menace to the national security of a contracting party.[2] The immediate examination of the situation by the Permanent Disarmament Commission (at the time well developed) would put the contracting states in a position to decide their own course of action. The subcommittee accepted the American draft with the single addition that notifications of an intended derogation should be made to the Permanent Commission through the Secretary-General of the League at the same time that it was made to the contracting parties.

The British[3] and French drafts passed over on first reading, the American proposal, and that proposal as amended by the subcommittee, came before the Preparatory Commission on November 25, 1930, when there was also pre-

[1] *Documents of the Preparatory Commission*, Series X, p. 452.
[2] The phraseology occurs in the Washington treaty, the French draft and the London treaty.
[3] There was also a second edition of the British draft printed.

sented a fifth proposal from the Yugoslav delegation, which had not been represented on the subcommittee.[1] The Yugoslav proposal recited three circumstances in which a state might increase its armaments. The first was "if it is threatened with imminent aggression or if a wrongful act of aggression has been committed against it." The second was "if it is faced with the threat of an organized rebellion or general rising." The third depended on the consent of the Council of the League. M. Politis, chairman of the subcommittee, in introducing the question expressed the hope "that, as the substance was the same," the Yugoslav proposal would be retired in favor of the American. The Yugoslav delegate did withdraw his own and accept the American proposal, which he considered "quite satisfactory." The idea of defining aggression once more faded from the picture.

American Formula Adopted

Everything was now set to vote on the American formula, but Viscount Cecil suggested that the discussion be postponed until the Preparatory Commission had taken its decisions respecting the constitution of the Permanent Disarmament Commission. This was agreed to, and the provisions respecting derogations were brought up immediately after the passage of those articles on the following day. On November 26, debate was resumed upon the now single (revised) American text which read as follows:[2]

If, during the life of the present convention, a change of circumstances constitutes, in the opinion of any high contracting party, a menace to its national security, such high contracting party may derogate temporarily, in so far as concerns itself, from any article or articles of the present convention, other than those expressly designed to apply in the event of war, provided:

(a) That such high contracting party shall immediately notify the other high contracting parties and at the same time the Permanent Disarmament Commission, through the Secretary-General of

[1] *Documents of the Preparatory Commission*, Series X, p. 237.

[2] *Documents of the Preparatory Commission*, Series X, p. 250. This text differs from the final Art. 50 only in drafting changes.

the League of Nations, of such temporary derogation, and of the extent thereof.

(b) That, simultaneously with the notification referred to in point (a), the high contracting party shall communicate to the other high contracting parties and, at the same time, to the Permanent Disarmament Commission, through the Secretary-General of the League of Nations, a full explanation of the change of circumstances referred to above.

Thereupon the other high contracting parties shall promptly take concerted counsel as to the situation thus presented.

When the reasons for such temporary derogation have ceased to exist, the said high contracting party shall reduce its armaments to the level agreed upon in the convention, and shall make immediate notification to the other high contracting parties.

The Preparatory Commission's debate took place under the conviction that the provisions would never have to be applied. It was Erik Colban of Norway who recalled that the cognate stipulation of the London Naval Conference had been inserted with such a hope and that it was with the same feeling that he would vote. The president indicated that the whole commission shared that sentiment.

Back of the remark lay considerable progress in drawing world policy together in a unified front toward the fears that breed national insecurity. It was a new stage in the meeting of the minds of states that feel themselves secure, and so are willing to stand on their record, and those which feel themselves insecure, and so are bidding to have their status quo underwritten. The easy and the uneasy found themselves on the same platform.

Hugh Gibson of the United States defined the meaning of the document before the vote. The formula was not the result of his own country's concern, and his government had accepted in the Washington and London treaties much more rigid — that is less elastic — forms of escape clauses. The United States was further prepared to accept much more rigid conditions than any thus far suggested.[1] But the present form was believed to be generally acceptable.

[1] The reader will perceive that what Mr. Gibson refers to as more rigid conditions indicate a willingness to be bound more fully without possibility of derogation. That is the typical attitude of the secure state.

The present clause, Mr. Gibson implied, sought to give a definite application to the doctrine of *rebus sic stantibus*.[1] "It is obvious," he said, "that the delicate problem of release from treaty obligations is one of infinite variety, applying in a different measure and in different ways to nearly every country." It was hopeless to attempt to set down provisions covering one set of conditions alone or an itemized statement of all the special sets of circumstances which would justify a country in seeking relief from the treaty obligations.

The point of departure of the article was that "when a menace to international security exists in the opinion of any people, no treaty provisions will survive as against the imperious demands of self-preservation." The doctrine of *rebus sic stantibus*, it may be parenthetically remarked, has created much confusion because its application has depended solely upon a state's own action, and there have been very few guiding lines of a general character for appraising proper or improper reliance upon it. Mr. Gibson remarked that if an itemized statement of the various sets of circumstances justifying a state in seeking relief from the treaty obligations were drawn up, many states would be reluctant to accept it. There were "unforeseen and unforeseeable circumstances which might arise menacing their very national existence, beyond any prescribed in our list." But, "aside from the clearly foreseen factors and those I have referred to as unforeseen and unforeseeable, there exists a third category, namely, definite apprehensions as to the future which can not be entered in any treaty."

The result was the broadest possible escape clause. "By broadening the opportunities for escape, we shall, in fact, increase the probability of observance." With its right to preservation fully guarded, low figures could be more

[1] This doctrine was not mentioned in the debate, but the doctrine of treaties remaining valid while conditions continue the same is the obvious substance of the article. The fundamental objection to that doctrine has been that it implicitly recognized a unilateral right to determine a change of conditions. Art. 50 starts from that premise, but establishes immediate responsibility for justifying the action.

fully justified to a nation's own people, and there would be a willingness to undertake the treaty's obligations "without specific reservations covering their national apprehensions." On the other hand, and as a practical matter, no state would be likely to undergo the heavy responsibility of upsetting a world-wide agreement for light and frivolous motives. Every state must give to the other contracting parties a full explanation of the reasons justifying its action, and that would deter resort to the clause for any except the most vital and serious causes, which "would surely be included within any list of derogations, were we gifted with sufficient vision of the future to draw up such a list."

The article was voted by the Preparatory Commission 23 to 1. The adverse vote was that of the Soviet Union. Mr. Lunacharsky had stated that the common object of the derogations was "to enable any particular state to cancel the whole convention at a favorable moment, and thus nullify its value, which is small enough already." To that statement Viscount Cecil replied that it was practically impossible that the derogations could be used "lightly, or casually, or dishonestly" and that no state would so act; "if it did it would suffer heavily for it." René Massigli of France emphasized that the necessity of a state applying the article required a justification of its action and that it would be in an awkward position if it could not satisfy the commission and contracting parties. To suggest that the clause was a means to avoid obligations was to misconstrue the work done. M. Politis, chairman of the subcommittee, confirmed these views, but the Soviet delegate in casting his adverse vote maintained that the commission should not provide for entirely exceptional cases.

Full Responsibility for Derogation

Art. 50 succeeds in accomplishing its purpose by relying upon the fact that no state can act irresponsibly under it and by avoiding any attempt either to lay down conditions entitling a state to act or to afford it in advance any authorization of action. Any derogation must emanate from a decision of the state making it and will take place on its sole responsibility. In order to suspend temporarily any provision of the convention, a contracting party must be convinced that a change of circumstances has taken place and that this change constitutes "a menace to its national security."[1] The suspension runs only with respect to the state making it, so that there is no likelihood of an argument respecting whether or not the unilateral action of one contracting party affects the obligations of others. Articles expressly applying to the event of war are not subject to derogation at all. Two articles only seem to be affected by this in the Draft Convention. Art. 20 prevents additions to a fleet from vessels under construction or in the jurisdiction of a state, and Art. 39 is the prohibition of chemical arms.

If a state should reach a unilateral decision to suspend any provision of the convention, it establishes new obligations for itself. The first obligation is the immediate notification of the temporary suspension and of its extent to the other contracting parties and the Permanent Disarmament Commission. The second is the simultaneous and identic notification of "a full explanation of the change of circumstances." Fulfillment of either or both obligations puts the derogating state under critical review with respect to its action. The Preparatory Commission would immediately convene, and, in making its report, the vote of the derogating state could not be counted in determining a majority.[2]

Upon the receipt of the notice of temporary suspension and of the explanation of circumstances, "the other high contracting parties shall promptly advise as to the situation

[1] It has been mentioned that security is a subjective emotion, in other words, that it consists very largely of what a nation chooses to think about its circumstances. The difficulty in handling such emotions in contracts, private or international, lies in getting hold of their objective content. Here by authorizing a state to base its derogation upon a menace to security, a basis is afforded for examining its content. The inevitable result should be a considerable deflation of the conception of security.

[2] Art. 45. Art. 50 does not provide in terms for the convening of the commission, but this was the intention of the subcommittee whose report says: "The situation thus created would have to be examined at once by the Permanent Commission" (*Documents of the Preparatory Commission*, Series X, p. 470).

thus presented." It is thus their duty under the treaty to enter into consultations, which would doubtless take place while the Permanent Disarmament Commission was preparing its report. The convention has no other provision, but the report of the drafting subcommittee comments that "the contracting parties would have to decide on a course of action,"[1] and it is, of course, obvious that a situation might be better handled without a definite decision than with one.

It is almost inconceivable that a state would make use of the derogation clause unless its governmental authorities were fully convinced that it was completely justified in taking the step. Unless they were calling far too extensively on their own ego, the justificatory circumstances would undoubtedly be of such a character that they were a disturbing factor in the part of the world affected. It is more than likely that the actual circumstances could be managed and controlled by some form of the growing fabric of pacific settlement. If not, the state's action would be found internationally to be justified or not justified. If the Permanent Disarmament Commission and the other contracting parties found its action justified, well and good.

But it is entirely obvious that a change of circumstances constituting a menace to national security could occur only on the initiative of another state. Now if state A were justified in recognizing a legitimate menace to its national security, state B, which had produced the menace, would not be in a happy situation. It would scarcely be in a position to derogate from the convention by expressing an opinion that a change of circumstances had created a menace to *its* national security. Its alternative then would be to menace state A with the armament which the convention afforded it, or flatly to violate its obligation.

Any menace it could create with its conventional armament would be far more likely to originate in the condition of state A's nerves than upon realities which the other contracting parties and the Permanent Disarmament Commission would be able to take into account. In that aspect,

[1] *Documents of the Preparatory Commission*, Series X, p. 470.

there is very little to encourage state A in sending a notification of suspension or in state B acting in such a way as to provoke it. Either of them in its own interest would find it far simpler, and infinitely less awkward, to think up a way to continue negotiations on whatever points of tension were involved or to leave the question at issue to some form of pacific settlement, with the odds on conciliation since the difference would probably be more in point of view than in substantive quality. State B would be in particularly bad if it simply violated the limitations to which it had bound itself under the convention. It would immediately find the governments of all other contracting parties opposed to its action, and under the convention it could not possibly have arrived at this point without having disregarded the entire chapter relating to the procedure as to complaints.

Case B. Violation the Concern of All

Part VI, Chapter C, is entitled "Procedure regarding Complaints" and consists of two articles. By the first of these the contracting states recognize that any violation of the convention "is a matter of concern to all the parties." This would have the effect of establishing a universal solidarity in favor of maintaining the obligations inviolate. A violation becomes an offense against every contracting party. The article appeared in the original British draft of 1927.[1] It was adopted by the subcommittee headed by M. Politis and was unanimously voted into the Draft Convention without any discussion.[2] It is certain to appear in the final convention.

The matter of complaints and their handling was before the Preparatory Commission from the outset. It was obvious all along that in a matter as novel and complicated as registering national armaments under an international standard, many debatable questions of fact might arise. A change in handling effectives or an alteration of material might seem entirely proper to the state effecting it and appear to another state to result in exceeding the engagement.

[1] *Documents of the Preparatory Commission*, Series X, p. 454, 471.
[2] *Ibid.*, p. 254, 318.

In armament rivalry there have always been two levels: the first and obvious one is based on general strength; the lesser, more puzzling and aggravating, is the rivalry in details, such, for instance, as the transformation of a certain number of men in infantry regiments into machine-gun detachments. The tensions which arise in this latter type of change were illustrated after the Washington naval treaty. "The 67th Congress made an appropriation of $6,500,000 to increase the elevation of the turret guns of 13 United States capital ships. Congress was informed erroneously but with candid intent (*sic*) that the guns of the British fleet had had their elevations similarly increased. The British Government stated that this information was incorrect."[1] In view of the misrepresentation accounting for the appropriation, it was not expended. The contemplated change was not illegal under the treaty, but would have disturbed the balance of strength. The incident, particularly in its public airing, left an impression which might well have justified formal examination if any machinery under the treaty had been provided for investigating complaints.

In a convention intended to be universal, the possibility of technical questions involving the effect of changes in organization or material are much increased. Provision for a method to examine such questions was made in both the French and British drafts, which were both carried through the first reading. The French draft[2] was very similar to the final American proposal relating to derogations and had a general effect of permitting a revision of conventional provisions to satisfy a claimant state. This idea was further applied to an authorization (by decision of a group of the parties) to exceed the limits fixed. The British draft contemplated a complaint of one party against another on the score that it was exceeding the agreed figures "or is making such changes in its armaments, or is embarking on such preparations as are likely to disturb international

[1] Memorandum by Capt. Frank H. Schofield, U.S.N., *Annual Report of the Secretary of the Navy, 1923*, p. 114.
[2] *Documents of the Preparatory Commission*, Series X, p. 454.

relations or the good understanding between nations, or is in any way violating the provisions of the convention." Such complaint was to result in a consultation. Use of the Permanent Disarmament Commission was included in a revised British draft put before the subcommittee,[1] while the French delegation presented there a new formula providing for the commission's consideration of any violation without any specification of its character. The subcommittee substantially adopted the British text, which came before the Preparatory Commission on November 26, when it was adopted.[2]

The result is if any high contracting party is of the opinion that another party is maintaining armament in excess of the figures agreed upon or is in any way violating or endeavoring to violate the provisions of the convention, the party holding that opinion may lay the matter before the Permanent Disarmament Commission. The commission hears a representative of the party whose action is questioned and any other contractant "which may be specially concerned in the matter and which asks to be heard." As soon as possible the commission is to present a report on the question to the contracting parties as a whole and to the Council of the League. The report, which is to embody conclusions, is to be published as soon as possible so that people everywhere will be informed.

Two alternative lines of action are indicated. The contracting parties are to advise as to the conclusions of the commission, which, of course, might be by any method from a diplomatic exchange of views to more formal consultation. The chances are in favor of the parties directly concerned being Members of the League of Nations; there are so many more of them than there are of non-Members. If the parties concerned are Members of the League, the Council "shall exercise the rights devolving upon it in such circumstances in virtue of the Covenant" with a view to insuring the observance of the present convention and the safeguarding of the peace of nations. The Preparatory Commission

[1] *Documents of the Preparatory Commission*, Series X, p. 417.
[2] *Ibid.*, p. 255.

stated that "it is understood, moreover, in this connection that the various pacific procedures provided for by the existing international agreements would, if necessary, be employed."

On second thought, the American delegation accepted this system with its two alternatives. In the subcommittee, the American delegation "expressed certain doubts as to the advisability of the clause on procedure" and reserved the matter for further consideration. That was on November 25.[1] On December 2, Mr. Gibson expressed pleasure in saying "that we have satisfied ourselves that the text as provided affords a satisfactory basis for our discussions at the coming conference, and that there will therefore be no need to include in the report any reference to the attitude of the American delegation."[2] The doubtful point was, of course, the provision for the recognition of the jurisdiction of the League Council.

System Insures Responsibility

Reverting to our hypothetical state B, which was contemplating violation instead of derogation from the convention, it will be perceived that its flirtation with the violative intention would give its opposite a full opportunity to set this machinery regarding complaints into motion. As both derogation and violation, on suspicion or in actuality, are to be dealt with by living organs, it is obvious that no state could in advance arrange a series of circumstances of so water-tight a character that it could certainly count upon a decision favorable to its contention. An assurance of being able to get away with the goods is a measurable incentive to embark on questionable enterprises. Any state desiring to deviate or derogate from or violate the Draft Convention would find itself completely incapable of securing that assurance. However good its case might seem to its own ego, it could have no guaranty that the counter case of its opposite would not have considerable, equal or superior merit, and it would be entirely unable to forecast what

[1] *Documents of the Preparatory Commission*, Series X, p. 470.
[2] *Ibid.*, p. 318.

conclusions the Permanent Disarmament Commission alone would reach in the premises. It would be entirely impossible for it to forecast whether the question would be reviewed by the Council of the League or by the states acting as contracting parties or whether the action of the latter would be confined to diplomatic exchanges or extended to a more formal gathering of delegates. No government wittingly starts anything which it does not see its way fairly clear to finish successfully, or at least advantageously. The complete inability to obtain any assurance of success or advantage in advance indicates that deviation, derogation or violation of the convention is a body of water in which fishing would probably be too troublesome to attempt.

As was suggested above, there will probably be many instances under the convention when alterations of armament appear to result in their maintenance in excess of technical figures. In view of the hazards inherent in raising questions under Arts. 50–52, it is more than probable that such questions will be raised and settled either by rulings of the Permanent Disarmament Commission or under the arbitration clause, Art. 54. Normally a question of obligations under the convention would be brought to attention in the annual reports coming before the Permanent Disarmament Commission or specially raised with it. In that case a general study would be made and a gloss as to the significance of the provision in question would thereafter exist for the guidance of all. It is quite probable that a change of practice would be assumed to affect a neighboring state. Art. 54 deals with disputes and provides negatively[1] for their settlement "directly between the parties." The way is thus open to a state in doubt as to the effects of a contemplated act upon another party to enter into bilateral negotiations and reach an understanding. This procedure is available for any matter concerning the interpretation or application of the convention's provisions. Art. 54 further contemplates that any method of friendly settlement is

[1] If the dispute can not be so solved, it goes to some formal method of pacific settlement. The capability of settling it directly is, therefore, implied as a first step.

available for the same purpose, that is, any bilateral jurisdiction of pacific settlement may be used for the purpose. The article as a whole, however, contemplates that such disputes shall be left to the Permanent Court of International Justice; thus a multilateral judicial jurisdiction is provided for the interpretation of the multilateral convention.

CHAPTER XIII

THE PAST IN THE FUTURE: A NECESSITY AND PROBLEM

Art. 53 of the Draft Convention reads:

The present convention shall not affect the provisions of previous treaties under which certain of the high contracting parties have agreed to limit their land, sea or air armaments, and have thus fixed in relation to one another their respective rights and obligations in this connection.

The following high contracting parties . . . signatory to the said treaties declare that the limits fixed for their armaments under the present convention are accepted by them in relation to the obligations referred to in the preceding paragraph, the maintenance of such provisions being for them an essential condition for the observance of the present convention.

This article is the only one on which a purely political controversy remains outstanding; other such controversies are outside the convention's actual terms. The German delegation states in respect to it "that, in so far as it does not refer to the Washington and London treaties, the German delegation would vote against the Draft Convention as a whole. The draft, as drawn up by the majority of the Preparatory Commission, excludes essential elements from the limitation and reduction of land armaments. Instead of leading to real disarmament, this draft would serve only to conceal the real state of world armaments or would even allow armaments to be increased. To accept it would at the same time be tantamount to a renewal of the German signature to the disarmament clauses of the treaty of Versailles."[1]

Before dealing with the substance of that statement, it will be convenient to account for the article and to analyze

[1] *Report*, par. 273.

its legal meaning in general. The original proposal was in the French draft of 1927, and it came before the third session of the commission, where Count Bernstorff on two occasions formulated his objection to it and indicated, unless the conditions which he had made were fulfilled, Germany would be unable to regard the convention as a first step toward general disarmament.[1] In the ensuing debate, Count Clauzel stated that the French draft owed its phraseology to Art. 19 of the convention of June 17, 1925, on trade in arms. In 1927 it was adopted on first reading with a clear reference to the peace treaties, the final clause reading "the present treaty being within these limits inapplicable between the said powers."

This Art. EA as it stood on first reading in 1927 was not reached on second reading until November 27, 1930, when Count Bernstorff asked for a public debate on it. A Bulgarian proposal to refer the article to the conference was passed over, and the Preparatory Commission opened the public debate requested by Germany forthwith. The German delegate in his statement vigorously asserted the substance of the reservation quoted above. He referred to the conditions which his Government considered "essential if this convention is to be regarded as discharging the obligations incurred by other nations toward disarmed Germany."[2] It could not "recognize anything as a first disarmament convention unless the solution which it provides is just and equitable, and pays regard to the security of all states." The value of the convention, said Count Bernstorff, would be "whether it is calculated to realize, at length, the principles of parity of security."

Viscount Cecil of Great Britain, who had given evidence of feeling that the procedure was artificially "created to enable Count Bernstorff to make a speech," began by asserting that if the parity referred to was to be attained, its realization would have to be in a special conference on the subject. But his main purpose was to protest "very earnestly" against the statement that the proposed convention would

[1] *Documents of the Preparatory Commission*, Series IV, p. 308, 352.
[2] *Ibid.*, X, p. 262.

not really amount to any limitation or reduction of land armaments. Limitation of total numbers was agreed to and also a separate limitation of officers, noncommissioned officers and professional soldiers in every army. As a necessary consequence, limitation in conscriptionist countries would take place. Total expenditure by budgetary limitation was agreed to and "it passes the wit of man to arm a force unless money is available for that purpose." And on the other aspect of the question, the parties to treaties providing for naval limitation "desire very strongly that nothing should be done to diminish their effect."

The debate then drifted to the proposals before the commission, concerning which the British delegate hoped for the active and practical cooperation of the German delegate in making "the best skeleton treaty for disarmament that is possible." René Massigli for France referred to the German speech only to note the German delegate's use of the word "security"[1] which he regarded "as an acceptance of a conception which the French Government has always defended." General Thadée Kasprzycki of Poland, one of the two military men on the Preparatory Commission, called attention to the fact that the "doctrine of existing security was the starting point of the disarmament obligations" under discussion, and that the one stable element among the present factors of security "is the military system of the countries disarmed in accordance with the peace treaties." The maintenance of that stable element was a prerequisite condition for the acceptance and maintenance in force of the coming convention by other states. He regarded the German estimate of the work as unjustified, since the convention, as General de Marinis of Italy — the sole other military delegate — had remarked, the Draft Convention was a skeleton without figures. There was another aspect of the question which he wished to emphasize as of far-reaching importance. "This is the first time that the sphere of national defense, hitherto reserved for the

[1] It may further be editorially noted that the adoption of the word brings nearer the time when states will have to explain exactly what they understand their security to involve.

sovereignty of states, has become the subject of international regulation."

Count Bernstorff, in view of his very old relations with Lord Cecil, expressed his regret at holding different opinions. He asked whether it was void of foundation:

(1) That sea and air armaments were directly limited and land armaments not;

(2) That budgetary limitation allows unlimited increase of armaments in stock;

(3) That the "central force of all the continental armies, trained reserves," was left out.

He had given up working with the commission because, to his regret, "the question of land armaments is to be sacrificed to the question of sea armaments . . . That is why I have absolutely nothing against security; only if there is to be security there must be parity of security and security for all."

Erik Colban of Norway stated that he was embarrassed by the debate, since he wished to vote for the text before the commission and found it difficult to know whether he could do so without expressing an opinion upon "a highly important political question." The Japanese, British and United States delegates all expressed the desire to have the binding force of the naval treaties mentioned in the convention, and it was agreed to vote without further political discussion, which was to be left to the conference.

The Bulgarian proposal to leave the article itself to the conference was defeated 12 to 5, and the article above was voted into the Draft Convention by 14 votes with some abstentions.

As a statement of inevitable legal obligation, Art. 53 seems to be unexceptional. As a legal statement, it says that previous treaties under which parties contracting to the disarmament convention have agreed to limit their armaments, and have thus established their relations with one another, are not to be affected by the provisions of the new convention. There are only two other possibilities: The first is that the disarmament convention should supersede the other treaties; but in that case a large number of provisions in previous treaties which go farther than the disarmament convention can expect to would cease to have effect, and the net result would be retrograde. Unless the Draft Convention is certainly to cover all phases of armament, its superseding other treaties is entirely impossible. If it were to supersede, it would throw out of force not only the peace treaties of the group to which Germany is a party, but the delicate arrangements of the naval limitation treaties, demilitarization and nonfortification clauses all around the world. If the article were to affect the provisions of previous treaties, the disarmament convention would have to state wherein they were affected. And that would reopen a multiplicity of questions which no one can accurately estimate. Beyond that, while all parties to the previous treaties will participate in the conference, the conference itself is not a possible forum in which to review a body of treaties which represent a most complicated network of engagements among some only of its membership. If that principle were followed, the Anglo-American agreement concerning naval forces on the Great Lakes; the Norwegian-Swedish demilitarization; the peace treaties between Estonia and Russia, and Finland and Russia, as well as the peace treaties of the Great War, would come under equivalent scrutiny. Clearly that is an impossible condition. There seems, then, to be no practical alternative to the idea of the first paragraph of the article.

By the second paragraph of Art. 53, contracting parties are enabled to make a special declaration as signatories to the previous treaties. The declaration is to the effect that the limits "fixed for their armaments under the present convention are accepted" by them in relation to the obligations referred to and that the maintenance of those obligations is "*for them* an essential condition for the observance of the present convention." In one direction, that is tantamount to saying that observance of the disarmament convention depends upon observance of previous conventions, but it is also a unilateral[1] escape clause, unless the parties

[1] The reader should bear in mind that A here states that B's maintenance of an obligation is an essential condition of A's loyalty to the disarmament convention. Negotiation in the conference may change the phraseology.

making the declaration should include all states parties to the previous treaties. As a legal statement, the paragraph is an expression of the doctrine of *rebus sic stantibus* that a treaty is binding during the conditions under which it was negotiated. In this aspect, any deviation from previous obligations could be reviewed as a "change of circumstances," as a derogation from the disarmament convention under Art. 50, and the mutual consultation of the contracting parties there might have the effect of bringing a question involving a previous treaty into the scope of a decision under the disarmament convention.

Art. 53, then, seems to contain sound enough legal doctrine. The political question it raises, however, can not be lost to sight, and it is proposed to narrate the salient facts concerning it.

Part V of the treaty of Versailles has a remarkable form. The treaty in general is built on the underlying fact that an armistice "was granted," on the request of the Imperial German Government; in other words, that Germany was a defeated state. Part V, however, the military, naval and air clauses, has a preamble of its own, which, as in the corresponding treaties with Austria, Bulgaria and Hungary, embodies this promissory condition:

> In order to render possible the initiation of a general limitation of the armaments of all nations, Germany undertakes strictly to observe the military, naval and air clauses which follow.

Arts. 159–202 are very thorough and complete provisions reducing the German army and navy to low levels and abolishing military aviation for the country. They apparently omit but one limitation, that of expenditure; by raising quality of material, Germany has on this account been able to establish greater efficiency than the victorious military experts planned for.[1] The victors established commissions under the treaty to see that the stipulated reductions were made. From 1919–1923 the commissions, which obviously had a thankless and unpopular task, received very little

[1] This consideration accounts in part for the concentration of attention upon budgetary limitation in the Preparatory Commission, but no one in 1919 knew how to handle the problem of budgetary limitation.

assistance from the German authorities and people, and France in particular was vociferous in protesting German bad faith in the matter.[1] Following the depreciation of the mark in 1923, the policy of the German Government became one of positive fulfillment of the military and naval clauses. The government perceived that the preamble to Part V enabled it to take the lead in disarmament, whereas it was clear to them that contesting the limits set for their own forces accomplished no useful national purpose. The reduction of men and material to the treaty limits was itself a very complicated process, and in November-December, 1925, an extensive list of conditions to be met was drawn up.[2]

The treaty in Art. 213 stipulates that the Council of the League shall have every facility for any investigation which it may consider necessary to insure the fulfillment of the disarmament conditions following the abolition of the military, naval and air commissions of control. Several of those commissions having been withdrawn from Austria, Bulgaria, Germany and Hungary, the League Council on September 27, 1924, established the organization for any exercise of the right of investigation that might be required.[3] Outstanding details in Germany resulted in the withdrawal of the Interallied Military Commission of Control from that country only on January 31, 1927. Since that date, the Conference of Ambassadors has transmitted to Geneva two reports respecting German military status. The first, dated July 22, 1927,[4] was the final report of the Military Control Commission. Until January 31, 1930, military experts were attached to the diplomatic missions at Berlin of Belgium, France, Great Britain, Italy and Japan — the states represented in the Conference of Ambassadors — for observation. The second report, supplemental to that of 1927, was dated March 16, 1931.[5] These reports are in the nature

[1] That note was repeatedly struck by Georges Clemenceau in his trip to the United States in November and December, 1922.

[2] *Cf. supra*, p. 39.

[3] *Official Journal*, V, p. 1592.

[4] *Official Journal*, VIII p. 1058.

[5] *Ibid.*, XII, p. 783.

of a judgment as to Germany's fulfillment of the conditions. Those conditions being multifarious, they are naturally subject to different viewpoints. The last report includes a supplementary note containing facts concerning which it says "the results secured on all these points can not be regarded as satisfactory." The points referred to are Arts. 160 (effectives and recruiting), 162 (police), 177 (activities of associations), 178 (military establishments). The Conference of Ambassadors comments that "it will rest with the Council to draw from the facts reported any conclusions it may think expedient." The Council did not think it either necessary or expedient to consider any of those points at its four following sessions. It may, therefore, be concluded that German disarmament under the terms of the treaty of Versailles is admitted to exist. The General Disarmament Conference may be regarded as taking place with the engagement of the preamble of Part V of the treaty of Versailles as a legal obligation fully in force running against the collective party of the first part of that treaty.[1]

Now, the defeated powers having fulfilled their side of the bargain, the question remains to determine what the bargain actually is. The conditions incumbent upon the defeated states were established "to render possible the initiation of a general limitation of the armaments of all nations." Strict observance of the conditions by Germany and the others is to be assumed unless there are specific allegations to the contrary. If no state has evidence of sufficient gravity to warrant requesting the Council of the League to exercise the right of investigation, it can hardly allege successfully that nonobservance by Germany or any other defeated state is sufficient cause for it to decline any engagement of disarmament. Nevertheless, such hints have been made and arguments based upon them.

[1] This statement runs for: Australia, Belgium, Bolivia, Brazil, Canada, Cuba, Czechoslovakia, France, Great Britain and Northern Ireland, Greece, Guatemala, Haiti, Honduras, India, the Irish Free State, Italy, Japan, Liberia, New Zealand, Nicaragua, Panama, Peru, Poland, Portugal, Rumania, Siam, South Africa, Uruguay and Yugoslavia.

It was signed, and repeatedly accepted as good policy, for the United States.

It is equally a legal obligation in the treaties of peace with Austria, Bulgaria and Hungary, the first of which China has ratified.

The preamble of Part V has been a universally admitted spur to the work of the Preparatory Commission. Implications of nonobservance as a basis for exaggerating insecurity have not been the serious difference of view concerning it. Germany has not claimed in so many words that the preamble necessitated the diminution of rival armed strengths to its own exact ratio, and in fact it would be a difficult task to weigh all the relevant factors so as to determine the relevant par of other states with relation to the German treaty standard. But Germany, as will be recalled, has asserted the right to "parity of security." This, in effect, makes the German interpretation of the preamble a positive obligation on the part of the other states. To a considerable extent they have avoided the issue. According to the interested states, the preamble expresses not so much an obligation as a condition precedent to enable them (the victors) to do something they are very anxious themselves to do. The maintenance of a stable position respecting some armament is, they say, an important consideration in reducing some more of it.

All the victors promised themselves to do was the "initiation" of a general limitation, and it is really on that idea that a difference of view persists. The Draft Convention is pictured as not only an initiation, but a long step forward and, therefore, a generous realization of the preamble. Germany holds that the treaty of Versailles set up the victors' own standard of what armament it was safe to intrust to a government and that there is reason to expect those states in good faith to conform to that standard. The truth seems to be that the standard is not obligatory upon any except the vanquished, but it affords a basis of comparison and has encouraged Germany in particular to take the lead in advocating drastic action.

Germany is to be a full and equal partner in the convention resulting from the Disarmament Conference. Part V of the treaty of Versailles, however, lays down the limits of its military and naval armament, and those limits are present law. On the other hand, Germany as a freely negotiating state in the conference is as much at liberty to introduce a new basis of armament regulation in modification of the treaty of Versailles as any state party to the Washington or London naval treaties has to bring forward a modification of them. Germany is not objecting to maintaining its present scale of armament in the convention, provided the figures adopted for other states give it "parity of security." If that should be realized, Germany would apparently willingly adopt the Versailles figures without demur, emphasizing that the relationship established was a matter of free agreement in the new convention. If the figures of others should not afford that parity of security, however, and Germany for some reason should be brought to sign the Geneva convention, the German view is that the act would be equivalent to re-signing the Versailles obligation. Rather than do that, the German spokesmen have stated that they would not become a party to the Geneva convention at all. None of these clear-cut alternatives is likely to be realized in the conference. Any convention is almost certain to supersede prior engagements in some degree and to create new armament relations. German policy will naturally weigh such conditions and may base its final judgment upon such considerations as the inclusion of provisions for reporting trained reserves or the treatment of heavy guns and offensive weapons in general.

The War-Guilt Issue

The relation of German policy to the treaty of Versailles is popularly associated with the so-called war-guilt issue. The extreme utterances of belligerent officials during the war, as well as a continuous debate of the subject, particularly with reference to the origin of the Great War, have contributed to fix German public opinion. A demand for a so-called revision of the treaty of Versailles has been built up, based so far as that treaty is concerned upon Art. 231, the beginning of Part VIII, which defines reparation. The treaty of Versailles is official in French and English, and the English at this point reads:

> The allied and associated governments affirm and Germany accepts the responsibility of Germany and her allies for causing all

the loss and damage to which the allied and associated governments and their nationals have been subjected as a consequence of the war imposed upon them by the aggression of Germany and her allies.

The same article *mutatis mutandis* appears in identical terms in the peace treaties with Austria and Hungary. The article was drafted by the Supreme Council. Paul Mantoux, that body's interpreter, in a review of its whole debate testifies that "there was never a question of the origins of the war, nor of a condemnation solemnly pronounced against Germany and aggravated by the obligation imposed upon Germany of subscribing to it, nor even of giving the system of reparation a moral basis . . . What they desired was to write into the treaty the theoretical principle of the pecuniary responsibility of Germany for all damages, so as to make it easier to get the parliaments to accept less extensive stipulations . . . The reason Art. 231 figures in the treaty is solely that it had been impossible to insert the figure for reparation."[1]

It may be doubted whether the article would have been given any other significance if the defeated states had been permitted to participate in the negotiation of the treaties. As it was, Germany correctly described the article in its *Comments on the Conditions of Peace*.[2]

The French-English text was handed on April 28, 1919, to the German delegation which was given the very limited time of one month in which to present all proposed changes to a most complicated and far-reaching document. A German text had to be prepared by the Germans for that purpose. The translation into German, made under great pressure, does not exactly correspond with the meaning of the French and English, and it is upon these differences that a controversy which bears directly upon the armament ques-

---

[1] *Le Temps*, November 29, 1931. On November 15, Camille Bloch and Pierre Renouvin had published in the French newspaper an extensive study of peace conference evidence, to which M. Mantoux added the record of the responsible negotiators. The Bloch-Renouvin article was republished in German in *Berliner Monatshefte für internationale Aufklärung* (IX, p. 1166), the periodical devoted to the "war-guilt" thesis.

[2] *International Conciliation*, No. 143, p. 62.

tion rests. The literal English of the official German text is:[1]

The allied and associated governments declare and Germany recognizes that Germany and its allies are responsible as originators for all losses and damages which the allied and associated governments and their nationals have sustained in consequence of the war imposed upon them by the attack of Germany and her allies.

The chief point on which this German version differed from the French and English was due to choice of expression with respect to the phrase "for causing[2] all the loss and damage." In the German version the causation of the loss and damage takes on the flavor of instigation. The use of the French-English word "aggression" was borrowed from the pre-armistice note of November 5, 1918, where an expression "aggression by land, by sea or from the air" is used as a derivation from the Supreme Council's original draft, which employed the word *invasion*.[3] The German word *Angriff* similarly means either attack or aggression. Since the articles in the treaties of St. Germain-en-Laye (Art. 177) and Trianon (Art. 161) are identic in phraseology with the Versailles text, it is clear that the article intended to do no more than to record the legal fact that the central states as a group struck the first blow.

In the popular German literature Art. 231 of Versailles is called the "Schuldartikel," the article on guilt. The word in the official French and English is "damage," which is properly enough translated in the German text (in the plural) as *Schäden*.

The question of responsibility for the war was one of the contentious points in the Paris peace conference and afterward so that as an incident of the German people's opposition to the charge and its association with the treaty of

[1] The German text is:
"Die alliierten und assoziierten Regierungen erklären, und Deutschland erkennt an, dass Deutschland und seine Verbündeten als Urheber für alle Verluste und Schäden verantwortlich sind, die die alliierten und assoziierten Regierungen und ihre Staatsangehörigen infolge des ihnen durch den Angriff Deutschlands und seiner Verbündeten aufgezwungenen Krieges erlitten haben." (*Reichsgesetzblatt, 1919*, Nr. 140, p. 985.)

[2] Alfred von Wegerer, the editor of *Berliner Monatshefte* and the director of the Central Office for Inquiry into the Origins of the War, renders "causing" by *verursacht* instead of *als Urheber* (*Berliner Monatshefte*, IX, p. 1189).

[3] Robert C. Binkley and A. C. Mahr, *Current History*, June, 1926, p. 399.

Versailles, Art. 231 came to be regarded as its official expression. This tendency was facilitated by the fact that the article is the basis of the very troublesome reparation obligation. In the popular German mind, at least, Part V and the "Schuldartikel" of the treaty of Versailles are closely associated.

CHAPTER XIV

DEVIATION AND NEW CONFERENCES

Arts. 55–60 of the Draft Convention are the formal articles relating to ratification, execution, duration, denunciation and fresh conferences. In a technical sense they represent a practical and fairly strong system as they stand, but are quite likely to be changed by the conference.

Ratification is to take place, as is customary, in accordance with the respective constitutional methods of the states, and the ratifications are to be deposited with the Secretary-General of the League. The convention is to enter into force as a multilateral engagement as a result of depositing the ratifications of a number of states to be determined by the conference. When the conference determines that list, it will in effect identify the states to which the limitation and reduction of armament positively applies in reality. Among the group on which the entrance of the convention into force will depend will be the large holders of military and/or naval strength, which are: China, Czechoslovakia, France, Germany, Great Britain, India, Italy, Japan, Poland, Rumania, the Soviet Union, Spain, Turkey, the United States and Yugoslavia.[1]

The final articles of the Draft Convention were based upon a first reading draft developed from the Synoptical Analysis of the original British and French suggestions, supplemented subsequently by British and French proposals, the whole of which were referred to the subcommittee of experts, of which M. Politis was chairman. They were coordinated rather than debated.[2]

The subcommittee considered the possibility that the

[1] The group mentioned in the original British proposal consisted of Germany, the United States, Great Britain, France, Italy and Japan (*Documents of the Preparatory Commission*, Series IV, p. 310).

[2] *Documents of the Preparatory Commission*, Series X, p. 266–279.

convention, after signature, might not have come into force after a certain lapse of time by the meeting of the condition of ratification by the group of states to be specified. In that case, a consultation will be held. When the convention comes into force, it naturally follows that each contracting party will take the necessary measures by legislation or administrative methods for carrying its provisions into effect within its own jurisdiction.

The convention is to remain in force for x years (to be fixed by the conference), but it will continue in force beyond that initial period in so far as it has not been amended, superseded or denounced. The Preparatory Commission was faced with a most delicate problem with respect to the initial period of x years. On the one hand, a convention representing so important a body of agreement should not be negotiated for so short a time that its usefulness could not be adequately tested by experience and that its effects could not be, as it were, digested. On the other hand, it was impossible to foresee what circumstances might arise which would change general conditions and render what might be called general rather than special derogation desirable. Some states in this regard betrayed a fear that the convention might bear down on them too hard, but there was a more general feeling that the lapse of a few years might enable governments to see their way to go farther. For either alternative an initial period of validity ought not to be too extended. The period of x years is left to the conference for determination, but in the explanation of M. Politis he calls attention to the fact that Art. 8 of the Covenant provides that the plans for reduction and limitation are to be subject to reconsideration and revision at least every 10 years. Half that time was also suggested, but it was convenient for explaining the rather complicated system which is provided to assume that x is 10 years.

Whatever happens, there is not to be another meeting of the conference before y years, a period indicated as between 6 and 9 years, if x is 10. The intention of non-Members of the League and the opinion of the Permanent Disarmament Commission were to be taken into account by the

Council of the League in fixing the date of a conference for the reexamination of the convention after the lapse of y years. In this conference revision of the convention or additions thereto might be made, as well as provisions for subsequent revision. This conference would be the second General Disarmament Conference and would have jurisdiction over the whole field.

For the sake of clarity, it was assumed that x is 10 and y 6 years. Within the y period, but not less than z years (say 2 or 3 years), a partial revision may take place under certain conditions. If conditions on which the convention was based had undergone changes on account of "technical transformations or special circumstances which justify a fresh examination" of some provisions of the convention, a conference may be convened and revision of specific engagements undertaken. Such a gathering is to be held at the request of a contracting party, "with the concurrence of the Permanent Disarmament Commission." The fundamental requisite for holding such a conference is that conditions have occurred which have resulted "in changes justifying a fresh examination," but no organ is designated for determining whether a fresh examination is justified by the changes. Such a request would, therefore, scarcely be made unless the case for examination were relatively clear.

Denunciation of the convention may be notified to the other contracting parties at a conference held after z years, or the one held after y years, to take effect only after the expiration of x years. Thus, the duration of the convention is assured for x years, though it may be modified in certain particulars after z (2 to 3) years or in general after y (6 to 9) years. Normal denunciation requires a 2-year notice, which would make it possible after 8 years, if x is 10.

The provision for a conference after z years on account of "technical transformations or special circumstances" was incorporated to take account of the rapid development of aviation. In the first-reading text,[1] Art. AD was a general reservation on this subject. "The limitations laid down,"

[1] *Documents of the Preparatory Commission*, Series X, p. 440.

in the whole convention, it said, "are accepted by each high contracting party in the light of the present development of civil aviation in other countries." The debates in the Preparatory Commission made it clear that such a general reservation was nugatory and undesirable. It was, however, impossible to disregard the development of civil aviation, and the Draft Convention contains Art. 37 providing for a collection of information respecting its extent and technical development, a body of fact which was available to the conference.[1] The first suggestion emanated from the French delegation. The discussions in the Preparatory Commission resulted in the general conclusion that it was not essential to make any definite condition, but that an orderly means for taking account of developments should be provided. Therefore, the device of the special conference after z years was invented. This safety valve was entirely satisfactory without definite reference to civil aviation. René Massigli, the French delegate, however, clearly defined the circumstances uppermost in the commission's mind when he said:[2]

We are going — for that is really the main result — by means of our convention, to bring the development of military aëronautics to a standstill. We are bringing it to a standstill before what I might call the "capital ship" of the air has been evolved. We shall therefore have none of these giant machines built specially for military objects, while, at the same time, civil aviation will continue its unrestrained march. And the time is at hand when we shall see great air liners, which may become auxiliary air cruisers and bombing machines.

The decision of the Preparatory Commission not to use the development of civil aviation as a formal excuse for not limiting other forms of armament is itself commendable. It is of great importance in principle for the future of disarmament, but it is perhaps of even larger significance as a principle. From time immemorial, the defensive-offensive habits of states have been highly acquisitive. Any change in economic, social, scientific or industrial fields has been

See *supra*, p. 171, 211.
[2] *Documents of the Preparatory Commission*, Series X, p. 286.

immediately seized on by the military experts and adapted for their own uses. The long continuing process resulted in giving almost everything from high-tension steel to trouser buttons a military significance, and in the prewar period military value took precedence not only in international relations, but throughout the national social economies. Society's civil interests tended to be subordinated to military considerations.

When the discussion of disarmament began, this all-pervading effect of the military predilection constituted a vested interest in policy and thought — both governmental and private — which took time to dislodge, even to the extent of being able to discuss the fundamental phases of the armament problem. It has been remarked above that scarcely any state is really seeking disarmament; what they are all anxious for is an increase of their own armament with relation to their opposites, which can most readily be done by the others reducing their strength. In the technical realms of armament not a little of the progress already recorded has been made possible by a state's belief that it will be possible to secure just as efficient military results in peace time from a lesser quantity of men or material than is at present in possession. Now that being the situation, the Preparatory Commission's decision to declare a divorce — or at least separate maintenance — between civil and military aviation represents the recognition of a very fruitful principle.

Military and naval experts are currently in great doubt as to the essential value of their present mechanism, considering the possibilities of aviation. Beyond question, much of the current military and naval apparatus occupies its place in the scheme of things by reason of inertia. Military and naval aviation have certainly changed the values of warlike operations, and there are enthusiasts who go so far as to claim that military and naval tactics and strategy should henceforth be frankly built around air operations. Be that as it may, there is no doubt but that this third arm of the military art is the one which will dictate the conditions of the future. The Preparatory Commission's decision amounts to a demonstration that the development of this new expression of organized force is not to absorb or take precedence over its civil development. The process of history by which civil development has been a direct feeder of military development is consciously altered.

The practical effect of this principle should not, however, be exaggerated. There is no way to prevent military and naval aviation from benefiting by the developments of civil aviation. Scientifically, they necessarily draw their technique from the same body of research, discovery and experimentation. The divorce between them is defined for the purposes of the Draft Convention by Art. 28 and insured by the publicity provision of Art. 37, which ought to have the effect of bringing out any national tendencies for civil aviation to play into the hands of military. Though the situation created is not complete as a divorce, it is a pretty thoroughgoing case of separate maintenance. Military and naval aviation will naturally make full use of all scientific, technological and industrial development to which the civil branch has access. But unless schemes for industrial procurement[1] are adjusted so as constructively to violate Art. 28 of the Draft Convention, military and naval aviation will have to depend upon their own budgets, their own planning boards and their own constructing staffs.

[1] See *supra*, p. 26-32.

APPENDIX

APPENDIX I

DRAFT CONVENTION FOR THE REDUCTION AND LIMITATION OF ARMAMENTS, DRAWN BY THE PREPARATORY COMMISSION FOR THE DISARMAMENT CONFERENCE, DATED DECEMBER 9, 1930[1]

Art. 1. The High Contracting Parties agree to limit and, so far as possible, to reduce their respective armaments as provided in the present convention.

PART I PERSONNEL[2]

CHAPTER A. EFFECTIVES

Art. 2. The average daily effectives in the land, sea and air armed forces and formations organized on a military basis of each of the High

---

[1] Text from C.687.M.288.1931.IX.8 and *Official Journal*, XII, p. 347.

The reservations referred to in the official print of the Draft Convention are printed in the *Report by the Commission* which is published in *Official Journal*, XII, p. 311–347, and *Documents of the Preparatory Commission*, Series X, p. 562–592. For clarity they are carried in full in the present reprint.

GENERAL RESERVATIONS: *Turkish delegation:* "41. The Turkish delegation reserved its Government's right to submit to the future Disarmament Conference the proposal it made with regard to standards for the reduction and limitation of armaments, and to require any modification of the text which might be rendered necessary in the event of the adoption of this proposal (see *Minutes of the Sixth Session* (first part), p. 206–208)."

German delegation: "42. The German delegation reserved its Government's right to submit to the future Disarmament Conference any proposals regarding the standards of reduction and limitation of armaments which it might consider likely to promote these aims (see *Minutes of the Sixth Session* (first part) p. 203–206)."

Norwegian and Irish Free State delegations: "43. Norway not having taken part in the earlier work of the commission, in particular the first part of the second reading of the Draft Convention, the Norwegian delegate made a general reservation concerning the attitude his Government might adopt at the conference.

"The delegate of the Irish Free State made a similar statement."

[2] RESERVATION: *German delegation:* "79. The German delegation has made the following general reservation on the whole of Part I and the annexed table:

"'The stipulations do not provide — either directly or by a reduction in the number of the annual contingent, or by a strict determination of the period of active service — for a reduction of limitation of trained reserves who, after having completed their service with the colors, continue to be registered and liable by law for military service, notwithstanding the fact that these reserves, though they do not exist in professional armies in the strict sense of the term, constitute the main body of the personnel in countries possessing conscript armies.

"'Moreover, the stipulations do not provide for any method whereby the effectives of conscript armies serving with the colors and in reserve, and professional effectives, whose military value is naturally not capable of comparison, could be reduced to comparable units of calculation.'"

Contracting Parties shall not exceed, in each of the categories of effectives defined in the tables annexed to this chapter, the figure laid down for such party in the corresponding column of the said tables.

Art. 3. The average daily effectives are reckoned by dividing the total number of days' duty performed in each year by the number of days in such year.

Art. 4. By formations organized on a military basis shall be understood police forces of all kinds, gendarmerie, customs officials, forest guards, which, whatever their legal purpose, are, in time of peace, by reason of their staff of officers, establishment, training, armament, equipment, capable of being employed for military purposes without measures of mobilization, as well as any other organization complying with the above condition.

By mobilization, within the meaning of the present article, shall be understood all the measures for the purpose of providing the whole or part of the various corps, services and units with the personnel and material required to pass from a peace-time footing to a war-time footing.

NOTE TO TABLES (P. 267)

[1] On certain tables annexed to Chap. A. of Part 1:

RESERVATIONS: *French delegation:* "65. The French delegation stated that it could not accept specific limitation of professional soldiers in land or air forces unless provision was made for similar limitation in the case of sea forces."

German and Italian delegations: "73. In regard to Tables I, II and III, the German and Italian delegations made the following statement:

" 'In connection with the distinction between the effectives and armaments of the home country and those stationed overseas, the German and Italian delegations formulated a general reservation to the effect that, for the purposes of the reduction and limitation of armaments, the importance of the forces and materials which one contracting party assigns to its oversea territories may vary, in relation to another contracting party, by reason of the geographical situation of its territory in relation to the home territories of the two contracting parties. Consequently, one contracting party will have every reason to regard the oversea forces of another contracting party as forming part of the latter's home forces, if the proximity of the oversea territories in relation to the home territories of the two parties justifies such an assumption.' "

German delegation: "74. The German delegation again draws attention to this reservation in connection with Tables V, IX and XII."

Italian delegation: "75. As regards Tables I, II and III, the Italian delegation considers that there should be added to the three columns (*b*), the words 'or officials assimilated to officers,' and to the three columns (*c*), after the words 'other soldiers' the words: 'or officials, employees or agents assimilated to soldiers.'

"76. As regards Tables VIII, IX and X, the Italian delegation is of opinion that no distinction should be made between armed air forces stationed in the home country and armed air forces stationed overseas."

Turkish delegation: "77. The Turkish delegation has made reservations regarding the tables annexed to Chap. A of Part I, both as regards the optional indication of land and air forces stationed overseas (Tables II and IX), and as regards the nonindication of the maximum forces stationed in each of the overseas territories (Tables II. V and IX)."

APPENDIX I

Tables annexed to Chapter A of Part 1[1]

TABLES OF THE AVERAGE DAILY EFFECTIVES WHICH ARE NOT TO BE EXCEEDED IN THE LAND ARMED FORCES

	TABLE I. Maximum Land Armed Forces stationed in the Home Country			*Table II* (optional). *Maximum Land Armed Forces stationed Overseas*			TABLE III. Maximum of the total Land Armed Forces		
	a	b	c	a	b	c	a	b	c
High Contracting Parties	Total effectives, including the effectives specified in columns b and c	Officers	Other effectives who have completed at least x^2 months of service	*Total effectives, including the effectives specified in columns b and c*	*Officers*	*Other effectives who have completed at least x^2 months of service*	Total effectives, including the effectives specified in columns b and c	Officers	Other effectives who have completed at least x^2 months of service
A. B. C. D. · ·									

TABLES OF THE AVERAGE DAILY EFFECTIVES WHICH ARE NOT TO BE EXCEEDED IN THE LAND FORMATIONS ORGANIZED ON A MILITARY BASIS

	TABLE IV. Maximum Formations organized on a Military Basis stationed in the Home Country			TABLE V. Maximum formations organized on a Military Basis stationed Overseas		
	a	b	c	a	b	c
High Contracting Parties	Total effectives, including the effectives specified in columns b and c	Officers or officials ranking as officers	Other effectives or officials who have completed at least x^2 months of service	Total effectives, including the effectives specified in columns b and c	Officers or officials ranking as officers	Other effectives or officials who have completed at least x^2 months of service
A. B. C. D. · ·						

[1] See note on p. 266.

Note. — This figure will be determined by the duration of the longest period of service which is in force in the conscript land army of any High Contracting Party at the time of the signature of the convention.

TABLES OF THE AVERAGE DAILY EFFECTIVES WHICH ARE NOT TO BE EXCEEDED IN THE SEA ARMED FORCES

	TABLE VI. Maximum Sea Armed Forces	TABLE VII. Maximum Sea Formations organized on a Military Basis
High Contracting Parties	Total effectives (officers, petty officers and men)	Total effectives (officers, petty officers and men and officials of every grade)
A. B. C. D.		

TABLES OF THE AVERAGE DAILY EFFECTIVES WHICH ARE NOT TO BE EXCEEDED IN THE AIR ARMED FORCES

	Table VIII (optional). *Maximum Air Armed Forces stationed in the Home Country*		*Table IX* (optional). *Maximum Air Armed Forces stationed Overseas*		TABLE X. Maximum of the Total Air Armed Forces	
	a	*b*	*a*	*b*	*a*	*b*
High Contracting Parties	Total effectives, including the effectives specified in column b	Effectives who have completed at least z^1 months of service (officers, noncommissioned officers and men)	Total effectives, including the effectives specified in column b	Effectives who have completed at least z^1 months of service (officers, noncommissioned officers and men)	Total effectives, including the effectives specified in column b	Effectives who have completed at least z^1 months of service (officers, noncommissioned officers and men)
A. B. C. D.						

[1] *Note.* — This figure will be determined by the duration of the longest period of service which is in force in the conscript air army of any High Contracting Party at the time of the signature of the convention.

TABLES OF THE AVERAGE DAILY EFFECTIVES WHICH ARE NOT TO BE EXCEEDED IN THE AIR FORMATIONS ORGANIZED ON A MILITARY BASIS

TABLE XI. Maximum Air Formations organized on a Military Basis stationed in the Home Country

TABLE XII. Maximum Air Formations organized on a Military Basis stationed Overseas

High Contracting Parties	a — Total effectives, including the effectives specified in column b	b — Effectives or officials who have completed at least z[1] months of service (officers, noncommissioned officers, men and officials of every grade)	a — Total effectives, including the effectives specified in column b	b — Effectives or officials who have completed at least z[1] months of service (officers, noncommissioned officers, men and officials of every grade)
A.				
B.				
C.				
D.				
..				
..				

CHAPTER B. PERIOD OF SERVICE

Art. 5. The provisions of this chapter apply only to effectives recruited by conscription.

Art. 6. For each of the High Contracting Parties concerned, the maximum total periods of service to which the effectives recruited by conscription are liable in the land, sea or air armed forces or formations organized on a military basis respectively, shall not exceed the figures laid down for such party in the table annexed to this chapter.

Art. 7. For each man, the total period of service is the total number of days comprised in the different periods of service which he is liable under the national law to perform.

Art. 8. As an exception, each of the High Contracting Parties concerned may exceed the limits which he has accepted by the table annexed to this chapter in so far as, owing to a falling-off in the number of births, such an increase may be necessary to enable the maximum total number of effectives fixed in his case by the tables annexed to Chapter A of this part to be attained.

It is understood that any High Contracting Party which avails itself of this option will immediately notify the measures taken and the reasons

---

[1] *Note.* — This figure will be determined by the duration of the longest period of service which is in force in the conscript air army of any High Contracting Party at the time of the signature of the convention.

justifying them to the other High Contracting Parties and to the Permanent Disarmament Commission referred to in Part VI of the present convention.

Art. 9. In any case, the total period of service shall not exceed ... months.

Table annexed to Chapter B of Part I

High Contracting Parties	Maximum total period of service to which the effectives recruited by conscription are liable in the armed forces or formations organized on a military basis		
	Land	Sea	Air
A. B. C. D.			

PART II MATERIAL

Chapter A. Land Armaments[1]

Art. 10.[2] (*Provisional text subject to the drafting of the annex.*) The annual expenditure of each High Contracting Party on the upkeep, purchase and manufacture of war material for land armaments shall be limited to the figures laid down for such party, and in accordance with the conditions prescribed, in the annex . . . to this article.[3]

---

[1] RESERVATIONS: *American delegation:* "94. The American delegation stated that, whereas they were unable to accept budgetary limitation in any form as far as the United States was concerned (see American reservations, pars. Nos. 171 and 181 [see Art. 29]), they did not wish their attitude to constitute an obstacle to agreement on the part of other powers. They therefore stated that they were prepared to apply, as far as they were themselves concerned, direct limitation instead of indirect limitation, provided that some practical budgetary method were generally agreed upon, which would be sufficiently detailed and precise to constitute an effective means of limitation."
German delegation: "102. The German delegation has made a general reservation in regard to Art. 10 since, notwithstanding its extraordinary importance, the material in service and in reserve of land armed forces and of land formations organized on a military basis is only covered — contrary to the method applied to air armaments and to naval floating material — by limitation of expenditure, and not by a reduction and limitation of specific articles and of numbers.
"103. As regards the limitation of expenditure, the German delegation reserves the right to take a decision after considering the report of the Committee of Budgetary Experts."
Turkish delegation: "99. Apart from the reservation in the footnote to the article, the Turkish delegation made its acceptance of any budgetary limitation of material and armaments expressly conditional upon account being taken — as also with any other method of limitation — of the special position of countries in which industry is not adequately developed."

[2] *Note.* — In pronouncing on this article, the governments will take into account at the conference the report requested from the Committee of Budgetary Experts, which will have been forwarded to them in order to permit of the drawing up of the annex to this article.
The Preparatory Commission, by sixteen votes to three and six abstentions, adopted the principle of limitation by expenditure. It also discussed the following resolution:
"The Preparatory Commission is of opinion that the principle of direct limitation should be applied to land war material."
When this resolution was put to the vote, there were nine votes in favor, nine against and seven abstentions.
Lastly, it examined the principle of a combination of the two methods. Nine members of the commission voted in favor of this principle; eleven voted against and five abstained.

[3] See Annex p. 306.

Chapter B. Naval Armaments [1] [2]

Art. 11. [3] [4] Throughout the duration of the present convention, the global tonnage of the vessels of war of each of the High Contracting Parties, other than the vessels exempt from limitation under Annex I to this chapter and the special vessels enumerated in Annex II, shall not exceed the figure laid down for such party in Table I annexed to this chapter.

Art. 12. [4] Table II annexed to this chapter shows, by tonnage per category, the way in which each High Contracting Party intends to distribute during the period of application of the present convention the global tonnage which is limited in the case of such party to the figure laid down in Table I.

Art. 13. Within the limits of the global tonnage fixed for such party in Table I, and failing any stricter conditions resulting from special

---

[1] *Note.* — Such figures and dates as appear in this chapter are only given as an illustration; most of them correspond to the figures and dates laid down in the treaties of Washington and London.

[2] GENERAL RESERVATIONS: *German delegation:* "109. The German delegation made a reservation in view of the great value of nonfloating material, on the ground that the latter — unlike floating material — would not be subject to any direct limitation by specific articles and by numbers, and would only be affected indirectly by limitation by expenditure. With regard to the latter, the German delegation reserved its opinion until it had studied the report of the Committee of Budgetary Experts."

Italian delegation: "108. The Italian delegation made a general reservation to the effect that the Italian Government could not finally agree to any specific method before all the powers had agreed on the proportions and the levels of maximum tonnage."

[3] RESERVATION: *Yugoslav delegation:* "116. The Yugoslav delegate emphasized the difference between recently created countries at present engaged in preparing a minimum naval program compatible with their national security, and countries having a maritime history and tradition and possessing a complete fleet. The figure of the total (global) tonnage to be inserted in Table I would, for the former countries, represent only the first stage in the execution of their minimum program, whereas for the latter, the figure will really indicate their maximum naval forces in the present state of international relations. In view of this essential difference, the Yugoslav delegation reserved the right to request at the conference that recently created countries, which are obliged to distribute their expenditure for the construction of a minimum tonnage compatible with their national security over a number of years exceeding the duration of the convention, should be accorded the right to mention separately, within the limits of the agreed total (global) tonnage, what portion of their program they intended to carry out during the period of the convention. Similarly, if, under Art. 57 of the Draft Convention, the convention remained in force for a further period, such prolongation should not debar the above-mentioned countries from continuing the execution of their naval program within the limits of the agreed tonnage."

[4] RESERVATION: *Italian delegation:* "112. The Italian delegation proposed that Arts. 11 and 12 should be replaced by a single article worded as follows:

" 'The limitation of naval armaments, accepted by each of the High Contracting Parties, is indicated in the following table . . . ' in the form of Table II of the text, Table I being omitted."

APPENDIX I

conventions to which it is or may become a party, each of the High Contracting Parties may modify the distribution shown for it in Table II, subject to the following conditions:

(1) The tonnages by category shown for each High Contracting Party in Table II shall in no case be the object of increase beyond the figures shown for it in Table III annexed to this chapter.

(2) Before the laying down of the ship or ships for the construction of which the transferred tonnage has been assigned, due notice must be given to all the other High Contracting Parties and the Secretary-General and the Permanent Disarmament Commission, of the amount of tonnage transferred, the length of such notice being that laid down for each of the High Contracting Parties in Table III.

Art. 14. No capital ship shall exceed 35,000 tons (35,560 metric tons) standard displacement or carry a gun exceeding 16 inches (406 mm.) in caliber.

Art. 15. No aircraft carrier shall exceed 27,000 tons (27,432 metric tons) standard displacement or carry a gun with a caliber in excess of 8 inches (203 mm.).

No aircraft carrier of 10,000 tons (10,160 metric tons) or less standard displacement shall carry a gun exceeding 6.1 inches (155 mm.) in caliber.

If the armament carried includes guns exceeding 6.1 inches (155 mm.) in caliber, the total number of guns carried, except anti-aircraft guns and guns not exceeding 5.1 inches (130 mm.), shall not exceed ten. If, alternatively, the armament contains no guns exceeding 6.1 inches (155 mm.) in caliber, the number of guns is not limited. In either case, the number of anti-aircraft guns and of guns not exceeding 5.1 inches (130 mm.) in caliber, is not limited.

Art. 16. No submarine shall exceed 2,000 tons (2,032 metric tons) standard displacement or carry a gun exceeding 5.1 inches (130 mm.) in caliber.

Art. 17. No vessel of war exceeding the limitations as to displacement or armament prescribed by the present convention shall be acquired by, or constructed by, for or within the jurisdiction of any of the High Contracting Parties.

Art. 18. In regard to the replacement of the vessels of war limited by the present convention, the High Contracting Parties will comply with the rules set out in Annex IV to this chapter.

Art. 19.[1] No preparation shall be made in merchant ships in time of peace for the installation of warlike armaments for the purpose of converting such ships into vessels of war, other than the necessary stiffening of decks for the mounting of guns not exceeding 6.1 inches (155 mm.) in caliber.

Art. 20. In the event of a High Contracting Party's being engaged in war, such party shall not use as a vessel of war any vessel of war which may be under construction within its jurisdiction for any other power, or which may have been constructed within its jurisdiction for another power and not delivered.

Art. 21. Each of the High Contracting Parties undertakes not to dispose, by gift, sale, or any mode of transfer, of any vessel of war in such a manner that such vessel may become a vessel of war in the navy of any foreign power.

Art. 22. Any vessels of war which have to be disposed of as being surplus to the tonnage figures allowed by the present convention shall be disposed of in accordance with the rules set out in Annex V to this chapter.

Art. 23. Existing ships of various types, which, prior to April, 1930, have been used as stationary training establishments or hulks, may be retained in a nonseagoing condition.

Art. 24.[2][3] (*Provisional text, subject to the drafting of the annex.*) The annual expenditure of each High Contracting Party on the upkeep,

[1] RESERVATION: *Japanese delegation:* "134. ... The Japanese delegation, however, reserved the right to raise the question of the limitation of aircraft equipment on merchant vessels, possibly at the conference itself. The Soviet delegation emphasized the importance of laying down that no preparations shall be made in merchant ships with a view to converting such ships in wartime into fighting units."

[2] In pronouncing on this article, the governments will take into account at the conference the report requested from the Committee of Budgetary Experts, which will have been forwarded to them in order to permit of the drawing up of the annex to this article, *infra*, p. 306.

[3] RESERVATIONS: *French delegation:* "139. The French delegation does not see its way to accept the special limitation of expenditure on upkeep, purchase and manufacture of war material for naval armaments. Apart from the technical difficulties, it observes that the limitation of naval material under satisfactory conditions is assured by the direct limitation of floating material, as well as indirectly by the limitation of the aggregate expenditure on armaments."
Japanese delegation: "140. The Japanese delegation also made a reservation in the same sense."
German delegation: "141. The German delegation reserves its opinion until it has studied the report of the Committee of Budgetary Experts."
British and Italian delegations: "142. The British and Italian delegations explained that their acceptance of this article depended on the attitude finally adopted by other maritime powers."

purchase and manufacture of war material for naval armaments shall be limited to the figures laid down for such party, and in accordance with the conditions prescribed, in annex . . .

Note. The two following articles appear in Part III of the London naval treaty, and are quoted as examples of supplementary restrictions which certain High Contracting Parties may be prepared to accept:[1]

Art. . . . "Not more than 25 per cent of the allowed total tonnage in the cruiser category may be fitted with a landing-on platform or deck for aircraft."

Art. . . . "In the destroyer category, not more than 16 per cent of the allowed total tonnage shall be employed in vessels of over 1,500 tons (1,524 metric tons) standard displacement."

Tables annexed to Chapter B of Part II

TABLE I.

High Contracting Party	Global Tonnage
A. B. C. D. E. F. G. . . .	

---

[1] RESERVATION: *Greek and Spanish delegations:* "143. . . . It is understood that these articles, which are binding solely upon the signatories of Part III of the London treaty, are only quoted by way of example, the commission not having expressed any view in regard to them. The representatives of Greece and Spain, however, have made a formal reservation in regard to the possibility of these supplementary restrictions being applied."

TABLE II.

Categories (defined in Annex III)	High Contracting Parties								
	A	B	C	D	E	F	G	.	.
(a) Capital ships (i)									
(ii)[1]									
(b) Aircraft carriers									
(cd) Light surface vessels — (c) Cruisers (i) Guns of more than 6.1 inches (155 mm.) (ii) Guns of 6.1 inches and less (155 mm.)									
(d) Destroyers									
(e) Submarines									

TABLE III. RULES FOR TRANSFER

The figures to be entered in this table will be calculated on the following principles:

1. Account must be taken of the special circumstances of each power, and of the classes of ships involved in the transfer.

2. Powers whose total tonnage does not exceed 100,000 tons[2] will have full freedom of transfer as regards surface ships.

3. As regards the other powers, the amount of the transfer should vary in inverse ratio to the amount of the total (global) tonnage of each of them.

---

[1] For parties who do not possess any capital ship of a standard displacement exceeding 8,000 tons (8,128 metric tons).

[2] This figure is given as an illustration.

APPENDIX I

Annexes to Chapter B of Part II

Annex I
Exempt Vessels

Subject to any special agreements which may submit them to limitation, the following vessels are exempt from limitation:

(*a*) Naval surface combatant vessels of 600 tons (610 metric tons) standard displacement and under;

(*b*) Naval surface combatant vessels exceeding 600 tons (610 metric tons), but not exceeding 2,000 tons (2,032 metric tons) standard displacement, provided they have none of the following characteristics:

  (1) Mount a gun above 6.1-inch (155 mm.) caliber;
  (2) Mount more than four guns above 3-inch (76 mm.) caliber;
  (3) Are designed or fitted to launch torpedoes;
  (4) Are designed for a speed greater than twenty knots.

(*c*) Naval surface vessels not specifically built as fighting ships which are employed on fleet duties or as troop transports or in some other way than as fighting ships, provided they have none of the following characteristics:

  (1) Mount a gun above 6.1-inch (155 mm.) caliber;
  (2) Mount more than four guns above 3-inch (76 mm.) caliber;
  (3) Are designed or fitted to launch torpedoes;
  (4) Are designed for a speed greater than twenty knots;
  (5) Are protected by armor plate;
  (6) Are designed or fitted to launch mines;
  (7) Are fitted to receive aircraft on board from the air;
  (8) Mount more than one aircraft-launching apparatus on the center line: or two, one on each broadside;
  (9) If fitted with any means of launching aircraft into the air, are designed or adopted to operate at sea more than three aircraft.

Annex II
List of Special Vessels

....
....
....

Annex III
Definitions

For the purposes of the present convention, the following expressions are to be understood in the sense defined in this annex:

(*a*) *Capital Ships*

(i) Vessels of war, not aircraft carriers, whose displacement exceeds 10,000 tons (10,160 metric tons) standard displacement, or which carry a gun with a caliber exceeding 8 inches (203 mm.).

(ii) For parties who do not possess any capital ship exceeding 8,000 tons (8,128 metric tons) standard displacement:

Vessels of war not exceeding 8,000 tons (8,128 metric tons) standard displacement and the caliber of whose guns exceeds 8 inches (203 mm.).

(*b*) *Aircraft Carriers*

Surface vessels of war, whatever their displacement, designed for the specific and exclusive purpose of carrying aircraft and so constructed that aircraft can be launched therefrom and landed thereon.

(*c*) *Cruisers*

Surface vessels of war, other than capital ships or aircraft carriers, the standard displacement of which exceeds 1,850 tons (1,880 metric tons) or with a gun above 5.1 inches (130 mm.) caliber.

The cruiser category is divided into two subcategories as follows:

(i) Cruisers carrying a gun above 6.1 inches (155 mm.) caliber.
(ii) Cruisers not carrying a gun above 6.1 inches (155 mm.) caliber.

(*d*) *Destroyers*

Surface vessels of war, the standard displacement of which does not exceed 1,850 tons (1,880 metric tons) and with a gun not above 5.1 inches (130 mm.) caliber.

(*cd*) *Light Surface Vessels*

Surface vessels of war, other than aircraft carriers, the standard displacement of which does not exceed 10,000 tons (10,160 metric tons), and with guns not exceeding 8 inches (203 mm.) caliber.

The category of light surface vessels is divided into two categories, as follows:

(i) Vessels carrying a gun above 6.1 inches (155 mm.) caliber.
(ii) Vessels not carrying a gun above 6.1 inches (155 mm.) caliber.

Standard Displacement.

1. The standard displacement of a surface vessel is the displacement of the vessel complete, fully manned, engined and equipped ready for sea, including all armament and ammunition, equipment, outfit, provisions and fresh water for crew, miscellaneous stores and implements of every description that are intended to be carried in war, but without fuel or reserve feed water on board.

2. The standard displacement of a submarine is the surface displacement of the vessel complete (exclusive of the water in nonwatertight structure), fully manned, engined and equipped ready for sea, including all armament and ammunition, equipment, outfit, provisions for crew, miscellaneous stores and implements of every description that are intended to be carried in war, but without fuel, lubricating oil, fresh water or ballast water of any kind on board.

3. Each naval combatant vessel shall be rated at its displacement tonnage when in the standard condition.

The word "ton," except in the expression "metric tons," shall be understood to be the ton of 2,240 pounds (1,016 kilos.)

Annex IV

Rules for Replacement

1. Except as provided in par. 4 of this annex, no vessel limited by this convention shall be replaced until it becomes "overage."

2. A vessel shall be deemed to be "overage" when the following number of years have elapsed since the date of its completion:
 (a) Capital ships: 20[1] years, subject to special provision as may be necessary for the replacement of existing ships.
 (b) Aircraft carriers: 20 years, subject to special provision as may be necessary for existing ships.
 (c) Surface vessels exceeding 3,000 tons (3,048 metric tons) but not exceeding 10,000 tons (10,160 metric tons) standard displacement:
  (i) If laid down before January 1, 1920, 16 years;
  (ii) If laid down after December 31, 1919, 20 years.
 (d) Surface vessels not exceeding 3,000 tons (3,048 metric tons) standard displacement:
  (i) If laid down before January 1, 1921, 12 years;
  (ii) If laid down after December 31, 1920, 16 years.
 (e) Submarines: 13 years.
3. The keels of replacement tonnage shall not be laid down more than three years before the year in which the vessel to be replaced becomes "overage": but this period is reduced to two years in the case of any replacement surface vessel not exceeding 3,000 tons (3,048 metric tons) standard displacement.

The right of replacement is not lost by delay in laying down replacement tonnage.
4. In the event of loss or accidental destruction, a vessel may be replaced immediately; but such replacement tonnage shall be subject to the limits of displacement and to the other provisions of this convention.

Annex V

Rules for Disposal of Vessels of War

The present convention provides for the disposal of vessels of war in the following ways:

(1) By scrapping (sinking or breaking up);
(2) By converting the vessel to a hulk;
(3) By converting the vessel to target use exclusively;
(4) By retaining the vessel exclusively for experimental purposes;
(5) By retaining the vessel exclusively for training purposes.

Any vessel of war to be disposed of may either be scrapped or converted to a hulk at the option of the High Contracting Party concerned.

Vessels which have been retained for target, experimental or training purposes, shall finally be scrapped or converted to hulks.

Section I. Vessels to be Scrapped

(a) A vessel to be disposed of by scrapping, by reason of its replacement, must be rendered incapable of warlike service within six months of the date of the completion of its successor, or of the first of its successors if there are more

---

[1] Under the London treaty, certain powers agreed not to exercise their rights to lay down the keels of capital ship replacement tonnage during the years 1931 to 1936 inclusive, as provided in the Washington treaty.

than one. If, however, the completion of the new vessel or vessels be delayed, the work of rendering the old vessel incapable of warlike service shall, nevertheless, be completed within four and a-half years from the date of laying the keel of the new vessel, or of the first of the new vessels; but should the new vessel, or any of the new vessels, be a surface vessel not exceeding 3,000 tons (3,048 metric tons) standard displacement, this period is reduced to three and a-half years.

(b) A vessel to be scrapped shall be considered incapable of warlike service when there shall have been removed and landed or else destroyed in the ship:

(1) All guns and essential parts of guns, fire-control tops and revolving parts of all barbettes and turrets;

(2) All hydraulic or electric machinery for operating turrets;

(3) All fire-control instruments and range finders;

(4) All ammunition, explosives, mines and mine rails;

(5) All torpedoes, war heads, torpedo tubes and training racks;

(6) All wireless telegraphy installations;

(7) All main propelling machinery, or alternatively the armored conning-tower and all side armor-plate;

(8) All aircraft cranes, derricks, lifts and launching apparatus. All landing-on or flying-off platforms and decks, or alternatively all main propelling machinery;

(9) In addition, in the case of submarines, all main storage batteries, air compressor plants and ballast pumps.

(c) Scrapping shall be finally effected in either of the following ways, within twelve months of the date of which the work of rendering the vessel incapable of warlike service is due for completion:

(1) Permanent sinking of the vessel;

(2) Breaking the vessel up; this shall always include the destruction or removal of all machinery, boilers and armor, and all deck, side and bottom plating.

Section II. *Vessels to be Converted to Hulks*

A vessel to be disposed of by conversion to a hulk shall be considered finally disposed of when the conditions prescribed in Section I, par. (b), of this annex, have been complied with, omitting subparagraphs (6), (7) and (8), and when the following have been effected:

(1) Mutilation beyond repair of all propeller-shafts, thrust-blocks, turbine-gearing or main propelling-motors and turbines or cylinders of main engines;

(2) Removal of propeller brackets;

(3) Removal and breaking up of all aircraft lifts, and the removal of all aircraft cranes, derricks and launching apparatus.

The vessel must be put in the above condition within the same limits of time as provided in Section I for rendering a vessel incapable of warlike service.

APPENDIX I

Section III. Vessels to be Converted to Target Use

(a) A vessel to be disposed of by conversion to target use exclusively shall be considered incapable of warlike service when there have been removed and landed, or rendered unserviceable on board, the following:
 (1) All guns;
 (2) All fire-control tops and instruments and main fire-control communication wiring;
 (3) All machinery for operating gun mountings or turrets;
 (4) All ammunition, explosives, mines, torpedoes and torpedo tubes;
 (5) All aviation facilities and accessories.

The vessel must be put into the above conditions within the same limits of time as provided in Section I for rendering a vessel incapable of warlike service.

(b) Each High Contracting Party is permitted to retain, for target use exclusively, at any one time:
 (1) Not more than three vessels (cruisers or destroyers), but of these three vessels only one may exceed 3,000 tons (3,048 metric tons) standard displacement;
 (2) One submarine.

(c) On retaining a vessel for target use, the High Contracting Party concerned undertakes not to recondition it for warlike service.

Section IV. Vessels Retained for Experimental Purposes

(a) A vessel to be disposed of by conversion to experimental purposes exclusively shall be dealt with in accordance with the provisions of Section III (a) of this annex.

(b) Without prejudice to the general rules, and provided that due notice be given to the other High Contracting Parties, reasonable variation from the conditions prescribed in Section III (a) of this annex, in so far as may be necessary for the purposes of a special experiment, may be permitted as a temporary measure.

Any High Contracting Party taking advantage of this provision is required to furnish full details of any such variation and the period for which they will be required.

(c) Each High Contracting Party is permitted to retain for experimental purposes exclusively at any one time:
 (1) Not more than two vessels (cruisers or destroyers), but of these two vessels only one may exceed 3,000 tons (3,048 metric tons) standard displacement;
 (2) One submarine.

(d) On retaining a vessel for experimental purposes, the High Contracting Party concerned undertakes not to recondition it for warlike service.

Section V. Vessels Retained for Training Purposes

(a) The following vessels may be retained, for training purposes exclusively, by the High Contracting Parties concerned:

....
....

(b) Vessels retained for training purposes under the provisions of par. (a) shall, within six months of the date on which they are required to be disposed of, be dealt with as follows:

1. *Capital Ships*

    The following is to be carried out:
    (1) Removal of main-armament guns, revolving parts of all barbettes and turrets; machinery for operating turrets; but three turrets with their armament may be retained in each ship;
    (2) Removal of all ammunition and explosives in excess of the quantity required for target-practice training for the guns remaining on board;
    (3) Removal of conning tower and the side-armor belt between the foremost and aftermost barbettes;
    (4) Removal or mutilation of all torpedo tubes;
    (5) Removal or mutilation on board of all boilers in excess of the number required for a maximum speed of 18 knots.

2. *Other Surface Vessels*

    The following is to be carried out:
    (1) Removal of one-half of the guns, but four guns of main caliber may be retained on each vessel;
    (2) Removal of all torpedo tubes;
    (3) Removal of all aviation facilities and accessories;
    (4) Removal of one-half of the boilers.

(c) The High Contracting Party concerned undertakes that vessels retained in accordance with the provisions of this section shall not be used for any combatant purpose.

Chapter C. Air Armaments

Art. 25. [1] [2] The number and total horse power of the aëroplanes, capable of use in war, in commission and in immediate reserve in the land, sea and air armed forces of each of the High Contracting Parties shall not exceed the figures laid down for such party in the corresponding columns of Table I annexed to this chapter.

The number and total horse power of the aëroplanes, capable of use in war, in commission and in immediate reserve in the land, sea and air formations organized on a military basis of each of the High Contracting Parties shall not exceed the figures laid down for such party in the corresponding columns of Table II annexed to this chapter.

[1] RESERVATION: *German delegation:* "148. The German delegation made a reservation in regard to these articles, on the ground that reduction and limitation do not apply to the aggregate of war material, including material in reserve, and that in its view the countries are left free to increase their stocks of aircraft not yet put together, and to arrange their air armaments as they please, without exceeding the limits fixed by the convention."

[2] RESERVATION: *Turkish delegation:* "149. The Turkish delegation reserved its opinion on the extension of the direct limitation provided for in Arts. 25 and 26 to armaments in reserve."

APPENDIX I

Art. 26.[1][2] The number, total horse power and total volume of dirigibles, capable of use in war, in commission in the land, sea and air armed forces of each of the High Contracting Parties shall not exceed the figures laid down for such party in the corresponding columns of Table III annexed to this chapter.

The number, total horse power and total volume of dirigibles capable of use in war, in commission in the land, sea and air formations organized on a military basis of each of the High Contracting Parties shall not exceed the figures laid down for such party in the corresponding columns of Table IV annexed to this chapter.

Art. 27. Horse power shall be measured according to the following rules . . .

The volume of dirigibles shall be expressed in cubic meters.

[FORMULA FOR ENGINE POWER OF AËROPLANES[3]

The formula giving the power rating of aëroplane engines is:

$$Wf = \sqrt{20\ Uf\ Pf}$$

Wf = power rating in horse power;
Uf = total volume of cylinders of the engine in dm^3;
Pf = weight in kilograms of the engine and its accessories as defined in the table below;
k = 20.

k is a constant fixed at 20 on the basis of the best information at the disposal of the committee, so that the product of this coefficient, multiplied by volume of cylinders and weight, would be approximately the square of the horse power.

TABLE FOR DEFINITION OF WEIGHT OF ENGINE

This weight is composed of:
(1) The engine in running order and having just been running, but empty of oil and water, complete with reduction gear, but without propeller hub.
(2) Feed supercharger of engine.
(3) Ignition, including casing of wireless. In the case of accumulators on board being used for other purposes, the portion for ignition shall be fixed at a round figure of 5 kilograms.

---

[1] RESERVATION: *German delegation:* "148. The German delegation made a reservation in segard to these articles, on the ground that reduction and limitation do not apply to the aggregate of war material, including material in reserve, and that in its view the countries are left free to increase their stocks of aircraft not yet put together, and to arrange their air armaments as they please, without exceeding the limits fixed by the convention."

[2] RESERVATION: *Turkish delegation:* "149. The Turkish delegation reserved its opinion on the extension of the direct limitation provided for in Arts. 25 and 26 to armaments in reserve."

[3] Prepared by a committee of experts to fix rules for the adoption of a standard horse power measurement for aëroplane and dirigible engines in pursuance of a Council resolution of January 24, 1931. The report of the experts was noted by Council resolution of May 22, 1931.
Text from *Official Journal*, XII, p. 1254.

(4) Oil radiator empty.
(5) Water radiator with all piping between pump and radiator and pump and engine, all the same being empty.
(6) Fuel pumps directly connected with the carburetor.
(7) Carburetors with heating appliance or equivalent feeding system.

The following, in particular, are not included in the weight:
Oil filters;
Indicator instruments and engine controls;
Starter and movable parts, whether or not connected with the engine;
Exhaust pipes and silencers;
Backflash baffles;
Extinguishers, etc.

Formula for Engine Power of Dirigibles

The formula giving the power rating of dirigible engines is:

$$Wf = \sqrt{8 \, Uf \, Pf}$$

Wf = power rating in horse power;
Uf = total volume of cylinders of the engine in dm^3;
Pf = weight in kilograms of the engine and its accessories as defined in the table below;
k = 8.

k is a constant fixed at 8 on the basis of the best information at the disposal of the committee, so that the product of this coefficient, multiplied by volume of cylinders and weight, would be approximately the square of the horse power.

Table for Definition of Weight of Engine

This weight is composed of:
(1) The engine in running order and having just been running, but empty of oil and water, complete with reduction gear, but without propeller hub.
(2) Feed supercharger of engine.
(3) Ignition, including casing of wireless. In the case of accumulators on board being used for other purposes, the portion for ignition shall be fixed at a round figure of 5 kilograms.
(4) Oil radiator empty.
(5) Water radiator with all piping between pump and radiator and pump and engine, all the same being empty.
(6) Fuel pumps directly connected with the carburetor.
(7) Carburetors with heating appliance or equivalent feeding system.

The following, in particular, are not included in the weight:
Oil filters;
Indicator instruments and engine controls;
Starter and movable parts, whether or not connected with the engine;
Exhaust pipes and silencers;
Backflash baffles;
Extinguishers, etc.]

Art. 28. 1. The High Contracting Parties shall refrain from prescribing the embodiment of military features in the construction of civil aviation material, so that this material may be constructed for purely civil purposes, more particularly with a view to providing the greatest possible measure of security and the most economic return. No preparations shall be made in civil aircraft in time of peace for the installation of warlike armaments for the purpose of converting such aircraft into military aircraft.

2. The High Contracting Parties undertake not to require civil aviation enterprises to employ personnel specially trained for military purposes. They undertake to authorize only as a provisional and temporary measure the seconding of personnel to, and the employment of military aviation material in, civil aviation undertakings. Any such personnel or military material which may thus be employed in civil aviation of whatever nature shall be included in the limitation applicable to the High Contracting Party concerned in virtue of Part I, or Arts. 25 and 26, of the present convention, as the case may be.[1]

3. The High Contracting Parties undertake not to subsidize, directly or indirectly, air lines principally established for military purposes instead of being established for economic, administrative or social purposes.

4. The High Contracting Parties undertake to encourage as far as possible the conclusion of economic agreements between civil aviation undertakings in the different countries and to confer together to this end.

[1] RESERVATION: *Canadian delegation:* "163. The Canadian delegation subsequently submitted a reservation in regard to the 'temporary and provisional' character of the seconding of personnel to, and the employment of military aviation material in, civil aviation undertakings. Canada, because of its special needs and problems, requires, for the reasons given in the minutes of December 2, 1930, the unrestricted right of seconding, in order to develop its country of vast distances and to protect its citizens and natural resources."

Tables annexed to Chapter C of Part II[1]

TABLE I. Aëroplanes of the Land, Sea and Air Armed Forces

High Contracting Parties	\multicolumn{2}{c}{a Total aëroplanes of the armed forces}	\multicolumn{2}{c}{b (Optional) Aëroplanes stationed in the home country}	\multicolumn{2}{c}{c (Optional) Aëroplanes stationed overseas}	\multicolumn{2}{c}{d (Optional) Aëroplanes in aircraft carriers}
	Number	Total horse power	Number	Total horse power	Number	Total horse power	Number	Total horse power
A. B. C. D. . .								

TABLE II. Aëroplanes of the Land, Sea and Air Formations organized on a Military Basis

High Contracting Parties	\multicolumn{2}{c}{a Total aëroplanes of the forces organized on a military basis}	\multicolumn{2}{c}{b (Optional) Aëroplanes stationed in the home country}	\multicolumn{2}{c}{c (Optional) Aëroplanes stationed overseas}
	Number	Total horse power	Number	Total horse power	Number	Total horse power
A. B. C. D. . .						

[1] RESERVATION: *German and Italian delegations:* "155. The German delegation makes a reservation of a general character in regard to Tables I*c*, II*c*, III*c*, IV*c*, attached to Chapter C of Part II. This reservation is to the following effect: for the purposes of reduction of armaments, the material which a contracting party may assign to its oversea territories may be of varying importance in relation to another contracting party by reason of the geographical situation of its territories in relation to the home country territories of the two contracting parties. One contracting party will therefore have every reason to regard the oversea material of another contracting party as forming part of the home country material of the latter, when such an assumption is justified by the proximity of the oversea terri-

TABLE III. Dirigibles of the Land, Sea and Air Forces

High Contracting Parties	a Total dirigibles of the armed forces			b (Optional) Dirigibles stationed in the home country			c (Optional) Dirigibles stationed overseas			d (Optional) Dirigibles in aircraft carriers		
	Number	Total horse power	Total volume	Number	Total horse power	Total volume	Number	Total horse power	Total volume	Number	Total horse-power	Total volume
A. B. C. D.												

TABLE IV. Dirigibles of the Land, Sea and Air Formations organized on a Military Basis

High Contracting Parties	a Total dirigibles of the formations organized on a military basis			b (Optional) Dirigibles stationed in the home country			c (Optional) Dirigibles stationed overseas		
	Number	Total horse power	Total volume	Number	Total horse power	Total volume	Number	Total horse power	Total volume
A. B. C. D.									

tories in relation to the home territories of the two parties (The Italian delegation called attention to the reservation presented by it with reference to the tables annexed to Part I, Chap. A (see par. 73 above, p. 266, n.))."

Turkish delegation: "156. The Turkish delegation repeated in regard to the tables attached to Chap. C the reservation it had made before (see par. 77 above, p. 266, n.) in regard to the tables in Part I (Chap. A)."

PART III BUDGETARY EXPENDITURE [1]

Art. 29.[2] (*Provisional text subject to the drafting of the annex.*) The total annual expenditure of each of the High Contracting Parties on his land, sea and air forces and formations organized on a military basis shall be limited to the figure laid down for such party and in accordance with the conditions prescribed in the annex. . . .

Editorial Note: — Articles assigned as 29A-C are additional suggestions made in the Report by the Committee of Experts on Budgetary Questions, Chaps. 6, 17 and 18.

[**Art. 29A.** The High Contracting Parties undertake not to employ the system of credit purchases or any other system of deferred payments in such a way as to increase their armaments, and, in particular, their war material, beyond the level which the parties would have been able to attain under the convention if the payments had not been deferred.

[**Art. 29B.** Each of the High Contracting Parties undertakes:

(*a*) To maintain during each consecutive period of four years[3] the average level of its annual expenditure within the limits laid down in Arts. 10, 24 and 29 of the Draft Convention of the Preparatory Commission for the Disarmament Conference;

(*b*) Not to exceed during any given year this average limit by more than a percentage fixed for the High Contracting Party in Table ....

[**Art. 29C.** (*a*) Whenever a High Contracting Party proves in the manner provided below that fluctuations in the purchasing power of currency have seriously increased the cost of its armaments and that in fact changes in the cost of certain items have not been compensated by changes in the opposite direction in the cost of other items, that High Contracting Party may submit a demand for a readjustment of its limits.

(*b*) Each High Contracting Party may demand a readjustment of the limits on the ground of an increase in the purchasing power of currency substantially reducing the cost of armaments of one or more High Contracting Parties.

[1] RESERVATION: *German delegation:* "182. The German delegation made a general reservation regarding this chapter pending the Committee of Budgetary Experts' report."

American delegation: "181. The American delegation made a general reservation on the subject of budgetary limitation and drew attention to its declaration of November 11, 1930 (*Minutes of the Sixth Session*, second part (fifth meeting))."

[2] *Note.* — In pronouncing on this article, and in particularly as regards the possibility of a distinct limitation of the expenditure on land, sea and air forces, the governments will take into account at the conference the report requested from the Committee of Budgetary Experts, which will have been forwarded to them in order to permit of the drawing up of annex . . .

[3] The committee proposes a period of four years, in view of the fact that limitation is based on payments and that the exact amount of the latter is not known until about 26 months after the beginning of the financial year.

(*c*) Any such demand shall be transmitted to the Financial Committee of the League of Nations, which shall give its opinion on this demand and also on the question whether, in the circumstances, a readjustment of the limits of other High Contracting Parties would also be justified. The demand of the High Contracting Party, together with the report of the Financial Committee, shall then be considered by a conference of all the High Contracting Parties.] [1]

PART IV EXCHANGE OF INFORMATION

Art. 30. For each category of effectives defined in the model tables annexed to this article, the exchange of information each year shall apply to the average daily number of effectives reached during the preceding year in the land, sea and air armed forces and formations organized on a military basis of each of the High Contracting Parties.

For this purpose, each of the High Contracting Parties will forward to the Secretary-General of the League of Nations, within .... months after the end of each year, the necessary information to enable the said tables to be drawn up in the case of such party. Each party shall attach to this statement an explanatory note showing the elements on which the figures supplied are based, and stating, in particular, for each sort of effectives (recruits, militiamen, reservists, territorials, etc.) the number of these effectives and the number of days' service they have performed.

The said tables shall be drawn up and published with the explanatory note referred to above by the Secretary-General not later than.......... in each year.

[1] The text submitted has been drafted more from the technical point of view and is not intended to deal exhaustively with questions of procedure.

NOTES TO MODEL TABLE ON P. 290

[1] RESERVATIONS: *French delegation:* "189. (*d*) The French delegation does not accept publicity for the effectives stationed in each overseas territory, as not being called for to any greater extent in the case of overseas territories than in the case of the various districts of the home country. The French delegation also desires to point out that detailed publicity in the case of each overseas territory, with a multitude of distinctions between the different categories of soldiers according to their rank and length of service, is even less acceptable, being materially impossible owing to the constant transfers from one territory to the other and the special conditions of the territories in question. An army of accountants would be required for the purpose. The inclusion in the convention of such minute rules is calculated to multiply involuntary errors in the information supplied by the contracting parties, and further threatens to lead to unnecessary and provocative discussion, which no one can desire, and which can not be the object the commission has in view."

British Empire delegation: "190. The British delegation concurred in the substance of this reservation."

Model Tables annexed to Art. 30 (Part IV)[1]

MODEL TABLES OF THE AVERAGE DAILY NUMBER OF EFFECTIVES REACHED
DURING THE YEAR IN THE LAND ARMED FORCES AND LAND
FORMATION ORGANIZED ON A MILITARY BASIS

TABLE I. Land Armed Forces Stationed in the Home Country

High Contracting Parties	a Total effectives, including the effectives specified separately in this Table	b Officers	c Other effectives who have completed at least x[2] months of service	d Soldiers whose period of service has exceeded the legal period of service but is less than x[2] months (*information to be supplied only for effectives recruited by conscription*)	e (Optional statement.) *Recruits not trained as defined in the national legislation*
A. B. C. D. . .					

---

[1] *Continued from p. 289.*

German delegation: "187. The following reservations were made in connection with Art. 30:

"(*a*) The German delegation made a reservation to the article on the ground that the tables mentioned therein do not provide for publicity regarding trained reserves and the figure of the annual contingent.

"The general reservation of the German delegation in regard to Chap. A, Part I (Table I (see par. 73 above)) applies to the following Tables of Part IV — Table II, Table V and the Annex to Tables II and V, Table IX and Table XII.

"(*b*) The German delegation also made a reservation in regard to the option allowed to states to show, if they desire, for purposes of information, in a special column of the tables annexed to Part IV (Table V*e*), the number of recruits not trained as defined in the national legislation.

"The German delegation considers that this option should not be allowed, unless the contracting parties are under obligation to publish at the same time and in the same tables similar information with regard to the number of their trained reserves. Failing such publicity, the German delegation considers it impossible to judge of the real military situation of the states."

Japanese delegation· "191. (*e*) The Japanese delegation also made a reservation as to the desirability of separate publication of the average daily effectives in each oversea territory."

Turkish delegation: "188. (*c*) The Turkish delegation repeated in regard to the tables annexed to Art. 29 the reservations made by it in regard to the tables in Chap. A, Part I (see par. 77 above, p. 266 n.).''

[2] *Note* — This figure will be determined by the duration of the longest period of service which is in force in the conscript army of any High Contracting Party at the time of the signature of the convention.

Table II. Land Armed forces Stationed Overseas

High Contracting Parties	Overseas territory	*a* Total effectives, including the effectives specified separately in this Table	*b* Officers	*c* Other effectives who have completed at least x^1 months of service	*d* Soldiers whose period of service has exceeded the legal period of service but is less than x^1 months (*information to be supplied only for effectives recruited by conscription*)	*e* (Optional statement.) (*Recruits not trained as defined in the national legislation*)
A.	M N O P …					
B.	… R S T …					

Table III. Total Land Armed Forces

High Contracting Parties	*a* Total effectives, including the effectives specified separately in this Table	*b* Officers	*c* Other effectives who have completed at least x^1 months of service	*d* Soldiers whose period of service has exceeded the legal period of service but is less than x^1 months (*information to be supplied only for effectives recruited by conscription*)	*e* (Optional statement.) *Recruits not trained as defined in the national legislation*
A. B. C. D.					

[1] *Note* — This figure will be determined by the duration of the longest period of service which is in force in the conscript army of any High Contracting Party at the time of the signature of the convention.

TABLE IV. Formations organized on a Military Basis

High Contracting Parties	a Total effectives, including the effectives specified separately in this Table	b Officers or officials ranking as officers	c Other effectives or officials who have completed at least x^1 months of service	d Soldiers or officials whose period of service has exceeded the legal period of service but is less than x^1 months (*information to be supplied only for effectives recruited by conscription*)	e (Optional statement.) *Recruits not trained as defined in the national legislation*
A. B. C. D. • •					

TABLE V. Formations organized on a Military Basis stationed Overseas

High Contracting Parties	a Total effectives, including the effectives specified separately in this Table	b Officers or officials ranking as officers	c Other effectives or officials who have completed at least x^1 months of service	d Soldiers or officials whose period of service has exceeded the legal period of service but is less than x^1 months (*information to be supplied only for effectives recruited by conscription*)	e (Optional statement.) *Recruits not trained as defined in the national legislation*
A.					

[1] *Note.* — This figure will be determined by the duration of the longest period of service which is in force in the conscript army of any High Contracting Party at the time of the signature of the convention.

APPENDIX I

Model Tables of the Average Daily Number of Effectives Reached during the Year in the Naval Forces

	Table VI. Naval Forces				Table VII. Sea Formations organized on a Military Basis			
	a	b	c	d	a	b	c	d
High Contracting Parties	Total effectives, including effectives specified separately in this table	Officers	Other effectives who have completed at least y[1] months of service	*(Optional statement.)* Recruits not trained as defined in the national legislation	Total effectives, including effectives specified separately in this table	Officers	Other effectives who have completed at least y[1] months of service	*(Optional statement.)* Recruits not trained as defined in the national legislation
A.								
B.								
C.								
D.								

Model Tables of the Average Daily Number of Effectives Reached during the Year in the Air Armed Forces

	Table VIII. Air Armed Forces stationed in the Home Country			Table IX. Air Armed Forces stationed Overseas			Table X. Total Air Armed Forces		
	a	b	c	a	b	c	a	b	c
High Contracting Parties	Total effectives, including the effectives specified separately in this table	Effectives who have completed at least z[1] months of service (officers, noncommissioned officers and men)	*(Optional statement.)* Recruits not trained as defined in the national legislation	Total effectives, including the effectives specified separately in this table	Effectives who have completed at least z[1] months of service (officers, noncommissioned officers and men)	*(Optional statement.)* Recruits not trained as defined in the national legislation	Total effectives, including the effectives specified separately in this table	Effectives who have completed at least z[1] months of service (officers, noncommissioned officers and men)	*(Optional statement.)* Recruits not trained as defined in the national legislation
A.									
B.									
C.									
D.									

[1] *Note.* — This figure will be determined by the duration of the longest period of service which is in force in the conscript navy army of any High Contracting Party at the time of signature of the convention.

Model Tables of the Average Daily Number of Effectives Reached during the Year in the Air Formations Organized on a Military Basis

High Contracting Parties	TABLE XI. Air Formations organized on a Military Basis stationed in the Home Country			TABLE XII. Air Formations organized on a Military Basis stationed Overseas		
	a	b	c	a	b	c
	Total effectives, including the effectives specified separately in this table	Effectives who have completed at least z^1 months of service (officers, noncommissioned officers and men and officials of all grades)	(Optional statement.) Recruits not trained as defined in the national legislation	Total effectives, including the effectives specified separately in this table	Effectives who have completed at least z^1 months of service (officers, noncommissioned officers and men and officials of all grades)	(Optional statement.) Recruits not trained as defined in the national legislation
A. B. C. D. . .						

Art. 31.[2] If any youths have compulsorily received, during any year, preparatory military training within the jurisdiction of any High Contracting Party, such party shall communicate to the Secretary-General of the League of Nations, within ..... x months after the end of each year, the number of youths who have received such instruction.

The above information shall be published by the Secretary-General not later than .... in each year.

Art. 32. The High Contracting Parties concerned shall forward to the Secretary-General of the League of Nations at the end of each year the following information as to the provisions of their law relating to the effectives recruited by conscription in their land, sea and air forces and formations organized on a military basis respectively;

(1) The total number of days comprised in the first period of service;
(2) The total duration in days of the ensuing periods.

[1] *Note.* — This figure will be determined by the duration of the longest period of service which is in force in the conscript air force of any High Contracting Party at the time of the signature of the convention.

[2] RESERVATION: *German and Italian delegations:* "194. The German and Italian delegations consider that particulars should be given, not only of the youths who have been subjected to compulsory preparatory military training, but of all who have received preparatory military training, whether voluntary or otherwise."

The above information shall be published by the Secretary-General not later than .... in each year.

Art. 33.[1][2] Each of the High Contracting Parties shall, within .... months from the end of each budgetary year, communicate to the Secretary-General of the League of Nations a statement drawn up in accordance with a standard model, showing by categories of materials the total actual expenditure in the course of the said year on the upkeep, purchase and manufacture of war materials of the land and sea armed forces and formations organized on a military basis of such party.

The information contained in this statement shall be published by the Secretary-General not later than .... in each year.

Art. 34. Within one month after the date of laying down and the date of completion respectively of each vessel of war, other than the vessels exempt from limitation under Annex I to Chapter B of Part II, laid down or completed by or for them or within their jurisdiction after the coming into force of the present convention, the High Contracting Parties shall communicate to the Secretary-General of the League of Nations the information detailed below:

(a) The date of laying down the keel and the following particulars:
Classification of the vessel and for whom built (if not for the High Contracting Party);
Standard displacement in tons and metric tons;
Principal dimensions — namely, length of water-line, extreme beam at or below water-line;
Mean draught at standard displacement;
Caliber of the largest gun.

(b) The date of completion, together with the foregoing particulars relating to the vessel at that date.

The above information shall be immediately communicated by the Secretary-General to all the High Contracting Parties and shall be published by the Secretary-General not later than ..... in each year.

Art. 35. Each of the High Contracting Parties shall communicate to the Secretariat of the League of Nations the name and the tonnage of any

---

[1] *Note.* — In giving an opinion on this article, the governments will take into account the report requested from the Committee of Budgetary Experts regarding the number and nature of the categories to be laid down and the methods of publicity thus adopted in connection with the provisions of the annex regarding limitation referred to in Art. 9 of the present convention.

[2] RESERVATION: *German delegation:* "201. The German delegation made a general reservation in regard to Art. 33. It considered that, in order to be effective, publicity should be given to the total of the land and air material and of non-floating material of the navies, and that this information should be published by categories and numbers.

"As regards publicity in respect of expenditure, it reserved its opinion until it had had an opportunity to study the Committee of Budgetary Experts' report."

vessel constructed in accordance with Art. 19. (Chapter II). With regard to existing vessels of this type, this communication shall be made within two months after ratification of the present convention. With regard to vessels to be constructed, the communication shall be made on the date of completion.

Art. 36.[1] For each of the categories of aircraft defined in the model tables annexed to this article, the exchange of information shall apply to the maximum figures attained in each year in respect of the number and total horse power, and for dirigibles the total volume, by the aircraft referred to in Arts. 25 and 26 of the present convention.

For this purpose, each of the High Contracting Parties will forward to the Secretary-General of the League of Nations within .... months after the end of each year the necessary information to enable the said tables to be drawn up in the case of such party.

The tables referred to in the preceding paragraph shall be drawn up and published by the Secretary-General not later than .... in each year.

[PARTICULARS WITH A VIEW TO ENABLING STATISTICS TO BE PREPARED REGARDING THE EFFECTIVES OF NONMILITARY AVIATION AND STATISTICS OF PUBLIC FUNDS EXPENDED ON SUCH AVIATION[2]

I. Effectives of Nonmilitary Aviation

A. COMMERCIAL AVIATION
  1. Aëroplanes and seaplanes carrying four persons or more:
     (a) Nominal horse power
         Number of passengers carried in normal service,
         Useful load permitted
         Freight permitted
         } According to the regulation certificates of airworthiness.
     (b) Normal contents of tanks
         Volume of compartments holding freight
     (c) Date of entry into service.

(The particulars grouped under (a) and (b) might be given in aggregate figures, the number of aircraft to which they refer being indicated.)

  2. Dirigibles:
     Volume
     Horse power
     Normal load
     Range of flight with normal load.
  3. Aëroplanes or seaplanes carrying from one to three persons:
     Number and total horse power.

---

[1] RESERVATIONS: *German delegation:* "206. The German delegation made a reservation concerning this article. It considers that publicity should apply to the total air material, including material in reserve (see also, in regard to Tables I*c*, II*c*, III*c*, IV*c*, the German delegation's general reservation concerning the tables annexed to Chapter C of Part II (par., p. 286, n. 155 above)."

[2] This list of particulars is provisional only, and is drawn up solely for purposes of detailed comparison between the replies received from the different governments.

4. Aëroplanes or seaplanes used for special purposes involving permanent installations (photography, spraying of crops or forests, wireless for patrolling purposes).

Number and horse power, by categories, according to purpose for which the aircraft are used.

B. PRIVATE AVIATION

Number and total horse power, by categories of single seaters, two seaters, three to five seaters and six seaters, aëroplanes, seaplanes and amphibians being classified separately.

Number and total horse power of dirigibles.

C. NONMILITARY AVIATION AT THE DISPOSAL OF THE STATE OR OF OFFICIAL SERVICES

This class would include, for instance, — enumerated by categories according to use, and the total horse power being indicated — police aircraft for forest patrols or attached to state meteorological or scientific services.

II. Expenditure of Public Funds Upon Nonmilitary Aviation

A. COMMERCIAL AVIATION

Direct assistance. — Mileage subventions; postal contracts; guaranties of minimum revenue from postal traffic; indemnities for crew or passenger accommodation placed at the disposal of contributing parties; subsidies to training schools for air transport crews; exemption from taxation; guaranteed interest on issues of bonds; Treasury advances.

Indirect assistance. — Establishment of air ports and air routes; meteorological services; insurance funds; other means of indirect assistance.

B. PRIVATE AVIATION

Expenditure on civil training centers.
Expenditure on subsidized schools for training pilots or specialists.
Expenditure on clubs possessing aircraft (engine driven only) placed at the disposal of their members for learning to fly or for free use.

Purchase, upkeep and efficiency bonuses granted to private persons, whether or not such bonuses render the aircraft so acquired liable for service.

Requisition bonuses.

C. NONMILITARY AVIATION AT THE DISPOSAL OF THE STATE OR OF OFFICIAL SERVICES

Relevant budget entries.

In each of the categories A, B and C, a distinction should be drawn between expenditure borne on the national or federal budget, on that of federated states, or of district, provincial or municipal organizations, according to the political and administrative structure of the country concerned.]

Model Tables annexed to Article 36[1]

MODEL TABLE I. Aëroplanes of the Land, Sea and Air Armed Forces

High Contracting Parties	a Total aëroplanes of the armed forces		b (Optional) Aëroplanes stationed in the home country		c (Optional) Aëroplanes stationed overseas		d (Optional) Aëroplanes in aircraft carriers	
	Number	Total horse power	Number	Total horse power	Number	Total horse power	Number	Total horse power
A. B. C. D. . .								

MODEL TABLE II. Aëroplanes of the Land, Sea and Air Formations organized on a Military Basis

High Contracting Parties	a Total aëroplanes of the forces organized on a military basis		b (Optional) Aëroplanes stationed in the home country		c (Optional) Aëroplanes stationed overseas	
	Number	Total horse power	Number	Total horse power	Number	Total horse power
A. B. C. D. . .						

[1] RESERVATION: *German delegation:* See Art. 36, par. 206 and Tables annexed to Chap. C of Part II, par. 155, p. 286, 296.

Turkish delegation: "207. The Turkish delegation repeated, in regard to the tables annexed to Art. 36, the reservations it had made concerning the tables in Chap. A, Part I (see par. 77, p. 266, above)."

MODEL TABLE III. Dirigibles of the Land, Sea and Air Forces

High Contracting Parties	a Total dirigibles of the armed forces			b (*Optional*) Dirigibles stationed in the home country			c (*Optional*) Dirigibles stationed overseas			d (*Optional*) Dirigibles in aircraft carriers		
	Number	Total horse power	Total volume	Number	Total horse power	Total volume	Number	Total horse power	Total volume	Number	Total horse power	Total volume
A. B. C. D. . .												

MODEL TABLE IV. Dirigibles of the Land, Sea and Air Formations organized on a Military Basis

High Contracting Parties	a Total dirigibles the formations organized on a military basis			b (*Optional*) Dirigibles stationed in the home country			c (*Optional*) Dirigibles stationed overseas		
	Number	Total horse power	Total volume	Number	Total horse power	Total volume	Number	Total horse power	Total volume
A. B. C. D. . .									

Art. 37.[1] In order to insure publicity as regards civil aviation, each of the High Contracting Parties shall indicate within x months after the end of each year to the Secretary-General of the League of Nations the number and total horse power of civil aëroplanes and dirigibles registered within the jurisdiction of such party. Each party shall also indicate the amounts expended on civil aviation by the government and by local authorities.

The above information shall be published by the Secretary-General not later than .... in each year.

Art. 38.[2] Each of the High Contracting Parties shall communicate to the Secretary-General of the League of Nations within .... months of the end of each budgetary year a statement drawn up in accordance with the standard model annexed to this article[3] showing the total amounts actually expended in the course of the said year on the land, sea and air armaments of such party.

The information supplied in this statement shall be published by the Secretary-General not later than .... in each year.

PART V. CHEMICAL ARMS [4]

Art. 39. The High Contracting Parties undertake, subject to reciprocity, to abstain from the use in war of asphyxiating, poisonous or similar gases, and of all analogous liquids, substances or processes.

They undertake unreservedly to abstain from the use of all bacteriological methods of warfare.

---

[1] RESERVATION: *German delegation:* "212. The German delegation ... considered that rules concerning publicity in regard to peace-time means of communication could not properly be included in a purely military convention, and that for this reason they should be dealt with in a special convention."

[2] RESERVATION: *German delegation:* "215. The German delegation reserved its opinion on the publication of expenditure until it had studied the report of the Committee of Budgetary Experts; it considered, however, that the standard model should not be used for purposes of comparison and limitation."

[3] See the standard model statement printed at p. 317.

[4] RESERVATIONS: *German delegation:* "229. With regard to Art. 39, the German delegation is of opinion that the effect of prohibiting the use of chemical weapons would be incomplete unless it referred also to preparations for the use of those weapons (instruction of troops, etc.).

"230. The same delegation stated that a scheme for the reduction and limitation of armaments should, in the first place, prohibit weapons of an essentially offensive character, the destructive efforts of which menaced not only armies but also the civilian population — *i.e.*, bombs from the air, large caliber guns and tanks of every kind."

PART VI. MISCELLANEOUS PROVISIONS

Chapter A. Permanent Disarmament Commission

Art. 40.[1] There shall be set up at the seat of the League of Nations a Permanent Disarmament Commission with the duty of following the execution of the present convention. It shall consist of x (figure to be fixed by the conference) members appointed respectively by the governments of .... (list to be drawn up by the conference).

Members of the commission shall not represent their governments. They shall be appointed for x years, but shall be reeligible. During their term of office, they may be replaced only on death or in the case of voluntary resignation or serious and permanent illness.

They may be assisted by technical experts.

Art. 41. The commission shall meet for the first time, on being summoned by the Secretary-General of the League of Nations, within three months from the entry into force of the present convention, to elect a provisional president and vice-president and to draw up its rules of procedure.

Thereafter it shall meet annually in ordinary session on the date fixed in its rules of procedure.

It may also, if summoned by its president, meet in extraordinary session in the cases provided for in the present convention and whenever an application to that effect is made by a High Contracting Party.

Art. 42. The commission shall have full power to lay down its own rules of procedure on the basis of the provisions of the present convention.

Art. 43. The commission may only transact business if at least two-thirds of its members are present.

Art. 44. Any High Contracting Party not having a member of its nationality on the commission shall be entitled to send a member appointed for the purpose to sit at any meeting of the commission during which a question specially affecting the interests of that party is considered.

Art. 45. Each member of the commission shall have only one vote.

All decisions of the commission shall be taken by a majority of the votes of the members present at the meeting.

In the cases provided for in Arts. 50 and 52 the votes of members ap-

---

[1] RESERVATIONS: *French delegation:* "238. The third paragraph provides that members of the commission may be 'assisted by technical experts.' The French delegation was in favor of a clause providing that members of the commission must themselves be technical experts, giving purely technical opinions and not prejudging any political conclusions that the governments might draw from those opinions. The French delegation stated that it still preferred this system, although the majority of the commission did not accept it."

pointed by the parties concerned in the discussion shall not be counted in determining the majority.

A minority report may be drawn up.

Art. 46. Each member of the commission shall be entitled on his own responsibility to have any person heard or consulted who is in a position to throw any light on the question which is being examined by the commission.

Art. 47. Each member of the commission shall be entitled to require that, in any report by the commission, account shall be taken of the opinions or suggestions put forward by him, if necessary in the form of a separate report.

Art 48. All reports by the commission shall, under conditions specified in each case in the present convention, or in the rules of procedure of the commission, be communicated to all the High Contracting Parties and to the Council of the League of Nations, and shall be published.

Art. 49. The Permanent Disarmament Commission shall receive all the information supplied by the High Contracting Parties to the Secretary-General of the League in pursuance of their international obligations in this regard.

Each year, the commission shall make at least one report on the information submitted to it and on any other information that may reach it from a responsible source and that it may consider worth attention, showing the situation as regards the fulfillment of the present convention.

This report shall be communicated forthwith to all the High Contracting Parties and to the Council of the League and shall be published on the date fixed in the rules of procedure of the commission.

Chapter B. Derogations

Art. 50. If, during the term of the present convention, a change of circumstances constitutes, in the opinion of any High Contracting Party, a menace to its national security, such High Contracting Party may suspend temporarily in so far as concerns itself, any provision or provisions of the present convention, other than those expressly designed to apply in the event of war, provided:

(a) That such contracting party shall immediately notify the other contracting parties and at the same time the Permanent Disarmament Commission, through the Secretary-General of the League of Nations of such temporary suspension, and of the extent thereof.

(b) That simultaneously with the said notification, the contracting party shall communicate to the other contracting parties, and at the same time, to the Permanent Disarmament Commission through the

Secretary-General, a full explanation of the change of circumstances referred to above.

Thereupon the other High Contracting Parties shall promptly advise as to the situation thus presented.

When the reasons for such temporary suspension have ceased to exist, the said High Contracting Party shall reduce its armaments to the level agreed upon in the convention, and shall make immediate notification to the other contracting parties.

Chapter C. Procedure Regarding Complaints

Art. 51. The High Contracting Parties recognize that any violation of the provisions of the present convention is a matter of concern to all the parties.

Art. 52. If, during the term of the present convention, a High Contracting Party is of opinion that another party to the convention is maintaining armaments in excess of the figures agreed upon or is in any way violating or endeavoring to violate the provisions of the present convention, such party may lay the matter, through the Secretary-General of the League of Nations, before the Permanent Disarmament Commission.

The commission, after hearing a representative of the High Contracting Party whose action is questioned, should such party so desire, and the representative of any other party which may be specially concerned in the matter and which asks to be heard, shall, as soon as possible, present a report thereon to the High Contracting Parties and to the Council of the League. The report and any proceedings thereon shall be published as soon as possible.

The High Contracting Parties shall promptly advise as to the conclusions of the report.

If the High Contracting Parties directly concerned are Members of the League of Nations, the Council shall exercise the rights devolving upon it in such circumstances in virtue of the Covenant with a view to insuring the observance of the present convention and to safeguarding the peace of nations.

Chapter D. Final Provisions

Art. 53.[1] The present convention shall not affect the provisions of previous treaties under which certain of the High Contracting Parties have agreed to limit their land, sea or air armaments, and have thus fixed in rela-

---

[1] RESERVATION: *German delegation:* "273. The German delegation stated, in connection with Art. 53, that, in so far as it does not refer to the Washington and London treaties, the German delegation would vote against the Draft Convention

tion to one another their respective rights and obligations in this connection.

The following High Contracting Parties . . . signatory to the said treaties declare that the limits fixed for their armaments under the present convention are accepted by them in relation to the obligations referred to in the preceding paragraph, the maintenance of such provisions being for them an essential condition for the observance of the present convention.

Art. 54. If a dispute arises between two or more of the High Contracting Parties concerning the interpretation or application of the provisions of the present convention, and cannot be settled either directly between the parties or by some other method of friendly settlement, the parties will, at the request of any one of them, submit such dispute to the decision of the Permanent Court of International Justice or to an arbitral tribunal chosen by them.

Art. 55. The present convention shall be ratified by the High Contracting Parties in accordance with their respective constitutional methods. The instruments of ratification shall be deposited with the Secretary-General of the League of Nations.

The present convention shall come into force, for each party whose instrument of ratification has been deposited, as soon as the instruments of ratification have been deposited by . . . (list to be drawn up by the conference).

(Should the present convention not have come into force in accordance with the preceding paragraph by . . . the High Contracting Parties shall be invited by the Secretary-General of the League of Nations to meet and consider the possibility of putting it into force. They undertake to participate in this consultation, which shall take place before. . . .)[1]

Art. 56. Each of the High Contracting Parties will take the necessary measures for carrying the provisions of the present convention into effect as soon as it has come into force for such party.

Art. 57. Subject to the provisions of Arts. 58 and 59, the present convention shall remain in force for [x] years. It shall remain in force after the expiration of that period except in so far as it may be amended, superseded or denounced under the conditions specified in the following articles.

---

as a whole. The draft, as drawn up by the majority of the Preparatory Commission, excludes essential elements from the limitation and reduction of land armaments. Instead of leading to real disarmament, this draft would serve only to conceal the real state of world armaments or would even allow armaments to be increased. To accept it would at the same time be tantamount to a renewal of the German signature to the disarmament clauses of the treaty of Versailles."

[1] *Note.* — It will be for the conference to decide whether this paragraph and any supplementary provisions which may be necessary would not be better placed in a protocol of signature.

Art. 58. Before the end of the period of x years provided for in the preceding article, and not less than y years after its entry into force, the present convention shall be reexamined by the High Contracting Parties meeting in conference. The date of this meeting shall be fixed by the Council of the League of Nations, after taking cognizance of the opinion of the Permanent Disarmament Commission and of the intentions of the High Contracting Parties non-Members of the League of Nations.

The above-mentioned conference may, if necessary, revise the present convention and establish fresh provisions in substitution therefor, fixing their period of duration and laying down general rules regarding their examination and subsequent revision, if the latter is required.

Art. 59.[1] Before the end of the period of y years provided for in the preceding article, but not less than z years after the entry into force of the present convention, the procedure for examination and revision laid down in that article may also be carried out at the request of a High Contracting Party with the concurrence of the Permanent Disarmament Commission, if the conditions under which the engagements stipulated in the convention were contracted have undergone, as the result of technical transformations or special circumstances, changes justifying a fresh examination and, if necessary, the revision of such engagements.

Art. 60. In the course of a conference held in the circumstances provided for in the two preceding articles, any High Contracting Party shall be entitled to notify its intention to denounce the present convention.

Such denunciation shall take effect two years after its date, but in no case before the expiration of the period of x years mentioned in Art. 57.

---

[1] RESERVATION: *German delegation:* "295. On the other hand, the German delegation submitted the following reservation:
"The German delegation is of opinion that the development of a peaceful means of communication must in no case be made a basis for armaments, especially as no account has been taken of the essential and purely military factors of material in reserve or in stock, trained reserves, etc., and other important means of communication, such as the mercantile marine, on which, indeed, preliminary warlike fittings have been authorized.'"

Draft Annex to Arts. 10, 24, 29 and 38 of the Draft Convention Elaborated by the Preparatory Commission for the Disarmament Conference, Together with the Model Statement (Land, Naval and Air Forces) and Annexed Tables.[1]

A. GENERAL PROVISIONS

1. The High Contracting Parties agree that the annual statements of expenditure on land, sea and air armaments required by Art. 38 of the convention shall be made in accordance with the model statement and appended tables and on the basis laid down in this annex. They further agree that the definitions of the total expenditure on land, sea and air armaments respectively and of the expenditure on war material for the land and sea forces respectively, for the purpose of the limitations provided in Arts. 10, 24 and 29 of the convention, shall be those laid down in the following paragraphs of this annex for the purpose of the filling in of the model statement.[2]

The expenditure to be entered in the model statements under the provisions of this annex shall correspond to the true and final utilization of the amounts involved; it shall comprise the whole of the expenditure on armaments.[3]

2. In filling in the model statement of national defense expenditure, each High Contracting Party undertakes to adhere as closely as possible to the definitions, given in the following paragraphs of this annex, of the expenditure to be entered under the various subheads, and only to depart therefrom in so far as its public accounting procedure renders unavoidable; it undertakes in particular not to make any change from year to year in the methods used for filling in the statement unless obliged to do so as a result of administrative improvements; in that case it shall be bound to notify the Permanent Disarmament Commission of the nature of such change.

Provided always that, except as may be otherwise agreed between the High Contracting Parties in accordance with the proposal in the report of the Budgetary Experts,[4] each High Contracting Party undertakes to adhere strictly to the definitions in this annex as regards (*i*) the cost of any of the three forces as a whole, and (*ii*) head IV of the model statement as a whole for each of the land and sea forces.

---

[1] From Preparatory Commission for the Disarmament Conference, *Report by the Committee of Experts on Budgetary Questions*, p. 28-40 (C.182.M.69.1931.IX.3) and *Official Journal*, XII, p. 700-712.

The Report of which the Draft Annex represents the conclusions is printed in both places ahead of it.

[2] See Chap. 1 of the *Report*, p. 6.

[3] See Chap. 3 of the *Report*, p. 7.

[4] This phrase would, of course, have to be modified when any such agreement is actually reached (see Chaps. 4 and 5, p. 8-10).

Provided also that these definitions shall be binding as regards the total cost of each force or the cost of war material limited under Arts. 10, 24 and 29 of the convention.

3. The annual expenditure, or the total amount actually expended in the course of any year, for the purposes of Arts. 10, 24, 29 and 38 of the convention, shall mean the payments recorded in the final accounts relating to that year. Provided, however, that in the case of any state which records in its accounts the issue of orders of payment but not the actual payments, and which satisfies the Disarmament Conference that such orders of payment are virtually equivalent to cash disbursements,[1] the annual expenditure above referred to shall mean the amount of the orders of payment recorded in the final accounts relating to that year.

4.[2] In those countries where the provision for gross expenditure (in the widest sense of the term) can be directly ascertained, this gross expenditure should be entered in the return.

In other countries, where it is the custom to allow certain receipts of the services to be applied to meet expenditure for national defence, governments shall reconstitute the gross amount of the expenditure by taking into account the expenditure effected out of these receipts and by adding such expenditure to the other expenditure in order to arrive at the sums to be entered in the return.

The above rules apply to expenditure effected out of all receipts, in respect either of services rendered, or of sale, or cession to other authorities, of property and material, new or old. They also apply to expenditure relating to the pay and allowances of all kinds of the personnel, whatever taxes, contributions to pension or social insurance funds, etc., may be due from this personnel, and whether such taxes or contributions are deducted from the pay or not.

Should the fact of the nondeduction of a particular receipt from the expenditure cause the repetition of a charge (in the same or a different guise) in the return, either of one armed force or of the armed forces of one country as a whole, the amount of the receipt in question may be deducted by way of exception.

Further, any government will be at liberty to state in a footnote to the return the amount of any receipts arising from cessions of property, etc., for purposes other than those of national defense.

5.[3] Where additional expenditure is incurred by the forces as a result of help given in emergency to the civil population, such additional expendi-

---

[1] This phrase would, of course, have to be modified when any such agreement is actually reached (see Chap. 4 and 5, p. 8–10).
[2] See Chap. 7 of the *Report* p. 11.
[3] See Chap. 7 of the *Report*, p. 11.

ture may be omitted from the returns, whether or not it is paid by the beneficiaries.

6.[1] Any grants and loans made to undertakings having among their objects the furnishing of goods or services for purposes of national defense, in accordance with the definitions given in the present annex, and any participation in the said undertakings (including the purchase of shares, bonds, etc., for payment in cash or in any other form) shall be deemed to be expenditure on the said goods or services, save only grants, loans or participations, etc., based on general economic, fiscal or social considerations or those representing purely temporary advances, provided always that these advances are not renewed. Whenever a High Contracting Party deems itself entitled not to include certain of these loans, participations and grants, etc., in the model statement, the sums thus omitted shall be shown in Table E with the necessary explanations in each case.

7.[2] All expenditure occasioned by reductions in the strength of the forces (other than pensions and allowances for loss of office or premature retirement or discharge, which will be excluded) will be included in the returns — *e.g.*, indemnities paid to towns for the withdrawal of garrisons.

8.[3] Expenditure for the purposes defined in this annex will be included whatever the source of the funds from which, or the authority under which, the expenditure is made, subject to the exceptions stated in par. 2 above. The expenditure should include that incurred out of:

(1) The budget votes, together with supplementary or extraordinary or excess votes, whether confined to one year or available for more than one year; including both the budgets of the defense departments and the budgets of other departments;

(2) Credits carried forward from previous years into the year in question;

(3) Credits opened by administrative action;

(4) Special funds or receipts applicable to armament expenditure outside the budget, including loans raised privately or on the markets, or made by other governments;

(5) Any corresponding resources made available by the authorities of states (in the case of federated countries), provinces, cities, municipalities, or by other local authorities, or by public institutions of any kind;

(6) Gifts, bequests or contribution by private institutions or persons.

9.[4] The list contained in this annex of expenditure to be included in each chapter of the model statement is purely indicative in character, and any

---

[1] See Chap. 8 of the *Report*, p. 11.
[2] See Chap. 9 of the *Report*, p. 12.
[3] See Chap. 10 of the *Report*, p. 13.
[4] See Chap. 12 of the *Report*, p. 14.

expenditure on new arms, or, in general any expenditure intended for national defense, must be included within the prescribed limits and within the scope of the model statement, even if it is not specially and explicitly indicated in this annex.

Similarly, all such expenditure, whether effected out of the resources enumerated in par. 8 above or not, shall be included within the limits and in the model statement.

B. INSTRUCTIONS ON THE DIFFERENT SUBHEADS

General Instruction on Pay and Allowances

10. Pay and allowances include, in the case both of the personnel of the land, sea and air forces and formations organized on a military basis and of civilian personnel, all pay, etc., paid to personnel seconded, or to personnel on leave, together with contributions paid by the state in respect of social insurance, etc., without deduction of contributions paid by the personnel toward the cost of their pensions or in respect of social insurance, etc. Family or separation allowances are also included.

HEAD I. EFFECTIVES

Subheads A. Payment and allowances of all kinds: officers; and B. — Ditto: N.C.O.s and men

11. Will include: Pay and allowances of all kinds granted in virtue of office, and other allowances (including subsistence allowances, but not pensions) of *officers, N.C.O.s,* and *men* normally forming an effective part of military formations, services and establishments, and of personnel holding corresponding ranks in formations organized on a military basis, excepting the officers, N.C.O.s and men falling under subheads L to N — namely:

In the case of the *land armed forces and formations organized on a military basis:* Central administration[1]; missions; military attachés; headquarters staff and staff of commands; infantry; cavalry; artillery; engineer and signal corps; tank corps; antigas units; intendance, transport, pay and accounting corps; recruiting services; medical and hospital services; remount and veterinary services; chaplains; military police; military law; schools and colleges; survey services so far as they work for the army;

All other services not enumerated above.

In the case of the *naval armed forces and formations organized on a military basis:* Central administration; missions, naval attachés; headquarters staff and staff of commands; combatant and noncombatant personnel of all branches (gunnery, mines, torpedo, engineer, etc.); coast defense, intendance, pay and accounting personnel; recruiting services; medical personnel; chaplains; naval police; martial law; naval schools and colleges; and, in so far as they work for the navy, scientific services, coastal and hydrographic surveys, chart printing,

---

[1] Central administration should include services dealing with administration and direction, but not operative services. For example, organizations carrying out scientific research should be included in head IV, whether situated in the same place or building as the central administration or not.

meteorological services, astronomical services, lighting and buoyage of the coasts;

All other services not enumerated above.

In the case of the *air armed forces and formations organized on a military basis:* Central administration; missions, air attachés; headquarters staff and staff of commands; flying and auxiliary personnel; military law; air force schools and colleges; survey and meteorological services so far as they work for the air force;

All other services not enumerated above.

Subhead C. Ditto: civilian personnel

12. Will include: Salaries, wages and allowances of all kinds granted in virtue of office and other allowances (including subsistence allowances, but not including pensions) of *civilian personnel*, forming part of the above forces and formations omitting, however:

    1. Workmen[1] who are shown:

        In subhead E (establishments and depots for provisions, clothing and medical stores);

        In subhead F (depots for animals, and forage depots);

        In subhead G (depots for coal, fuel oil, petrol and lubricants, etc.);

        In subhead H and K (building);

        If any countries find it impossible to comply with this instruction, they may include workmen in the civilian personnel.

    2. All civilian personnel which has to be shown in subheads L to N.

Subhead D. Persons undergoing preparatory military training, reservists and reserve organizations

13. Will include: Pay and allowances of all kinds and other expenses for *personnel not normally forming an effective part of formations* (persons undergoing preparatory military training, reservists, territorial and other reserve organizations, associated with the respective armed forces or formations organized on a military basis) — namely:

Expenditure on military training for persons not serving with the colors (*e.g.*, expenditure relating to rifle clubs, physical training clubs, etc.).

Remuneration outside periods of training of personnel not employed, but receiving remuneration; and remuneration during periods of training of reservists called up.

Also administrative expenditure on certain reserve organizations, if this expenditure cannot be split up and shown in other subheads, provided always that any expenditure proper to head IV is shown under that head.

Subhead E. Maintenance of personnel referred to in Subheads A to D

14. Will include: *Maintenance* expenses for meeting the personal requirements of the normal effectives of armed forces and formations organized on a military basis and of reservists called up for training (provisions, clothing, medical expenses, office and miscellaneous expenses) and also expenses relating to the maintenance and creation for military purposes of reserves of goods, raw

---

[1] This term does not include office staff.

materials or products relating to provisions, clothing and medical requirements — namely:

As regards *provisions* and *clothing:* Purchase of materials and goods, hand tools; payments to private firms in respect of the purchase and repair of all manufactured products; wages and allowances of workmen employed in the manufacture or maintenance of any of the above-named products in state or regimental workshops and depots (manufacture, repair, cleaning, handling and care); all other expenditure relating to provisions and clothing.

In the case of *medical expenses:* Expenditure relating to provisions, washing, office stores and consumable stores, drugs and medical stores of all kinds for military hospitals and infirmaries; fees of approved civilian doctors, chemists and dentists; miscellaneous expenses; wages and allowances of workmen employed in the hospitals and medical store depots; all other expenditure relating to medical services.

Office and miscellaneous expenses of all descriptions.

15. In countries which have no separate Air Ministry and in which only a portion of air expenditure is shown separately in the army and navy budgets (the general expenditure on air personnel and the greater part of the maintenance expenses being included in the totals) proportionate figures will be worked out based on the numbers of the civil and military air personnel, making due allowance for rank in the case of military personnel and for grades in the case of civilian personnel.

HEAD II. TRANSPORT

Subhead F. Horses and other animals, forage, harness and shoeing

16. Will include, in the case of the respective forces or formations: Expenditure on the purchase of horses and other animals, of harness (including purchase of raw materials, such as leather, hemp, etc.), of hand tools, manufactured articles, shoeing, veterinary charges, forage, including provision for current services and for stock, subsidies for horse breeding; and all other expenditure relating to horses and other animals.

Omitting, however, all expenditure on personnel (but including workmen).

Omitting also such draft animals and their harness and maintenance, as are included under head IV.

Subhead G. Coal, fuel, oil, petrol, lubricants, etc., and other transport expenses

17. Will include, in the case of the respective forces or formations: Expenditure on coal, fuel, oil, petrol, lubricants, etc., including provision for current services and for stock; apparatus for distributing fuel on land (petrol pumps, etc.); postal services, telegraphs and telephones (wire or radio), harbor and pilotage dues, hire of vessels; payments to nonmilitary and nonnaval organizations (railway, tramways, boats, motor-cars, air navigation companies, etc.), in respect of all transport of personnel, animals or material; subsidies or other expenditure on the organization of communications for the purpose of defense against air, gas[1] or other attacks; and all other expenditure relating to fuel, transport and communications.

[1] See Chap. 11 of the *Report*, p. 14.

Omitting, however, expenditure of the same nature included in head IV. Transport of all these materials as far as the place of delivery will be included.

18. In the case of air and sea forces and formations, the expenditure on animals as defined in subhead F above will be shown in whatever subhead is most convenient for the country concerned, but not however in head IV.

As regards expenditure on liquid fuel, petrol and lubricants and other expenditure under this head, countries which have no separate Air Ministry should show these expenses in the following manner: the figure required will be made up by first taking any amounts which appear separately in the army and navy budgets, and then adding the other items of expense, the necessary division being made with the help of information supplied by the departments concerned.

Head III. Buildings

Subhead H. Construction of new fortifications and defense works

19. Will include: Only expenses relating to the construction of new fortifications and defense works, whether or not these fortifications and works contain shelters for troops (casemates). For upkeep of fortifications, see subhead K.

Expenditure on coast defense works will be entered under expenditure on naval forces.[1]

Subhead K. Barracks, other buildings, upkeep, furniture

20. Will include: In the case of the respective forces or formations:

Cost of upkeep of fortifications, expenditure relating to the purchase and hire of land and buildings, erection, equipment, improvement, extension, upkeep and repairs of works of all descriptions (buildings, piers, quays, platforms, signal stations, canals, etc., marine works in naval ports and naval bases including dry docks and floating jetties, and all other works for the land, sea or air forces and formations).

Expenditure relating to fixed machinery and to heavy plant, and expenditure relating to the interior economy of buildings (water, heating, lighting, bedding, furniture, power).

Subsidies or other expenditure for the construction, modification or upkeep, for defense purposes, of railways, roads, bridges, canals, drainage, forestry works, or any analogous expenditure.

21. These different categories of expenditure include training or musketry camps, aërodromes, accommodation for troops and for military, naval and air services, sheds for stores and adjacent areas, and also state establishments which provide for the personal needs of the troops.

They do not include, however, state factories and yards for the manufacture, upkeep and repair of munitions or other warlike stores, and for the building or maintenance of ships.

Expenditure on coast defense works will be entered under expenditure on naval forces.[1]

---

[1] See Chap. 11 of the *Report*, p. 14.

22. As regards subsidies to private industry or other expenditure for the improvement, extension or construction of plant or machinery for shipbuilding or for the manufacture of munitions or other warlike stores, see head IV.

23. As regards air forces, subheads H and K will be combined. If the expenses relating to buildings, etc., for the air services are not shown separately, either among the separate items for air services or in one of the chapters of the army or navy budgets, they must be extracted from those budgets, either by obtaining the necessary information from the departments concerned or by calculating a proportionate amount based on the pay of the air service.

Head IV. War Material

24. In the case of each of the categories of material enumerated for land, sea and air armed forces, or formations organized on a military basis, in pars. 30 *et seq.*, these headings will include:

Expenses of maintenance, repair, purchase from traders or manufacturers, and of manufacture in state factories (including cost of research and experiment, inspection of materials delivered, and design, and subsidies to manufacturers or other equivalent expenditure) of ships, goods, materials and ammunition whether complete or in parts intended either for training purposes in peace time, or for the completion or increase of mobilization stocks and replacements for forces on a war footing, and also the expenses of creation and maintenance (in state or private hands) of stocks and plant, useful only for the construction of warlike stores.

The cost of war material for coast defense purposes will be entered under expenditure on naval forces.[1]

25. In so far as war material is purchased from or repaired by outside industry or state establishments possessing autonomous budgets, the expenditure to be included is that allocated to cover the purchase prices or cost of repairs.

26. There should also be included all costs of transport as far as the place where delivery to the army, naval or air administrations is required under the purchase contracts; or, in the case of supplies and deliveries of goods made by state establishments possessing autonomous budgets, under the regulations or standing orders, etc.

27. In so far as these stocks are manufactured, maintained and repaired by state establishments not possessing autonomous budgets, all the working expenses of the establishment (in respect of manufacture, maintenance, etc., of the material shown under these headings) should be included, in particular:

Labor
Office staff
General subordinate staff } Military or civil
Supervisory staff
Purchase of raw materials
Construction, maintenance and repairs of premises
Rents payable
Purchase, erection, maintenance and repair of fixed plant

[1] See Chap. 11 of the *Report*, p. 14.

Purchase, maintenance and repair of machinery, movable equipment and tools
Transport for internal services
Fuel
Gas
Electricity
Other motive power
Water
Washing, cleaning and scavenging
Rates actually paid to municipalities
Furniture
Stationery, printing and office expenses
Medical expenses
Postal, telegraph and telephone expenses
Delivery to the factory of all articles purchased
All other auxiliary services necessary for the working of the factories

28. The following must also be included:

(*a*) Subsidies paid to outside industry or autonomous state establishments, and other expenditure, with a view to increasing or maintaining the capacity of production or the stocks available for government use, relating to any of the war material specified in par. 30 *et seq.*

(*b*) Subsidies to transport companies and other expenditure for procuring war material, *e.g.*, subsidies to the mercantile marine and other expenditure for the construction and maintenance of vessels held at the disposal of the state for use in warlike operations or for stiffening the decks of merchant ships, subsidies to owners and other expenditure for the upkeep of motor vehicles available for government uses in case of war, etc.

29. Cost of inspection of goods purchased or manufactured and cost of research and experiment relating to these goods should be included. The items to be taken into account are those which correspond to the list in par. 27. The cost of inspection, research and experiment must be divided according to the category to which the material belongs, this division being estimated if necessary.

30. In the case of the *army* or *land formations organized on a military basis*, the stores in question come under the following headings:

Subhead M. *Arms, ammunition and fighting material*

Small arms and automatic firearms: rifles, muskets, carbines, revolvers and pistols, machine rifles, automatic pistols, machine guns, apparatus and appliances used for throwing projectiles.

Long and short guns, howitzers, mortars, infantry guns, anti-aircraft guns in use in army formations, etc.

Ammunition for small arms and guns, also ammunition wagons, vehicles, boxes, etc., for their transport, bombs, grenades and other projectiles, explosives, etc.

Cutting weapons, such as swords, spears, lances, bayonets and daggers.

Tanks, armored cars, armored trains.

Motor tractors.

APPENDIX I

All other arms, ammunition, apparatus and appliances for throwing projectiles, land mines, equipment and spare parts, etc.

Subhead M (a). *Engineer and other warlike stores* (not including explosives)

This subhead will include:
Boats
Railway material
Searchlight equipment
Pioneer equipment
Bridging equipment
Signal and radio stores
Optical instruments (including gun sights)
Antigas stores[1]
Mining stores
Horse or motor transport vehicles, specialized or not (not belonging to the manufacturing establishments covered by subheads M and N)
Accessories and spare parts
All other engineer and warlike stores

31. In the case of *air forces* or *formations organized on a military basis*, subhead M will include the following stores when intended for air services belonging to armed forces or formations organized on a military basis:
Aëroplanes and airships
Motors
Instruments
Stores for aircraft: radio, electricity, photographic, oxygen, heating, parachutes
Arms and ammunition, including bombs and torpedoes and anti-aircraft guns belonging to air formations
Ground equipment
Balloons (free or captive)
Motor and horse transport vehicles (specialized or not)
Hydrogen and helium
Accessories and spare parts of the above stores
All other warlike stores

32. Countries which do not possess a separate Air Ministry must endeavor to extract the expenditure relating to air material from the other accounts where this expenditure is not shown separately by calculating the proportion of these stores which is intended for the air services.

33. In the case of the *navy* or *sea formations organized on a military basis,* subhead L will include:
New construction and maintenance of:
    War vessels of all types
    Aircraft carriers
    Victualling craft
    Fuelling craft
    Naval armament vessels

[1] See Chap. 11 of the *Report*, p. 14.

Repair ships
Tugs
Barges and lighters
Floating docks
All other vessels intended for naval use

Including their:
Propelling machinery
Auxiliary engines
Hulls
Armor
Gun mountings
Boats and launches
Navigating instruments
Furniture
Electrical and radio equipment
Torpedo tubes and equipment
Fire-control apparatus
Searchlights
Optical and sound apparatus of every kind for naval purposes
All other equipment, accessories, spare parts, etc., for the vessels, described

34. In the case of the *navy* or *sea formations organized on a military basis* subhead M, "Arms and Ammunition," will include:

Guns, howitzers, mortars, machine guns, rifles and other small arms
Projectiles and ammunition
Torpedoes, mines and bombs of all sorts, paravanes and explosives
Electrical equipment belonging to the above articles
Motor vehicles and boats employed in naval armament depots
Motor vehicles (not belonging to manufacturing establishments covered by subheads L and N)
Antigas stores[1]
All other types of arms and ammunition
Accessories and spare parts

35. In the case of the *army* and *navy* and of *land and sea formations organized on a military basis,* subhead N will only be used to show expenditure relating to manufacturing establishments which do not possess budgetary autonomy, when such expenditure can not be divided between subheads M and M (*a*) or subheads L and M.

36. The expenditure on depots of war material should not be shown under head IV. However, as an exception, the wages and allowances of *workmen* occupied on storage duties should be given under this head. These expenses should, if possible, be divided between subheads M and M (*a*) or L and M, according to the nature of the materials stored in each case. Where this division can not be effected, the cost of the workmen in these depots must be shown in subhead N.

[1] See Chap. 11 of the *Report,* p. 14.

INSTRUCTIONS CONCERNING ANNEXED TABLE B.

This table must indicate exactly, or approximately, the sums expended respectively on "new construction" and on "maintenance and repairs" of vessels.

"New construction" includes all expenditure on vessels up to the moment of the first commission.

The following charges will be included among others in maintenance: Compensation for damage by ships; supply of water for ships; the removal of ashes from ships; motor transport vehicles used in naval establishments (not including naval armament depots and dockyards).

MODEL STATEMENT
A
RETURN OF ACTUAL EXPENDITURE FOR THE YEAR ......

Total

LAND FORCES..

NAVAL FORCES..

AIR FORCES..

GRAND TOTAL..

B. LAND FORCES

Subhead	Category of Expenditure	Armed forces stationed in the home country (optional) (1)	Armed forces stationed overseas (optional) (2)	Formations organized on a military basis stationed in the home country (optional) (3)	Formations organized on a military basis stationed overseas (optional) (4)	Total (5)

HEAD I
Effectives

Personnel normally forming part of formations and services:

A Pay and allowances of all kinds: Officers..
B Ditto: N.C.O.s and men................
C Ditto: Civilian personnel..............

Personnel not normally forming part of formations and services:

D Persons undergoing preparatory military training, reservists and reserve organizations....................................
E *Maintenance of personnel referred to in subheads A to D*.......................

HEAD II
Transport

F Horses and other animals, forage, harness and shoeing........................
G Coal, fuel, oil, petrol, lubricants, etc., and other transport expenses............

HEAD III
Buildings

H Construction of new fortifications and defense works........................
K Barracks, other buildings, upkeep, furniture..............................

TOTAL: HEADS I TO III...................

APPENDIX I

Subheads	Category of Expenditure	(1)	(2)	(3)	(4)	Total (5)

HEAD IV
War Material

M Arms, ammunition and fighting material
M(a) Engineer and other warlike stores .....
W Manufacture of war material in "non-autonomous" state establishments (expenditure not divisible between subheads M and M(a)) ....

TOTAL: HEAD IV ....

GRAND TOTAL .... [1]

C. NAVAL FORCES

Subhead	Category of Expenditure	Armed Forces (optional) (1)	Formations organized on a military basis (optional) (2)	Total (3)

HEAD I
Effectives

Personnel normally forming part of formations and services:

A Pay and allowances of all kinds: Officers ....
B Ditto: N.C.O.'s and men ....
C Ditto: Civilian personnel ....

[1] Black lines inclose amounts subject to limitation under Arts. **10**, **24** and **29** of the Draft Convention.

Subhead	Category of Expenditure	(1)	(2)	Total (3)

Personnel not normally forming part of formations and services:

D Persons undergoing preparatory military training, reservists and reserve organizations ....

E *Maintenance of personnel referred to in subheads A to D* ....

HEAD II

Transport

G Coal, fuel, oil, petrol, lubricants, etc., and other transport expenses ....

HEAD III

Buildings

H Construction of new fortifications and defense works
    ....

K Barracks, other buildings, upkeep, furniture ....

HEAD IV

War Material

L Ships: new construction and maintenance ....

M Arms, ammunition and fighting material ....

N Manufacture of war material in nonautonomous state establishments (expenditure not divisible between subheads L and M) ....

TOTAL: HEAD I .... [1]

GRAND TOTAL ....

[1] Black lines inclose amounts subject to limitation under Arts. 10, 24 and 29 of the Draft Convention.

D. AIR FORCES

Subhead	Category of Expenditure	Armed forces stationed in the home country (optional)	Armed forces stationed overseas (optional)	Formations organized on a military basis stationed in the home country (optional)	Formations organized on a military basis stationed overseas (optional)	Total
		(1)	(2)	(3)	(4)	(5)

HEAD I
Effectives

Personnel normally forming part of formations and services:

A   Pay and allowances of all kinds: Officers .

B   Ditto: N.C.O.s and men ....

C   Ditto: Civilian personnel ....

Personnel not normally forming part of formations and services:

D   Persons undergoing preparatory military training, reservists and reserve organizations........................

E   *Maintenance of personnel referred to in subheads A to D*......................

HEAD II
Transport

G   Coal, fuel, oil, petrol, lubricants, etc., and other transport expenses ....

HEAD III
Buildings

K   Barracks, other buildings, upkeep, furniture...............................

TOTAL: HEADS I TO III..................

Subhead	Category of Expenditure	(1)	(2)	(3)	(4)	Total (5)
	HEAD IV					
	War Material					
M	Arms, ammunition and fighting material.					
	TOTAL: HEAD IV......................					[1]
	GRAND TOTAL........................					

ANNEXED TABLES

TABLE A [2]. EXPENDITURE ON PAY OF RESERVES FOR THE YEAR.. ....
1. Remuneration outside periods of training of personnel not employed.................................. ....
2. Remuneration during training of reservists called up.. ....

TABLE B [2]. EXPENDITURE ON SHIPBUILDING FOR THE YEAR ....
1. New construction............................... ....
2. Maintenance and repairs........................ ....

TABLE C [2]. STATEMENT OF THE AMOUNT OUTSTANDING, AT THE END OF THE FINANCIAL YEAR . . . OF BLOCK CREDITS VOTED IN RESPECT OF EXPENDITURE FOR MORE THAN ONE YEAR...................................... ....

TABLE D [3]. STATEMENT OF THE AMOUNT OUTSTANDING ON THE . . . (DATE) IN RESPECT OF PURCHASES ON CREDIT OR DEFERRED PAYMENTS RELATING TO GOODS DELIVERED OR SERVICES RENDERED, IN CASES WHERE THE DUE DATES OF PAYMENT ARE LATER THAN THOSE CUSTOMARY IN CONTRACTS OF THE SAME KIND WHICH DO NOT PROVIDE ANY SPECIAL CREDIT FACILITIES......................... ....

[1] Black line incloses amount subject to limitation under Arts. 10, 24 and 29 of the Draft Convention.
[2] See Chap. 20 of the *Report*, p. 22.
[3] See Chaps. 6 and 20 of the *Report*, p. 10, 22.

APPENDIX I

TABLE E[1]. STATEMENT FOR THE FINANCIAL YEAR ... OF LOANS MADE TO, OR PARTICIPATIONS ACQUIRED IN, ENTERPRISES HAVING AMONG THEIR OBJECTS THE FURNISHING OF GOODS OR SERVICES FOR ARMAMENT PURPOSES, WHERE THESE HAVE BEEN EXCLUDED FROM THE RETURN ON THE GROUND THAT THEY ARE NOT REGARDED AS ARMAMENT EXPENDITURE............................... ....

TABLE F[2]. EXPENDITURE IN RESPECT OF PENSIONS FOR THE YEAR... ....
   I. Military personnel:
      (a) Service pensions; ....
      (b) Invalidity pensions; ....
      (c) Mixed pensions; ....
  II. Civil personnel: pensions; ....
 III. War pensions, if a distinction is made in the national budget between ordinary pensions and war pensions (if not, these pensions must appear under headings I and II); ....
 IV. Pensions or other compensation granted, apart from the regulations regarding normal pensions, for premature retirement, discharge or loss of office resulting from a reduction of the forces. ....

TABLE G[2]. PRINCIPAL MODIFICATIONS MADE SINCE THE LAST RETURN IN:
1. Provisions relating to the grant of pensions of any contributions made by the personnel towards the cost of these pensions............................... ....
2. Provisions relating to the taxation of the pay or pensions of the personnel.......................... ....
3. Provisions relating to social insurance or analogous benefits of the personnel, and to the contributions made by the personnel for this purpose........... ....

[1] See Chaps. 8 and 20 of the *Report*, p. 11, 22.
[2] See Chap. 20 of the *Report*, p. 22.

APPENDIX II

ARBITRATION AND SECURITY TEXTS

1. General Act for the Pacific Settlement of International Disputes, Geneva, September 26, 1928.[1]

In force from August 16, 1929, between Belgium and Sweden; and 90 days after date noted for: Australia, May 21, 1931; Belgium, May 18, 1929; Canada, July 1, 1931; Denmark, April 14, 1930; Estonia, September 3, 1931; Finland, September 6, 1931; France, May 21, 1931; Great Britain and Northern Ireland, May 21, 1931; Greece, September 14, 1931; India, May 21, 1931; Irish Free State, September 26, 1931; Italy, September 7, 1931; Luxemburg, September 15, 1930; Netherlands (Chap. I, II and IV), August 8, 1930; New Zealand, May 21, 1931; Norway (Chap. I, II and IV), June 11, 1929, and Chap. III, June 11, 1930; Peru, November 21, 1931; Spain, September 16, 1930; Sweden (Chap. I, II and IV), May 13, 1929.

CHAPTER I. CONCILIATION

Art. 1. Disputes of every kind between two or more parties to the present General Act which it has not been possible to settle by diplomacy shall, subject to such reservations as may be made under Art. 39, be submitted, under the conditions laid down in the present chapter, to the procedure of conciliation.

Art. 2. The disputes referred to in the preceding article shall be submitted to a permanent or special Conciliation Commission constituted by the parties to the dispute.

Art. 3. On a request to that effect being made by one of the contracting parties to another party, a permanent Conciliation Commission shall be constituted within a period of six months.

Art. 4. Unless the parties concerned agree otherwise, the Conciliation Commission shall be constituted as follows:

1. The commission shall be composed of five members. The parties shall each nominate one commissioner, who may be chosen from among their respective nationals. The three other commissioners shall be appointed by agreement from among the nationals of third powers. These three commissioners must be of different nationalities and must not be habitually resident in the territory nor be in the service of the parties. The parties shall appoint the president of the commission from among them.

---

[1] *Treaty Series*, XCIII, p. 343; Reg. No. 2123, under which subsequent accessions may be found in the annexes published at the end of each 100 treaties in the *Treaty Series*, C, p. 260; CVII, p. 529; CXI, p. 414, etc.

2. The commissioners shall be appointed for three years. They shall be reeligible. The commissioners appointed jointly may be replaced during the course of their mandate by agreement between the parties. Either party may, however, at any time replace a commissioner whom it has appointed. Even if replaced, the commissioners shall continue to exercise their functions until the termination of the work in hand.

3. Vacancies which may occur as a result of death, resignation or any other cause shall be filled within the shortest possible time in the manner fixed for the nominations.

Art. 5. If, when a dispute arises, no permanent Conciliation Commission appointed by the parties is in existence, a special commission shall be constituted for the examination of the dispute within a period of three months from the date at which a request to that effect is made by one of the parties to the other party. The necessary appointments shall be made in the manner laid down in the preceding article, unless the parties decide otherwise.

Art. 6. 1. If the appointment of the commissioners to be designated jointly is not made within the periods provided for in Arts. 3 and 5, the making of the necessary appointments shall be intrusted to a third power, chosen by agreement between the parties, or on request of the parties, to the acting president of the Council of the League of Nations.

2. If no agreement is reached on either of these procedures, each party shall designate a different power, and the appointment shall be made in concert by the powers thus chosen.

3. If, within a period of three months, the two powers have been unable to reach an agreement, each of them shall submit a number of candidates equal to the number of members to be appointed. It shall then be decided by lot which of the candidates thus designated shall be appointed.

Art. 7. 1. Disputes shall be brought before the Conciliation Commission by means of an application addressed to the president by the two parties acting in agreement, or in default thereof by one or other of the parties.

2. The application, after giving a summary account of the subject of the dispute, shall contain the invitation to the commission to take all necessary measures with a view to arriving at an amicable solution.

3. If the application emanates from only one of the parties, the other party shall, without delay, be notified by it.

Art. 8. 1. Within fifteen days from the date on which a dispute has been brought by one of the parties before a permanent Conciliation Commission, either party may replace its own commissioner, for the examination of the particular dispute, by a person possessing special competence in the matter.

2. The party making use of this right shall immediately notify the other party; the latter shall, in such case, be entitled to take similar action within fifteen days from the date on which it received the notification.

Art. 9. 1. In the absence of agreement to the contrary between the parties, the Conciliation Commission shall meet at the seat of the League of Nations, or at some other place selected by its president.

2. The commission may in all circumstances request the Secretary-General of the League of Nations to afford it his assistance.

Art. 10. The work of the Conciliation Commission shall not be conducted in public unless a decision to that effect is taken by the commission with the consent of the parties.

Art. 11. 1. In the absence of agreement to the contrary between the parties, the Conciliation Commission shall lay down its own procedure, which in any case must provide for both parties being heard. In regard to inquiries, the commission, unless it decides unanimously to the contrary, shall act in accordance with the provisions of Part III of the Hague Convention of October 18, 1907, for the Pacific Settlement of International Disputes.

2. The parties shall be represented before the Conciliation Commission by agents, whose duty shall be to act as intermediaries between them and the commission; they may, moreover, be assisted by counsel and experts appointed by them for that purpose and may request that all persons whose evidence appears to them desirable shall be heard.

3. The commission, for its part, shall be entitled to request oral explanations from the agents, counsel and experts of both parties, as well as from all persons it may think desirable to summon with the consent of their governments.

Art. 12. In the absence of agreement to the contrary between the parties, the decisions of the Conciliation Commission shall be taken by a majority vote, and the commission may only take decisions on the substance of the dispute if all its members are present.

Art. 13. The parties undertake to facilitate the work of the Conciliation Commission, and particularly to supply it to the greatest possible extent with all relevant documents and information, as well as to use the means at their disposal to allow it to proceed in their territory, and in accordance with their law, to the summoning and hearing of witnesses or experts and to visit the localities in question.

Art. 14. 1. During the proceedings of the commission, each of the commissioners shall receive emoluments the amount of which shall be fixed by agreement between the parties, each of which shall contribute an equal share.

2. The general expenses arising out of the working of the commission shall be divided in the same manner.

Art. 15. 1. The task of the Conciliation Commission shall be to elucidate the questions in dispute, to collect with that object all necessary information by means of inquiry or otherwise, and to endeavor to bring the parties to an agreement. It may, after the case has been examined, inform the parties of the terms of settlement which seem suitable to it, and lay down the period within which they are to make their decision.

2. At the close of the proceedings, the commission shall draw up a *procès-verbal* stating, as the case may be, either that the parties have come to an agreement and, if need arises, the terms of the agreement, or that it has been impossible to effect a settlement. No mention shall be made in the *procès-verbal* of whether the commission's decisions were taken unanimously or by a majority vote.

3. The proceedings of the commission must, unless the parties otherwise agree, be terminated within six months from the date on which the commission shall have been given cognizance of the dispute.

Art. 16. The commission's *procès-verbal* shall be communicated without delay to the parties. The parties shall decide whether it shall be published.

Chapter II. Judicial Settlement

Art. 17. All disputes with regard to which the parties are in conflict as to their respective rights shall, subject to any reservations which may be made under Art. 39, be submitted for decision to the Permanent Court of International Justice, unless the parties agree, in the manner hereinafter provided, to have resort to an arbitral tribunal.

It is understood that the disputes referred to above include in particular those mentioned in Art. 36 of the Statute of the Permanent Court of International Justice.

Art. 18. If the parties agree to submit the disputes mentioned in the preceding article to an arbitral tribunal, they shall draw up a special agreement in which they shall specify the subject of the dispute, the arbitrators selected, and the procedure to be followed. In the absence of sufficient particulars in the special agreement, the provisions of the Hague Convention of October 18, 1907, for the Pacific Settlement of International Disputes shall apply so far as is necessary. If nothing is laid down in the special agreement as to the rules regarding the substance of the dispute to be followed by the arbitrators, the tribunal shall apply the substantive rules enumerated in Art. 38 of the Statute of the Permanent Court of International Justice.

Art. 19. If the parties fail to agree concerning the special agreement referred to in the preceding article, or fail to appoint arbitrators, either party shall be at liberty, after giving three months' notice, to bring the dispute by an application direct before the Permanent Court of International Justice.

Art. 20. 1. Notwithstanding the provisions of Art. 1, disputes of the kind referred to in Art. 17 arising between parties who have acceded to the obligations contained in the present chapter shall only be subject to the procedure of conciliation if the parties so agree.

2. The obligation to resort to the procedure of conciliation remains applicable to disputes which are excluded from judicial settlement only by the operation of reservations under the provisions of Art. 39.

3. In the event of recourse to and failure of conciliation, neither party may bring the dispute before the Permanent Court of International Justice or call for the constitution of the arbitral tribunal referred to in Art. 18 before the expiration of one month from the termination of the proceedings of the Conciliation Commission.

Chapter III. Arbitration

Art. 21. Any dispute not of the kind referred to in Art. 17 which does not, within the month following the termination of the work of the Conciliation Commission provided for in Chap. I, form the object of an agreement between the parties, shall, subject to such reservations as may be made under Art. 39, be brought before an arbitral tribunal which, unless the parties otherwise agree, shall be constituted in the manner set out below.

Art. 22. The Arbitral Tribunal shall consist of five members. The parties shall each nominate one member, who may be chosen from among their respective nationals. The two other arbitrators and the chairman shall be chosen by common agreement from among the nationals of third powers. They must be of different nationalities and must not be habitually resident in the territory nor be in the service of the parties.

Art. 23. 1. If the appointment of the members of the Arbitral Tribunal is not made within a period of three months from the date on which one of the parties requested the other party to constitute an arbitral tribunal, a third power, chosen by agreement between the parties, shall be requested to make the necessary appointments.

2. If no agreement is reached on this point, each party shall designate a different power, and the appointments shall be made in concert by the powers thus chosen.

3. If, within a period of three months, the two powers so chosen have been unable to reach an agreement, the necessary appointments shall be

made by the President of the Permanent Court of International Justice. If the latter is prevented from acting or is a subject of one of the parties, the nomination shall be made by the Vice-President. If the latter is prevented from acting or is a subject of one of the parties, the appointments shall be made by the oldest member of the Court who is not a subject of either party.

Art. 24. Vacancies which may occur as a result of death, resignation or any other cause shall be filled within the shortest possible time in the manner fixed for the nominations.

Art. 25. The parties shall draw up a special agreement determining the subject of the disputes and the details of procedure.

Art. 26. In the absence of sufficient particulars in the special agreement regarding the matters referred to in the preceding article, the provisions of the Hague Convention of October 18, 1907, for the Pacific Settlement of International Disputes shall apply so far as is necessary.

Art. 27. Failing the conclusion of a special agreement within a period of three months from the date on which the tribunal was constituted, the dispute may be brought before the tribunal by an application by one or other party.

Art. 28. If nothing is laid down in the special agreement or no special agreement has been made, the tribunal shall apply the rules in regard to the substance of the dispute enumerated in Art. 38 of the Statute of the Permanent Court of International Justice. In so far as there exists no such rule applicable to the dispute, the tribunal shall decide *ex aequo et bono*.

Chapter IV. General Provisions

Art. 29. 1. Disputes for the settlement of which a special procedure is laid down in other conventions in force between the parties to the dispute shall be settled in conformity with the provisions of those conventions.

2. The present General Act shall not affect any agreements in force by which conciliation procedure is established between the parties or they are bound by obligations to resort to arbitration or judicial settlement which insure the settlement of the dispute. If, however, these agreements provide only for a procedure of conciliation, after such procedure has been followed without result, the provisions of the present General Act concerning judicial settlement or arbitration shall be applied in so far as the parties have acceded thereto.

Art. 30. If a party brings before a Conciliation Commission a dispute, which the other party, relying on conventions in force between the parties has submitted to the Permanent Court of International Justice or an Arbitral Tribunal, the commission shall defer consideration of the dispute until the Court or the Arbitral Tribunal has pronounced upon the conflict of competence. The same rule shall apply if the Court or the tribunal is seized of the case by one of the parties during the conciliation proceedings.

Art. 31. 1. In the case of a dispute the occasion of which, according to the municipal law of one of the parties, falls within the competence of its judicial or administrative authorities, the party in question may object to the matter in dispute being submitted for settlement by the different methods laid down in the present General Act until a decision with final effect has been pronounced, within a reasonable time, by the competent authority.

2. In such a case, the party which desires to resort to the procedures laid down in the present General Act must notify the other party of its intention within a period of one year from the date of the aforementioned decision.

Art. 32. If, in a judicial sentence or arbitral award, it is declared that a judgment, or a measure enjoined by a court of law or other authority of one of the parties to the dispute, is wholly or in part contrary to international law, and if the constitutional law of that party does not permit or only partially permits the consequences of the judgment or measure in question to be annulled, the parties agree that the judicial sentence or arbitral award shall grant the injured party equitable satisfaction.

Art. 33. 1. In all cases where a dispute forms the object of arbitration or judicial proceedings, and particularly if the question on which the parties differ arises out of acts already committed or on the point of being committed, the Permanent Court of International Justice, acting in accordance with Art. 41 of its Statute, or the Arbitral Tribunal, shall lay down within the shortest possible time the provisional measures to be adopted. The parties to the dispute shall be bound to accept such measures.

2. If the dispute is brought before a Conciliation Commission, the latter may recommend to the parties the adoption of such provisional measures as it considers suitable.

3. The parties undertake to abstain from all measures likely to react prejudicially upon the execution of the judicial or arbitral decision or upon the arrangements proposed by the Conciliation Commission and, in general, to abstain from any sort of action whatsoever which may aggravate or extend the dispute.

Art. 34. Should a dispute arise between more than two parties to the present General Act, the following rules shall be observed for the application of the forms of procedure described in the foregoing provisions:

(*a*) In the case of conciliation procedure, a special commission shall invariably be constituted. The composition of such commission shall differ according as the parties all have separate interests or as two or more of their number act together.

In the former case, the parties shall each appoint one commissioner and shall jointly appoint commissioners, nationals of third powers not parties to the dispute, whose number shall always exceed by one the number of commissioners appointed separately by the parties.

In the second case, the parties who act together shall appoint their commissioner jointly by agreement between themselves and shall combine with the other party or parties in appointing third commissioners.

In either event, the parties, unless they agree otherwise, shall apply Art. 5 and the following articles of the present act, so far as they are compatible with the provisions of the present article.

(b) In the case of judicial procedure, the Statute of the Permanent Court of International Justice shall apply.

(c) In the case of arbitral procedure, if agreement is not secured as to the composition of the tribunal, in the case of the disputes mentioned in Art. 17, each party shall have the right, by means of an application, to submit the dispute to the Permanent Court of International Justice; in the case of the disputes mentioned in Art. 21, the above Art. 22 and following articles shall apply, but each party having separate interests shall appoint one arbitrator and the number of arbitrators separately appointed by the parties to the dispute shall always be one less than that of the other arbitrators.

Art. 35. 1. The present General Act shall be applicable as between the parties thereto, even though a third power, whether a party to the act, or not, has an interest in the dispute.

2. In conciliation procedure, the parties may agree to invite such third power to intervene.

Art. 36. 1. In judicial or arbitral procedure, if a third power should consider that it has an interest of a legal nature which may be affected by the decision in the case, it may submit to the Permanent Court of International Justice or to the Arbitral Tribunal a request to intervene as a third party.

2. It will be for the Court or the tribunal to decide upon this request.

Art. 37. 1. Whenever the construction of a convention to which states other than those concerned in the case are parties is in question, the Registrar of the Permanent Court of International Justice or the Arbitral Tribunal shall notify all such states forthwith.

2. Every state so notified has the right to intervene in the proceedings; but, if it uses this right, the construction given by the decision will be binding upon it.

Art. 38. Accessions to the present General Act may extend:

A. Either to all the provisions of the act (Chaps. I, II, III and IV);

B. Or to those provisions only which relate to conciliation and judicial settlement (Chaps. I and II), together with the general provisions dealing with these procedures (Chap. IV);

C. Or to those provisions only which relate to conciliation (Chap. I), together with the general provisions concerning that procedure (Chap. IV).

The contracting parties may benefit by the accessions of other parties only in so far as they have themselves assumed the same obligations.

Art. 39. 1. In addition to the power given in the preceding article, a party, in acceding to the present General Act, may make his acceptance conditional upon the reservations exhaustively enumerated in the following paragraph. These reservations must be indicated at the time of accession.

2. These reservations may be such as to exclude from the procedure described in the present act:

(a) Disputes arising out of facts prior to the accession either of the party making the reservation or of any other party with whom the said party may have a dispute;

(b) Disputes concerning questions which by international law are solely within the domestic jurisdiction of states;

(c) Disputes concerning particular cases or clearly specified subject-matters, such as territorial status, or disputes falling within clearly defined categories.

3. If one of the parties to a dispute has made a reservation, the other parties may enforce the same reservation in regard to that party.

4. In the case of parties who have acceded to the provisions of the present General Act relating to judicial settlement or to arbitration, such reservations as they may have made shall, unless otherwise expressly stated, be deemed not to apply to the procedure of conciliation.

Art. 40. A party whose accession has been only partial, or was made subject to reservations, may at any moment, by means of a simple declaration, either extend the scope of his accession or abandon all or part of his reservations.

Art. 41. Disputes relating to the interpretation or application of the present General Act, including those concerning the classification of disputes and the scope of reservations, shall be submitted to the Permanent Court of International Justice.

Art. 42. The present General Act of which the French and English texts shall both be authentic, shall bear the date of the 26th of September, 1928.

Art. 43. 1. The present General Act shall be open to accession by all the heads of states or other competent authorities of the Members of the League of Nations and the non-Member states to which the Council of the League of Nations has communicated a copy for this purpose.

2. The instruments of accession and the additional declarations provided for by Art. 40 shall be transmitted to the Secretary-General of the League of Nations, who shall notify their receipt to all the Members of the League and to the non-Member states referred to in the preceding paragraph.

3. The Secretary-General of the League of Nations shall draw up three lists, denominated respectively by the letters A, B and C, corresponding to the three forms of accession to the present act provided for in Art. 38, in which shall be shown the accessions and additional declarations of the contracting parties. These lists, which shall be continually kept up to date, shall be published in the annual report presented to the Assembly of the League of Nations by the Secretary-General.

Art. 44. 1. The present General Act shall come into force on the ninetieth day following the receipt by the Secretary-General of the League of Nations of the accession of not less than two contracting parties.

2. Accessions received after the entry into force of the act, in accordance with the previous paragraph, shall become effective as from the ninetieth day following the date of receipt by the Secretary-General of the League of Nations. The same rule shall apply to the additional declarations provided for by Art. 40.

Art. 45. 1. The present General Act shall be concluded for a period of five years, dating from its entry into force.

2. It shall remain in force for further successive periods of five years in the case of contracting parties which do not denounce it at least six months before the expiration of the current period.

3. Denunciation shall be effected by a written notification addressed to the Secretary-General of the League of Nations, who shall inform all the Members of the League and the non-Member states referred to in Art. 43.

4. A denunciation may be partial only, or may consist in notification of reservations not previously made.

5. Notwithstanding denunciation by one of the contracting parties concerned in a dispute, all proceedings pending at the expiration of the current period of the General Act shall be duly completed.

Art. 46. A copy of the present General Act, signed by the president of the Assembly and by the Secretary-General of the League of Nations, shall be deposited in the archives of the Secretariat; a certified true copy shall be delivered by the Secretary-General to all the Members of the

League of Nations and to the non-Member states indicated by the Council of the League of Nations.

Art. 47. The present General Act shall be registered by the Secretary-General of the League of Nations on the date of its entry into force.

The President of the ninth ordinary session of the Assembly of the League of Nations:
(*Signed*)   Herluf ZAHLE.

The Secretary-General:
(*Signed*)   Eric DRUMMOND.

RESERVATIONS

[Accessions to the General Act may extend to all or certain chapters in accordance with Art. 38, A, B or C; the list of accessions in the head note indicates all states which have limited accessions to particular chapters. In addition reservations may be expressed in accordance with Art. 39 to exclude from the procedure of the General Act disputes of specified categories. The following record gives the text of reservations indicated at the time of accession:]

Australia: Identic with United Kingdom, except:

"(I, iii) Disputes between His Majesty's Government in the Commonwealth of Australia and the government of any other Member of the League which is a member of the British Commonwealth of Nations, all of which disputes shall be settled in such a manner as the parties have agreed or shall agree."

Belgium: The accession by Belgium is only subject to the sole reservation provided for under Art. 39, (2), (*a*) the effect of which is to exclude from the procedures described in this act, disputes arising out of facts prior to the accession of Belgium or prior to the accession of any other party with whom Belgium may have a dispute.

Canada: Identic with the United Kingdom, except:

"(I, i) Disputes arising prior to the accession in respect of Canada to the said General Act, or relating to situations or facts prior to the said accession;

"(I, iii) Disputes between His Majesty's Government in Canada and the government of any other Member of the League which is a member of the British Commonwealth of Nations, all of which disputes shall be settled in such a manner as the parties have agreed or shall agree."

Denmark: No reservations.

Estonia: The following disputes are excluded from the procedures described in the General Act, including the procedure of conciliation:

(*a*) disputes resulting from facts prior either to the accession of Estonia or to the accession of another party with whom Estonia might have a dispute;

(*b*) disputes concerning questions which by international law are solely within the domestic jurisdiction of states.

Finland: No reservations.

France: The said accession concerning all disputes that may arise after the said accession with regard to situations or facts subsequent thereto, other than those which the Permanent Court of International Justice may recognize as bearing on a question left by international law to the exclusive competence of the state, it being understood that in application of Art. 39 of the said act the disputes which the parties or one of them may have referred to the Council of the League of Nations will not be submitted to the procedures described in this act unless the Council has been unable to pronounce a decision under the conditions laid down in Art. 15, par. 6, of the Covenant.

Furthermore, in accordance with the resolution adopted by the Assembly of the League of Nations "on the submission and recommendation of the General Act," Art. 28 of this act is interpreted by the French Government as meaning in particular that "respect for rights established by treaty or resulting from international law" is obligatory upon arbitral tribunals constituted in application of Chap. 3 of the said General Act.[1]

Great Britain and Northern Ireland, United Kingdom of and all parts of the British Empire which are not separate Members of the League of Nations: —
(1) That the following disputes are excluded from the procedure described in the General Act, including the procedure of conciliation:

(i) Disputes arising prior to the accession of His Majesty to the said General Act, or relating to situations or facts prior to the said accession;

(ii) Disputes in regard to which the parties to the dispute have agreed or shall agree to have recourse to some other method of peaceful settlement;

(iii) Disputes between His Majesty's Government in the United Kingdom and the government of any other Member of the League which is a member of the British Commonwealth of Nations, all of which disputes shall be settled in such a manner as the parties have agreed or shall agree;

(iv) Disputes concerning questions which by international law are solely within the domestic jurisdiction of states; and

(v) Disputes with any party to the General Act who is not a member of the League of Nations.

(2) That His Majesty reserves the right in relation to the disputes mentioned in Art. 17 of the General Act to require that the procedure prescribed in Chap. II of the said act shall be suspended in respect of any dispute which has been submitted to and is under consideration by the Council of the League of Nations, provided that notice to suspend is given after the dispute has been submitted to the Council and is given within ten days of the notification of the initiation of the procedure, and provided also that such suspension shall be limited to a period of twelve months or such longer period as may be agreed by the parties to the dispute or determined by a decision of all the members of the Council other than the parties to the dispute.

(3) (i) That, in the case of a dispute, not being a dispute mentioned in Art. 17 of the General Act, which is brought before the Council of the League of

[1] For an account of the original proposal of the French Government see Myers, *Origin and conclusion of the Paris Pact,* p. 29.

Nations in accordance with the provisions of the Covenant, the procedure prescribed in Chap. I of the General Act, shall not be applied, and, if already commenced, shall be suspended, unless the Council determines that the said procedure shall be adopted.

(ii) That in the case of such a dispute, the procedure described in Chap. III of the General Act shall not be applied unless the Council has failed to effect a settlement of the dispute within twelve months from the date on which it was first submitted to the Council, or, in a case where the procedure prescribed in Chap. I has been adopted without producing an agreement between the parties, within six months from the termination of the work of the Conciliation Commission. The Council may extend either of the above periods by a decision of all its members other than the parties to the dispute.

Greece: The following disputes are excluded from the procedures described in the General Act, including the procedure of conciliation referred to in Chap. I:

(*a*) Disputes resulting from facts prior either to the accession of Greece or to the accession of another party with whom Greece might have a dispute;

(*b*) Disputes concerning questions which by international law are solely within the domestic jurisdiction of states, and in particular disputes relating to the territorial status of Greece, including disputes relating to its rights of sovereignty over its ports and lines of communication.

India: Identic with United Kingdom, except:

"(I, iii) Disputes between the Government of India and the government of any other Member of the League which is a member of the British Commonwealth of Nations, all of which disputes shall be settled in such a manner as the parties have agreed or shall agree."

Irish Free State: No reservations.

Italy: I — The following disputes shall be excluded from the procedures described in the said act:

a. Disputes arising out of facts or situations prior to the present accession;

b. Disputes relating to questions which international law leaves to the sole jurisdiction of states;

c. Disputes affecting the relations between Italy and any third power.

II — It is understood that, in conformity with Art. 29 of the said act, disputes for the solution of which a special procedure is provided by other conventions shall be settled in accordance with the provisions of those conventions; and that, in particular, disputes which may be submitted to the Council or Assembly of the League of Nations in virtue of one of the provisions of the Covenant shall be settled in accordance with those provisions.

III — It is further understood that the present accession in no way affects Italy's accession to the Statute of the Permanent Court of International justice and to the clause in that Statute concerning the compulsory jurisdiction of the Court.

Luxemburg: No reservations.

Netherlands: No reservations; accepts Chaps. I, II and IV; accession also effective for Netherlands, Indies, Surinam and Curaçao.

New Zealand: Identic with United Kingdom, except:

"(I, iii) Disputes between His Majesty's Government in New Zealand and the government of any other Member of the League which is a member of the British Commonwealth of Nations, all of which disputes shall be settled in such a manner as the parties have agreed or shall agree."

Norway: No reservations; accepts Chaps. I, II and IV.

Peru: Subject to reservation (*b*) provided for in the second paragraph of Art. 39.

Spain: Subject to the reservations (*a*) and (*b*) provided for in the second paragraph of Art. 39.

Sweden: No reservations; accepts Chaps. I, II and IV.

2. Convention on Financial Assistance, Geneva, October 2, 1930.[1]

Not in force; enters into force with the Disarmament Convention.

Open for signature until December 31, 1931; thereafter to accession by Members of the League.

Ratified by: Denmark, May 15, 1931; Finland, July 30, 1931.

Signed by: Albania, Australia, Austria, Belgium, Bolivia, Bulgaria, Cuba, Czecho-slovakia, Estonia, Ethiopia, France, Germany, Great Britain (and all nonmember parts of British Empire), Greece, Irish Free State, Italy, Latvia, Lithuania, Netherlands, Norway, Persia, Peru, Poland, Portugal, Rumania, Spain, Sweden, Yugoslavia.

[Heads of States.]

Recognizing the importance, as a means of safeguarding or, if necessary, restoring peace between nations, of creating a system of financial assistance in the form of guaranties for loans to be given in the event of international disputes likely to lead to a rupture or in case of war;

Considering that such a system of assistance can best be organized by the conclusion of an international convention;

Have appointed as their plenipotentiaries for this purpose:

[Here follow the names of the plenipotentiaries.]

Who, having communicated their full powers found in good and due form, have agreed as follows:

Cases in Which Financial Assistance is Granted

Art. 1. 1. If, despite the efforts which the Council of the League of Nations has found it possible to make for the maintenance or the reestab-

[1]Text from C.611.M.237.1930.IX.7. and *Official Journal*, XI, p. 1649.

lishment of peaceful relations, a state, in violation of its international obligations, resorts to war against a High Contracting Party, the latter shall at his request receive the financial assistance provided for in the present convention, unless the Council decides otherwise.

2. The High Contracting Party to whom financial assistance is granted undertakes, for his part, to submit the dispute to judicial or arbitral settlement, or to any other pacific procedure which the Council may deem suitable.

Art. 2. 1. If the Council, in the performance of its duties under the Covenant, and acting within the limit of its rights under the Covenant or under general or special conventions applicable in the circumstances shall, in any international dispute likely to lead to a rupture, have taken steps to safeguard peace, including resort to mediation or any other means of peaceful settlement, and if one of the parties shall refuse or neglect to conform to such steps, the Council may, at the request of the other party, if the latter is a party to the present convention, grant financial assistance to the last-named party, provided it considers that peace can not be safeguarded otherwise.

2. The High Contracting Party to whom financial assistance is granted undertakes, for his part, to submit the dispute to judicial or arbitral settlement or to any other pacific procedure which the Council may deem suitable and to conform to any provisional measures that may be recommended by the Council with a view to safeguarding peace.

Art. 3. The financial assistance of the High Contracting Parties shall take the form of ordinary guarantees and special guarantees covering, as hereafter provided, the service of loans (which term shall include short-term credits) contracted in accordance with the present convention.

Art. 4. For the purpose of the present convention, the service of a loan comprises the sums payable in each year for interest and amortization, under the terms of the loan contracts.

Art. 5. No loan contracted under the present convention shall be for a period exceeding thirty years. In order to facilitate, so soon as circumstances permit, the discharge of the ordinary guarantor and special guarantor governments from their obligations in regard to the loan, a government contracting a loan under this convention shall, if possible, reserve the right to repay it before the end of its full period of maturity.

ORDINARY GUARANTIES

Art. 6. Each High Contracting Party undertakes and recognizes that the governments for which he becomes a party to the present convention severally guarantee as ordinary guarantors, to the extent and in the manner set out in the following articles, the due payment of the annual service of the loans which are contracted. The said ordinary guaranties attach to each loan in virtue of the present convention from the moment at which the loan is authorized, without any further action or consent on the part of the guarantor government.

Art. 7. 1. (*a*) Subject to the provisions of Art. 19 regarding payment of interest in the event of default, the annual liability which can fall to the charge of any government in the capacity of an ordinary guarantor in respect of all the loans contracted in accordance with the present convention, is limited to a maximum. This maximum shall be a sum bearing the same proportion to 100 million gold francs as the contribution to the League's expenses payable by the government, under the scale of allocation applicable on January 1, 1930, bears to the total contributions due from all the Members of the League.

(*b*) In the case of a government which was not liable to contribute to the League's expenses under the scale mentioned in the preceding paragraph, the scale of allocation in force on the date on which it became bound by the obligations of the present convention shall be applied to it.

2. The Council shall, as soon as possible, notify to the various governments the maximum annual liabilities which result for them from the provisions of par. 1.

SPECIAL GUARANTIES

Art. 8. Subject to the provisions of Art. 11, a High Contracting Party may accept the obligations of a special guarantor in respect of the government of any of his territories. Such government is thereby constituted a special guarantor, and the guaranty which it accords to loans to be contracted in accordance with the present convention shall be a special guaranty within the meaning of the present convention, without any further action or consent on the part of the government.

Art. 9. The special guaranties are created for the purpose of strengthening the security on which a loan contracted in accordance with the present convention is issued, by insuring that the service of such loan shall be guaranteed for its full amount, not merely by all the guaranteeing governments as ordinary guarantors, but also by a small number of governments which, as special guarantors, will bear, within the limits of their special guaranties, the risk of any delay in the payment of the amounts due from any of the other governments as ordinary guarantors. The amount covered by each special guaranty accordingly includes the amount of the government's liability as an ordinary guarantor together with an additional amount, and it is determined, as provided below, in such manner that the total of the additional amounts thus guaranteed by the special guarantor governments will equal the total amount guaranteed by the governments which are ordinary guarantors only. In the event of a default by the borrowing government on the service of the loan, the total amount covered by a special guaranty is payable in full; but the sum paid by a special guarantor government in excess of its liability as an ordinary guarantor is reimbursable, after the service has been met, out of the balance of the amounts collected from the guaranteeing governments.

Art. 10. 1. Subject to the provisions of Art. 19 regarding the payment of interest in the event of default, the annual liability which may fall to the charge of any special guarantor government in respect of all the loans contracted in accordance with the present convention is limited to a maximum which includes the government's obligation as an ordinary guarantor and the additional amount covered by its special guaranty. This maximum shall be determined by dividing the sum total of the maximum obligations of all the governments, as ordinary guarantors, among the special guarantor governments in proportion to their respective maximum obligations as ordinary guarantors.

2. The said maximum liabilities of the special guarantor governments shall be notified to them by the Council of the League of Nations as soon as possible. They shall be revised by the Council, in the event of any change in the number of governments which are ordinary guarantors or of those which are special guarantors, as soon as possible after such change has occurred.

Art. 11. 1. The following governments may be special guarantors under the present convention:

(a) The governments of permanent members of the Council of the League of Nations;

(b) The governments of other Members of the League which are unanimously invited to become special guarantors by those governments which themselves are special guarantors.

Such invitation may be given either before or after the entry into force of the convention.

2. Acceptance of the obligations of a special guarantor may be intimated at the moment of signature or at that of ratification or at the moment of accession to the convention, or subsequently by a declaration in writing deposited with the Secretary-General of the League of Nations, who shall notify such acceptance to all the other Members of the League.

Art. 12. The Secretary-General of the League of Nations shall send to the trustees provided for in Art. 13 a certified true copy of each notification of its maximum liability made to a government in execution of Art. 7 or Art. 10.

TRUSTEES

Art. 13. 1. Upon the entry into force of the present convention, the Council of the League of Nations shall appoint five persons to act as trustees of loans contracted in accordance with the present convention. The trustees shall be nationals of the Swiss Confederation and habitually resident in Switzerland.

2. (a) The trustees shall be appointed for periods of five years. At the end of their term of office, they may be reappointed for the like or any less period. A trustee may at any time resign on giving three months' previous notice in writing to the Council of the League of Nations.

(b) The Council of the League of Nations may at any time remove a trustee.

(c) In the event of a vacancy occurring for any reason in the office of trustee, the Council of the League of Nations shall without delay appoint another trustee. If, in his opinion, it is necessary to do so, the acting president of the Council may appoint a person to act until the vacancy is filled by the Council.

3. (a) The trustees shall appoint from their number a chairman and deputy-chairman and draw up their rules of procedure subject to the provisions of the present convention. Except in the case mentioned in Art. 16, par. 1, meetings shall be convened by the chairman or, if he is unable to act, by the deputy-chairman.

(b) Three trustees shall constitute a quorum. All decisions may be taken by a majority; in case of equality of votes, the presiding trustee shall have a casting vote.

(c) The Secretary-General of the League of Nations shall be entitled to be present or be represented at all meetings of the trustees.

(d) The expenses incurred by the trustees in executing their functions in connection with any loan and such honoraria for the performance of those functions as may be fixed by the Council of the League of Nations shall be paid by the borrowing government.

(e) The Council of the League of Nations may advance to the trustees the amounts referred to in par. (d); any sum so advanced shall be repaid to the League by the borrowing government.

(f) No trustee shall incur any personal liability in the execution of his functions as trustee, except for a breach of his duties knowingly and intentionally committed by him.

(g) The trustees shall report annually to the Council of the League of Nations upon the execution of their functions as trustees of each loan contracted in accordance with the present convention; they shall be entitled at any time to bring to the attention of the Council any difficulties experienced by them in performing such functions.

AUTHORIZATION OF LOANS

Art. 14. 1. Where the Council of the League of Nations recognizes that, in virtue of Arts. 1 or 2, a High Contracting Party should receive financial assistance under the present convention, it shall authorize the Government of such High Contracting Party to issue a loan enjoying the ordinary guaranties and the special guaranties resulting from the present convention. The Council may exclude the ordinary guaranty or special guaranty of any government if, in its opinion, it would not be desirable in the interest of the success of the loan that such ordinary guaranty or special guaranty should attach to the loan.

2. (a) The maximum sum to which the service of the loan may amount in each year shall be fixed by the Council. The sum fixed by the Council shall be expressed in gold francs as defined in Art. 26, and, for the purpose of determining the sum to which the service may amount in the currencies in which the loan is actually contracted, the value of those currencies shall in all cases be assumed to be, at the moment of signature of the loan contracts, that of their legal weight in pure gold.

(b) The annual sum fixed for the service of the loan in any year shall not exceed the amount which can be covered by special as well as by ordinary guaranties without imposing on any government a liability in excess of the maximum fixed by the present convention.

(c) The amount for each year of each government's liability as an ordinary guarantor shall be determined by dividing the service of the loan among all the guaranteeing governments in the proportion of their maximum possible annual liabilities as ordinary guarantors under this convention, as fixed by Art. 7. The total amount covered by each special guaranty shall be determined by dividing the said service among the special guarantor governments in the proportion of their maximum possible annual liabilities as special guarantors as fixed by Art. 10. For the purpose, however, of simplifying the application of the special guaranties, the Council, with the consent of the special guarantor governments whose liabilities are affected, may make minor fractional adjustments of the percentages attributable to the special guarantor governments to the extent necessary to convert such percentages into convenient whole numbers.

3. For the purpose of the preceding provisions, no account shall be taken of the liability for interest which may result under the provisions of Art. 19 from a default by a government in meeting its obligations as an ordinary or as a special guarantor.

Issue of Authorized Loans

Art. 15. 1. The Council shall require that the conditions and terms of issue of a loan contracted in accordance with the present convention, that is to say, *inter alia*, the method of issue, the securities (if any) on which the loan is raised, the issue price, the rate of interest, the amortization (including any stipulations as to repayment before maturity), the expenses of issue, negotiation and delivery, and the currency or currencies in which the loan is issued, shall be submitted for approval to it or to a person or persons appointed by it for the purpose. As provided in Art. 14 par. 2. (*a*), the value of the currencies in which the loan is issued and in which its service is payable shall in every case, for the purpose of determining the maximum to which the service may amount, be assumed to be, at the moment of signature of the loan contracts, that of their legal weight in pure gold. The arrangement made by the Council with the borrowing government in question shall be embodied in a protocol duly accepted by the latter.

2. The Council may make conditions as to the employment of the proceeds of the loan and the supervision of such employment. These conditions shall be embodied in the protocol mentioned in par. 1.

3. In the case of a loan issued in execution of Art. 2 of the present convention, the protocol provided for in par. 1 above shall contain provisions enabling the Council to suspend at any moment the payment to the government receiving the loan of such part of the proceeds of the loan as is not yet paid if the Council considers that such a measure is rendered necessary by the attitude of that government after financial assistance has been granted to it.

4. The loan shall not possess the ordinary guaranties and special guaranties resulting from the convention, unless the contracts relating to it shall have been certified in writing by a person or persons appointed by the Council — and acting in the second case by majority — to be in conformity with the decisions of the Council and the protocol provided for by par. 1 above, and the provisions of the present convention. A signed duplicate of the certificate shall be delivered to the Secretary-General of the League of Nations for communication to the trustees, together with copies of each contract authenticated by the borrowing government in sufficient number to enable him to send one to each trustee.

5. The following provisions shall be obligatory in all cases:

(*a*) The trustees appointed under the present convention, acting as provided therein, shall be trustees of the loan for all purposes for which trustees are appointed, and in particular shall make all payments for interest or amortization due on the loan out of the funds supplied by the borrowing government or, in the event of its default, by the governments guaranteeing the loan as special or ordinary guarantors.

(*b*) Except in the case of short-term credits of a currency not exceeding two years, a reserve shall be constituted in the hands of the trustees by the direct transfer to them by the issuing houses out of the yield of the loan of an amount sufficient to pay one-half of the annual service of the loan as issued. Any sums drawn from this reserve by the trustees shall immediately be refunded to them by the borrowing government.

(c) The borrowing government shall provide the trustees with the funds necessary to meet the service of the loan in time of war as well as in time of peace. Such remittances shall be in the hands of the trustees not later than thirty days before each payment falls due.

Deposit of Bonds in respect of Particular Loans

Art. 16. 1. As soon as possible after a contract for the issue of all or part of an authorized loan has been certified in accordance with Art. 15, par. 4, the trustees, convened by the Secretary-General of the League of Nations, shall examine the contract and the relevant decisions of the Council and ascertain and notify to the governments whose guaranties attached to the loan:

(a) What is the total amount of each payment due in respect of that issue in each year;

(b) What is the maximum sum for which each government, whether it be an ordinary or a special guarantor, may be liable as an ordinary guarantor in respect of each such payment;

(c) What is the maximum sum for which each special guarantor government may be liable as a special guarantor in respect of each such payment.

The sums mentioned in (b) and (c) shall be determined in the manner provided in Art. 14, par. 2 (c).

2. Within four months of the receipt of the above notification, each government, according as it is solely an ordinary guarantor or a special guarantor, shall deposit to the order of the trustees with such bank or other body as the Council, as soon as the convention comes into force, or subsequently, may choose, either an "Ordinary Guaranty Bond" in the form given in Annex I [1] or a "Special Guaranty Bond" in the form given in Annex II,[2] bearing a separate coupon for each payment for which the government may be liable in each year. The coupons shall be expressed and be payable in the currency in which payment is due to the bondholders. If the issue is made in more than one currency, separate bonds shall be deposited in respect of the service due in each currency.

3. The coupons of the said bonds shall be payable at an address satisfactory to the trustees fixed by the government.

4. The omission to deposit bonds, as provided above, shall in no way affect the obligations of the governments, whether as ordinary or as special guarantors, or prevent the issue of the loan on the security of the

---

[1] Not reprinted; for form see C.611.M.237.1930.IX.7, p. 19 and *Official Journal*, XI, p. 1671.
[2] Not reprinted; for form see C.611.M.237.1930.IX.7, p. 21 and *Official Journal*, XI, p. 1675.

ordinary guaranties and special guaranties which attach to it in virtue of the present convention.

OPERATION OF THE ORDINARY GUARANTIES AND SPECIAL GUARANTIES IN THE EVENT OF DEFAULT BY THE BORROWING GOVERNMENT

Art. 17. 1. (*a*) The service of loans contracted in accordance with the present convention shall always continue to be primarily a charge upon the borrowing government. The guaranties provided under the convention shall enter into operation only if, and to the extent to which, the trustees are neither provided with the necessary funds by the borrowing government nor able to meet the service out of the reserve constituted in accordance with Art. 15, par. 5 (*b*).

(*b*) In such a case, the trustees shall call simultaneously on all the guaranteeing governments, whether they be ordinary or special guarantors. They shall apply the yield of the calls to meet the service of the loan and shall then reimburse to the special guarantor governments *pro rata* out of the balance of such yield the amounts paid by them in excess of their liabilities as ordinary guarantors. Delay by a guarantor government in meeting a call is recognized as creating a duty to compensate special guarantor governments as provided in Arts. 19 and 21 for the prejudice caused to them by the resulting delay in the reimbursement of the amounts paid by them in excess of their liability as ordinary guarantors.

(*c*) All amounts obtained by the trustees from the guaranteeing governments, with the exception of the amounts reimbursed as contemplated in par. (*b*) and of amounts paid to them by way of interest under Art. 19, shall constitute a debt due, with interest, from the borrowing government.

(*d*) The liabilities between governments which result from the present convention shall be settled through the intermediary of the trustees.

2. The principles set out in par. 1 shall be applied in accordance with the provisions of Arts. 18 to 22 below.

Art. 18. 1. In the event of a default by the borrowing government in providing funds to pay the annual service of an authorized loan, the trustees shall draw on the reserve constituted by application of Art. 15, par. 5 (*b*), until that reserve is exhausted. They shall at once notify the default to the governments whose ordinary guaranties or special guaranties attach to the loan. They shall likewise notify any payments into the reserve.

2. If, thirty days before the date at which a payment for interest or amortization falls due, the trustees have neither received from the borrowing government nor possess in the reserve sufficient funds to make the payment, they shall inform each guarantor government of the amount

of the deficiency and the amount for which it will be liable if the deficiency is not made good. If, twenty days before the due date of the payment, the trustees still are unable to make it in full, they shall present for payment those coupons of the ordinary guaranty and special guaranty bonds which cover the service payment in question. If the deficiency is not total, the trustees shall reduce *pro rata* the amounts which they call upon the guarantor governments to pay on the said coupons, and the coupons shall be endorsed accordingly. If a guarantor government has not yet deposited its bond as required by Art. 16, the trustees shall nevertheless call upon it and it shall be liable to make the payment due from it.

3. The calls which are made by the trustees upon the ordinary guarantor and special guarantor governments shall be paid immediately by the said governments to the trustees notwithstanding that they may be at war with the borrowing government or with any country or countries in which a part of the loan has been issued, and notwithstanding that the holders of any or all of the bonds of the series of the loan in the service of which the default has occurred may be subjects of, or resident in, a country or countries with which they are at war.

4. The trustees shall meet the service of the loan out of the yield of the calls made upon the governments and shall apply the balance, and their receipts from any calls which are paid at a later date, to reimbursing *pro rata* to the special guarantor governments the amounts paid by them in excess of their liabilities as ordinary guarantors.

Art. 19. If an ordinary guarantor or special guarantor government fails to meet in full a call by the trustees by a date not later than ten days before the interest or amortization payment in question falls due, the trustees shall charge the said government, and the government shall pay to them, compound interest on the amount in arrears at the rate fixed by Art. 21. This charge shall be considered as interest due to those special guarantor governments which met their obligations by the said date, in consideration of the fact that the delay was calculated to retard payment of the sums reimbursable to them, and the sums received shall be paid over to the said special guarantor governments in proportion to the amount paid by them in excess of their liabilities as ordinary guarantors.

Art. 20. 1. The amount of each default by the borrowing government in meeting a guaranteed payment due on a loan shall constitute a debt of that government to the trustees, bearing compound interest, at the rate mentioned in Art. 21, as from the date at which the government was due to provide the trustees with the funds necessary for the service of the loan.

2. The payments received by the trustees from the borrowing govern-

ment after it has defaulted in meeting the guaranteed service of its loan shall, if necessary, be applied in the first instance to making good any arrears in the guaranteed service of the loan which have occurred, notwithstanding the ordinary guaranties and special guaranties provided by the present convention, and, secondly, to reconstituting the reserve provided for by Art. 15, par. 5 (*b*). Subject to this provision, any amounts not required for meeting the current service of the loan shall be used to reimburse to the special guarantor and ordinary guarantor governments, with the appropriate interest, the amounts which they have furnished to meet defaults in the service of the loan and which have not been reimbursed to them. Each government shall be entitled to be reimbursed the sum paid by it in the capacity of an ordinary guarantor with compound interest at the rate mentioned in Art. 21, as from the date of its payment to the trustees. Each special guarantor government shall, in addition, be entitled to receive the amount paid in excess of its liability as an ordinary guarantor, together with its share of any interest chargeable to other governments under Art. 19. Priority shall be given to reimbursement to the special guarantor governments of the amounts paid by them in excess of their liabilities as ordinary guarantors, and the sums due in respect of earlier defaults shall be met in full before any payment is made in respect of later defaults. Subject to the above provisions, the reimbursement shall be effected *pro rata* to the sums due to the various governments.

3. A reimbursement to the special guarantor governments effected under par. 2 shall cancel *pro rata* the claims of these governments against other ordinary or special guarantor governments. The trustees shall determine what liabilities are extinguished or reduced and notify the governments concerned.

Art. 21. The compound interest provided for in Arts. 19 and 20 shall be calculated half-yearly and shall be at a rate one per cent higher than the rate of interest payable on the guaranteed loan, or, if the loan was issued in several series, on the particular series in the service of which the default occurs.

Art. 22. All questions arising in the execution of Arts. 16 to 21 inclusive shall be settled by the trustees, subject to appeal by any government concerned to the Council of the League of Nations, whose decision shall be final. The appeal to the Council shall not suspend the execution of the trustees' decision.

GUARANTY OF STATES NOT MEMBERS OF THE LEAGUE OF NATIONS

Art. 23. The Council of the League of Nations, with the consent of those governments which are interested in the particular loan as special guarantors, may accept an offer by a state which is not a Member of the

League to participate in guaranteeing the annual service of a particular loan which the Council decides to authorize in application of the present convention. The acceptance of the offer shall not entail the assumption by any government, whether as an ordinary or as a special guarantor, of liability to make payments greater than it would have been liable to make if the non-Member state had not agreed to participate.

General Provisions

Art. 24. The trustees shall, if so directed by the Council of the League of Nations, suspend all payments to, or for the benefit of, the government or inhabitants of a territory to which the financial sanctions provided for in Art. 16 of the Covenant have become applicable; the sums retained by the trustees shall become payable, together with any interest which they may have earned, so soon as the Council shall be of opinion that the maintenance of the said sanctions is no longer justified.

Art. 25. The ordinary or special guarantor governments undertake to facilitate to the fullest possible extent the issue of loans authorized under the present convention, both by opening their financial markets to such loans and by abstaining from any measure capable of compromising the efficacy of the financial assistance provided for by the present convention.

Art. 26. For the purposes of the present convention, the gold franc shall mean a monetary value equivalent to 0.322581 gramme or 4.97818 grains of gold nine-tenths fine.

Art. 27. Any dispute as to the interpretation or as to the method of application of the present convention shall be settled by a decision of the Council of the League of Nations.

Art. 28. 1. Decisions of the Council under Arts. 1 or 2 or those suspending the loan in accordance with Art. 15, par. 3 shall be taken by the unanimous vote of the Members represented at the meeting, the votes of representatives of the parties to the dispute not being counted in determining such unanimity.

2. All other decisions taken by the Council in virtue of the present convention shall be taken by a simple majority vote of the Members represented at the meeting, the votes of the representatives of the parties to the dispute not being counted.

3. A Member of the League which is not a member of the Council can not claim to sit on the Council, when the latter discusses questions arising under the present convention, in virtue solely of the fact that it is an ordinary guarantor or special guarantor under the present convention.

Art. 29. The provisions of the present convention may not be interpreted as affecting the rights and obligations of the High Contracting

Parties under the provisions of Art. 16 of the Covenant of the League of Nations.

Final Provisions

Art. 30. 1. The present convention of which the French and English texts shall both be authentic, shall bear to-day's date; it may, until December 31, 1931, be signed on behalf of any Member of the League of Nations.

2. The present convention shall be ratified. The instruments of ratification shall be transmitted to the Secretary-General of the League of Nations, who shall notify their receipt to all the Members of the League.

Art. 31. As from January 1, 1932, the present convention may be acceded to on behalf of any Member of the League of Nations. The instruments of accession shall be transmitted to the Secretary-General of the League of Nations, who shall notify their receipt to all the Members of the League.

Art. 32. It shall be a condition of the entry into force of the present convention that the ratifications or accessions which it has received shall have resulted in causing a sum of not less than 50 million gold francs, for the annual service of loans, to be covered by ordinary guaranties and also by the special guaranties of not less than three governments.

Art. 33. 1. The present convention shall enter into force ninety days after the date on which the conditions provided for in Art. 32 are satisfied and subject to the provisions of Art. 35.

2. The Secretary-General shall make the calculations necessary for the purpose of Art. 32. He shall notify the entry into force of the convention to all the Members of the League.

3. In the case of a Member of the League of Nations on whose behalf a ratification or accession is subsequently deposited, the convention shall take effect on the day on which the instrument of ratification or accession is deposited with the Secretary-General of the League of Nations.

4. The total maximum amount covered by ordinary guaranties in accordance with Art. 7 on the date of entry into force of the convention, and any subsequent increase in that amount resulting from a new ratification or accession, shall be notified to all the Members of the League by the Secretary-General.

Art. 34. Subject to the conditions laid down in Art. 35, the following provisions shall apply:

1. The present convention shall be concluded for a period continuing until the end of the year 1945.

2. It shall continue in force for further successive periods of five years as between such High Contracting Parties as do not denounce it at least two years before the expiration of the current period.

3. Denunciation shall be effected by a written notification deposited with the Secretary-General of the League of Nations, who shall notify its receipt to all the Members of the League. A denunciation may relate merely to the guaranty of the government of a particular territory of the High Contracting Party.

4. Notwithstanding the provisions of par. 2, the convention shall cease to be in force, so far as it relates to the authorization of new loans, at the end of the original period for which it is concluded, or of any successive period for which it continues in force, if at that date, as a result of denunciations, or of the operation of par. 7 below, the annual sum to which the ordinary guaranties amount is less than 50 million gold francs or the number of special guarantor governments has fallen below three.

5. (a) The obligations of any government in respect of loans already authorized in virtue of the present convention shall not be affected by denunciation of the convention, or by its ceasing to be in force, under the provisions of par. 4 above or of Art. 35.

(b) The Council of the League of Nations and the trustees shall continue to exercise in respect of loans already authorized all the functions attributed to them by the present convention until such loans have been repaid in full.

6. If the ratifications or accessions necessary to bring the present convention into force have not been received before the end of the year 1935, the Council of the League of Nations shall convene a conference to examine the situation.

7. Withdrawal or exclusion from the League of Nations shall, on the date on which it becomes effective, terminate all the rights and obligations of the government concerned under the present convention, except such obligations as already rest upon it in consequence of the previous authorization of a loan in application of the convention.

Art. 35. 1. The entry into force of the present convention, and its maintenance in force as regards the authorization of new loans, shall be conditional, in respect of each of the High Contracting Parties, upon the entry into force and maintenance in force, in respect of that party, of a plan for the reduction of armaments adopted in execution of Art. 8 of the Covenant of the League of Nations.

2. Notwithstanding the provisions of Arts. 1, 2 and 14, if, after the expiration of one year from the entry into force of the plan referred to above, a High Contracting Party is not acting in conformity with his obligations under such plan, he shall not benefit by the financial assistance provided for by the present convention.

Art. 36. The present convention shall be registered by the Secretary-General of the League of Nations on the date of its entry into force.

IN FAITH WHEREOF, the above-mentioned plenipotentiaries have signed the present convention.

DONE at Geneva on the second day of October, one thousand nine hundred and thirty, in a single copy, which shall be kept in the archives of the Secretariat of the League of Nations, and of which certified true copies shall be delivered to all the Members of the League.

[Here follow signatures.]

3. General Convention to Improve the Means of Preventing War, Geneva, September 26, 1931.[1]

Not in force; enters into force on deposit of 10 ratifications or accessions. Open for signature until February 2, 1932; thereafter to accession.

Signed by: Albania, Austria, Belgium, Bulgaria, Colombia, Czechoslovakia, Denmark, France, Germany, Greece, Lithuania, Luxemburg, Netherlands, Norway, Panama, Peru, Portugal, Siam, Spain, Sweden, Switzerland and Uruguay.

[Names of the High Contracting Parties.]

Being sincerely desirous of developing mutual confidence by increasing the efficacy of the means of preventing war,

Noting that, for this purpose, the task of the Council of the League of Nations in insuring peace and conciliation might be facilitated by undertakings assumed voluntarily in advance by the states,

Have decided to conclude a convention and have for that purpose appointed as their plenipotentiaries:

[Designation of plenipotentiaries.]

Who, having deposited their full powers, found in good and true form, have agreed as follows:

Art. 1. The High Contracting Parties undertake, in the event of a dispute arising between them and being brought before the Council of the League of Nations, to accept and apply the conservatory measures of a nonmilitary nature relating to the substance of the dispute which the Council, acting in accordance with the powers conferred upon it by the Covenant of the League of Nations, may recommend with a view to preventing the aggravation of the dispute.

The Council shall fix the period of duration of these conservatory measures. It may extend this period should circumstances render it necessary.

---

[1] *Resolutions and Recommendations adopted by the Assembly . . . 1931*, p. 24 (*Official Journal*, Spec. Sup. No. 92); certified true copy is C.658(1).M.269(1). 1931.IX.1932.IX.17.

Art. 2. If, in circumstances which, in the Council's opinion, do not create a state of war between the powers at issue which are parties to the present convention, the forces of one of those powers enter the territory or territorial waters of the other or a zone demilitarized in virtue of international agreements, or fly over them, the Council may prescribe measures to insure their evacuation by those forces. The High Contracting Parties undertake to carry out without delay the measures so prescribed, without prejudice to the other powers vested in the Council under Art. 11 of the Covenant.

Art. 3. If the circumstances referred to in Art. 2 have arisen, or, if in the event of a threat of war, special conditions, and in particular the possibilities of contact between the forces of the parties to the dispute, render it necessary, the Council may fix lines which must not be passed by their land, naval or air forces and, where necessary in order to avoid incidents, by their civil aircraft. The High Contracting Parties undertake to comply with the Council's recommendations in this matter.

The lines referred to in the previous paragraph shall, if possible, be fixed by agreement with the parties at issue.

Failing such agreement, the Council shall fix the lines with the consent of the party whose forces are affected, provided always that this does not involve the withdrawal of the forces further back than the exterior lines of the defense organizations existing on the frontier of the High Contracting Parties concerned at the time when the Council of the League of Nations takes its decision, and that the lines do not involve the abandonment of any other work, position or line of communication essential to the security or the supplies of the party concerned.

It shall, in every case, rest with the Council to determine the period within which the said lines shall be fixed under the conditions specified above.

The High Contracting Parties further agree to give strict orders to the commanders of their forces, if the Council so recommends, to take all necessary precautions to avoid incidents.

Art. 4. The Council shall, if it thinks fit, or if one of the parties at issue so requests before the Council has reached any of the decisions referred to in Arts. 2 and 3, appoint commissioners for the sole purpose of verifying on the spot the execution of the conservatory measures of a military character recommended by the Council under the conditions specified in Arts. 2 and 3.

When regulating the execution of the measures it has prescribed, the Council shall, at the reasoned request of a High Contracting Party which is a party to the dispute, cause that execution to coincide with the arrival of the commissioners on the spot, so far as it may think necessary.

The High Contracting Parties undertake to afford these commissioners every facility for the performance of their duties.

The commissioners may not make a more extensive inspection than is necessary to enable them to carry out the duty defined in par. 1. Nor may they make any inspection of a naval or air base, nor may they inspect military works or establishments for any purpose other than to verify the withdrawal of the forces.

The rules to be followed for the composition and working of commissions of inspection shall be embodied in executive regulations which shall be prepared by the competent organs of the League of Nations so as to enter into force at the same time as the present convention.

Art. 5. If any violation of the measures defined in Arts. 2 and 3 is noted by the Council and continues in spite of its injunctions, the Council shall consider what means of all kinds are necessary to insure the execution of the present convention.

Should war break out as a consequence of this violation, such violation shall be regarded by the High Contracting Parties as *prima facie* evidence that the party guilty thereof has resorted to war within the meaning of Art. 16 of the Covenant.

Art. 6. The High Contracting Parties undertake to provide, by the means at their disposal, such publicity as the Council may think fit for its proceedings, decisions and recommendations when a dispute is brought before it in the cases contemplated by the present convention.

Art. 7. In the cases referred to in Arts. 1, 2, 3, 4, 5 and 6, the Council's decisions and recommendations shall, except as otherwise provided in those articles, be binding for the purposes of the present convention, provided that they are concurred in by all the Members voting other than the parties to the dispute.

Art. 8. The provisions of the present convention shall only apply as between the High Contracting Parties.

Art. 9. The present convention may not be interpreted as restricting the task or the powers of the Council of the League of Nations as laid down in the Covenant.

Nor should it affect the right of free passage through the Suez Canal provided for in the Convention on the Free Navigation of the Suez Maritime Canal signed at Constantinople on October 29, 1888.

Art. 10. The present convention shall remain open until February 2, 1932, for signatures on behalf of any Member of the League of Nations or of any non-Member state to which the Council of the League of Nations has communicated a copy of the convention for this purpose.

Art. 11. The present convention is subject to ratification. Ratifications shall be deposited with the Secretariat of the League of Nations.

The Secretary-General shall give notice of the deposit of each ratification to the Members of the League of Nations and to the non-Member states mentioned in Art. 10, indicating the date of its deposit.

Art. 12. As from February 3, 1932, any Member of the League of Nations and any non-Member state mentioned in Art. 10 on whose behalf the convention has not been signed before that date may accede thereto.

Accession shall be effected by an instrument deposited with the Secretariat of the League of Nations. The Secretary-General of the League of Nations shall give notice of each accession to the Members of the League of Nations and to the non-Member states mentioned in Art. 10, indicating the date of the deposit of the instrument.

Art. 13. A *procès-verbal* shall be drawn up by the Secretary-General of the League of Nations as soon as ratifications or accessions on behalf of 10 Members of the League of Nations or non-Member states have been deposited.

A certified copy of this *procès-verbal* shall be sent by the Secretary-General of the League of Nations to each Member of the League of Nations and to each non-Member state mentioned in Art. 10.

Art. 14. The present convention shall be registered by the Secretary-General of the League of Nations ninety days after the date mentioned in Art. 13. It will then enter into force as regards all Members of the League of Nations or non-Member states on whose behalf ratifications or accessions have been deposited on the date of the *procès-verbal*.

As regards any Member of the League or non-Member state on whose behalf a ratification or accession is subsequently deposited, the convention shall enter into force on the ninetieth day after the date of the deposit of a ratification or accession on its behalf.

Each of the High Contracting Parties shall have the right to inform the Secretary-General of the League of Nations at the moment of the deposit of his ratification or of the notification of his accession, to the exclusion of all other reservations, that he makes the entry into force of the convention, in so far as he is concerned, conditional on ratification or accession on behalf of certain countries named by him.

Art. 15. The present convention may not be denounced before the expiration of five years from its coming into force in accordance with Art. 14.

Denunciation shall be effected by a notification in writing addressed to the Secretary-General of the League of Nations, who shall inform all Members of the League of Nations and the non-Member states mentioned in Art. 10. Each denunciation shall take effect one year after the receipt by the Secretary-General of the notification, but only as regards the High Contracting Party on whose behalf it has been notified.

Art. 16. The French and English texts of the present convention shall both be authoritative.

IN FAITH WHEREOF the above-mentioned plenipotentiaries have signed the present convention.

DONE at Geneva on the 26th day of September, one thousand nine hundred and thirty-one, in a single copy, which shall be deposited in the archives of the Secretariat of the League of Nations, and of which certified true copies shall be transmitted by the Secretary-General to all the Members of the League of Nations and to any non-Member state to which the Council of the League of Nations has decided to communicate a copy of the present convention, in accordance with Art. 10.

[Here follow signatures]

RESERVATIONS ON SIGNING

France — On signing the present convention, I declare, on behalf of the Government of the Republic, that ratification can not take place until it has been possible to ascertain that the settlement provided for in Art. 4 and which must be elaborated in order to enter into force at the same time as the convention, insures the guaranties of control which are deemed necessary by the French Government.

January 30, 1932.   RENÉ MASSIGLI

Panama — On signing the present convention, I declare, on behalf of my Government, that my signature does not affect in any way the provisions of the treaties of conciliation and arbitration concluded up to this date by the Republic of Panama with other powers.

January 30, 1932.   NARCISO GARAY

APPENDIX III

STATISTICAL NOTES

N. B. As emphasized in the text, there exist no really trustworthy records of armament statistics for accurate purposes of comparison. An essential result of any agreement made by the conference will be improvement in this respect. The following tables have been compiled to illustrate discrepancies between methods more than to provide absolute figures.

The anarchy in armament statistics is due to natural causes. Each government has produced figures in accordance with its own system of administration and accounting, modified by imitative conformity, in the annual memoranda furnished for the *Armaments Year-Book*. The *Particulars* furnished in accordance with the model tables of the Draft Convention provide relatively comparable statistics, which will improve in respect of uniformity with further application to national accounts.

The following statistics are, therefore, presented with all reserves as to scientific accounting accuracy, though they carefully report the governmental figures. The figures from the seventh *Armaments Year-Book*, representing national methods of accounting, are comparable only because they are the best evidence made available by governments themselves. The figures from the *Particulars* (repeated in the eighth *Armaments Year-Book* (1932), are comparable only because they were compilations by governments applying international formulas for the first time, but with many differences of practice. Where the national and international figures are presented in parallel they illustrate the different results secured by the application of the two methods rather than any absolute difference in experience.

WORLD ARMAMENT STRENGTH
As reported by Governments in the Seventh *Armaments Year-Book*

	Fiscal year ending	Land Budgetary effectives absolute figures	Reserves, gendarmes, etc.	Naval Tonnage	Depreciated and Superannuated Tonnage [1]
Albania	1931	10,335	3,131	184	
Argentine Republic	1930	27,484		113,400	19,253
Australia	1931	1,614	56,800	52,373	28,162
Austria	1931	21,432			
Belgium	1930	85,310	6,439		
Bolivia	1928	8,000			
Brazil	1931	46,532	4,273	60,100	1,088
Bulgaria	1931	32,412		100	
Canada	1931	5,214	53,160	1,810	151

[1] Depreciated tonnage is calculated for each year of service as follows: capital ship, aircraft carriers, coast guard and other minor craft, 1/20 per year; cruisers and light cruisers, 1/17 per year; destroyers, torpedo boats and submarines, 1/12 per year.

For the definition of exempt and special vessels, see *Draft Convention*, Part II, Chapter B, Annexes I, II.

APPENDIX III

	Fiscal year ending	Land Budgetary effectives absolute figures	Reserves, gendarmes, etc.	Naval Tonnage	Depreciated and Superannuated Tonnage [1]
Chile	1927	22,380	18,349	75,800	13,800
China	1929	1,800,000		40,300	4,383
Colombia	1929	8,909	2,242	1,443	
Costa Rica		500	37,280		
Cuba		12,458	2,376	4,351	38
Czechoslovakia	1930	130,080			
Denmark		11,115	3,065	23,897	4,696
Dominican Republic	1929	2,128			
Ecuador	1930	5,323	4,204	1,050	
Egypt	1929	11,380	18,450	3,460	
Estonia		12,000	1,200	5,418	180
Finland		27,653	100,000	7,218	
France	1930	522,737	55,145[2]	504,441	199,909
Germany	1930	94,900		150,900	26,906
Great Britain and Northern Ireland	1931	139,513	132,200	1,274,500	493,400
Greece	1931	61,684[3]		24,995	3,735
Guatemala	1931	6,649			
Haiti	1930	2,715			
Honduras	1926	2,253			
Hungary	1931	34,993	25,091		
India	1930	226,479	24,381	5,775	3,097
Irish Free State	1931	6,219	7,800		
Italy	1929	234,700	387,236	391,837	
Japan	1928	210,880	66,450	769,777	374,097
Latvia	1929	20,000		1,305	802
Liberia	1928	6,386			
Lithuania	1931	17,839			
Luxemburg	1930	405	8,978		
Mexico	1930	64,203		5,682	
Netherlands	1930	59,030[4]	44,800	68,214	26,968
New Zealand	1931	561	16,990	9,700	3,994
Nicaragua	1924	337	828		
Norway	1930	3,740	9,250	25,481	1,785
Panama	1927	756			
Paraguay	1928	2,915			
Persia	1931	40,000	12,415	1,579	
Peru	1930	9,045	6,627	9,541	1,867
Poland	1931	265,871	63,826	25,613	7,498
Portugal	1931	47,363[5]	16,085	18,010	2,602

[1] Depreciated tonnage is calculated for each year of service as follows: capital ship, aircraft carriers, coast guard and other minor craft, 1/20 per year; cruisers and light cruisers, 1/17 per year; destroyers, torpedo boats and submarines, 1/12 per year.

For the definition of exempt and special vessels, see *Draft Convention*, Part II, Chapter B, Annexes I, II.

[2] Gendarmerie, republican guard and irregulars only.
[3] To be 59,612 in 1931–32.
[4] Includes 35,573 troops in overseas territory.
[5] Includes 12,746 troops in overseas colonies.

	Fiscal year ending	Land Budgetary effectives absolute figures	Reserves, gendarmes, etc.	Naval Tonnage	Depreciated and Superannuated Tonnage [1]
Rumania	1929	186,143	30,150	16,595	7,051
Salvador	1931	3,000	1,108		
Siam		25,000		6,100	
South Africa, Union of	1930	1,424	8,396	800	
Soviet Union	1927	562,000	(1930)	166,247	28,925
Spain	1930	177,820[2]	51,235	117,432	50,459
Sweden	1930	23,686	7,000	66,949	12,247
Switzerland	1931	33,182[3]	152,436[3]		
Turkey		140,000		44,500	3,279
United States	1930	139,374	287,799	1,308,671	679,911
Uruguay	1926	8,132		(1930) 3,500	
Venezuela	1930	6,000		2,075	
Yugoslavia	1931	111,749	25,497	10,695	3,052
		5,781,989	1,752,692	5,423,856	2,003,335

[1] Depreciated tonnage is calculated for each year of service as follows: capital ship, aircraft carriers, coast guard and other minor craft, 1/20 per year; cruisers and light cruisers, 1/17 per year; destroyers, torpedo boats and submarines, 1/12 per year.

For the definition of exempt and special vessels, see *Draft Convention*, Part II, Chapter B, Annexes I, II.

[2] Includes 63,177 troops overseas. In 1931 eight out of sixteen divisions were disbanded and two-thirds of the officers retired by the republic.

[3] In one sense the Swiss army consisted of 309 permanent training staff and officers and men under limited periods of training. In 1930, 8,002 officers and men performed 253,681 parade days of duty and 25,180 recruits parade days to a total of 1,649,720. In addition, 152,436 men had refresher training for a total of 2,059,358 days. The average daily effectives were 11,130.

APPENDIX III
NATIONAL EXPENDITURES ON ARMAMENT[1]

Country	National Report Fiscal Year	Currency	$ Equivalent	By Experts' Formulas Fiscal Year	Currency	$ Equivalent
Albania				1930–31	14,529,613 gold francs	2,803,126
Argentine Rep.	1930–31	114,403,000 paper pesos	42,031,662			
Australia	1930–31	£3,785,000	15,136,972	1929–30	4,761,659	22,522,647
Austria	1930	103,623,000 schillings	14,610,843	1930	103,622,700	14,610,800
Belgium	1930	1,223,000,000 francs	34,244,000	1930	1,443,521,079	40,418,590
Bolivia	1930	8,703,000 Bolivianos	3,167,892			
Brazil	1930	459,216,000 papermilreis	10,681,763			
Bulgaria	1930–31	1,087,000,000 levas	7,818,791	1930–31	1,033,418,000	7,432,77
Canada	1929–30	$21,069,200	20,893,483	1930–31	19,274,397	19,272,470
Chile	1930	241,004,000 pesos	9,720,495			
China	1928–29	209,537,000 Chinese dollars	94,291,650			
Colombia	1930	6,452,000 pesos	6,226,180	1931	4,300,000	4,152,510
Costa Rica	1929–30	2,752,000 colones	688,000	1931	470,557	117,639
Cuba	1930–31	12,031,000 pesos	12,031,000	1930–31	11,427,282	11,427,282
Czechoslovakia	1930	1,706,300,000 koruna	50,506,480	1930	1,813,260,121	53,672,500
Denmark	1930–31	44,900,000 kroner	12,028,832	1930–31	{45,265,127[1] / 20,780,147}	12,116,569 / 5,562,430
Dominican Rep.	1930	1,056,838 pesos	211,368			
Ecuador	1930	9,071,100 sucres	1,814,220			
Egypt	1930–31	£E2,119,700	10,559,921	1931–32	981,988	4,854,065
Estonia	1930–31	18,400,000 krooni	4,918,320			
Finland	1931	658,300,000 marks	16,569,411	1930	639,481,996	16,114,946
France	1930–31	11,674,500,000 francs	458,078,194	1930–31	13,809,598,000	541,854,102
Germany	1930–31	716,346,000 R.Mks.	170,698,088	1930–31	707,722,624	168,643,224
Great Britain and Northern Ireland	1930–31	£94,950,000	461,475,990	1929–30	108,553,924	527,599,209
Greece	1930–31	1,641,600,000 drachmai	21,291,552			
Guatemala	1930–31	2,001,000 quetzals	2,001,000			
Haiti	1929–30	5,789,600 gourdes	1,157,920	1930–31	2,150,539	430,108
Hejaz and Nejd					930,151 guineas	4,752,967
Honduras	1930–31	1,974,048 pesos	973,524			
Hungary	1930–31	101,100,000 pengo	17,667,225		121,600,045	21,219,208
India	1930–31	579,708,000 rupees	208,767,344	1929–30	537,751,057	194,397,007
Irish Free State	1930–31	£1,445,000	7,022,700	1930–31	1,251,739	6,083,802
Italy	1930–31	4,978,931,000 lire	260,746,616	1930–31	6,328,987,862	331,449,094

[1] The first figure is the budget; the second is the estimate when the new program is in effect.

NATIONAL EXPENDITURES ON ARMAMENT [1]
(Continued)

Country	National Report Fiscal Year	National Report Currency	National Report $ Equivalent	By Experts' Formulas Fiscal Year	By Experts' Formulas Currency	By Experts' Formulas $ Equivalent
Japan	1930–31	473,723,000 yen	234,256,024	1929–30	527,671,515	248,744,352
Latvia	1930–31	39,300,000 lats	7,580,970	1928–29	41,986,291	8,103,354
Liberia	1928	$126,071	126,071		102,090	102,090
Lithuania	1931	56,800,000 lits	5,685,680	1930	56,678,911	5,667,891
Luxemburg	1930	9,900,000 francs	277,200			
Mexico	1930	92,671,000 pesos	43,648,041			
Netherlands	1930	77,200,000 florins	31,034,400	1929	190,931,300	76,754,382
New Zealand	1930–31	£713,500	3,282,628	1930–31	859,806	3,955,709
Nicaragua	1928–29	77,687 cordobas	77,687			
Norway	1930–31	38,400,000 kroner	10,275,840	1930–31	47,500,000	12,692,000
Panama	1926–27	650,720 balboas	650,720			
Paraguay	1928–29	62,662,000 paper pesos	1,405,888			13,598,751
Persia	1929–30	123,700,000 krans	10,640,921		{ 16,998,439 tomans	
Peru	1930	£P2449,000	8,889,870			
Poland	1930–31	844,300,000 zloty	94,561,600	1931–32	{ 847,600,000[2] 996,304,309	95,083,768[2] 111,765,417[2]
Portugal	1930–31	409,491,000 escudos	18,354,206	1931–32	490,537,634	21,960,086
Rumania	1930	8,941,200,000 lei	53,647,200[3]	1931	{ £12,439,281[4] 10,204,029,936	60,713,978
Salvador	1930–31	4,391,200 colones	2,195,600			
Siam	1930–31	21,171,000 baht	9,414,534	1930–31	27,047,788	11,965,941
Union of South Africa	1930–31	£1,008,300	4,875,937	1930–31	867,094	4,193,093
Soviet Union	1929–30	1,125,100,000 rubles	578,920,205	1931	1,290,000,000	663,769,500
Spain	1930	962,248,000 pesetas	112,583,016	1930	750,873,299	87,852,176
Sweden	1930–31	132,500,000 kronor	35,543,125	1929–30	137,696,009	36,971,378
Switzerland	1931	98,300,000 francs	19,014,169	1930	113,586,207	22,035,724
Turkey	1929	£T69,295,100	33,538,828	1931	55,452,008	26,117,896
United States	1930–31	$707,425,000	707,425,000	1929–30	700,237,191	700,237,191
Uruguay	1929–30	8,638,000 pesos	8,262,247	1930–32	8,529,630	6,892,453
Venezuela	1930–31	30,452,000 bolivars	5,539,219			
Yugoslavia	1930–31	2,522,900,000 dinars	44,612,441	1929–30	3,211,112,248	56,595,853

[1] The first figure is the budget; the second is the estimate when the new program is in effect.
[2] Includes estimates for frontier guard and state police force in addition to 847,600,000 zloty for land, naval and air forces.
[3] Calculated at par.
[4] Average rate £1 = 816.50 lei.

LAND EFFECTIVES

Contrasting Totals Given by States Under National and International Methods of Calculation

	Armaments Year-Book *Absolute figures* Total	Officers	Draft Convention Total Table III *Average daily effectives* Total	Officers
Albania	10,335	650	12,629	771
Argentina	27,484	1,501	32,712	1,827
Australia	1,614	281	2,574	436
Austria	21,432	1,487	21,463	1,415
Belgium	85,310	4,204	86,384	5,025
Bulgaria	32,412	1,493	19,532	980
Canada	5,214	570	4,644	570
Costa Rica	500	44	318	58
Cuba	12,458	786	13,155	867
Czechoslovakia	130,080	10,079	138,788	10,221
Denmark	11,115	2,245	{8,093 / 1,182}	{1,574[1] / 221}
Dominican Republic	2,128	115	2,000	179
Egypt	12,485	550	24,292	565
Estonia	12,000	1,200	13,533	1,290
Finland	27,653		31,575	1,818
France	522,737	29,156	651,320[2]	33,570
Germany	94,900	3,798	100,500	4,500
Great Britain and Northern Ireland	139,513	7,217	144,522	9,393
Haiti	2,715	178	2,555	199
Hejaz and Nejd			43,437	734
Hungary	34,993	1,780	35,000	1,750
India	226,479	7,534	259,818	12,650
Irish Free State	6,219	519	6,440	515
Italy	234,700	16,470	491,398[3]	22,137
Japan	210,880	15,340	259,304	17,343
Latvia	20,000	2,000	23,000	2,200
Liberia	6,386		4,751	409
Lithuania	17,839	1,351	18,603	1,158
Luxemburg	405		500	
Netherlands	59,030	2,623	55,376	2,698
New Zealand	561	119	469	94
Nicaragua	337	48	2,404	204
Norway	3,740	2,896	5,731	893
Panama	756		0	0

[1] The first figure is the present strength; the second the estimated strength when the new program becomes effective.

[2] Includes 249,065 effectives intended for police purposes in overseas territories, and excludes 155,535 not trained as defined in national legislation.

[3] Owing to a complicated system of calling up and releasing men, while holding all eligible recruits liable to service, the Italian Government did not report its figures in terms of average daily effectives. The total land forces, at home and overseas, for 1930–31 seems to have been 414,859 for five months and 250,890 for seven months. No statement is given to show the number of men serving in both periods. These are presumptively the equivalent of 319,210.5 men for 12 months.

	Armaments Year-Book Absolute figures		Draft Convention Total Table III Average daily effectives	
	Total	Officers	Total	Officers
Poland................	265,871	17,905	⎰329,451[1] ⎱59,980	⎰19,923[1] ⎱17,895
Portugal..............	47,363	4,896	61,143	5,283
Rumania...............	186,143	14,729	240,501	14,185
Siam..................	25,000		24,468	1,933
South Africa...........	1,424	139	2,487	151
Soviet Union..........	562,000		504,303	30,354
Spain.................	177,820	12,702	195,393	23,993
Sweden................	23,686	4,036	24,869	2,340
Switzerland...........	33,182		12,290	662
Turkey................	140,000	20,000	194,000	20,000
United States..........	139,374	12,255	139,957	13,080
Uruguay...............	8,132	818	6,629	785
Yugoslavia.............	111,749	7,527	184,448	6,741

NAVAL TONNAGE

Contrasting Totals Given by States Under National and International Methods of Calculation

	Armaments Year-Book		Draft Convention Part II, Chapter B	
	Tonnage	Depreciated	Tonnage	Exempt and Special
Albania...............	184			184
Argentina..............	113,400	19,253	88,707	34,640
Australia..............	52,373	28,162	38,478	
Austria................	0		0	
Belgium...............	0		0	
Bulgaria...............	100		0	
Canada................	1,810	151	4,466m.	942
Cuba..................	4,351	38	3,255	2,425
Czechoslovakia.........	0			
Denmark..............	23,897	4,696	⎰16,208 ⎱8,000	⎰5,520 ⎱5,100
Estonia................	5,418	180	2,585	2,087
Finland...............	27,218	0	9,569	6,273
France................	504,441	199,909	628,603[2]	47,911
Germany..............	150,900	26,906	125,780	46,810
Great Britain and Northern Ireland...............	1,274,500	493,400	1,250,247	587,989
Hungary...............	0	0	0	0
India..................	5,775	3,097	0	13,448
Irish Free State.........	0	0	0	0
Italy..................	391,837		404,005	188,260
Japan.................	769,777	74,097	850,328	340,343
Latvia.................	1,305	802	756	
Netherlands............	68,214	26,968	59,432	38,950

[1] These figures include formations organized on a military basis of special character.

[2] Does not include 27,739 tons and 1 capital ship.

APPENDIX III

	Armaments Year-Book		Draft Convention Part II, Chapter B	
	Tonnage	Depreciated	Tonnage	Exempt and Special
New Zealand	9,700	3,994	9,415	4,894
Norway	25,481	1,785	19,936[1]	8,730
Panama	0	0	0	0
Poland	25,613	7,498	6,020	19,944
Portugal	18,010	2,602	50,000	not reported
Rumania	16,595	7,051	6,350	7,745
Siam	6,100		1,730	
Soviet Union	166,247	28,925	160,892	
Turkey	44,500	3,279	60,304	9,695
Spain	117,432	50,459	129,783	56,060
Sweden	66,949	12,247	82,836m.[2]	23,590[3]
United States	1,308,671	679,911	1,251,840	864,135
Uruguay	3,500		1,761	
Yugoslavia	10,695	3,052	2,880	10,970

AIR STRENGTH

Total of Military Aëroplanes (dirigibles omitted) and their horse power for all forces

	Number	Horse power
Albania	0	0
Argentina	86	32,460
Australia	38	19,571
Austria	0	0
Belgium	195	85,600
Bulgaria	0	0
Canada	355	100,692
Cuba	16	5,590
Czechoslovakia	546	263,069
Denmark	78 / 24[4]	25,000 / 9,840
Estonia	74	24,600[4]
France	2,375	1,235,123
Germany	0	0
Great Britain and Northern Ireland	1,434	740,215
Hejaz, and Nejd	9	3,780
Hungary	0	0
India	196	103,900
Irish Free State	24	8,641
Italy	1,507	876,847
Japan	1,639	0
Latvia	79	41,050
Netherlands	321	126,692

[1] All over-age; exempt vessels reported in global tonnage.
[2] Less 20,315 exempt by Draft Convention. The metric and standard tons contain 1,000 and 1,016 kilograms respectively.
[3] Plus 20,315 included in regular tonnage but exempt under Draft Convention.
[4] Figures to be attained when legislative reduction is effective.

	Number	Horse power
New Zealand	21	5,100
Norway	179	88,650
Poland	700	262,290
Portugal	24	6,570
Rumania	799	264,413
Siam	344	72,320
South Africa	66	13,353
Soviet Union	750	310,400
Spain	533	276,870
Sweden	167	41,430
Switzerland	125	75,000
Turkey	370	185,000
United States	1,752	1,028,745
Uruguay	42	9,520
Yugoslavia	627	293,291

INDEX

Afghanistan:
    naval status of.................. 18
    statistics on armaments of not available.................... 17
    treaty with Soviet Union....... 44
Aggression:
    attempts to define............72, 110
    problem of, considered in Draft Convention.................. 230
    treaties to prevent.....74–88, 337–355
Air armaments:
    budgetary limitation of........ 175
    comparative forces............ 19
    control under Draft Convention. 8
    future of................18, 261–262
    material...........171–174, 282–287
    personnel..................... 268
    provision for special conference on......................259–260
    statistical notes on..........363–364
Albania, naval status of.......... 18
Alsace-Lorraine.................. 36
Anglo-American Agreement of 1817, influence of..................50–51
Anglo-Japanese Alliance.......... 228
Arbitration:
    as substitute for war........... 69
    development of treaties of...... 88
Arbitration treaties:
    listed......................94–100
    model treaties................ 116
    postwar development of........88–90
    texts of....................324–355
Argentine Republic:
    armaments of.................. 17
    naval tonnage of.............. 166
    treaty with Chile.............. 52
Armament truce:
    as preparation for conference.... 9
    development of.............127–129
Armaments Year-Book:
    extent of information in........ 197
    nature of data in............125, 126
    quoted.......................18, 25
    statistical notes.............356–364
Austria:
    air forces forbidden............ 19
    armaments of................. 61
    naval status of................ 18
Aviation:
    Civil—
        and Draft Convention.......8, 225
        publicity on..............211–212
        relation to military aviation... 172
    Military—
        see Air Armaments

Bacteriological warfare, prohibition of......................213, 216, 300
Baker, Newton D...............30, 32
Battleships..................... 162
    see also Capital ships.
Belgium:
    armaments of.................17, 18
    attitude on manufacture of arms 67
    conscription in..............139, 144
        affected by falling birth rate.. 143
    neutralization of.............. 51
    reserves of.................... 204
    signatory of treaty of Locarno.. 115
Bernstorff, Count Johann von...245, 247
Birth rate, effect on conscription... 143
Bismarck, Prince von............ 36
Bloch, Camille.................. 254
Brazil:
    arbitration in Constitution of.... 90
    armaments of................. 17
    law regarding incitement to war . 91
    signatory of armament truce.... 127
Briand, Aristide..............117, 124
Brussels Act regarding traffic in arms 63
Budgetary expenditure:
    attitude of United States toward 148–150
    in Draft Convention........176–189, 288, 289, 306–317
    land armaments.........146–150, 271
    naval armaments.............. 171
    omitted from treaty of Versailles. 249
    relation to technological change.. 31
    statistics for United States....190–196
    statistics for world..........359–360
Bulgaria:
    air forces forbidden............ 19
    armaments of.............17, 18, 61
Canada:
    armaments of................. 18
    demilitarized frontier of........ 52
Capital ships:
    construction of postponed....... 15
    evolution of................164–165
Catholic women's organizations, petitions on disarmament......... 16
Cecil, Viscount of Chelwood.......5, 245
Chemical arms:
    attitude of United States.....214–215
    Draft Convention...........216, 300
    protocol of 1925............... 214
    uncertainty regarding some gases 218
China:
    armaments of................. 17
    proposal for permanent commission....................221, 226

INDEX

Civilian control, increased reliance on..........................8, 36–40
Clausewitz, Karl von............ 36
Clauzel, Count.................. 245
Clemenceau, Georges........36–37, 250
Colban, Erik...................233, 247
Colombia, naval status of........ 18
Commission on Private Manufacture of Arms.................. 63
Committee on Arbitration and Security:
    appointment of............... 105
    financial aid..................32, 75
    model treaties................ 115
    preparatory work for disarmament...................... 6
    prevention of war considered.... 83
Committee of Experts on Budgetary Questions:
    analysis of budgetary practises. 178–189
    report........................8, 152
Committees working toward disarmament................... 105
Conference of Ambassadors:
    during Locarno conference...... 39
    reports on German disarmament. 250
    revision of treaty of Versailles...57–60
Conscription:
    comparison with other forms of service....................133–134
    data on...................... 199
    problems of..................142–144
    text of Draft Convention.....269–270
Convention on Financial Assistance:
    analysis......................76–81
    history......................74–76
    reference to Council........... 73
    signatories.................... 82
    text........................337–351
"Conversion lag"................ 34
Coolidge, Calvin................ 38
Coolidge conference, *see* Geneva conference.
Cost of armaments..............31–32
    see also Budgetary expenditure.
Costa Rica:
    naval status of................ 18
    signatory of armament truce.... 127
Council for National Defense (United States).............26, 27
Covenant of the League of Nations:
    as treaty of arbitration......... 89
    obligations under—
        Article 8.................104–105
        Article 11...............77, 83, 85
        Article 15.................77, 78
        Article 16..............71, 85, 87
        Article 17................. 85
Currency fluctuations, provision for 185–186, 288–289

Curtius, Julius.................. 124
Czechoslovakia:
    armaments of.................17, 18
    attitude on manufacture of arms. 67
    signatory of treaty of Locarno... 115
Danzig, status of regarding armaments...................... 2
Dawes Plan..................... 113
Derogations to Disarmament Convention, provision for......227–238, 302–303
Dominican Republic:
    arbitration in constitution of.... 90
    naval status of................ 18
Draft Convention for Limitation and Reduction of Armaments:
    adoption..................... 121
    divisions..................... 7
    importance.................103–104
    preliminary drafts............. 131
    reference to Council........... 73
    reservations before Russian accession....................41–43
    signatures.................... 5
    supplementary reports......... 8
    text.......................265–305
    annex......................306–323
Draft Convention regarding Private Manufacture of Arms........65–68
Draft Treaty of Mutual Assistance 110–112
Ecuador, naval status of......... 18
Effectives:
    analysis of Draft Convention..131–144
    statistical tables.............361–362
    text of convention...........265–270
Estonia:
    at Moscow conference......... 43
    reservation in Draft Convention regarding................... 42
Ethiopia, limitation on armaments of........................ 50
Finland:
    at Moscow conference......... 43
    report on armaments of....... 48
    reservation in Draft Convention. 42
    suggestion for mutual aid....... 31
    treaty with Soviet Union....... 44
Foch, Marshal Ferdinand 36–38
France:
    armaments of.................17–18
    attitude on—
        manufacture of arms......... 67
        on revision of treaty of Versailles.................... 60
    proposals—
        for budgetary limitation...... 156
        for Permanent Commission.220–221
    rapprochements with Germany and Italy................... 9

INDEX

reduction in period of service.... 143
signatory of treaty of Locarno... 115
trained reserves of.............. 204
treaty with Soviet Union....... 44
General Act for Pacific Settlement of Dixputes:
    analysis....................116–117
    multilateral treaty.............. 89
    preparation for Disarmament Conference 6
    text........................324–337
General Convention to Improve the Means of Preventing War:
    analysis......................83–87
    reference to Council........... 73
    text.......................351–355
Geneva Conference of 1927:
    effect on disarmament......... 119
    military delegates to........... 8, 39
    reaction in United States....... 41
Geneva Protocol...............113–114
Genoa conference............... 43
Germany:
    air force forbidden............. 19
    armaments of.................. 17
    attitude on—
        conscription..............200–201
        chemical warfare............ 217
    criticism of Draft Convention. 132, 140
    launching of *Deutschland*....... 32
    moratorium................... 9
    proposals—
        regarding conscription....... 143
        regarding land armaments.... 150
    report on armaments of......... 49
    Rhineland zone...............38–39
    signatory of—
        treaties of Locarno 115
        treaty of Rapallo............ 43
    war-guilt thesis.............253–256
    see also Treaty of Versailles.
Gibson, Hugh S.:
    explanation of escape clause..233–235
    speeches on—
        budgetary limitation.......148–149
        continuing nature of disarmament problem............ 10
        need for concessions.......... 119
Grandi, Dino................... 3
Great Britain:
    armaments of.................17–19
    battleships of.................. 162
    budgetary limitation........... 155
    guarantor of financial assistance. 81
    reserves of.................... 138
Great powers:
    attitude of toward disarmament. 6
    reasons for special activity of....22–23
Greco-Bulgarian incident......... 83

Greece, attitude on budgetary limitation..................... 154
Guatemala, naval status of........ 18
Hague Conference of 1899........ 31
Haiti, naval status of............ 18
Henderson, Arthur............... 124
Herriot, Édouard 113
Honduras, naval status of........ 18
Hoover moratorium............. 9
Hungary:
    air force forbidden............. 19
    armaments of.............17, 18, 61
Iceland, status regarding armaments...................... 2
India, armaments of............. 17
Insular possessions in Pacific Ocean, treaty relating to............ 74
Intergovernmental indebtedness...9, 110
International Agricultural Mortgage Credit Company............ 72
International Cooperative Alliance. 16
Irish Free State:
    naval status of................ 18
    reservation on Draft Convention. 132
Italy:
    armaments of.................17–19
    attitude on manufacture of arms. 67
    criticism of Draft Convention... 140
    rapprochement with France...... 9
Japan:
    armaments of.................17–18
    attitude on private manufacture of arms.................... 66
    constitutional position on declaration of war................ 34
    exercise of veto................ 20
    military influence in............ 39
    petitions for disarmament in.... 16
    signatory of treaty of Washington 14
Kasprzycki, Gen. Thadée........39, 246
Kellogg-Briand Pact, *see* Treaty for Renunciation of War.
Kellogg, Frank B..............117, 227
Labor organizations, petitions for disarmament of............. 16
Land armaments:
    effectives...............133–134, 267
    figures for 1930–31............. 17
    material...................160, 271
    reportable weapons............ 207
    statistical notes.....356–358, 361–362
Lange, Christian L............... 111
Latvia:
    at Moscow conference......... 43
    reservation in Draft Convention. 42
League of Nations:
    Organization for Communications and Transit................ 8
Lefebure, Maj. Victor............ 34
Lerroux, Alejandro.............. 125

INDEX

Limitation of armaments, benefit of..........................14–15
Lithuania:
  at Moscow conference.......... 43
  naval status of................ 18
  treaty with Soviet Union.......44–45
London Naval Conference:
  and postponement of General Conference................... 121
  consultative pact discussed at... 229
  see also Treaty of London.
Lunacharsky, A. V............... 42
Luxemburg:
  naval status of................ 18
  neutralization of.............. 51
MacArthur, Gen. Douglas........ 29
MacDonald, J. Ramsay.......... 113
Madariaga, Salvador de.......... 4
Mantoux, Paul.................. 254
Marinis, Gen. Alberto de 39, 246
Nassigli, René...............246, 260
Material:
  air armaments......171–175, 282–287
  land armaments........145–160, 271
  naval armaments....160–171, 272–282
Methodists, disarmament petitions of........................ 16
Mexico:
  admission to League of Nations.. 9
  armaments of.................. 17
Mobilization, definition of........ 136
Moltke, Helmuth von............ 36
"Moral disarmament," importance of.:........................3, 110
Moscow conference on limitation of armaments.................. 43
Moseley, Gen. George V. H....... 33
Naval armaments:
  budgetary limitation regarding.. 171
  effectives...................141–142
  material..........160–171, 272–282
  merchant shipping in relation to. 169
  reduction in.................. 164
  statistical notes.............362–363
Netherlands, proposal of regarding publicity.................... 205
Neutralization treaties............51–56
Nicaragua, naval status of........ 18
Norway:
  criticism of Draft Convention... 132
  provisions for derogation....... 233
Optional clause to World Court Protocol 117
Panama, naval status of.......... 18
Permanent Advisory Commission:
  appointment of............... 108
  examination of armaments by... 48
Paraguay, naval status of......... 18
Permanent Court of International Justice:

compulsory jurisdiction........ 6
disputes regarding derogation... 243
in arbitral system............. 89
in treaties of Locarno.......... 115
Permanent Disarmament Commission:
  functions and organization....219–226
  supervision of complaints and derogations...........236–237, 240
  text of Draft Convention.....301–302
Pershing, Gen. John J............ 14
Persia:
  armaments of.................17, 18
  exercise of veto............... 20
  treaty with Soviet Union....... 44
Personnel, *see* Effectives
Peru, armaments of.............. 17
Petitions for disarmament........ 16
Poland:
  armaments of.................. 17
  at Moscow conference......... 43
  attitude on manufacture of arms. 67
  fear of attack................. 107
  law regarding incitement to war.. 91
  proposal regarding publicity..... 87
  reservation in Draft Convention. 42
  signatory of treaty of Locarno... 115
  treaty with Soviet Union....... 44
Political aspects of disarmament:
  armaments in politics..........11–12
  control of agreements........227–228
  efforts to relieve tension........ 9
  speech by Dino Grandi......... 3
Politis, Nicolas................42, 257
Popular attitude toward disarmament:
  desire for reduction............16, 22
  importance of................. 5
  need of further education in.....12–13
Portugal:
  arbitration in constitution of.... 90
  armaments of.................. 17
Pratt, Admiral William V......... 14
Preparatory Commission for the Disarmament Conference:
  preponderance of civilians in.... 8
  term of service................ 105
Private manufacture of arms:
  postponement of treaty on...... 205
  questions of supervision........62–67
Professional soldiers compared with conscripts................199–200
Publicity:
  as antidote to suspicion......... 198
  effects of during threat of war...87–88
  regarding manufacture of arms..63–64
  see also Statistics on armaments.
Ratification of Disarmament Convention, provisions for......257–258
Raw materials essential to war..25, 28–29

INDEX

Renouvin, Pierre.............. 254
Reserves:
  extent and variety of......... 134–139
  German attitude toward........ 201
  provisions in certain countries for
                                     203–204
Revision of peace treaties......... 56–61
Rule of unanimity............... 20–22
Rumania:
  armaments of................. 17
  attitude on manufacture of arms. 67
  law regarding incitement to war.. 91
  reservation in Draft Convention. 41
  willingness to conclude nonaggression pacts............... 45
Russia, *see* Union of Socialist Soviet Republics
Salvador, naval status of.......... 18
Security:
  as international problem...... 71–73, 106–107
  German use of term......... 245–246
  relation to disarmament........ 69–70
  subjective nature of.......... 70, 107
  see also Arbitration treaties.
Serbia, *see* Yugoslavia
Siam, armaments of............. 17
Small states, influence of......... 23
South Africa, naval status of...... 18
Spain:
  armaments of................. 17
  naval tonnage of.............. 166
  renunciation of war in constitution....................... 90
Statistical Year-Book of Trade in Arms and Ammunition....... 64
Statistics on armaments:
  figures for 1930 and 1931....... 17–19
  model statement............ 317–322
  Part IV of Draft Convention—
    analysis.................. 197–212
    text..................... 289–300
  preparation for conference.... 121–127
  private manufacture of arms.... 64
  statistical notes............. 356–364
Stimson, Henry L............... 9
Students' organizations and disarmament petitions.......... 16
Suez Canal.................... 52, 87
Sweden, proposal of regarding incitement to war............. 88
Switzerland:
  armaments of................. 17, 18
  neutralization of.............. 52
  reserves of................... 204
Technological obsolescence.... 29–31, 33
Temporary Mixed Commission:
  and effort to define aggression... 230
  and principle of demilitarization. 52
  appointment of............... 109

recommendation of regarding private manufacture........... 63
Treaties of Locarno:
  lessened military control....... 39
  regional guaranty............115–116
Treaties of neutralization and demilitarization................ 52–56
Treaty for Renunciation of War:
  implied consultation........... 74
  incomplete acceptance of....... 4
  model for nonaggression treaties. 45
  place in arbitral system......... 89
  provisions.................... 118
Treaty of London, 1930:
  and capital ships.............. 14
  as a consultative pact.......... 74
  preserved in Draft Convention.. 244
  ratified by Japan.............. 39
  results of.................. 160–161
  transfer of tonnage under....... 165
  see also London Naval Conference.
Treaty of Neuilly:
  prohibition of—
    air forces................... 19
    naval forces................ 61
Treaty of Rapallo............... 44
Treaty of St. Germain-en-Laye:
  prohibition of—
    air forces................... 19
    naval forces................ 61
  war guilt implied by
Treaty of Trianon:
  prohibition of—
    air forces................... 19
    naval forces................ 61
  war guilt implied by........... 255
Treaty of Versailles:
  obligation of general disarmament under................249, 251–252
  omission of budgetary limitation. 32
  prohibition of air forces........ 19
  relation to Draft Convention.. 244–247
  revision of to date............. 56–61
  trained reserves under......... 201
  war-guilt thesis in........... 253–256
Treaty of Washington:
  beneficial result............... 14
  capital ships under............ 15
  consultative feature of......... 84
  preserved in Draft Convention.. 244
  see also Washington Conference.
Turkey:
  armaments of................. 17
  attitude on budgetary limitation. 154
  criticism of Draft Convention. 132, 141
  proposal for permanent commission...................... 221
  signatory of armament truce.... 128
Union of Socialist Soviet Republics:
  armaments of................. 17

conscription in.................. 139
criticism of Draft Treaty......104, 132
nonaggression pacts signed by...43–46
opposition to escape clauses..... 235
position at conference.......... 24
proposal for complete disarmament..................... 118
reservation in Draft Convention. 42
United States:
armaments of.................17–19
attitude on—
  budgetary limitation...155, 158–159
  land armaments...........147–150
  size of battleships........... 162
  chemical warfare..........214–215
  manufacture of arms........66, 67
civilian heads of departments in.. 35, 37–38
cost of occupation of Germany... 61
naval policies of...............40–41
proportion of officers in army of.. 141
proposals for derogation......231–232
reserves of...................137–138
raw material essential to war. 25, 28–29
tables of expenditure of......190–196
War Department studies....... 26
war potential of...............26–29
Uruguay, arbitration in constitution of......................... 90
Venezuela, arbitration in constitution of..................... 90
War-guilt issue................253–256
War potential in United States....26–29
Washington Conference:
civilian influence at............ 38
concurrent political and technical success of................110, 228
effect of....................... 160
preparation for by State Department...................... 40
see also Treaty of Washington.
Women's organizations, disarmament petitions from......... 16
Yoshizawa, Kenkichi............ 125
Yugoslavia:
armaments of................. 17
proposal for derogation......... 232